DIGITAL MARKETING

Sara Miller McCune founded SAGE Publishing in 1965 to support the dissemination of usable knowledge and educate a global community. SAGE publishes more than 1000 journals and over 800 new books each year, spanning a wide range of subject areas. Our growing selection of library products includes archives, data, case studies and video. SAGE remains majority owned by our founder and after her lifetime will become owned by a charitable trust that secures the company's continued independence.

Los Angeles | London | New Delhi | Singapore | Washington DC | Melbourne

Annmarie Hanlon

DIGITAL MARKETING

SECOND EDITION

STRATEGIC PLANNING & INTEGRATION

$SAGE

Los Angeles | London | New Delhi
Singapore | Washington DC | Melbourne

Los Angeles | London | New Delhi
Singapore | Washington DC | Melbourne

SAGE Publications Ltd
1 Oliver's Yard
55 City Road
London EC1Y 1SP

SAGE Publications Inc.
2455 Teller Road
Thousand Oaks, California 91320

SAGE Publications India Pvt Ltd
B 1/I 1 Mohan Cooperative Industrial Area
Mathura Road
New Delhi 110 044

SAGE Publications Asia-Pacific Pte Ltd
3 Church Street
#10-04 Samsung Hub
Singapore 049483

Editor: Matthew Waters
Development editor: Martha Cunneen
Assistant editor: Jasleen Kaur
Production editor: Sarah Cooke
Copyeditor: Neil Dowden
Proofreader: Sharon Cawood
Indexer: Silvia Benvenuto
Marketing manager: Lucia Sweet
Cover design: Francis Kenney
Typeset by: C&M Digitals (P) Ltd, Chennai, India
Printed in the UK

Library of Congress Control Number: 2021943757

British Library Cataloguing in Publication data

A catalogue record for this book is available from the British Library

ISBN 978-1-5297-4281-7
ISBN 978-1-5297-4280-0 (pbk)

At SAGE we take sustainability seriously. Most of our products are printed in the UK using responsibly sourced papers and boards. When we print overseas we ensure sustainable papers are used as measured by the PREPS grading system. We undertake an annual audit to monitor our sustainability.

To Nick

Positively making all things possible

To my sister

Separated by sweeping sea

Together with technology

To the students and teachers reading this book

May the road rise up to meet you in your digital journey

CONTENTS

List of Cases — viii

List of Figures — ix

List of Tables — xi

About the Author — xiii

Preface to the Second Edition — xiv

Acknowledgements — xvi

Praise for Digital Marketing — xviii

Online Resources — xix

Part 1 Digital Marketing Essentials — 1

1 The Digital Marketing Environment — 3

2 The Digital Consumer — 31

Part 2 Digital Marketing Tools and Channels — 57

3 Email, Websites, SEO and Paid Search — 59

4 Content Marketing — 91

5 Social Media Marketing — 121

6 Online Communities — 149

7 Mobile Marketing — 181

8 Augmented, Virtual and Mixed Reality — 211

Part 3 Digital Marketing Strategy and Planning — 239

9 Digital Marketing Audit — 241

10 Digital Marketing Strategy and Objectives — 269

11 Building the Digital Marketing Plan — 299

Part 4 Digital Marketing Management — 331

12 Managing Resources and Reporting — 333

13 Digital Marketing Metrics and Analytics — 365

14 Integrating and Transforming Digital Marketing — 395

References — 423

Index — 445

LIST OF CASES

Case title	Company	Country	Page
Unilever's big datacentres	Unilever	USA	14
Klarna's digital payments	Klarna	Scandinavia	17
Uber and the sharing economy	Uber	USA	39
Moving customers from pre-purchase to purchase with Reviews.io	Reviews.io	UK	42
The failure of the Track and Trace app	NHS	UK	71
MoneySavingExpert and the fake ads	MoneySavingExpert	UK	85
TikTok the ultimate short form content	TikTok	USA, China	111
ASOS Insiders	ASOS	UK	116
M&S and Social Media	M&S	UK	139
Gymshark's social media adoption	Gymshark	UK	142
Wikipedia the largest online community of practice	Wikipedia	USA	162
Lego® Ideas Community	Lego	Scandinavia	168
FatSecret	FatSecret	Australia	195
#TextForHumanity	Sinch, Mental Health America	Scandinavia, USA	200
Zeekit the virtual fitting room	Zeekit	Gulf Region	219
YouVisit	YouVisit	USA	223
Helly Hansen's Digital PESTLE	Helly Hansen	Scandinavia	248
The Winning Group – we say YES in a no world	The Winning Group	Australia	254
Orange Money Africa	Orange Money Africa	Africa	276
Just Eat Takeaway.com	Just Eat Takeaway.com	Scandinavia	285
MUD Jeans	MUD Jeans	Netherlands	309
Petpuls – The crowdfunded AI dog collar	Petpuls	South Korea	324
Bellingcat	Bellingcat	Netherlands	338
ArcticZymes Technologies	ArcticZymes Technologies	Scandinavia	355
Microsoft's traditional metrics	Microsoft	USA	374
Hootsuite social media reporting	Hootsuite	Canada	383
Ikea's approach to co-creation	IKEA	Scandinavia	405
Japan's Digital Transformation Journey	Japan government	Japan	412

FIGURES

1.1   The blended data   24

2.1   Framework of the different elements in the sharing economy   36
2.2   Example of a customer journey map   46
2.3   Technology Acceptance Model (TAM)   53

3.1   The adapted digital marketing toolbox   61
3.2   Theoretical model of email opening   65

4.1   Key factors in content marketing   92
4.2   Types of influencers   104
4.3   Examples on the vividness to interactivity scale   111

5.1   The honeycomb model of social media functionality applied
      to individuals   128
5.2   Classification of social media by social presence/media richness and
      self-presentation/self-disclosure   132
5.3   Strategic framework for social media application in organisations   137

6.1   Building social capital in communities   154
6.2   Community life cycle   164
6.3   The place of social media in the customer complaining process   174

7.1   The 5Ps framework for personalised mobile marketing   185
7.2   Mobile advertising effectiveness framework   198
7.3   Characterisation of push notifications   201

8.1   Technology Readiness Scale   217
8.2   Conceptual model for an adoption framework for mobile
      augmented reality games   225
8.3   Typology of experiential value   226
8.4   The differences between conventional and skin electronic
      VR/AR devices   235

9.1   Market sensing framework   244
9.2   Manual social listening process   252
9.3   The digital 7Cs for competitor evaluation   256

10.1 The link between strategy and the hierarchy of objectives   272
10.2 Traditional and digital approaches to strategy   281
10.3 The digital marketing strategy framework   282
10.4 The McKinsey consumer decision journey   288

FIGURES

11.1	Building the digital marketing plan	301
11.2	Digital marketing mix objectives transformed into tactics	307
11.3	MUD Jeans circular mission	310
11.4	Digital marketing campaign planning process	315
11.5	Two-dimensional brand positioning map	316
12.1	The 9Ms of resource planning	335
12.2	Types of work in the platform economy	341
12.3	Impact and effort matrix	347
13.1	Types of customer value	369
13.2	Example of web address using UTMs	380
13.3	Weak, acceptable and strong metrics	387
13.4	Application of the PDCA to an advertising campaign	391
14.1	Enhancing value through digital marketing	398
14.2	The 6Cs of integration	400
14.3	Exit strategy archetypes	404
14.4	The process of digital transformation	407

TABLES

1.1 The move from traditional to digital marketing tools   5
1.2 Examples of sectors experiencing disruption   10
1.3 Examples of weak behaviour based on abuse of data   13

2.1 How the customer journey has changed   45
2.2 Digital persona elements   50
2.3 Initial scale items for perceived usefulness and for perceived
     ease of use   53

3.1 Examples of triggered emails based on the customer journey stage   62
3.2 Core attributes of web usability based on the components of UX   69

4.1 Types of fake news with examples   94
4.2 Storybox Selection   97
4.3 Types of storytellers, content and media   99

5.1 Social media network types and their utilities   124
5.2 Uses and gratifications theory applied to individuals   126
5.3 Critical benefits of social media for organisations   135
5.4 Stage model of social media adoption   141

6.1 Summary of user roles and contribution behaviour   166
6.2 Rules of engagement examples   172

7.1 Use of wearables for marketing   187
7.2 Mobile advertising options   197
7.3 Types of social commerce   204

8.1 Dimensions of interactivity   228

10.1 Orange Money Africa TOWS framework   277
10.2 Digital marketing mix objectives   290

11.1 Crowdfunding platforms, audiences and fees   305
11.2 Gantt chart to add five digital products to the product offer
      by September   308
11.3 MUD Jeans digital marketing mix objectives and digital
      marketing campaign concept   314
11.4 Digital media plan example   320
11.5 Strategy, digital marketing objectives and tactics   325
11.6 Example of a one-page digital marketing plan   327

TABLES

12.1 Examples of MarTech stacks and products, applied to areas of digital marketing management   343
12.2 SAF framework scoring example applied to Natura   350
12.3 RACI roles and responsibilities example   352
12.4 Strava budget to achieve the objectives   361

13.1 Traditional to digital marketing metrics   367
13.2 Examples of attribution measures and how they work   371
13.3 Email analytics data available   385
13.4 Metrics and how to use them to create an actionable plan 388

14.1 Companies failing to adopt digital marketing   396

ABOUT THE AUTHOR

Annmarie Hanlon PhD is a Senior Lecturer in Digital Marketing at the Cranfield School of Management and a practitioner working on digital marketing strategy projects.

Originally a graduate in French and Linguistics, she gained a master's in Business Administration, focusing on marketing planning. She studied for the Chartered Institute of Marketing Diploma for which she won the Worshipful Company of Marketors' award for the best worldwide results. Subsequently, she was awarded the Mais Scholarship for her PhD which investigated social media marketing within organisations.

As an early adopter, working in 'online marketing' since 1990, she is a Fellow of the Chartered Institute of Marketing, a Member of the Marketing Institute Ireland and a Liveryman of the Worshipful Company of Marketors. Annmarie's research interests include the business application of social media and digital transformation within organisations.

Follow her updates on Twitter @AnnmarieHanlon

PREFACE TO THE SECOND EDITION

Three hundred billion emails. Two billion websites. More mobile phones than tooth-brushes. Hundreds of social media networks. This is not a million miles away, it's our digital day.

Digital marketing gained importance during the pandemic. Some organisations were well prepared and others less so, scrambling to adapt to our digital world.

As a student of digital marketing, you're in an area that's growing. Take the opportunities in front of you, read, study and find your digital niche.

This textbook is in four parts. You can read these in order or navigate between chapters based on your knowledge and needs. Each builds on the previous part to provide a strong overview of digital marketing, as a student or a practitioner.

1. **Digital Marketing Essentials** provides the background, context and understanding of key concepts.

2. **Digital Marketing Tools and Channels** explores the tactical aspects of the digital marketing toolbox. It explains and evaluates the different elements and alerts you to areas to consider.

3. **Digital Marketing Strategy and Planning** enables you to create real plans for real organisations.

4. **Digital Marketing Management** shows the critical factors involved when managing digital marketing.

You'll notice different elements in each chapter:

*   Each chapter starts with **Learning Outcomes** based on Bloom's taxonomy, enabling students to progress from understanding to creation.

*   **Professional Skills** are useful additions to a CV or LinkedIn profile.

*   **Smartphone Sixty Seconds®** are designed as class icebreakers, whether you're online or offline.

*   **Digital Tools** highlight useful online sites or devices.

*   The **Activities** can be used as in-class sessions or for homework, moving from knowledge to application.

*   **Ethical Insights** provide glimpses into areas to be discussed further, as topics for debate.

*   **Key Terms** aim to remove the jargon and explain what things mean.

- The **Case Examples** contextualise specific areas in the chapter, showing real-life application.

- **Discover More** offers the curious further information on specific topics.

- **Journal of Note** shines a light on specific academic journals to investigate further.

- Throughout the book, there is a running **Case Study** that looks at Strava. This is my own creation based on publicly available information and my imagination.

- **Further Exercises** include three tasks for students to demonstrate their understanding of the chapter. Task 4 stretches this into a discussion question which could be a 1,000- to 2,000-word essay to examine an area in greater depth.

- Finally, the **References** section at the end includes those mentioned in the text that should be available via your university libraries.

Digital marketing is everywhere. In your world and mine, from when we wake until we rest our heads. This textbook aims to guide you along your digital path. Lean forward and start reading.

ACKNOWLEDGEMENTS

It's a blank page and then the keyboard moves into action.

Tapping, scrolling, clicking and deleting.

The book opens.

It's made possible with readers and reviewers. To the students and teachers who adopted the first edition of this textbook, then requested this second edition, thank you so much. I've enjoyed your enthusiastic comments and positive reactions. Plus, the anonymous peer reviewer feedback inspired and enhanced the chapters.

The book evolves.

It's made possible with the SAGE Publishing team. Special thanks to Matthew Waters and Martha Cunneen for their encouragement, wisdom and care.

The book expands.

It's made possible with ideas: Amani Loukou who introduced me to Orange Money Africa, Lynette Sraha with her insights on influencers, Mark Wakelin and Frans Riemersma for their advice on Martech.

The book ends.

It's not possible without inspiration. Thank you for the texts and emails, Teams and Zoom meetings, tweets and WhatsApps, posts and hashtags: James and Susan Herbert, Dr Karen Jones, Professor Stan Maklan, the Mackie family, Dr David Peck, Peter Rees, Richard Shambler, Adrian Stores and the many marvellous marketing academics on Twitter.

PUBLISHER'S ACKNOWLEDGEMENTS

The author and SAGE would like to thank all the instructors who reviewed the content of this textbook to ensure it is of the highest value for students and educators:

Vicki Andonopoulos, University of Sydney

Red Barrington, Oxford College of Marketing

Sree Beg, University of Roehampton

Scott Cowley, Western Michigan University

Franco Curmi, University of Malta

Ronnie Das, Newcastle University

Paul Davies, Swansea University

Jon Engström, Stockholm University

Shelton Giwa, De Montfort University

Clive Helm, University of Westminster

Dawn McCartie, Newcastle University

James Pressly, University of Hertfordshire

Michelle Renton, Victoria University of Wellington

Billy Sung, Curtin University

Silviu Tierean, Queen's University Belfast

PRAISE FOR DIGITAL MARKETING

'*Digital Marketing* is an invaluable resource for those who want to discover more about this exciting, emerging and rapidly evolving subject. The logical structure and presentation make it easy to read each topic in depth or to dip into for quick reference. Case studies about recognisable brands increase engagement and application of theoretical concepts, making learning and teaching enjoyable and valuable for students and lecturers alike. Highly recommended!'

Sarah Evans-Howe, Lecturer in Business and Marketing, The University of Buckingham

'Annmarie Hanlon has mastered effectively conveying the most crucial digital marketing concepts in a way that is grounded in theory and real-world applications. This second edition text is a must for students exploring the evolving world of all things digital.'

Megan F. Hill, M.S., Professor of Practice in Marketing, Grenon School of Business, Assumption University

'*Digital Marketing* is a flexible book, written to enhance our theoretical understanding and prepping us for the practical skills we need to deliver great digital results in organizations. The second edition solidly elaborates on classical and core theoretical models, and the new cases enlighten students understanding of the need to have good frameworks when creating unique content with competitive advantage.'

Cathrine von Ibenfeldt, Lecturer in Marketing, BI Norwegian Business School

'The book has a sound theoretical basis, covering the foundations of the subject in a clear and accessible manner. The Digital Tools regularly provide opportunities for students to apply what they have learned in practice. The book is also up to date in its content, with a selection of recent, global case studies, to engage modern students.'

Desmond J. Laffey, Senior Lecturer in E-Commerce, University of Kent

'Annmarie Hanlon is placed at the unique intersection of academic and practice. *Digital Marketing* integrates contemporary examples in the dynamic digital ecosystem to bring alive relevant concepts and theories into practical situations clearly and persuasively. This book is an essential read for both students and tutors.'

Wilson Ndasi, Senior Lecturer in Digital Marketing, Oxford Brookes University

ONLINE RESOURCES

Head online to access a wealth of online resources that will aid study and support teaching. All resources have been designed and formatted to upload easily into your LMS or VLE, and are available at: **https://study.sagepub.com/Hanlon2e**.

FOR LECTURERS

- **Editable PowerPoint slides** will allow you to easily **integrate each chapter into your lessons** and provide access to **figures and tables from the book**.

- **Testbank** of multiple-choice questions will help you test **students' knowledge and understanding** of the materials.

- **Instructor's manual** containing tutor notes will provide further support when **teaching each chapter**, and **encourage discussion** in sessions.

- Links to **SAGE journal articles** selected by the author to help supplement students' reading and **deepen their understanding** of the key topics outlined.

- **Downloadable template**s that can be added to course resources or printed out for use in class.

FOR STUDENTS

- Access **helpful websites and video links** with lots of extra information to reference in your assignments.

- A **worked digital marketing strategy** to help you get your project off the ground and see the **theory in action**.

PART 1

DIGITAL MARKETING ESSENTIALS

CONTENTS

1   The Digital Marketing Environment   3
2   The Digital Consumer   31

Evaluate being digital during the pandemic

Manage your privacy

Understanding digital generations and the digital divide

ACTIVITIES

OVERVIEW
Chapter 1 introduces the concept of digital marketing and sets the scene providing the historical context and highlighting key issues around data and privacy.

Choose your digital products

KEY CONCEPTS

The characteristics of big data

Why nothing to hide in digital privacy matters

DIGITAL TOOLS

Explore the Wayback Machine and review older versions of brand websites

Examine how the search engines' right to be forgotten process works

1

THE DIGITAL MARKETING ENVIRONMENT

LEARNING OUTCOMES

When you have read this chapter, you will be able to:

Understand key issues in the digital environment

Apply nudge theory

Analyse opportunities for buy now pay later (BNPL)

Evaluate the impact of the digital environment

Create a plan to develop digital products

PROFESSIONAL SKILLS

When you have worked through this chapter, you should be able to:

- Evaluate options to develop digital goods
- Create a campaign using nudge theory

1.1 INTRODUCTION TO THE DIGITAL MARKETING ENVIRONMENT

Digital marketing is satisfying customers' needs and wants using digital means. Our digits tap, swipe and pinch our devices for many hours each day. We depend on technology to work, rest and play. Airbnb, Klarna, Dropbox and Uber were founded over 10 years ago. Amazon is approaching its 30th birthday and Google is nearly 25 years old. If you're using an Apple device, did you realise the company is nearly 50 years old? The company that invented the first PCs, IBM, is over 100 years old. Computing is now ubiquitous (Weiser, 1991), there are computers everywhere – in our homes and cars, offices and universities, on our trains and buses, in our shops, streets and cities, yet we don't even notice their presence.

Digital marketing 'can be defined as using any digital technology to facilitate the marketing process, with the end goal of customer interaction, engagement and measurement' (Zahay, 2021, p. 125).

One major change in digital marketing is the move from the traditional 7Ps (Booms and Bitner, 1980) towards a digital marketing mix. In this chapter, we'll look at products and places, payments (pricing) and processes. Chapters 3 to 6 look at digital promotion and physical evidence is addressed when considering websites in Chapter 3. People is explored in Chapter 12, 'Managing Resources and Reporting'.

But first, let's explore how digital marketing started and changed our environment with the implications for digital marketing.

1.2 A NEW ERA

Digital marketing did not happen instantly. The origins of digital marketing can be found in direct marketing where companies tried to connect with individuals on a one-to-one basis through traditional letters. In an online context, this was known as internet marketing and was based on Web 1.0 and enabled direct communication from organisations to customers.

1.2.1 WEB 1.0

Web 1.0 was one-way with no opportunities to have conversations. Spanning from 1989 until about 2004, Web 1.0 is often referred to as the 'read only' web. The first websites were launched, such as Amazon and Google. As a simple system with slow internet speeds, it enabled organisations to share brochures online with basic shopping carts. This was an online version of direct marketing and one major benefit that Web 1.0 introduced was removing barriers between customers and companies (known as disintermediation).

However, Web 1.0 also presented new ways of keeping the broker in the middle which is called re-intermediation. One of the earliest examples was MoneySuperMarket.com which launched in the UK in 1993. Re-intermediation still happens today and is how Just Eat Takeaway works. You no longer contact your local food takeaway restaurant, instead you look at your Just Eat Takeaway app and decide what's for supper this evening.

1.2.2 WEB 2.0

Technology improved and Web 2.0 was identified in 2004, offering two-way communication and interactive marketing. Many social media networks launched and changed buyer behaviour further, as customers or fans could add comments to company content. The first version of Facebook was launched along with Twitter, which was initially as a text-only service designed as a messaging tool. Online systems like the picture-sharing site Flickr emerged, allowing users to upload, save and share photos.

1.2.3 WEB 3.0

Web 3.0 witnessed a change as online technology became more intelligent, finding meaning in the content, which was known as the semantic web. This was identified by the father of the World Wide Web, Sir Tim Berners-Lee, some years before in 1999 and is when the term internet marketing started appearing.

These concepts took until 2006 before computer-to-computer interaction or online marketing was possible. Web 3.0 is here now and is considered to be the next generation of the web due to its ability to process information using technologies like machine learning (ML) and big data. The careers page of any well-known brand shows they're hiring data scientists to manage their online data. We could say that Web 3.0 enabled digital marketing.

1.2.4 WEB 4.0

We don't have a formal version of Web 4.0 although this is considered as part of the Internet of Things (IoT), where devices are seamlessly connected. The IoT ecosystem relies on sensors such as barcodes and RFID tags (radio-frequency identification) within a WiFi zone. From this it can identify physical properties such as: Are there people in the building? Is your heart beating at the usual rate? What's the date on the barcode? This is combined with autonomous machines being accessed via a remote-control source such as an app on your phone or your wearable device.

Our fast-changing digital environment provides many opportunities for marketers and the growth of technology has changed the relationship between businesses and customers. Plus, new technology has heralded changes in behaviour (see Chapter 2, 'The Digital Consumer'), resulting in the decline of traditional marketing tools, as shown in Table 1.1.

Table 1.1 The move from traditional to digital marketing tools

Traditional	Digital	Why the change?
Newspaper and magazine adverts	Online adverts; social media, PPC	Newspaper and magazine sales have declined and it's easier to target people online
Door-to-door sales people	Email	Door-to-door is expensive and we can now personalise offers to existing customers via email

(Continued)

Table 1.1   (Continued)

Traditional	Digital	Why the change?
Company brochures	Websites	Printing brochures is expensive, so is creating websites, but they are agile and easier to change as needed
Traditional PR	Online PR, blogs	With the decline in newspaper and magazine sales, the number of staff has declined too; online PR makes the process easier
Directories like the Yellow Pages	Search engine marketing	The default is to search online and voice search is growing, so directories have become smaller and are rarely used
Community groups	Social networks	We live in a more mobile world where people move from home towns to find work, so traditional community groups have declined, but social media networks increased

Digital promotion is explored in more detail in Chapters 3, 4 and 5.

We have 24/7 access to the internet, our documents are automatically saved online, we trust the words of strangers rather than companies, we create digital products, we have digital payments as well as digital products, and companies will hire you based on your digital skills and capabilities.

DIGITAL TOOL   The Wayback Machine

Since 1996 the Internet Archive has collected snapshots of websites and is known as the Wayback Machine. Described as 'a digital library of Internet sites and other cultural artifacts in digital form', it's free to access and contains nearly 500 billion web pages! It's a great way to turn back time and look at early editions of brands' websites.

- Go to https://archive.org/web
- Add in a web address
- Click browse history
- Explore older versions of the website that are no longer available

1.3 DIGITAL PEOPLE

1.3.1 DIGITAL GENERATIONS

If you're a student at university now, there's a good chance that you're a digital native. You've been born into a time when mobile phones, tablets and wearables are the norm. The research says that you rarely watch TV in real time, you'd rather view YouTube. You don't send letters, you use WhatsApp. You don't use printed business directories, you ask Siri.

But not everyone was born when computers were the norm, so we have two digital peoples: 'digital natives' and 'digital immigrants' which are part of a range of generational cohorts, shown here with when they were born:

- Baby Boomers: mid-1946 to mid-1964
- Generation X: mid-1960s to the late 1970s/early 1980s
- Digital Immigrants: before 1980
- Digital Natives: after 1980
- Net Generation: between 1982 and 1991
- Millennials: in or after 1982
- Google Generation: after 1993
- Generation Y: between 1981 and 1999
- Generation C: after 1990
- Gen Z: mid-1990s to early 2010s
- Generation Alpha: early 2010s to mid-2020s

Some cohorts cross into another generation. This is because there is no official agreement on the terms, nor are they formally defined by governments, but mainly by researchers and consultants working in advertising who see the different behaviours developing.

The terms 'digital native' and digital immigrant' are considered by some as being controversial and by others as divisive. The work has been criticised due to the phraseology and as some people objected to the labels. Marc Prensky was teaching groups of students and realised there was a marked difference between the students who had always used technology and teachers who were new to this. He described the situation as similar to learning a new language, where immigrants move into a new country and learn the language but it is never their mother tongue, so they might always retain an accent. In the same way, he thought that those who had to learn about technology would retain this 'accent'.

1.3.2 THE DIGITAL DIVIDE

Amongst our digital generations we have a digital divide. Not everyone has access to the internet. Not everyone has access to computers or smartphones. Not everyone knows how to gain information from the internet. This phenomenon was named the digital divide by the Organisation for Economic Co-operation and Development (OECD, 2001), an intergovernmental economic organisation with member countries worldwide. Typically the digital divide occurs due to:

- Location – weak access or lack of access to the internet in the region
- Education – lack of digital skills and capabilities
- Technology adoption – lack of understanding of the internet mainly by older digital immigrants
- Economy – lack of financial ability to access computers or devices

During the COVID-19 pandemic, the divide changed. In some cases it was reduced, but in others it increased. We're aware that researchers have identified location as a factor because 'developed countries of the world have more access to fixed telephony connections' (Inegbedion, 2021, p. 83). However, even in wealthier countries there are gaps with internet provision in rural areas and small villages (Lai and Widmar, 2021) where internet speeds are slow or because the service cannot support multiple devices at the same time.

The lack of digital skills is a key factor in the digital divide. Most countries have been upskilling their populations to gain digital skills. During the pandemic, many people gained new digital skills – how to use Zoom or Teams, how to adjust cameras, how to add more people to calls.

In the same way that digital skills improved during the pandemic, technology adoption increased as families stayed in contact using digital devices, removing barriers to adoption and demonstrating the usefulness of technology.

One area where the divide increased was in access to computers or devices. Understandably many families did not have multiple devices for home schooling and the idea of buying a new laptop – or two – was outside the budget of most households. Several organisations tried to help by providing recycled laptops, but this may not have reached all households. This was one reason why governments worldwide were keen to ensure school children could return to their classrooms as soon as possible. Even so, this lack of ability to access computers or devices may have ongoing consequences that future researchers will most likely explore.

Activity 1.1   Being digital during the pandemic

During the pandemic, you may have been studying or working from home. This may have brought benefits and difficulties which you can reflect on and assess:

1. What were the main skills you gained and how are these relevant for your future?
2. What were the main challenges you faced and how did you overcome these issues?
3. Evaluate the impact of the digital divide in your home town or local area and make recommendations for improvements to reduce the barriers.

1.4 DIGITAL PRODUCTS AND PLACES

The development of cloud computing enables software and services to run on the internet which means that we can access our digital technology at any time in any location. Our data is stored on the cloud, whether that's Alibaba Cloud, Amazon Web Services, Dropbox, Google Drive, iCloud or OneDrive. And many of the programs we access are cloud based, from Office365 to Dropbox, Netflix to our health records.

The main advantages are that you can work at home, at a friend's house or in a coffee shop and when you arrive at work or at university, you can continue where you left off, on the same page of the same document – as long as you saved it! However, the technology has created digital disruption which has created both advantages and disadvantages for product offers worldwide.

Digital products include a range of materials that we use for work, study and play, such as:

- Audio-visual: TV shows, movies, online videos (e.g. YouTube, Twitch, TikTok)
- Business or educational: Computer software (e.g. Microsoft, Google)
- Entertainment: Video games (e.g. Xbox, PlayStation, Amazon, Google)
- Recreational: Sports, cooking or lifestyle apps (e.g. any app store)
- Sound: Recordings, audio books, podcasts, musical compositions, ringtones (e.g. Spotify, Apple, SoundCloud, Clubhouse)
- Theatrical: Dramas, plays, musicals (e.g. Netflix, Hulu)
- Visual: Paintings, posters, advertisements (e.g. on social media sites or via specialist retailers)
- Written: Lectures, articles, ebooks (e.g. your university's online learning environment such as Blackboard, Brightspace, Canvas, Moodle)

Many are online-only and need internet access to function fully. For example, while at university you have access to thousands of digital products in the form of academic articles from journals. The journals charge the libraries a fee and, in return, share material with academics and students. When you leave university, you no longer have access to this material. You may subscribe to digital products including apps from Netflix to Strava, paying a monthly amount in return for using the product. The difference with these products is that they have all been created as a result of digital marketing – finding a need and satisfying this online.

Activity 1.2   Choose your digital products

Consider your digital products, in particular where you're paying a fee or regular subscription. If you were only allowed to keep three of these, which three would you choose and why?

ETHICAL INSIGHTS   Digital theft

Easy access to digital products has resulted in an increase in theft. This is more than an image taken from another website, it's downloading eBooks and games but failing to pay for the goods.

(Continued)

Students are aware of plagiarism – stealing someone else's words without correctly acknowledging the authors, which can result in expulsion from university and damage careers. Yet there is said to be a lack of understanding around downloading online materials (Geçer and Topal, 2021, p. 92).

Digital theft destroys businesses; for example, copied eBooks can be stored on poor websites that at worst may include viruses or at best fail to acknowledge the hard work of the author. However, this is commonplace and considered fun – it's called piracy, which sounds romantic rather than like theft or stealing, which is what it is. Stealing risks reputational damage and can result in heavy costs as many digital goods include embedded codes so they can be tracked. Why does digital theft occur?

- Do you feel it's acceptable to steal someone else's work?
- What are the best ways to educate students about digital theft?
- How do you feel about digital theft?

1.4.1 DIGITAL DISRUPTION

In addition to digital products, we have witnessed traditional products evolving to meet consumers' needs. Every era sees disruption from newer technologies that replace outmoded methods of delivery, service, production or communication. We could describe digital disruption as 'major marketplace changes or sector transformation, following the application of technology'.

All digital disruption is driven by technology, especially as it becomes smaller, faster and easier to access. Amazon is heralded as the next new, easy-to-use online supermarket, yet it has existed for over 20 years which demonstrates that disruption can take years to gain scale. Examples of technology-driven digital disruption include those shown in Table 1.2:

Table 1.2   Examples of sectors experiencing disruption

Sector	Example of disruptive service	Traditional businesses in this sector
Accommodation	Airbnb	Hotels
Car rental	Zipcar	Car rental companies
Clothing swap	Vinted	Swap with friends
General services	Taskrabbit	Local people
Personal transport	Uber	Regular taxi companies
Ride-sharing	Via	Car-pooling with colleagues

Many disruptive digital products are often a variation of traditional products; the difference is that they offer more choice. For example, Airbnb offers accommodation, but via a digital app. Plus the accommodation is peer to peer, so no hotel groups are involved.

Uber offers taxi services, a business type that has existed for centuries! Yet the difference is place, physical evidence, processes and people as the product is accessed via an app, you know the drivers' details and can see where they are on a map. Another example is Zipcar who compete with traditional car rental companies, which were perceived as complex to use and the contracts were often for a minimum number of days. Zipcar changed this by adopting a digital-first approach, adapting the traditional 7Ps:

- Place and processes: Moving the access point – picking up the vehicle from a nearby street rather than having to get to a depot which may be in an inconvenient location
- Place: Changing access to the service – booking via an app
- Product and price: Adapting the offer – removing longer contracts and allowing customers to hire a car or van by the hour, rather than the day, week or month.

As these sectors are disrupted, some traditional businesses decide to fight back, such as the battle between taxi companies and Uber. Other disrupters are acquired by companies that benefit from their services, such as Taskrabbit which was purchased by IKEA, as an easier way to offer furniture assembly services to its customers. Or in the case of Zipcar, its direct competitor, the Avis Budget Group took more direct action and purchased the company!

1.4.2 CRYPTOASSETS

In our digital world, we've seen the development of new types of digital products or cryptoassets that are known as non-fungible tokens (see Key Term **NFT**). An NFT is a one-off creation and can't be divided or shared. This can be a piece of artwork, a sound or other collectible item which is only available to access online.

These gained worldwide attention when an artist known as Beeple turned a collage of many thousands of images that he created into an NFT and placed it for auction via the international art company Christie's. The bidding started at $100 and the artwork sold for $69 million, yet the owner will never physically touch the piece – they will keep it in their digital wallet. Just like physical artwork, they can collect or re-sell if they wish.

However, we're not sure how cryptoassets will develop as the use of NFTs is still in its early stages and there are issues about their environmental credentials due to the energy required to create and store the assets.

KEY TERM   NON-FUNGIBLE TOKEN (NFT)

NFTs are tokens that represent ownership of unique items. They enable the tokenisation of things such as works of art or other collectible items. They are secured by a **blockchain** so that no one can modify the record of ownership and they can only have one official owner at a time. Owners store their NFTs in their digital wallet and retain a crypto key as proof of ownership, so the item can be re-sold.

Smartphone Sixty Seconds® – Find the NFTs

Search online for NFTs and see if you can find Beeple's 'Everydays: The First 5000 Days'. This sold for nearly $70 million.

- What's your view on this?

1.4.3 BIG DATA

Having all this material online, whether it's our digital products, NTFs or our online behaviour, has resulted in the growth of digital data which has grown and is known as big data. Big data refers to large data sets that computers can barely handle (Cox and Ellsworth, 1997). This isn't a large Excel sheet, but data that's measured in gigabytes (1000^3 bytes), terabytes (1000^4 bytes) or petabytes (1000^5 bytes).

The characteristics of big data are referred to as the 4Vs and include the size of the data (volume), the speed at which the data is generated (velocity), the different types (variety) of structured and unstructured data (Laney, 2001), and the quality of the data being analysed (veracity). The data is so large that it may not be possible to scroll through to find useful insights and you may need coding skills (e.g. R or Python) or special software such as Hadoop to make sense of the data.

Big data is all around us. Social media companies including Facebook, Twitter and Google gather big data. For example, Facebook stores your data securely in data warehouses. They generate significant volumes daily, when you add a post or an image, or like a page – that's all data. The velocity is hard to keep up with, as over a billion users add data every second. The variety of data includes structured elements (liking pages, clicking on links) and unstructured elements (adding free text content). The quality or veracity varies – you might 'like' a page to add complaints, you might not accurately add all your details. Your profile shows your personal details, plus your buying behaviour is captured and this can be overlaid with additional data from third-party sources. This all feeds into companies' datasets and is how data is acquired.

This data is fed back to data specialists where the data is integrated, to better inform market research companies. For example, health insurance companies know your age, job role, where you live, whether you drive far for work, your family composition, typical diet, height, weight, health problems and where you visit on holidays. Some companies offer free fitness trackers for cheaper insurance premiums, which allows them to assemble a full profile of your daily life. Assembling and managing the data requires expertise, and professional data specialists include:

- CACI, whose database named 'Ocean' provides lifestyle and demographic details on 48 million adults in the UK
- Nielsen, a worldwide data specialist, which has amassed data on consumers in 47 countries
- Kantar who have captured data around the world on how people think, feel and act, globally and locally in over 90 markets

These companies are invaluable resources when you are a busy marketing manager and want to target the right customers with the right message. As professional organisations, they abide by strict codes of conduct. However, there are less scrupulous firms capturing and selling data without consent. Within five days of having my academic email address published on a university website, my data had been gathered using web scraping software which visits websites, identifies email addresses and adds to a local database. From here the data is sold as 'new data' and those making the purchase might think these companies have permission to sell the data. Whilst web scraping is not technically illegal, using the data may be and often results in getting emails blocked and reported as spam.

The challenge with big data for consumers and companies occurs on several levels and potential weak behaviour can occur (De Cremer et al., 2017, p. 150), such as the elements identified in Table 1.3 which are applied to elements of the PESTLE framework.

Table 1.3 Examples of weak behaviour based on abuse of data

Weak behaviour	What this means	Examples	PESTLE Factors
Barriers to switching	Making it less attractive or difficult to switch providers	Difficulty in switching banks or mobile phone providers	Economic
Financial penalties	Only benefiting consumers using the products and penalising those that don't	Special offers for clients wearing fitness devices	Economic, Technological
Privacy issues	Collecting personal data and selling online	Fitness providers collecting health data and potentially sharing with insurance companies	Social
Favouritism and discrimination	Micro-segmentation based on shared customer behaviour	One gender charged more than another for the same products	Social
Unfairness	Discriminating against certain user types	Charging higher prices to Mac users	Social, Technological
Confusing customers	Only providing complex pricing models	Utilities providers (e.g. electricity, water) using pricing models based on units that are difficult to understand	Social
Information misuse	Abusing the data held about the customer	Companies selling data to influence elections	Legal
Dishonesty	Cross-selling potentially unwanted or unneeded products based on behaviour	Promoting plastic surgery to young girls	Legal

Source: Adapted from De Cremer et al. (2017, p. 150)

Big data matters to marketers as we can make informed decisions by understanding customer behaviour. Whether that's knowing the best times to send emails, add offers or change advertising images, big data enables organisations to make informed decisions about all aspects of marketing.

CASE EXAMPLE 1.1   Unilever's big datacentres

Unilever is a global business with 400 household name brand products in nearly 200 countries and over 2.5 billion consumers. Its consumers outnumber most social networks, other than Facebook. Its largest market is the USA, followed by India and China. Unsurprisingly, Unilever is one of the world's largest advertisers and it leads the market in three areas:

- Beauty and personal care with brands such as Dove, Sunsilk, Axe, Lifebuoy, Dermalogica, Living Proof
- Food and refreshment with brands such as Ben & Jerry's, Wall's and Magnum ice cream, Knorr products, Hellman's mayonnaise
- Home care with brands such as Persil clothes' washing products, Domestos cleaning products.

Unilever is successful because it listens closely to its customers' needs and identifies market trends and responds to these trends. Its global presence provides 40 billion consumer reach points which it says is more than any other competitor.

Unilever understands the value of data and so the social listening and customer conversations take place in many ways and, in a typical year, this can include:

- Around 3 million interactions with customers captured online
- Millions of conversations about different Unilever brands online in forums and groups
- 2.5 million interactions through calls, emails, letters, social media and webchats
- Millions of enquiries from its consumer carelines, which are old-fashioned telephone call centres
- Nearly 1.8 million data points gathered when consulting consumers through regular surveys using partners like Kantar, Nielsen and Ipsos

This is a huge amount of data gathered from different channels, from different people, in different locations, about different products. To make sense of the data, Unilever has invested heavily in big data. To manage the data, it has over 35 datacentres worldwide. The raw data is added to 'data lakes' where vast amounts of unstructured data start their journey. From here, specialist data managers, architects, engineers, experts and analysts process the data, using **machine learning** (see Key Term), and it is categorised and added to 'data warehouses'. The data scientists work in the data warehouses to arrange or classify the material by themes, products, customers' feelings or other factors. From this they make sense of the data by generating insights (see Chapter 13) which are used by their marketing and research teams to develop new products. For a company that launched 600 new products worldwide in 2020, analysing its big data is essential.

Unilever has formed a partnership with Amazon which involves co-investment in data and has explained more about its use of data, how this is shared and informs product development:

> We're sharing increasingly sophisticated insights with customers around shopper preferences and behaviours gained through social listening and other tools. This is helping our larger customers make data-driven decisions about how and where best to bring value to shoppers. We partnered with Walmart in the US, for example, to co-create and launch a new bath product range based on insights around people needing 'me time' at home during lockdown.

However, gathering such vast amounts of data raises issues about data protection which was recognised in the company's 2020 Annual Report:

> Increasing digital interactions with customers, suppliers and consumers place ever greater emphasis on the need for secure and reliable IT systems and infrastructure and careful management of the information that is in our possession to ensure data privacy.

It's certain that the Unilever data lake will continue to grow, as will the data warehouses. The company will continue to recruit digital marketing staff that understand the impact of data and the insights it brings.

Case questions

- What types of data might Unilever gather online? Select the social media page for one of its brands and find examples of data and discuss how this could be used.
- Unilever ensures it manages its data carefully but what risks might occur with sharing data with third parties such as Amazon and Walmart?
- Have you ever asked a question, added a comment or made a remark about a brand online? Can you describe what you did and why, as well as considering how this might be used by the brand?

KEY TERM   MACHINE LEARNING

According to Professor Tom Mitchell who wrote the best-selling book on the subject, 'Machine Learning is the study of computer algorithms that improve automatically through experience' (Mitchell, 1997, p. 1).

IBM suggests that 'Machine learning is a branch of artificial intelligence (AI) focused on building applications that learn from data and improve their accuracy over time without being programmed to do so', adding that 'Machine learning focuses on applications that learn from experience and improve their decision-making or predictive accuracy over time' (IBM, 2020, p. 1).

1.5 DIGITAL PAYMENTS AND PROCESSES

1.5.1 E-MONEY AND DIGITAL WALLETS

Shopping on the internet required online payment systems and although credit cards were established in the last century by Diners' Club in the 1950s, not all ecommerce sites accepted all card types, at the start. Plus, what if you didn't qualify for a credit card? In 1998 PayPal became the first online payment system offering an e-money facility. You added credit to the account to use for shopping, just like a pre-loaded credit card (e.g. Starling, Travelex), and could use it for buying goods online.

Beyond e-money, digital wallets evolved. Not just storing money, but keeping all your items in one place in a single app. This could include your address details, passwords, multiple credit cards, event or travel tickets and membership cards.

E-money has evolved as PayPal is an accepted payment method across many websites, alongside credit and debit cards backed by Visa, MasterCard and Amex. Plus, PayPal did more than regular credit cards and offered peer-to-peer payments, enabling you to send and accept money to and from friends. In addition to PayPal, there are other systems such as Alipay, Google Pay and Apple Pay. These are more like digital wallets and can be used for contactless payments offline.

The social media networks are getting involved too. In China, WeChat Pay is well established and Facebook Pay is available in some locations. The social network payment systems are other ways of sending money to friends to pay for goods via WeChat, Facebook, Instagram, WhatsApp or Messenger, and these are likely to grow, offering access to those without banking services and removing a barrier to online shopping.

New options for digital payments are evolving such as allowing consumers to shop and pay in instalments. This is known as buy now pay later (**BNPL** – see Key Term) and BNPL companies include Afterpay, Klarna, Laybuy, Payright and Zip Money. These companies offer different payment options and use push notifications to tell you when a payment is due. Many well-known retailers use BNPL methods on their online stores to encourage an immediate rather than a delayed purchase.

KEY TERM   BUY NOW PAY LATER (BNPL)

Buy now pay later (BNPL) allows consumers to buy items in a series of instalments. It's not a new concept and in the United Kingdom was known as 'buying on tick' where the tick represented a ticket. Your name was added in a book, the total cost noted and you paid back in weekly sums.

The digital version allows you to download and pay via an app. You choose the BNPL company as your payment method (instead of credit card or online banking) and decide how to pay. This may be 'Pay in 4' – that's four equal payments over two months or pay in full 30 days later.

The downside is that if you miss a payment, you're charged a default fee and this could get out of control if not managed well.

CASE EXAMPLE 1.2   Klarna digital payments

Klarna is a digital-born business. It was founded in Stockholm, Sweden in 2005, and now has over 3,500 employees, known as Klarnauts, and offices across three continents. The business is recognised as one of Europe's largest banks and was started by three master's students at Stockholm School of Economics: Sebastian Siemiatkowski, Niklas Adalberth and Victor Jacobsson.

The Stockholm School of Economics had an entrepreneurship competition, similar to *Dragon's Den* or *Shark Tank*, and Siemiatkowski, who had worked in a financial services telephone call centre, thought there could be an opportunity for easier online payments. The team presented their business idea known as InvoiceMe which was an idea for an easy (smooth) online payment system that allowed online shoppers to pay in instalments.

But the presentation didn't go well and the trio's idea of 'Buy now pay later' online was not popular with the jury. In fact, it came last, but one of the people at the event said that traditional banks would never offer the service, so the trio should go for it. The three friends decided to see if the business worked and agreed a trial. If it didn't work after six months, they would get proper jobs.

Later that year, the company launched and in 2010 Klarna opened offices in Germany and the Netherlands. The company continuously innovates and in 2017 the app was launched. More investors joined the business, including the retailer H&M and the rapper Snoop Dogg – who temporarily changed his name to Smooth Dogg (for an advertising campaign)!

The product offer allows customers to spread payments and to do one of three things:

- 'Pay Later' which means between 14 to 30 days after purchasing
- 'Pay in Three' where they repay in three equal statements
- 'Slice It' where customers repay in instalments for anything from three months to three years

Klarna has two customer groups: the consumers who use the buy now pay later system to manage their finances and the online stores that offer Klarna as a payment system.

Nearly one billion consumers use Klarna for shopping. In its own research, Klarna found that 67 per cent of its customers use the payment option as a method of spreading the cost of a purchase into smaller, more manageable amounts.

Over 250,000 retailers trust Klarna globally, including ASOS, Etsy, IKEA, Nike, North Face, Ralph Lauren, Samsung and Sephora. Well established in Europe and North America, the service is growing in Australia and New Zealand.

There are growing concerns about buy now pay later systems which has become an area where regulation is moving in, and Klarna works closely with official financial authorities providing advice and sharing its insights.

(Continued)

Case questions

- Evaluate the advantages and disadvantages for consumers in using a BNPL like Klarna.
- How do buy now pay later systems add value for online retailers? What are the critical factors to consider when signing up for a BNPL system?
- Klarna has demonstrated that it's an innovative company and is a keen adopter of new technology. How else might the company make use of online data and technology?

DISCOVER MORE ON HOW BNPL SCHEMES WORK

An article by researchers in Australia examined the regulations around BNPL with a background to the history of the schemes. Read 'Analyzing the Impacts of Financial Services Regulation to Make the Case That Buy-Now-Pay-Later Regulation Is Failing' by Johnson et al. (2021) in the journal *Sustainability*.

1.5.2 CRYPTOCURRENCIES

In 2009 a new form of digital currency was introduced to the world, a cryptocurrency called Bitcoin. Created anonymously, it works on the basis of peer-to-peer financing. There are no banks, no third parties, no bank vaults and no cash machines involved with Bitcoin.

Your cryptocurrency is stored in a digital wallet which is kept on your computer or stored in the cloud. You buy, store or sell cryptocurrency on digital currency exchanges. For example, billionaire twins Cameron and Tyler Winklevoss, known for suing Facebook as they believed that Mark Zuckerberg had stolen their idea (this became a film, *The Social Network*), formed a digital currency exchange in 2014. Aptly named Gemini, it was founded and is regulated by the New York State Department of Financial Services to allow customers to buy, sell and store digital assets such as Bitcoin.

Although Bitcoin may be the best known, there are over 4,000 cryptocurrencies available for purchase in any currency, such as Ethereum and Litecoin. Transactions are recorded online in a transparent register or ledger, which is called a blockchain, and all transactions are checked electronically.

Using Bitcoin as the example, new Bitcoins are created by mining and an industry of Bitcoin miners has developed. Bitcoin miners de-code online encrypted mathematical challenges using algorithmic processes. In exchange for their work in finding and recording Bitcoins on the blockchain, they are given Bitcoins.

There are downsides to Bitcoin as the whole process is anonymous, giving rise to the potential for money laundering as well as illegal or terrorist uses, and this has resulted in many mainstream banks refusing to accept Bitcoin or closing accounts trading in the currency. A major challenge is that there are no guarantees if the coins are lost, and there have been many issues with all aspects of Bitcoin, from hacked wallets to software scams. Although some universities have accepted payment in Bitcoin, it's a complex area and you could lose all your money! It's an area that you need to investigate in detail before getting involved, although Bitcoin has created awareness of a new, disruptive digital currency.

1.5.3 BLOCKCHAIN

One technological innovation within digital processes is blockchain or distributed ledger technology (DLT). Generated through the development of Bitcoin, a blockchain is a distributed database where no one person or organisation stores all the data; it is securely shared in the cloud over several systems, records all actions and is open for verification (Workie and Jain, 2017).

Blockchain was initially aimed at securely recording all Bitcoin transactions but its usefulness on a wider scale for 'interorganizational cooperation' was then realised (Gupta, 2017, p. 3). The benefits of DLT are:

- One single person does not control all the data
- Data sets are portable
- Records are transparent
- It has greater data integrity as records cannot be changed later
- It is a more efficient system

Blockchain technology is already used in food safety, for example the French supermarket Carrefour uses blockchain to track foodstuffs including milk and fruit from the farmer to its stores. The farmers can add when the goods were harvested, picked or packed, the distributor can add collection times and the supermarket can record when the goods were placed on the shelves.

Other ways it can be used include:

- Medical records: Every specialist, every appointment, diagnosis, treatment and prescription history can be viewed in one place
- Education and training data: All results, certificates, accreditations, memberships and awards are in one place
- Property records: A property passport can be established that lists all safety checks, mortgages attached to the property, equipment installed (and removed), planning permissions and ownership

There are drawbacks to blockchain technology too: supercomputers use a lot of energy; some say as much as a small country! The database keeps growing and it is getting slower; if you make a mistake, it is there forever and can't be changed. Once content is added, it can't be corrected – whilst that has advantages, it is also a disadvantage.

> **DISCOVER MORE ON BLOCKCHAIN PRODUCTS**
>
> The legendary computer company IBM is working on blockchain products. Its website provides examples of how this is working, as well as offering more details on the basics of blockchain.
>   Visit ibm.com/uk-en/blockchain

1.6 DIGITAL PRIVACY

As we leave footprints across the internet when we are looking at websites, liking social media pages or messaging friends, our digital privacy has become more of a concern. We rarely check the terms and conditions (T&Cs) and, in any case, they're too long! Facebook's T&Cs are around 10 pages, WeChat has over 20, Microsoft and Twitter have 30-plus pages. Seriously, does anyone read these?

We probably should as they explain how our data is used. But the challenge is, even if we go ahead and read the T&Cs, we'd ignore the details to gain access to the service. This is known as the privacy paradox where we realise we're giving away our digital data, but do so in return for gaining access to the platform (see Chapter 6 for more on the privacy paradox). Perhaps an alternative approach is needed such as nudge theory.

1.6.1 NUDGE THEORY

Nudge theory was originally proposed by Professors Thaler and Sunstein in 2008. Rooted in psychology, the idea was that someone could be gently encouraged or nudged to do something, rather than being forced, if choices were presented in a different way. This has become a key method used in marketing campaigns by governments where they are seeking behaviour change. Often, this is for health purposes, such as diabetes management, stopping smoking or losing weight.

During the pandemic, we saw campaigns reminding us to socially distance, wear a mask and wash our hands. While wearing a mask might have been mandatory in some places, washing our hands wasn't, and many governments used different examples – nudge campaigns to motivate behavioural change.

The same has been tried with digital data. Banks and financial institutions have launched campaigns that explain how data can be misused, and provide best practice on password management. Yet data leaks, breaches and mismanagement occur. How many people do you know that potentially overshare, providing enough details for their data to be misused?

DISCOVER MORE ON NUDGE THEORY

The article 'Nudging the financial market? A review of the nudge theory' by Cynthia Weiyi Cai provides a useful background to nudge theory and where it has been used, as well as many examples. It was published in the journal *Accounting and Finance* in 2020.

1.6.2 WE HAVE NOTHING TO HIDE

At the same time, there is the argument that if we have nothing to hide, it doesn't matter (see Ethical Insights), but privacy is designed to protect us, not to hide us.

Privacy is complicated. An older article by Daniel Solove suggested that privacy could be invaded in many different forms (Solove, 2011). He noted that the focus seems to be on hiding bad things, rather than retaining or protecting private or personal things you don't want to share.

Imagine that you have an online diary that keeps your deepest secrets. This belongs to you and contains your hopes, thoughts and dreams. Although you have nothing to hide, sharing it could be embarrassing and cause you personal distress – this would be an invasion of privacy. In the same way, if you've mentioned or described friends and these details were exposed, although you may not be harming anyone, it could be embarrassing if this was shared.

Or perhaps when you were younger, you shared snaps with someone that you'd rather weren't seen now. Or maybe you're being watched without your permission through your phone or video cam, by your government, even if no secrets are revealed.

The social media networks are hacked probably more than any other platforms online and these networks contain our personal images, friends' information, thoughts, likes and dislikes, yet this data has been leaked many times.

Privacy is personal to each of us and it has a value. In our online world, this has real implications for how we work, rest and play. As a result, there are several themes connected to data and privacy (Garratt and Lee, 2021) which we will explore further in the next few sections:

- Data protection
- Acquisition of data and targeted advertising
- The right to be forgotten

Activity 1.3   Manage your privacy

Think back to your younger self. Is there content that you created that perhaps now you wish you hadn't? Assess your own privacy status. Check the settings on the apps you use most.

1.   What have you permitted and who can access your data?

2.   What have you blocked?

3.   Based on this, what changes are you likely to make in the future?

1.6.3 DATA PROTECTION

Weak behaviour around the care of data has been recognised worldwide, following multiple data breaches such as the Cambridge Analytica scandal, as well as well-known brands admitting to being hacked and losing customer data.

While there is data protection legislation in most countries, it is fragmented, as these examples show:

- The African Union (AU) Convention on Cybersecurity and Data Protection (known as the AU Convention) was proposed in 2014 and some African countries have adopted this or have created country-specific data privacy legislation.

- China has several legal frameworks governing data, including the Cybersecurity Law (2016). Recently, the country has created laws governing data security and personal information.

- Australia has Australian Privacy Principles (APPs) which provide guidelines on what is and is not acceptable. This is supported by the Privacy Act which includes the ability for courts to levy fines of up to AUD 2.1 million (that's around 1 million euros, pounds or US dollars) for those breaking the law and misusing data.

- New Zealand has Privacy Principles and introduced a Privacy Act in 2020 along with an ad campaign 'Privacy is Precious – Protect it. Respect it' to explain why it matters.

- Europe (including the UK) has the General Data Protection Regulation. Under GDPR, the maximum fine is 20 million euros or 4 per cent of turnover, whichever is greater.

- The United States has a fragmented approach, due to the lack of country-wide data protection law, instead providing differing approaches across individual states.

However, one state in America has created new legislation to provide greater protection for consumers: the California Consumer Privacy Act of 2018 (CCPA).

According to the State of California's Department of Justice, Office of the Attorney General (2021), this provides:

- The right to know about the personal information a business collects about them and how it is used and shared
- The right to delete personal information collected from them (with some exceptions)
- The right to opt out of the sale of their personal information
- The right to non-discrimination for exercising their CCPA rights

The challenge is that this applies only to a single state in the USA, but it's the state where Facebook (which owns Instagram, Messenger, WhatsApp), Microsoft (which owns LinkedIn, Hololens), Google (which owns YouTube, Android) and Apple have their headquarters. This means that they are governed by these laws, so if they decide to leave California, we should be worried!

The aim of these different laws is to offer consumers more control over the personal data that businesses collect. It moves the power from organisations to consumers who need to give consent about being contacted, so if you have allowed a company to contact you about an online sale and its staff contact you about a totally different subject, the law is being broken.

There are consequences and if organisations mismanage the data and it is accidentally shared, leaked or hacked, there may be large fines. The largest penalties are in Europe and can impact on large companies too. For example, for a large tech company with a turnover of 150 billion euros, 20 million euros may not seem great. But when that's 4 per cent of turnover or 6 billion euros, that gains attention and ensures these companies take privacy more seriously. However, at the other end of the scale, these fines could result in smaller businesses ceasing to trade if their data is not properly secured.

Smartphone Sixty Seconds® – Leaky data

- Take out your smartphone and search for *data leak*.
- What are the latest data breaches?
- Were you aware of these already?
- Who did this impact and does this matter?

1.6.4 ACQUISITION OF DATA AND TARGETED ADVERTISING

In an online context, we have to consider how the data for targeted or personalised advertising is gathered. Nothing is ever free. If you're offered software, apps or games that are free, you are the product. This means that social media platforms won't charge you to access Instagram, Clubhouse, Pinterest or Snapchat, but they will gather your data in the T&Cs we considered earlier. I can launch an Instagram advertising campaign in around 30 minutes that's targeted at students in your university or location. Or the campaign could target individuals that have downloaded K-pop music, played Cards Against Humanity or like Depop. Your online behaviour is tracked and added to online audiences, making it easier for advertising to present relevant content to you. Your online search history is remembered and can be used as part of an advertising campaign to increase awareness of a brand, encourage you to consider that brand over others, go to the website to complete a conversion action or share your enthusiasm for the brand with your friends.

So, you might add various pieces of data to a social media platform (e.g. name, location, date of birth), you might behave in a certain way on that platform (e.g. likes, follows, reactions), you might buy products online, and your data in one place might be shared with others and blended together. Figure 1.1 shows the overlap between the different areas, and on their own the information or data may not paint a full picture, but when combined this can be powerful and enable laser-focused targeting online.

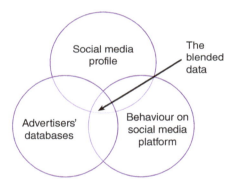

Figure 1.1   The blended data

As a marketer, this saves time and means you promote relevant goods to relevant people. Your granny might not be interested in Depop, but your friends might be. So, being able to advertise to specific audiences means campaigns can be better focused and more effective.

One thing to consider is that while much of this data is shared, it's at an aggregated level. This means that you're targeting groups of people who match those characteristics, rather than individuals. This is as a result of the privacy legislation, but does mean that locations without these laws have little respect for our privacy.

One change we are likely to see in the future is consumers being better able to control the sale of their data. The California Consumer Privacy Act (2018) allows individuals 'the right to opt-out of the sale of their personal information'. So we may see companies offering you vouchers, discounts or rewards in return for access to your data.

1.6.5 THE RIGHT TO BE FORGOTTEN

Having considered our digital privacy, data protection and data acquisition issues, we might decide we'd prefer that some pieces of online content are removed. As researchers have noticed, this is needed as 'Individuals could perpetually or periodically face stigmatization as a consequence of a specific past action, even one that has already been adequately penalized' (Garg et al., 2020, p. 1).

Under the GDPR legislation across Europe and the California Consumer Privacy Act, individuals have rights to 'have personal data erased' and 'delete personal information collected from them'. This is commonly referred to as 'the right to be forgotten', which enables individuals to remove unnecessary personal data from search engines.

There are exceptions and the right to be forgotten can conflict with freedom of information. So if the content serves public interest, it is harder to remove and we could argue that greater online transparency can protect us too.

One example in the UK was when the first Youth Police and Crime Commissioner was appointed in the south of England in 2013. This role represented the voice of the people, to hold the police to account, for younger people. So you'd imagine the candidates had unimpeachable reputations and were upstanding young members of the wider community. But when 17-year-old Paris Brown was appointed, it caused a media storm, not just because everyone wanted to know more about this teenager who was the first person in the role, but because a few online searches of her social media revealed unacceptable racist and homophobic comments made when she was younger. So, just seven days after getting the job, as police officers interviewed her, 17-year-old Ms Brown apologised, said she had made mistakes and resigned. Without the online content being found and reported, she may have continued in the role which was designed to represent all young people.

While the right to be forgotten matters, at times it can help inform decisions. Yet it is based on legislation in certain locations only such as Europe and California, which means that the information may still be available in other countries or states.

Digital privacy will continue to be a major issue for organisations, especially as consumers understand the consequences. This means that companies need to ensure they protect and respect our data and that we learn how to better manage our information.

DIGITAL TOOL The right to be forgotten

See how the right to be forgotten process takes place through the search engines' request forms for removal of content:

Google: https://is.gd/righttobe

Bing: bing.com/webmaster/tools/eu-privacy-request

JOURNAL OF NOTE

Originally called the *Journal of Direct Marketing*, in 1988 its name changed to the *Journal of Interactive Marketing*, to better reflect the wider impact of digital marketing on consumers. It's likely to be available via your university or study centre to access and explore further.

CASE STUDY

SEAT NUMBER 9: INTRODUCING STRAVA, INC.

This case study continues in all chapters.

One cold Tuesday morning in November 1986, Michael Horvath and Mark Gainey, students at Harvard University, were rowing with six crew members in a Resolute along the Charles River. Rowing was an escape from class, a break from mental activities and a space to think. They were literally all in the same boat, having to work together to achieve their goal. From seat number 9, the cox called out commands and at the end of the session told them their times. The challenge was knowing if they'd achieved a personal best or not, so some chilly mornings it was difficult to get motivated and row faster.

Horvath and Gainey had an idea to develop an internet tool that could foster motivation and track performance, but back in 1986 the internet was slow and mobile phones were still analogue, with Nokia and Mitsubishi dominating the market. Real life got in the way as Horvath and Gainey graduated and went their separate ways until 1996 when they co-founded Kana Communications, which became a successful software company. This gave them an insight into technology firms, as well as how to grow and market a digital business.

Skipping ahead to 2009, two decades after rowing together at university, they decided the time was right and the technology was in place to revisit their earlier idea. Mobile phones were more widely available and the Global Positioning System (GPS) was easy to access. Both Horvath and Gainey were competitive fitness fans and the idea was for some form of tool that would track performance. They selected cycling, because they'd seen that cyclists had true passion and a real energy for their workouts.

In the past, enthusiastic cyclists who were keen to measure how far they'd travelled would use a map, pieces of string and a ruler to calculate the distance. Using these measurement tools when out cycling created challenges as paper maps could get damaged in the rain and needed greater attention to view (and not fall off). Creative cyclists would place the maps under plastic that was fixed to their handlebars and soon bicycle companies were selling accessories to make this easier. As technology evolved and computers became smaller, personal navigation devices (PNDs) were developed and in 1989 Garmin was launched, selling hand-held GPS units, but these weren't accessible to everyone as the starting price at that time was over £2,000.

Horvath and Gainey developed a free app that could see where you went, how far, how high and for how long. The business started as mobile first – users could take a mobile device on their ride and plug into their computer when they returned from their workout to see their performance. According to Mark Gainey (Smedley, 2020), the business focus was 'Inch wide mile deep', meaning their aim was to focus on one sport and create a rich experience for that audience.

For the first three to four years, Strava only offered cycling as an activity until in 2012–13 they added running as a second fitness activity. Mark Gainey commented that they had made many mistakes along the way as they were trying to support different audiences. Today, Strava has a better-managed and expanded product offer and includes dozens of sports: running, walking, canoeing, kitesurfing, snowboarding, swimming and rowing. It has since added some accessibility features with wheelchair activities.

With these additional activities, Strava collects between 10 and 20 billion pieces of data every day on a global basis. Athletes can opt out of sharing their data, although it's anonymised and aggregated, so in theory single individuals could not be identified. The data includes GPS locations, activity type, duration, speed, comparative information, popular routes, connected devices and more.

Strava shares its data with researchers on a dedicated projects website (see https://labs.strava.com) and this data is being used to help urban planners improve cycling and running routes. Strava has created a separate website for urban planning (see https://metro.strava.com) to enable governments, consultants and researchers to review transport planning, cycle paths and tourism.

There have been stories online that fitness fans working for military organisations who are sharing their activities have accidentally exposed military bases and popular running routes for those working for the secret service.

Strava started as a free app but in 2020 this changed and the business started charging users $50 or £50 for a 12-month subscription to access key features. There have been many negative blog posts about this latest change, with users saying they will delete their Strava app.

You'll discover more about Strava at the end of each chapter as the case continues throughout the book, applying the different concepts that are covered.

CASE QUESTIONS

- What item of technology do you have that replaced some other method of performing a task? How long did it take you to adopt this new technology?

- Strava gathers large amounts of data from its users. What actions should they take to ensure this is protected and not misused?

- Businesses have to generate an income to pay their staff. How do you feel about Strava's move towards monetising its services?

FURTHER EXERCISES

1. Evaluate the impact of the digital environment on an organisation you are familiar with.

2. Applying nudge theory, create a campaign targeted at students to encourage better digital privacy management.

3. For an organisation of your choice that sells digital goods, analyse the opportunities and relevance of using buy now pay later (BNPL) options.

4. Online personalised pricing is unfair as some groups gain an advantage with lower prices being offered whilst some groups are charged more. Discuss and justify your response.

SUMMARY

This chapter has explored:

* Key issues in the digital environment
* Factors in digital people
* Types of digital products and ethical issues around digital theft
* Different types of digital payments and currencies
* Big data and issues concerning digital privacy

GO ONLINE

Visit **study.sagepub.com/hanlon2e** to access links to interesting articles, websites and videos related to this chapter.

OVERVIEW
Chapter 2 discusses the digitial consumer and how behaviour has changed in a digital environment. Customer journeys are discussed with visual examples.

KEY CONCEPTS

Showrooming and webrooming

Net Promoter Score

Technology Acceptance Model

ACTIVITIES

Construct a simple customer journey

Create a digital persona

Apply the Technology Acceptance Model

DIGITAL TOOLS

Explore Review Skeptic to see the difference between genuine and fake reviews

Use Uxpressia to create a customer journey map

2

THE DIGITAL CONSUMER

LEARNING OUTCOMES

When you have read this chapter, you will be able to:

Understand digital consumer behaviour

Apply the Technology Acceptance Model

Analyse the digital customer experience

Evaluate the sharing economy

Create an online customer journey

PROFESSIONAL SKILLS

When you have worked through this chapter, you should be able to:

- Understand critical touchpoints in organisations
- Create a digital persona

2.1 INTRODUCTION TO THE DIGITAL CONSUMER

We have moved from a time when companies made as many products as they could and sold as many as possible in the mass production era, when there were few options for shopping other than local stores. We can now access products from any place at any time and often on any device. There is a culture of sharing what we have; from cars to spare rooms. Plus we accept technology and understand the usefulness it contributes to our lives.

So who or what is the digital consumer? Consumers include you and me: people who consume things in a digital environment, from food to fashion, online fitness streams to our favourite brand forums. Consumption is the process of buying or using goods, which, in a digital environment, may involve watching, downloading, playing, adding, collaborating, commenting, liking, following, sharing, posting, storing or shopping.

2.1.1 WE'RE ALL CONNECTED

An experiment to assess how we're connected, using old-fashioned letters (Travers and Milgram, 1969), demonstrated that the number of degrees of separation between one random person and another was six. 'Six Degrees of Separation' was later the title of a play and a movie. It quickly became a meme, as, in an online world, we're all connected.

The idea of six degrees of separation is based on the concept of living in a small world where everyone knows someone who knows that person. The first online social network was called Six Degrees but it failed due to the technology and infrastructure available back in 1997 (Heidemann et al., 2012). Today, social networks like LinkedIn facilitate these connections. So when you're looking for a new job, always check out the degrees of separation between you and the people you'll be working with!

In this chapter, we will explore how digital marketing has changed consumer behaviour. We'll consider the sharing economy as well as our customer journeys and digital personas. Finally, we'll examine the Technology Acceptance Model to better understand why we do, or don't, accept new technology.

Smartphone Sixty Seconds® – Degrees of separation

- Use your mobile phone to log in to LinkedIn and look at the vice-chancellor (VC) of your university.
- How many degrees of separation are there between you and the VC?
- Who in the class has fewest degrees of separation between themselves and the VC?

2.2 CHANGING DIGITAL CONSUMER BEHAVIOUR

Consumer behaviour has changed with the introduction of new technology and examples of this include:

- Consumer power
- Second screening
- Showrooming and webrooming
- Liquid and solid consumption

These are discussed in the following sections.

2.2.1 CONSUMER POWER

In the past, organisations controlled their messaging, branding and information. They were created by the organisation, placed by the organisation in a suitable location (newspapers, magazines, websites) and, other than letters to the editor, consumers had few opportunities for feedback.

A typology of consumer communication identifies voicers, activists and irates (Naylor, 2017, p. 134). Voicers share opinions online, both good and bad. Activists take legal action and share their messages using hashtags. Irates may have previously taken forms of direct action to gain attention and ensure their point of view was heard, as well as using social media.

In a digital setting, the power has moved from company to consumer and we have seen an increase in consumer power.

2.2.2 SECOND SCREENING

Second screening is also called dual screening, media meshing, sofalising or connecting media. The concept is watching a TV screen (or a programme via Netflix on your laptop) while messaging friends on your mobile and using a tablet to search for content mentioned on the programme.

Second screening has become commonplace. Initially considered information-seeking behaviour, a new form of usage is emerging – discussion. According to Liu, Zhou and Zhang (2020), second screening is impacting on political events and live news consumption is being augmented. Individuals have moved beyond seeking information: they are actively sharing opinions and adding content. In a political context, this can change points of view and potentially influence elections.

2.2.3 SHOWROOMING AND WEBROOMING

The concepts of showrooming and webrooming first emerged in 2011 from consultancy studies where consumer buying behaviour and preferences were explored. Showrooming means searching in store and buying online.

Reasons for showrooming include answering questions before purchasing, such as: What will it look like? Will it fit? Is it heavy? These gaps in your knowledge are due to the mental model, which is the picture that the consumer builds in their mind of how something works, such as how a product will function – whether that's the fabric of a jacket, a new laptop or an app. If someone cannot see how an item will work, they may adopt showrooming to check out the item in more detail and, when they are satisfied that it meets their needs, buy the item online.

This concurs with research from Verhoef et al. (2015) who considered showrooming to be a form of research shopper behaviour where a consumer would visit a store, explore the required goods and the purchase would take place online. The benefits of showrooming for consumers include:

- It is easy to search at any time
- It is quick to find information
- There may be offers or better prices online

However, not all showrooming behaviour is the same. A study by Schneider and Zielke (2020) considered (a) the impact of where consumers buy which they called locational factors (in store or at home) and (b) loyalty to specific stores. From this their study identified four types of showroomer:

- Conservative showroomers mainly use devices at home and stay with the same retailer. So they might explore in store, make a note and return home to carry out further research.
- Loyal showroomers are less concerned about the location but prefer to shop with one retailer.
- Comfort-oriented economic showroomers prefer to buy from home but they are price conscious so will take time to search online for better prices.
- Mobile economic showroomers mainly shop using mobile devices and have no loyalty to specific retailers, so they price check to seek cheaper items elsewhere.

The opposite of showrooming occurs, which is known as webrooming (Verhoef et al., 2015), where consumers search online and buy offline in a physical store. The reason for the in-store purchase is said to be a lack of confidence about buying online (Orús, Gurrea and Ibáñez-Sánchez, 2019). Arora and Sahney (2017) suggest that webrooming, or ROBO (Research Online Buy Offline), exists for several reasons:

- Consumers gather more information about the product choices
- Online reviews make it easier to choose products
- It reduces the risk of buying online
- It helps to reduce the different options available

Ways to manage showrooming include creating special online or offline only products, or grouping products together to make comparison difficult, or price matching. But there are challenges with tracking the in-store shopper who makes the purchase online. Plus, consumers can be both a showroomer and a webroomer!

A luxury brand transforming its retail stores into experiences is Ralph Lauren who has reduced showrooming by encouraging shoppers to stay longer and complete the purchase. They've incorporated coffee shops and restaurants in their flagship stores in New York, Tokyo and Beijing. They've addressed webrooming and added the 'RL Virtual Experience', using technology normally associated with selling property to provide 360-degree walkthroughs of flagship stores, with opportunities to 'add to cart' along the journey. These luxury brands are recognising that our shopping behaviour has changed and they're ensuring they can manage both online and offline shoppers, in a similar way.

2.2.4 LIQUID AND SOLID CONSUMPTION

We no longer buy physical products only and may subscribe to digital-only items. This is known as liquid consumption. Access to the products is 'ephemeral, access based, and dematerialized' (Bardhi and Eckhardt, 2017, p. 582). This is the opposite of solid consumption, 'which is enduring, ownership based, and tangible' (Bardhi and Eckhardt, 2017, p. 582).

This is a step change which Bardhi and Eckhardt argue has partly occurred with the increase in the digital economy and that consumers, in some cases, place greater dependence on digital access than physical ownership. The absence of physical goods, or fluid consumption, is known as dematerialisation. Instead of acquiring items, we consume in a digital setting.

An example of dematerialisation is music. There was a time when people owned vinyl records, cassette tapes or CDs, whereas today most of us don't physically own any music; we rent playlists via Spotify, Amazon or iTunes accounts, or we ask Alexa, Google Home or other smart speakers to play our favourite music. We have removed the need to own material goods.

One other issue is digital clutter. It's great adopting a fluid perspective, but how many photos have you stored on Instagram? How many emails have you archived? As it is easier to retain liquid possessions, do we ever review and remove, as we would do with old clothing? What will happen to charity shops or thrift stores if a generation moves towards liquid possessions? These shops, from health research associations to animal charities, depend upon the acquisition of solid possessions.

Smartphone Sixty Seconds® – Check your digital clutter

- On your mobile phone open your photos.
- How many are there?
- What other digital clutter is on your mobile phone?
- Do you back up your mobile or store your photos, contacts and messages somewhere else in case your mobile phone breaks and can't be repaired?

Students often move between solid and liquid consumption. Some bring many possessions to university whereas others travel light, often due to necessity, with a laptop, mobile phone and clothes. Those towards the fluid end of the scale can access music and films online, with their contacts and memories stored in their mobile phone.

2.3 THE SHARING ECONOMY

Another change in our behaviour is that we share items owned by others. This is known as the sharing economy, which involves a temporary peer-to-peer exchange accessed via technology. The exchange needs three parties: the platform operator, the provider offering the service and the consumer. The operator – such as Airbnb – creates a peer-to-peer platform where you can offer your home, as well as find new places to stay.

It has been defined as 'a consumption-production mode in a city, in which value is generated through transactions between actors (both organisations and individuals) involving temporary access to idling or underutilised rivalrous physical assets' (Voytenko Palgan et al., 2021, p. 1) and as 'a scalable socioeconomic system that employs technology-enabled platforms to provide users with temporary access to tangible and intangible resources that may be crowdsourced' (Eckhardt et al., 2019, p. 7).

According to Eckhardt et al. (2019), the characteristics of an organisation in the sharing economy are based on: technology, the changing role of consumers as prosumers, money for the service, the temporary nature of the service and crowdsourcing the supply. Figure 2.1 shows a framework of the different elements in the sharing economy, with the exchange taking place between the provider and consumer which is facilitated through the platform operator.

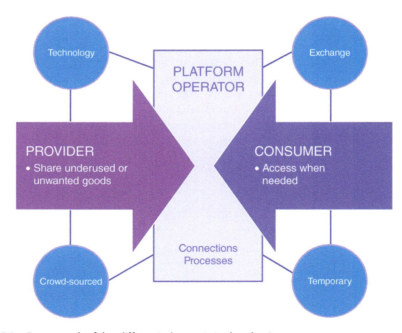

Figure 2.1 Framework of the different elements in the sharing economy

Let's explore these elements.

The sharing economy only works with technology, often via an app, which is why this is considered to be part of digital disruption (see Chapter 1). For example, taxi cabs in various forms have existed in England since the 1600s. So Uber's service is not new, but accessed in a different way.

The technology needs to be easy to use for both service providers and consumers. Ideally service providers either have free time to share their cars or skills, or, in the case of Airbnb, their accommodation is not used 100 per cent of the time, so providers can share their space to generate an additional income.

Although Eckhardt et al. (2019) argue that money must change hands, this is not always the case. Yet, there is always an exchange which can involve payment, in the cases of Uber and Airbnb, but there are other exchanges too. One example is the Freecycle Network which is a platform operator that allows consumers to share unwanted items with others though its website – turning trash into treasure. There is no payment and the Freecycle Network makes its money through adverts on its website and donations.

In the sharing economy, the connections are not one-to-one but from many-to-many which involves the crowd – wider groups that wouldn't normally find each other. Another element is the ephemeral or temporary nature of the exchange. The items are not sold, but shared on a temporary basis. This could be a one-off ride, a short stay or skill that's needed at that specific time.

2.3.1 WHY CONSUMERS SHARE

We share cars, sofas, playlists, film accounts, clothes and books. The notion of a sharing economy is not new; for example, libraries are probably the oldest form of a sharing system. We have always borrowed or loaned goods between friends and neighbours but today's sharing economy is more sophisticated. Instead of sharing with neighbours, you are sharing with strangers; this is known as **collaborative consumption** (see **Discover More**), which has been described as 'people coordinating the acquisition and distribution of a resource for a fee or other compensation' (Belk, 2014, p. 1597).

Two of the success factors for collaborative consumption are: (a) critical mass so there were enough people signing onto the platform; and (b) social proof as potential community members heard, saw or read about others using the platform (Botsman and Rogers, 2010).

DISCOVER MORE ON COLLABORATIVE CONSUMPTION

Researchers Eleonora Pantano and Nikolaos Stylos have explored the motivations of people renting goods rather than owning them in 'The Cinderella moment: Exploring consumers' motivations to engage with renting as collaborative luxury consumption mode', which provides further background to this area and was published in the journal *Psychology and Marketing* in 2020.

Researchers found three main reasons why people participate in the sharing economy: to save money, for the social interaction as part of a community, and because they understand sustainable consumption and want to do good within society (Hallem et al., 2020). These researchers identified types of sharers or collaborative consumers:

- **Committed**: Conscious of ecological issues and seeking ways to reduce consumption
- **Pragmatist**: Take a practical approach and like the ease of using the platforms
- **Intermittent**: Busy people who sometimes use the platforms
- **Sceptical**: Don't see the need and prefer traditional consumption

Some companies are already following types of collaborative consumption. For example, Amazon has sold second-hand books for over a decade and IKEA has created a 'BuyBack & resell service' to recycle more of its furniture.

2.3.2 PROSUMERS

Digital consumers can be prosumers (Toffler, 1980), a combination of the words 'producer' and 'consumer'. This is because consumers don't just consume, they have become producers of goods and services too. Prosumers are often considered within the context of the sharing economy – I can share my car or rent your car (Uber), share my home or rent your home (Airbnb), share my clothes and rent your clothes (ByRotation.com).

2.3.3 ADVANTAGES AND DISADVANTAGES OF THE SHARING ECONOMY

One advantage of the sharing economy is that it can enhance sustainability. Consumers reduce waste or over-consumption by sharing or trading unwanted goods.

For providers, disadvantages include making temporary solutions permanent. For example, some Uber drivers turned their occasional ride-sharing into a full-time business. But during 2020 many sharing services stopped. Travel to work or for leisure stopped and many sharing providers lost income. For instance, the Airbnb hosts who had borrowed money to buy additional accommodation faced cancellations, plus no income for many months.

The sharing economy works when we're a safe and secure world, but as soon as one major factor changes this, such as COVID-19, the difficulties are highlighted. For the providers who moved from being occasional sharers to full-time business managers, the sharing economy may become a lost economy.

CASE EXAMPLE 2.1   Uber and the sharing economy

Uber is a technology company that took a traditional method of hailing taxis – waving your arm in the air when you managed to see a cab nearby – and made it digital, making it easy to find a cab when you need one. The concept is known as 'ridesourcing' (Button, 2020, p. 76) and the numbers are impressive, with nearly 1 billion people using the app in over 70 countries across 10,000 cities.

The initial concept was much more than a tech company: it was a central part of the sharing economy, encouraging consumers to be both producers of the service and consumers – prosumers. Drivers shared their clean cars with someone travelling in the same direction. On your regular journey to work, you could use your car and register to become an Uber driver and perhaps earn extra money at the weekends. The Uber app enables people to share their cars and as a rider you open the app, request a trip and pay through the app. So you can be both a rider and a driver, a prosumer.

But it's become a business with drivers signing up in the hope of gaining a fantastic salary, yet often working for less than the minimum wage with much time waiting for bookings, hence the legal challenges. Kenneth Button calls this 'Ubernomics' and notes that 'Uber does not own vehicles, give training, pay driver expenses, provide insurance, or accept liability' (Button, 2020, p. 77), so all the risk is with the provider.

For the platform operators, it's not an easy business to start as every town, city and region has its own licensing authority. So a taxi firm could gain a licence in London or New York, but that doesn't mean they can operate in Birmingham or San Francisco. There's a separate process every step of the way and a lot of red tape.

Uber has faced many licensing and legal challenges. At the start, there were concerns that drivers had not been properly verified, and the London licensing authority withdrew Uber's permission to operate as it claimed it failed to carry out background checks. Uber contested the claim and won, but like the variations in licensing, the verification process varies from place to place. For instance, in California, drivers are vetted by the Justice Department with fingerprint scanning, drug and alcohol testing, and additional searches. In London, checks are conducted through a third party which looks at the driver's previous addresses, passport and driving licence to highlight misdemeanours or criminal records.

Some drivers have taken Uber to court to challenge driver classification which considers whether drivers are employees, workers or quasi-employees, rather than being self-employed or independent contractors choosing when to work. Uber won its first battle in California, but lost in the UK, and there are more cases on the way. If Uber loses these legal cases, the business model no longer works and the company may withdraw from some locations which may result in the end of the business.

(Continued)

Case questions

- As many Uber drivers seem to be offering rides full-time, is Uber still part of the sharing economy?
- Have you participated in the sharing economy as a producer, sharing your resources? How did this work for you?
- What are the downsides of the sharing economy, as a consumer?

ETHICAL INSIGHTS   The dark side of the sharing economy

The sharing economy is often considered positively as it helps people gain an income (providers) and keeps costs lower for those using the service (consumers). But there is a dark side and, according to Buhalis, Andreu and Gnoth (2020), providers have little training and consumers can be rude or abusive, leading to 'co-destruction'. For example, in Airbnb guests might complain about hosts, and hosts might add guests to a blocklist to discourage others from providing accommodation. Hosts might exaggerate the space available or use fake photos and guests can post negative reviews advising others to stay elsewhere. Each party destroys the other in this unregulated setting.

- Imagine you've secured a job managing a hotel brand and your boss has asked you to create positive reviews to combat negative comments on an international website. How do you feel about this?
- Have you ever experienced a service where fake photos were used? What do you think about this?
- Are there any benefits of co-destruction?

2.4 CUSTOMER EXPERIENCE

Customer experience management (CEM) considers the entire customer experience, whether offline, online or blended, such as the showrooming and webrooming examples. Customer journeys are a sub-set of the customer experience.

Although we talk about customers and consumers interchangeably, customers are those who make the purchase (in B2B they are clients) and consumers are those who use the purchase. Your friend can buy a gift for you, so they're the customer and you're the consumer. In this section, we will first explore the notion of customer experience and then look at customer journeys.

There is no agreement on what customer experience (CX) means. Described as 'a multi-dimensional construct that involves cognitive, emotional, behavioral, sensorial, and social components' (Lemon and Verhoef, 2016, p. 70), this construct covers many bases from online to offline as well as virtual.

Earlier definitions include 'an evolution of the concept of relationship between the company and the customer' (Gentile et al., 2007, p. 397) and it 'encompasses every aspect of a company's offering – the quality of customer care, of course, but also advertising, packaging, product and service features, ease of use, and reliability' (Meyer and Schwager, 2007, p. 118).

2.4.1 TOUCHPOINTS

Differences between the idea of customer relationship and experience management are what a customer thinks about a company, the times when this happens and the touchpoints that are encountered (Meyer and Schwager, 2007). This is where we start hearing 'touchpoints' – the interactions between organisations and customers that occur in multiple channels. Lemon and Verhoef (2016) proposed four types of touchpoints:

- **Brand-owned**: managed by the brand such as its website or advertising. Brands can pay for keywords you might use to search for their products (see Chapter 3) to make the customer experience easier.

- **Partner-owned**: jointly owned by the brand and a partner, such as appearing on an affiliate or other website. Brands still control most of the content within the restrictions of the brand site, such as Tripadvisor®.

- **Customer-owned**: actions controlled by the customer, such as their choice of payment (credit card, Apple Pay, PayPal) or the device used to access the website or app. One issue is that the customer's dynamic external environment can have a significant influence on customer experience. Imagine that you're viewing a website and about to buy, but you're on a bus and suddenly it becomes crowded and others are looking at your mobile; this might make you abandon the purchase.

- **Social/external touchpoints**: content appearing across social media or other external sites such as review platforms. We know that we read and assess reviews and they are an essential factor when making purchase decisions.

When moving through the customer journey, customers both use and are exposed to multiple touchpoints. These have direct and indirect effects on their purchase and other customer behaviours (Lemon and Verhoef, 2016).

If a touchpoint has a negative effect, such as the consumer abandoning the shopping cart, it's important to understand why, so that it can be remedied.

CASE EXAMPLE 2.2 Moving customers from pre-purchase to purchase with Reviews.io

Consumer reviews help potential customers move from the pre-purchase to purchase stage by reading or watching feedback from other customers. These are social or external touchpoints and are part of online word of mouth or eWOM, which is any positive or negative statement made by potential, actual or former customers about a product or company, which is made available to a multitude of people and institutions via the Internet (Hennig-Thurau et al., 2004, p. 39).

Typically, a customer review includes a star rating, some comments or a show-and-tell video. These are gathered post-purchase and often via email or text message. Reviews can be applied to the whole business (usually about customer service) or individual products. Companies are notified about new reviews and access the data via a dashboard, which allows companies to respond.

Reviews.io wasn't the first platform that enabled companies to collect verified customer feedback, but their focus was making it easier and collecting different types of reviews. In addition to the star ratings and written remarks, Reviews.io captures feedback via SMS and video. Collecting comments by text message works well where people are shopping via an app or mobile and don't use email as often. Reviews.io encourages video reviews and although these are used less frequently, they are powerful steps in the customer journey, as real customers upload videos to share how they use, wear and consume. Another innovative service is automatically turning reviews into social media posts. In the company dashboard, companies can select great reviews, choose the social media platform and posts are automatically created, ready to share.

However, as reviews have become so valuable, one of the challenges is the growth of fake reviews and many major organisations have fallen foul of this practice, including Tripadvisor®, Amazon and tech product company HTC (Wu et al., 2020). An entire business based on trying to combat fake reviews has emerged, mainly led by researchers seeking algorithms to better identify the fakes (see Digital Tool **Review Skeptic**). Fake reviews can be created by companies, by people paid by companies to make an organisation look good, or automated where online programs use machine learning to add positive words to describe products.

Companies such as Reviews.io try to combat this weak practice by only accepting verified reviews which are collected through automation after a purchase is made. This aims to reduce inauthentic and deceptive comments as they are a 'verified purchase'.

Case questions

- Have you ever made a decision to buy – or not to buy – an item because of a review?
- What do you think are the key components of a good and a fake review?
- In addition to written reviews, video testimonials and star ratings, what other formats could be used to create reviews?

DIGITAL TOOL   Review Skeptic

A team at Cornell University created a 'review checker' which was designed to identify genuine and fake reviews based on the language used in the consumer comments. Although this was an experiment to see if a computer could see the difference between authentic and bogus hotel reviews, it is a useful way of understanding what fake reviews look like.

- You can try it here: www.reviewskeptic.com

2.4.2 CUSTOMER SERVICE ENCOUNTERS

A variation of the customer service experience is the idea of customer service *encounters*. A study suggested that the difference between service encounter and service experience was about the period of time the service lasted (Voorhees et al., 2016). An ongoing or continuous service was an experience, whereas a specific service was an encounter.

The encounters were divided into three phases:

- Pre-core service encounter – the time before the main service where the customer engages with the firm and seeks information such as online reviews.
- Core service encounter – the time at which the primary service is provided.
- Post-core service encounter – the time after the service has been received where the consumer reflects, assesses the service and may complete online feedback.

A popular way to measure whether customers are satisfied with the service encounter is **Net Promoter Score**® (see Key Term).

KEY TERM   NET PROMOTER SCORE® (NPS)

A Net Promoter Score® is often based on a single-question survey asking customers how likely they are to recommend the product or service on a scale of 1 to 10, and is used by major retailers including Apple.

There are three categories of customers:

- Promoters (score 9–10) are happy customers who are likely to keep buying and recommend the company
- Passives (score 7–8) are satisfied but not delighted and may switch to other companies
- Detractors (score 0–6) are unhappy customers who may have voiced their feelings on social media

The percentage of all scores from 1 to 6 is subtracted from the percentage of 9s and 10s; 7s and 8s are ignored (Reichheld, 2003). The scores range from –100 to +100. The downside with the NPS is that it doesn't explain why the customers may be promoters or detractors.

2.5 CUSTOMER JOURNEYS

Part of the customer experience are customer journeys which are the process or sequence of events that consumers take from searching for an item to concluding with a successful outcome, such as a purchase, a download or sharing data. The concept was identified by a consultancy team from McKinsey who developed a strategic model from the initial consideration set to the post-purchase experience, moving away from traditional linear sales funnels.

Customer journeys should be as smooth as possible, providing a good customer experience. This is often referred to as seamless, effortless or frictionless.

One challenge with customer journey terminology is that it lacks consistency, because the customer journey and the process of understanding the steps that customers take to complete an action is described in different ways. Sometimes the customer journey is referred to as the buyer journey, the consumer journey, the consumer decision journey or the path to purchase. The changes tend to be based on different types of business models – whether that's B2C or B2B.

Regardless of the terminology, according to Lemon and Verhoef (2016), the customer journey is in three main stages, as discussed in this next section.

2.5.1 CUSTOMER JOURNEY STAGES

Stage 1: Pre-purchase

This stage starts with problem or need recognition, understanding that you have a problem to solve, or a need to be fulfilled. The pre-purchase stage is where customers interact with the brand and encounter the first touchpoints, whether owned by the brand or partner, or from external or social sources in their search and initial consideration steps.

In this stage, consumers are actively evaluating the brand or product and in a B2B setting it could include a login to LinkedIn to check out a sales associate or the managing director. In B2C consumers could search for online reviews or look at the company Instagram page to see the shared comments.

If this stage is not successful or the touchpoints are negative, the search may be abandoned, or another brand selected instead.

Stage 2: Purchase or conversion

If the pre-purchase stage is successful, the consumer moves towards the purchase stage, often known as the conversion. The purchase stage concerns all customer inter-actions with varied touchpoints during the purchase: the online user experience, ease of purchase, delivery choices and confirmation of delivery if relevant. The experience of the purchase process is another factor.

An earlier description of the customer journey was 'the buyer journey'. This was a transactional perspective and was seen as the final stage to complete a sale. We may think of a customer journey as a visit to a website to buy a product, but in some cases no physical or immediate purchase is made because a customer journey can involve conversion actions including:

- Downloading a brochure
- Signing up for a newsletter
- Filling in a form
- Submitting information
- Registering interest or support

Buyer journeys are often used in commercial organisations where the goal is an instant conversion.

Stage 3: Post-purchase

The final stage, which is a newer aspect found in digital marketing, is the post-purchase stage. According to Lemon and Verhoef, this comprises behaviours such as usage and consumption – you bought it but did you use it? Did you leave a review? Sign up for the newsletter? Share the purchase with friends? Again, the customer experience of how the process was managed is a contributing factor towards future purchasing.

The digital environment has provided consumers with access to greater choice. The customer journey has therefore changed, as shown in Table 2.1, which indicates the different customer journey stages and touchpoints applied to a traditional and digital setting.

Table 2.1 How the customer journey has changed

Customer journey stage	Touchpoints	Traditional consumer	Digital consumer
Pre-purchase	Search	High street or shopping mall, items in magazines	• We search online for products • We use voice search and ask our devices to search for us • We explore products our friends recommend on social media
Pre-purchase	Selection	Examine products in real life and decide whether to buy	• We compare delivery times, costs, overall costs • We check reviews and ratings
Pre-purchase	Decision making and choice	Decision making with fixed store times	• Based on ratings and ease of purchase we decide and choose • We save items for later with 'wish lists'
Purchase	Shopping	Physical visits to stores	• We use branded websites and comparison websites to shop online • We use store apps for instant shopping • We buy during live video streaming (LVS)
Purchase	Purchase	Involves queuing to pay	• One-click delivery systems, next-day delivery, delivery to lockers
Purchase	Gift	Requires additional effort to take away, wrap, pack and post	• Automatic gift options and reminders, purchase from one address and delivery to another address
Purchase	Rental	Physically visit a store to organise a rental agreement	• We rent music, properties, cars and more, at the click of a mouse

2.5.2 CUSTOMER JOURNEY MAPPING

Customer journey mapping is generally acknowledged to have been devised by Barry Kibel (2000) where he suggested that results mapping could be used as an approach for assessing the work of social, health and education programmes. The process was to map, score, analyse and provide feedback about a programme and the key factor was using a visual representation of the journey or process.

Let's examine an online customer journey, step by step, that I've mapped out and which is shown in Figure 2.2. This online customer journey is based on buying a laptop – not an everyday purchase and one that requires some investigation. This shows the pre-purchase, purchase and post-purchase stages, which highlight the different brand, partner and customer-owned touchpoints along with the social and external touchpoints.

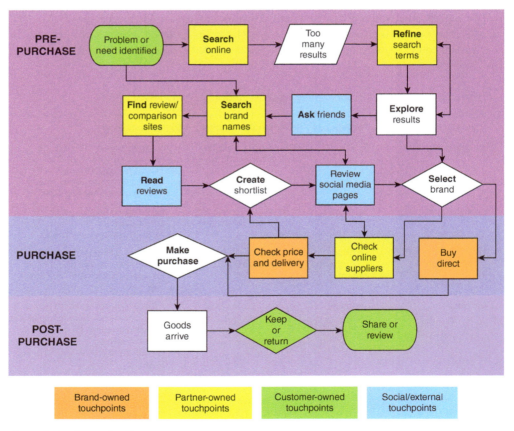

Figure 2.2 Example of a customer journey map

Figure 2.2 is based on a digital journey, so no showrooming or webrooming is involved. In this example, the first step is identifying a problem or a need – perhaps your laptop has broken and you need a new one. This is the beginning of the pre-purchase stage which is often the longest part of the customer journey.

The pre-purchase journey usually starts with an online search, adding words into a search engine – in this case using the words 'laptop for studying'. With millions of shopping websites available, this provides too many results and you refine the search terms and add more words; for example, 'lightweight laptop for studying with good battery life' or 'laptop for studying with touchscreen'. These are known as search terms and the results are based on the keywords and key phrases used (see Chapter 3). These are partner-owned touchpoints which may be controlled by Google, Bing or Baidu – whatever search engine the customer chooses to use.

You explore the search results further, but you seek social or external touchpoints by asking friends for recommendations. From this you start to search for specific brand names. Perhaps you knew the brand you wanted and visited its social media to read feedback from other people? If not, you might look at review sites or comparison sites where they have star ratings for the different products. When you've read the reviews and gathered more information, you create a shortlist – that's the first decision, as you have removed some of the brands from your potential selection.

If you haven't already, you might explore brands' social media pages and make the next decision as to which brand to select.

You move into the purchase stage. You've decided to buy, you're ready to spend some money. You might explore online suppliers and check the options for price and delivery. The next decision takes place, which often involves brand-owned touchpoints such as its website, and the purchase is made. When the laptop arrives, there is another decision or customer-owned touchpoint – to keep it or return it.

Finally, you reach the post-purchase stage and may provide feedback, add a review or share on social media, contributing future social touchpoints for other consumers.

This seems logical although there are some back and forward steps, so there may be steps missing. This highlights several factors; for example, the stages are complicated. In the laptop example, the pre-purchase stage could take one hour or several days. The customer journey is not linear. It rarely follows a straight line as customers can change their mind during the process, return to earlier steps or something else may occur and interrupt the journey – friends send a message to meet up and you abandon the search.

When discussing customer journeys, researchers David Norton and Joseph Pine described them as 'the sequence of events – whether designed or not – that customers go through to learn about, purchase and interact with company offerings – including commodities, goods, services or experiences' (Norton and Pine, 2013, p. 12). The key here is the concept of a sequence of events, regardless of whether the customer journey is online, offline or multi-channel.

Activity 2.1   Construct a customer journey

Assess your activity as an online customer. Consider your most expensive recent purchase and map out your pre-purchase, purchase and post-purchase stages.

DIGITAL TOOL   Customer journey maps

Uxpressia offers a free tool which can be useful to create professional customer journey maps.

Access and sign up here: https://uxpressia.com

2.5.3 PATH TO PURCHASE

Another type of customer journey mapping is path to purchase. Borrowed from computing terms, path data contains information about a user's search behaviour, interests and visits. In marketing parlance, the 'path to purchase' concept is similar to a non-linear customer journey; the difference is trying to attribute the elements or touchpoints which have had an impact on the journey. Was it the email? The pop-up offer on the website? Perhaps **dark social** (see Key Term) with a message from a friend? If the specific steps can be correctly attributed, more investment can be made where needed.

Google, as a major seller of online advertising, was an early pioneer of sharing path to purchase data and provides free access to aggregate data, to inform marketers about latest trends and insights.

Researchers created a conceptual framework for the path to purchase which combined the customer journey with stages initiated by the firm to influence and direct the purchase (Li and Kannan, 2013). They reviewed the channels connected to online purchases of high-involvement goods such as consumer durables and travel services.

This study used a linear model from the channels considered, which were identified through search, so, in the example of trying to find a short vacation, the consumer might search online for flights and they may visit a firm's own website, such as American Airlines or British Airways, or they may use a flight search engine such as SkyScanner. If the consumer goes backwards and forwards between the different sites, modifying their search terms, to gain the best price, they are leaving a trail of **cookies** (see Key Term) for the firms to add them to their online advertising campaigns. Ever noticed that ad following you around when you've just looked at a website? It's all based on your online behaviour and this is the area that Li and Kannan explored further as 'firm-initiated' behaviour, which we could call brand-owned touchpoints.

In some cases, this may have been display ads, like the follow-me marketing. But if a user responded to another channel, such as email, the firm may have subsequently sent a nudge email to encourage the web visitor to return to the website and complete their purchase.

KEY TERM   COOKIE

A web cookie is a small piece of data that is stored temporarily or for a period of time on your device when you have visited a website.

   There are two kinds of cookie: (a) session cookies, which are temporary whilst you are browsing and do not store your data; and (b) persistent cookies, which remember who you are. Persistent cookies remember usernames and passwords, automatically log in to websites and recall what is in your shopping basket.

Dark social

One of the greatest challenges in the online customer journey is when the organisation does not know how the customer arrived at the site – this is known as **dark social**. Dark social matters as marketers need to know what drives traffic to a website. In the pre-purchase stage, what's the most effective method of gaining new visits? If you don't know, it's difficult to manage!

To mitigate dark social, organisations need to re-think how the tracking works. It may be that they provide exclusive content to specific groups, using links that can be connected back to the group. Other methods include testing product promotion on different social media channels at different times, creating different links using link shorteners (bit.ly or Owl.y) to see the impact. Another method is to make sharing really simple. Buttons to 'share this' are often at the top or the end of a page, but these could be adapted to include sharing buttons in places such as mid-way through product descriptions, articles and posts.

KEY TERM   DARK SOCIAL

Dark social occurs when the tracking information (metadata) to report on the source of the visitor is lost. This occurs when a new customer arrives at your website, but you do not know how they heard of you – the source of the visit or relevant touchpoints. They are invisible on your analytics data and therefore cannot be attributed to a specific campaign (Madrigal, 2012).

   This happens when a friend copies a link and pastes it into an encrypted platform or private channel such as instant messages, text messages, email and message boards. So when the link is clicked, it is not obvious how the visitor found the web page. It can occur when someone screenshots a page and shares it, the receiver types out the web address and there is no indication as to the source. It's also known as invisible traffic.

2.6 DIGITAL PERSONAS

Historically, we considered customer segments or segmenting of marketing into groups. Customer segments divide customers into groups based on demographics. Personas take this further and consider the emotional elements (psychographics) and online behavioural (webographics) which is why they are more relevant in a digital marketing context.

Personas are 'representations of archetypical users; they bring "people to life" in the minds of the people who use them' (Hendriks and Peelen, 2013, p. 60). They are used by businesses to create content, build websites, develop advertising messages – to assess their likely reactions to the touchpoints along the customer journey.

2.6.1 WHY DO YOU NEED PERSONAS?

Personas 'enable organizations to view and see their products and services from the customer perspective' (Parise et al., 2016, p. 416). If you're 20 or 21 and you're writing a blog article aimed at a wealthy couple in their sixties, it's a stretch to imagine what their life is really like. As a student, you may be on a budget and you have no idea of the challenges faced by older people. That's where personas are invaluable, allowing you to step into the shoes of the customer.

2.6.2 HOW DO YOU CREATE A PERSONA?

The first step is to collect and analyse data about the customer groups. The data should be genuine and secondary research such as industry reports can help. You may seek primary data, which takes longer to organise and often requires an investment.

From the data, you should extract and identify patterns of behaviour to describe different 'types' of user. Typically, digital personas are based on three elements, as shown in Table 2.2, which also suggests examples of data sources (see Discover More on **Demographic Research Sources**).

Table 2.2   Digital persona elements

Persona element	What this means	Data source
Demographics	Age, gender, income, education, ethnicity, marital status, household (or business) size, geographical location, occupation	Mintel, Keynote, government data, sales data, in-house metrics and shopping statistics
Psychographics	Personality and emotionally based behaviour linked to buying habits, purchase choices, attitudes, beliefs, lifestyle, hobbies, holidays, values	Mintel, Keynote, government data showing hobbies and interests
Webographics	Internet usage, social media usage, websites visited, browsers used, devices and systems used, time of day and duration online, action on site (downloads, comments, likes), other media used	Online data sources such as Statista, Pew Internet, Google Analytics or offsite analytics, interviews and observation sessions with existing and potential users, user testing sessions

DISCOVER MORE ON DEMOGRAPHIC RESEARCH SOURCES

Many government bodies worldwide capture statistics that are free to access. They include the following:

- The Office for National Statistics is 'the recognised national statistical institute of the UK', providing data from leisure and finance to education and well-being. See www.ons.gov.uk.
- The European Union gathers data from country profiles to population details. See https://ec.europa.eu/info/statistics_en.
- The United Nations statistics division gathers and assembles worldwide demographic data. See https://unstats.un.org/home.
- The United Nations has links to national statistical offices' websites which cover Africa, the Americas, Asia, Europe and Oceania. See https://unstats.un.org/home/nso_sites.

Activity 2.2   Create a digital persona

1. For an organisation of your choice, construct a digital persona.

2. Conduct some research to identify data about the target audience and distil key demographic and psychographic features.

3. Based on additional research, propose webographic characteristics.

4. Provide an appropriate name and provide a suitable image to support a realistic persona.

2.7 THE EVOLUTION OF THE DIGITAL CONSUMER

There are different types of consumption and many theories about consumer behaviour. These often consider motivations for the decision; for example, did you need the item, or simply want to own it? If it was an essential purchase that's needed for survival, such as food, clothing or a mobile phone, this is described as utilitarian consumption. You may buy essential items from ecommerce websites, or from auction sites, or from an app where your last shopping list was stored.

The opposite of utilitarian consumption is hedonic, where goods are purchased for pleasure and, although these are not vital, they make you happy (e.g. flowers, designer noise-cancelling headphones or a limited-edition gift set). Hedonic purchases may take place on specialist ecommerce websites, luxury private sales websites or invitation-only apps.

The purchase may be limited by your resources: your time and money. The time you have varies depending on your life stage; for example, whether you're a full-time student, or if you're working, or a part-time student juggling family, work and studies.

Another layer of consumer behaviour is derived from personality traits such as being adventurous, being cautious or seeking excitement, which influences whether you plan your purchases or impulse buy. Impulse purchases can be utilitarian or hedonic and it may be that you're watching a live streaming video, looking at social media and participating in social commerce. You see the item on Instagram or an other visual platform, want it immediately and click to buy! Or you pin it, save it and take time to decide.

> ## DISCOVER MORE ON CONSUMER BEHAVIOUR
>
> For more on the psychological and sociological issues, see Zubin Sethna and Jim Blythe's helpful textbook *Consumer Behaviour* (2019) by SAGE Publications; the latest edition may be available in your online library.

2.7.1 ACCEPTING NEW TECHNOLOGY

These changes in behaviour show our acceptance of technology, and back in 1989 this was a major challenge. This was when computers were being introduced into the workplace, where there were difficulties understanding their benefit.

A researcher at the University of Michigan in the United States was exploring ways to predict system usage by measuring attitudes towards the technology, combined with the user experience. The measurement framework is called the Technology Acceptance Model (TAM) (Davis, 1989).

The model considers positive attitudes towards two specific measures: (a) perceived usefulness; and (b) perceived ease of use. One of the major criticisms of this model is that it is seen as being too basic. Yet TAM has been used by many researchers in digital marketing who have developed it so it's more relevant to today's environment.

People accept or reject different technologies and Davis's research explained that people will use an application that they feel will help them perform their job better. This was named 'perceived usefulness' and was originally suggested by other researchers.

The second part considers whether the application is too difficult to use as the benefits may be outweighed by the effort needed. This was called 'perceived ease of use'. Davis explained that a TAM should discover the impact of external factors; and so the model starts with the external variables which could include items such as individual or group training and user guides. The flow of the model is shown in Figure 2.3 and this initial framing from the external variables contributes to perceptions of usefulness and ease of use, which in turn lead to an attitude toward using the system. Finally, positive attitudes contribute to a behavioural intention to use the system.

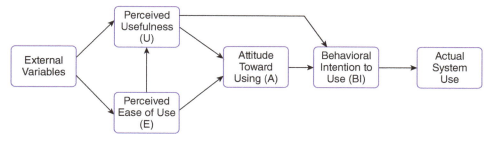

Figure 2.3 Technology Acceptance Model (TAM)

Source: Republished with permission of *Management Science*, from 'User acceptance of computer technology: A comparison of two theoretical models',
Davis, F.D., Bagozzi, R.P. and Warshaw, P.R., 35 (8), 1989; permission conveyed through Copyright Clearance Center, Inc.

In the research, Davis explored electronic mail (or email) and asked 14 questions to assess the perceived usefulness and perceived ease of use. The questions are shown in Table 2.3. The words 'electronic mail' could be replaced with another type of technology such as augmented reality, personal drones or specific apps.

Table 2.3 Initial scale items for perceived usefulness and for perceived ease of use

Initial scale items for perceived usefulness	Initial scale items for perceived ease of use
1. My job would be difficult to perform without electronic mail.	1. I often become confused when I use the electronic mail system.
2. Using electronic mail gives me greater control over my work.	2. I make errors frequently when using electronic mail.
3. Using electronic mail improves my job performance.	3. Interacting with the electronic mail system is often frustrating.
4. The electronic mail system addresses my job-related needs.	4. I need to consult the user manual often when using electronic mail.
5. Using electronic mail saves me time.	5. Interacting with the electronic mail system requires a lot of my mental effort.
6. Electronic mail enables me to accomplish tasks more quickly.	6. I find it easy to recover from errors encountered while using electronic mail.
7. Electronic mail supports critical aspects of my job.	7. The electronic mail system is rigid and inflexible to interact with.
8. Using electronic mail allows me to accomplish more work than would otherwise be possible.	8. I find it easy to get the electronic mail system to do what I want it to do.
9. Using electronic mail reduces the time I spend on unproductive activities.	9. The electronic mail system often behaves in unexpected ways.
10. Using electronic mail enhances my effectiveness on the job.	10. I find it cumbersome to use the electronic mail system.
11. Using electronic mail improves the quality of the work I do.	11. My interaction with the electronic mail system is easy for me to understand.
12. Using electronic mail increases my productivity.	12. It is easy to remember how to perform tasks using the electronic mail system.
13. Using electronic mail makes it easier to do my job.	13. The electronic mail system provides helpful guidance in performing tasks.
14. Overall, I find the electronic mail system useful in my job.	14. Overall, I find the electronic mail system easy to use.

Source: Republished with permission of *MIS Quarterly*, from 'Perceived usefulness, perceived ease of use, and user acceptance of information technology' Davis, F.D., 13 (3), 1989; permission conveyed through Copyright Clearance Center, Inc.

In both cases, respondents rate the scale items which are subsequently ranked on a 'highly likely' to 'highly unlikely' scale, to deliver a statistically recognised measure. The numerical analysis is beneficial if you have access to statistical packages (and know how to use them!) but, if not, the model can be adapted and the questions used in a survey format, with simple yes or no responses.

The Technology Acceptance Model is a useful framework to test the development of new apps as it enables companies to create better systems.

Activity 2.3   Apply the Technology Acceptance Model

1. Think of an app, a software program or a device that has failed.

2. In Table 2.3, replace 'electronic mail' with your selected technology.

3. Use the questions in Table 2.3 and score the items either yes or no.

4. Analyse the factors: where are the main yes or no responses? Is it with the overall perceived usefulness? Or the perceived ease of use?

5. Which specific factors do you feel contributed to the failure of the technology, app or device?

We're all digital now

As digital consumers, our lives have become surrounded by online tools, technology and systems – from the moment we wake until the day is over. Can you imagine a world without WiFi?

Governments and businesses are harnessing digital technology too. The European Union publishes an annual Digital Economy and Society Index (DESI) and keeps a scorecard of where European countries feature in terms of the available connectivity, digital skills, use of internet by citizens, integration of digital technology by businesses and digital public services (European Commission, 2020).

And now the digital genie is out of the bottle, it's difficult to give up our online lives. As digital consumers, even if we adopt greater liquid consumption we're unlikely to give up second screening and showrooming.

JOURNAL OF NOTE

To dig deeper into the digital consumer, look at the journal *Psychology and Marketing* which combines the application of psychological theories to marketing.

CASE STUDY

STRAVA: THE USER PERSPECTIVE

This continues our long case study and you may find it helpful to read the first part in Chapter 1.

It's Wednesday lunchtime and Claire is sitting outside a coffee shop in the city centre waiting for her dad to arrive. He's working nearby today. For Claire, it's sort of a day off as she has no classes on Wednesdays, although she should be working on her digital marketing plan assignment.

She arrived early so she could pick a table with plenty of space. She knows her dad will probably be five minutes late, stuck in traffic and trying to find a parking space. Her mum is busy at work and couldn't get the day off. While she waits, she checks her phone. There are several notifications on her Strava app. She looks at her training log as she went for a run earlier today. The matched activities show that her performance has improved. Claire is pleased with today's activity and her classmates, Georgios and Argyris have just completed a long cycle ride and she sends them Kudos (a digital thumbs-up). They've sent her Kudos for her activity too. As they say, if it isn't on Strava, it never happened!

The monthly cost of the app is about the same as two coffees from a high street café which she thinks is OK, but many people have complained online about the subscription.

Exploring the Strava app, she looks at the 'challenges' and she knows that these are activities that can be joined virtually and they are interesting because they change each month. She could run a marathon in New York, in Oslo or Milan, all from her university in Swansea in Wales. Or she could just complete a standard September half-marathon. The challenges are fun, keep you motivated and sometimes there are rewards. She read a blog online that mentioned that Strava partners offer 'secret prizes' if you complete one of their challenges. One of her friends claimed a secret prize and was given branded shorts and a t-shirt when she redeemed a 'branded challenge', so maybe it's worth exploring.

Her mum doesn't use Strava because she can't see how it's useful. Perhaps Claire should try the Technology Acceptance Model on her mum! Replace the words 'electronic mail' with 'Strava' and see what happens! She knows her mum took a quick look and decided it was too complicated. Perhaps she's just concerned about using the technology or maybe something else. The TAM survey would help. At the moment, her mum goes for a run, looks at her watch and makes a note of her time when she gets home.

Claire is considering buying new running shoes. She's looked online but can't decide what to buy. She's seen some brands and read their feedback and the online reviews; some of it is good, some isn't. She hasn't got the budget to buy immediately but some websites offer BNPL so perhaps she could buy the running shoes and pay for them over three months, rather than all at once. Having looked at Nike, ASICS and New Balance, she's starting to see adverts for Saucony. She could visit some of the running shops and then buy online as that will always be cheaper. She wonders how some of these stores stay in business. If they close, she would just buy online anyway as it's so easy to return things.

CASE QUESTIONS

- Claire has started her customer journey and is in pre-purchase stage. What touchpoints might help move her to the purchase stage?
- How might Strava support smaller sports stores that sell running shoes, that are often used as places to try not buy, to encourage digital consumers like Claire to stop showrooming?
- What steps could Strava take to convert non-users, such as Claire's mum, to adopt new technology?

FURTHER EXERCISES

1. Evaluate different elements of the sharing economy for an organisation of your choice. Highlight opportunities and challenges the organisation may encounter.

2. Working in small groups, analyse the digital customer experience for (a) a food delivery app that you access via your mobile phone or (b) a local coffee shop. Identify where there are any possible difficulties and make recommendations to address these issues.

3. Imagine you are responsible for introducing a new technology into university. This could be a new payment system or a new library access system or something else. Considering the users, identify three objections you are likely to encounter. Write robust responses to all the objections that could be used across social media. Prepare a promotional one-page website to explain the new system.

4. 'Retail stores are dead, the future of shopping is online.' Evaluate this statement and present your views in a 1,500-word individual essay. You should support your argument with evidence from textbooks and academic journal articles.

SUMMARY

This chapter has explored:

- How changing digital behaviour affects marketing
- The characteristics of the sharing economy
- The difference between the customer experience and customer journeys
- How to create a digital persona
- How the Technology Acceptance Model can be applied

GO ONLINE

Visit **study.sagepub.com/hanlon2e** to access links to interesting articles, websites and videos related to this chapter.

PART 2

DIGITAL MARKETING TOOLS AND CHANNELS

CONTENTS

3 Email, Websites, SEO and Paid Search   59
4 Content Marketing   91
5 Social Media Marketing   121
6 Online Communities   149
7 Mobile Marketing   181
8 Augmented, Virtual and Mixed Reality   211

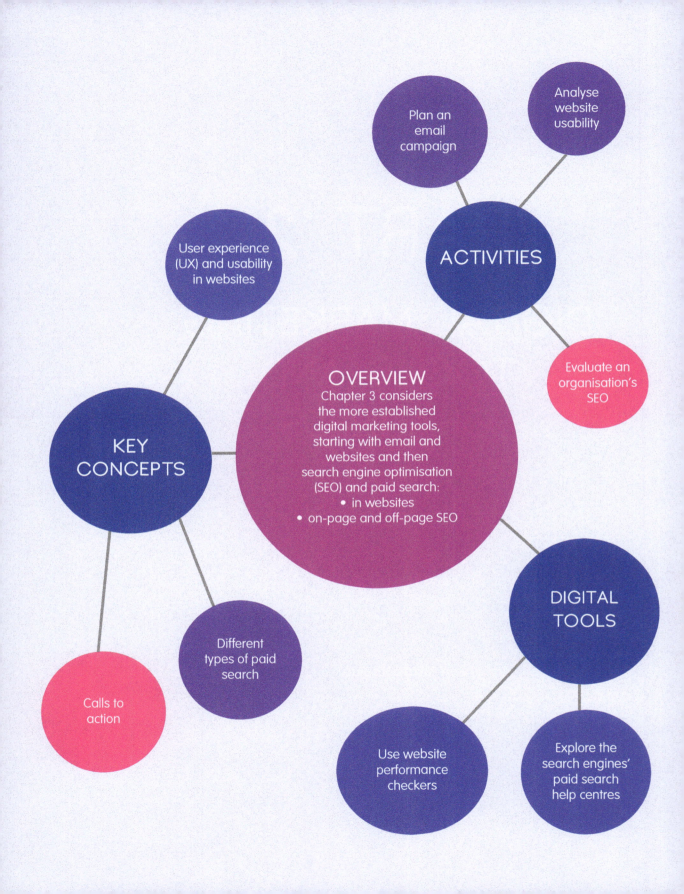

OVERVIEW
Chapter 3 considers the more established digital marketing tools, starting with email and websites and then search engine optimisation (SEO) and paid search:
• in websites
• on-page and off-page SEO

ACTIVITIES

Plan an email campaign

Analyse website usability

Evaluate an organisation's SEO

KEY CONCEPTS

User experience (UX) and usability in websites

Calls to action

Different types of paid search

DIGITAL TOOLS

Use website performance checkers

Explore the search engines' paid search help centres

3

EMAIL, WEBSITES, SEO AND PAID SEARCH

PROFESSIONAL SKILLS

When you have worked through this chapter, you should be able to:

- Plan an email campaign
- Use website performance checkers to assess SEO
- Recommend improvements to websites

3.1 INTRODUCTION TO THE DIGITAL MARKETING TOOLBOX

Originally, digital marketing was called e-marketing (the 'e' being short for 'electronic') and it was also known as internet marketing. We have expanded beyond internet marketing to a much wider array of connected devices, hence the term digital marketing.

Traditional marketing communications tools included advertising, sales promotion, public relations (PR), sponsorship, direct marketing and personal selling. This was considered to be the marketing communications toolbox – the tools available for marketers to communicate with customers.

As digital marketing has evolved, so has the marketing communications toolbox. The first digital communication tool was email which later expanded to include websites, blogs and search engines. Social networks followed and then social media advertising. These newer digital tools were no longer just about simple communications; they enabled two-way or multiple-conversations, they provided rich data and the ability to see which tools were most successful, which is why this is known as the digital marketing toolbox.

The impact of digital technology has changed the way many organisations execute their marketing campaigns. Traditional marketing such as newspaper and magazine advertising is at an all-time low and letter writing has declined, although the postal service is busy delivering our online shopping parcels. Business-to-business exhibitions have reduced, with many taking place every two years, instead of annually, as buyers can more easily search online for new ideas, products and suppliers.

However, we now have digital marketing tools which started over 50 years ago (email, websites, SEO and paid search) as well as newer digital tools: content marketing has become a key factor in many organisations, along with the growth of agencies managing paid influencers. So I have adapted the digital marketing toolbox, as shown in Figure 3.1.

Changes from the earlier version of the digital marketing toolbox are: online PR and blogs are part of content marketing, and social media advertising is included in paid search. In the adapted digital marketing toolbox, there are seven overarching tools.

This chapter will explore email, websites, search engine optimisation and paid search. Chapter 4 will explore content marketing, including influencers and blogs. Chapter 5 addresses social media marketing and Chapter 6 will examine online communities. These chapters will allow you to better understand each of the digital toolbox components.

3.2 EMAIL MARKETING

Nearly 300 billion emails are sent every day, yet one of the challenges is encouraging people to check their emails. The number of email users globally is over 4 billion – when you register for a webinar, shop online or make other transactions, your email account is often needed as verification. Marketing emails can be planned, triggered or one-offs, as discussed in this section.

Figure 3.1   The adapted digital marketing toolbox

3.2.1 PLANNED EMAILS

Planned emails are prepared in advance and organised on a schedule. In a business-to-consumer (B2B) or business-to-business (B2B) context, the aim is usually to encourage the recipient to take action or to provide information; for example:

- Promotions or offers
- Brand stories
- Customer stories
- Tips and advice
- Links to blog articles
- Events and invitations

For expensive items that can only be purchased in a store or where a service is provided, the email purpose may be for lead nurturing, to encourage the recipient to register online, make a booking via a form or telephone the organisation.

3.2.2 TRIGGERED EMAILS

Triggered emails, also known as transactional or behaviour-based emails, occur when an event, activity or response to a **Call to action** (see Key Term) has taken place.

These emails can be dynamic or automated and built into online customer relationship management systems. For example, when a customer makes an enquiry a specific email is sent. If they respond within three days, they receive the next email in the sequence; and if they fail to respond within 10 days, a different email is despatched. Triggered emails are usually connected to the customer journey (see Chapter 2), as shown in Table 3.1.

Table 3.1   Examples of triggered emails based on the customer journey stage

Customer journey stage	Examples of triggered emails
Pre-purchase	Welcome – thanks for signing up
	Transcriptional – downloading chat content
	Process – filling in an online form to request a download
Purchase	Password reminders
	Forgotten products in your shopping cart
	Thank you for the purchase
	Shipping confirmation
Post-purchase	Receipt from a store purchase
	Request for a review after a purchase
	Please like us, follow us on …
	Re-engagement (we've missed you)

KEY TERM   CALL TO ACTION (CTA)

A call to action (CTA) is an instruction to do something. These are words, buttons, images that are placed in an email, as well as being on a web page or on a video. They are usually 'action verbs' and are often two-word phrases, aimed at the person reading the email, exploring the web page or watching the video, such as: learn more, read more, see more, watch now, send message, sign up, join today, follow, swipe up, download now, get offer, tap to unlock and shop now.

Calls to action are useful devices in email automation. Triggered emails can respond to **CTAs** (see Key Term) and three primary types of CTAs have been identified (Chen et al., 2020):

- Link to a web page – learn more
- Take action after browsing a web page – contact us
- Clickable buttons to perform an action – shop now

Smartphone Sixty Seconds® – Identify the CTAs

- On your mobile phone, open your emails.
- Find an email that you opened that was sent to you from an organisation, perhaps where you have bought something or made contact.
- Count the calls to action. How many can you see?
- Did you respond to the CTA?

3.2.3 ONE-OFF EMAILS

These emails are often a response to unplanned incidents or external factors, such as company announcements or urgent news. One-off emails can be used for research by companies sending surveys to learn more about their customers.

Within a digital marketing strategy, email marketing can have specific, measurable and timed objectives for individual campaigns, but what are the advantages and disadvantages of email as a marketing tool?

3.2.4 ADVANTAGES OF EMAIL MARKETING

Email is an important marketing tool that provides advantages to organisations as a method of communicating with customers. Email marketing is popular with marketers because:

- The email or content is delivered direct to the consumer's mobile or desktop and – unless it's spam – it is not intercepted by a third party.
- The email process provides key metrics, so that you can see: who opened the email; how many times they looked at the message; and if they clicked on any links. These metrics mean that every single email campaign can be compared to understand what worked.
- Email is easy to share, as consumers can click on the forward button and send immediately to a friend or colleague.

3.2.5 DISADVANTAGES OF EMAIL MARKETING

Equally, there are disadvantages of email marketing, such as getting through the spam filters. Other challenges are producing relevant and regular content, plus trying to think of captivating headlines and finding words that trigger responses.

Email is often perceived as being 'free of charge' as there seem to be no immediate costs, as there would be if placing an advertisement. But this is not the case.

There are many resources required to deliver successful email, both direct costs and indirect costs such as:

- Copywriters to create the headlines and content
- Imagery or video material
- An email software system (this may be free for smaller volumes of emails)
- People to upload the content, add the correct list and schedule the email delivery
- Data controllers to manage the data and ensure no rules are broken

Emails are part of the customer journey and may send the reader to a specific web page or **landing page** (see Key Term). This means that some technical web help is needed to create these pages.

KEY TERM   LANDING PAGE

A landing page is a dedicated conversion page inside a website or social media platform that is used for tracking visitors, and is defined as 'where consumers are directed to after they have clicked on the brand hyperlink' (Stubb and Colliander, 2019, p. 211). For example, someone receiving an email might click on a link in the email and they visit a landing page, or see a social media advert and click on the link which directs them to the landing page.

Accuracy and the numbers of email addresses are an issue. How many email addresses do you have? The average person has at least two email addresses: one for work and one for home.

Another critical challenge is safeguarding data, such as your email address, name, address, purchasing history and possibly credit card data. Many companies have accidentally released personal information, resulting in big fines based on local data protection legislation.

3.2.6 WHY AND HOW EMAIL WORKS

One model that explored why email works is shown in Figure 3.2 (Miquel-Romero and Adame-Sánchez, 2013). This is in three sections: antecedents (what happened before); action (what happened); and consequence (what happened afterwards).

Antecedents consider that if you know who is sending the email (H1), have positive associations of the sender (H2), believe there is some benefit in the email (H3), are feeling good when the email arrives (H4) and are in a location where you can easily open the email (H5), then you are more likely to open the email!

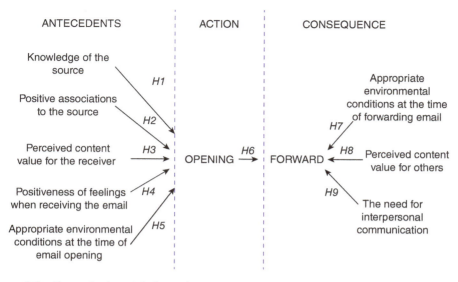

Figure 3.2 Theoretical model of email opening

Source: Miquel-Romero and Adame-Sánchez (2013)

In the third part of the model, the researchers explored how likely you might be to share or forward the email, which was based on additional conditions: if you are in a location where you can easily open the email (H7), if you think a friend or colleague might benefit from the email (H8) and if it is perhaps a while since you have been in contact or just want to say hello, then sending the email may be useful (H9).

Logically the model makes sense. If you know the sender, it is less likely to be spam and if it is from a favourite online store, you might be keen to open the email. And whilst we think about the way we can reach people at any place at any time with email, if you are on the train and it is a complicated message, you might ignore it, save it until later (and perhaps forget) or simply delete it; this is why the idea of 'appropriate environmental conditions at the time' is relevant. This is a useful checklist before starting a campaign.

3.2.7 PLANNING AN EMAIL CAMPAIGN

The main steps in planning an email campaign are as follows.

Capture data with consent

You can legally only collect and use someone's email address with their permission due to local data protection rules but data protection varies across the world – see Chapter 1.

Add into email system

Once the data has been gathered, it needs to be added into the email programme or customer management system. The email system can include the email address, the person's first and last name.

Segment lists into relevant groups or personas

Not all customers are the same and it may be useful to add descriptive tags to customer data to enable you to send more targeted email campaigns. Tags can note the status of the customer, e.g. 'existing customer', or the purchase behaviour, e.g. 'buys for friends'.

Create winning subject lines

Subject lines require careful creation to ensure they don't end up in the trash or spam folder. Make it personal by adding the individual's name, e.g. 'An offer for Annmarie'.

Build in instructions – calls to action

An email has no purpose unless it provides instructions for the reader – what do you want them to do? These are often two-word instructions, e.g. buy now or read more.

Create content

Once the subject line and CTAs have been agreed, it's time to create the body content of the email. Typically this focuses on one theme, so the reader isn't confused. The content should have value for the reader and be useful, whether that's 'top looks for summer' or 'perfect gifts this holiday season for sisters'.

Test to see which subject lines or images work best

Most email software systems allow you to test two or more subject lines. You can do the same with images to see which resonates best with your audience. Mailchimp allows you to try subject line A and subject line B (see Chapter 11).

Measure the results

Email software systems will provide a dashboard showing the number of opens and allow you to measure these results. The results from one campaign can be measured against a later campaign to provide greater understanding of what works.

Update the database

If any of your audience unsubscribe after the email, make sure they are removed and not emailed again.

Email software systems will do this for you automatically.

Examples of popular email software systems, which start with free options when smaller numbers are used, or offer a free trial, include: campaignmonitor.com, dotmailer.com, emailit.co, and mailchimp.com. These email management systems usually work via a wizard, with a step-by-step approach to creating an email campaign.

DISCOVER MORE ON SUCCESSFUL EMAIL CAMPAIGNS

Mailchimp, a commercial organisation that provides a free and paid-for email marketing platform, has a helpful guide to creating successful email campaigns. It describes the steps and best practice. See mailchimp.com/resources/email-marketing-field-guide.

Activity 3.1   Plan an email campaign

Follow these steps to plan an email campaign to promote a new juice bar. You can do this in a document, as a slideshow or sign up for one of the free email tools.

1. Create a name for your campaign. Pick something you will be able to understand later.

2. Who are you sending this campaign to? Consider the recipients.

3. Who is sending this campaign? Say clearly who this is from. This is usually a person or a company name.

4. What's the subject line for this campaign? The subject should be easy to understand; make it too cryptic and it's more likely to be deleted.

5. Plan the content for your email and decide if this includes words, images, videos and/or links to landing pages.

6. Identify any remaining questions you may have before being able to send the campaign!

3.3 WEBSITES

In the last century, around 1990, a handful of companies created basic websites which were little more than static brochures. They were expensive, complicated and few people had internet access. Today you can create a site for free using Wordpress.com in less than a day and there are over one billion websites worldwide (InternetLiveStats. com, 2020). The challenge is trying to ensure your organisation's website can be found, especially as websites are owned media, the one element of the digital marketing toolbox that is totally under the control of the organisation.

Websites exist for many reasons and can provide dynamic insights into organisations, such as:

*   The aims of the organisation (about us)
*   Who works there (our team)

- What they do (our work)
- Who they work for (our customers)

Shopping websites offer opportunities to instantly buy online which can be enhanced with:

- Multiple product images
- Videos showing different product views
- Verified reviews from happy customers
- Options for customers to message or chat online to customer service assistants

But websites are created for many reasons, such as:

- An information site, providing information for existing and potential customers (e.g. a government or traditional manufacturing website)
- A repository of information or materials (e.g. Wikipedia, your university's online system)
- A shopping site (e.g. your favourite online retailer)
- A utility site (e.g. currency conversion websites)

Specific aims for commercial websites are based around business growth, whether that's customer acquisition, conversion or retention (see Chapter 10, 'Digital Marketing Strategy and Objectives' for more on this model), and may be to acquire new customers, convert potential customers and retain existing customers.

Website aims may involve market development and product development strategies (Ansoff, 1957), such as to move into new markets or to launch new products.

Non-commercial websites such as those providing a public service will have different aims, often focused around changing behaviour, encouraging participation and providing information. Typically, these include health information websites (lose weight, stay fit, stop smoking) and government websites to register personal information to access documents (driving licences, passports).

Regardless of the type or purpose of the website, user experience and usability are key factors that ensure visitors return, or not, to your website. The next section looks at these concepts in more detail.

3.3.1 USER EXPERIENCE (UX) AND USABILITY IN WEBSITES

The foundation of user experience (UX) in websites came from usability (Hassenzahl and Tractinsky, 2006; Law and Van Schaik, 2010). This concerned examining the ease of use and usefulness of the websites and is connected to the Technology Acceptance Model (see Chapter 2). This was considered as the instrumental view – measuring the instrument – whether that was a website or piece of software.

UX concerns every aspect of a user's experience when on a website, whereas usability traditionally concerned the task-driven factors, ease of use and usefulness.

However, usability has incorporated many of the features of UX which is why these terms ore often confused.

Some early websites were challenging to use and the first guidelines on website usability were created by Kevin Keeker in the Microsoft Usability & Marketing team (Keeker, 1997), and three years later American professor of marketing Charles Hofacker created a model of how consumers would process information online. Known as 'Hofacker's 5 stages of information processing' (Hofacker, 2001), this was a blueprint for usability and contained elements of the Technology Acceptance Model (see Chapter 2). Researchers Venkatesh and Ramesh (2006) combined the Microsoft Usability Guidelines (MUG) with the Technology Acceptance Model (you can see a recurring theme here) to provide guidelines for practitioners. These guidelines were further enhanced by Tung, Xu and Tan (2009). Although academic researchers explored usability, this was popularised by Dr Jakob Nielsen, a software engineer who is largely credited with defining usability based on five quality components (Nielsen, 2012). Table 3.2 combines these core attributes.

Table 3.2   Core attributes of web usability based on the components of UX

The components of UX	Hofacker (2001)	Venkatesh and Ramesh (2006)	Tung, Xu and Tan (2009)	Nielsen (2012)
Instrumental – usability	Comprehension and perception, how users understand content	Ease of use and made for the medium, being able to customise the site as needed	Ease of use and made for the medium, whether accessed via a desktop or mobile should include options for personalisation, to log in and see previous orders	Learnability; ease of use Efficiency – how quickly can users perform tasks?
Non-instrumental, aesthetics and pleasure	Physical factors such as movement and intensity that attract attention when users are on a website	Content, relevant material with appropriate breadth or depth	Relevant and high-quality content	Satisfaction – how pleasant is it to use the design?
Affect and emotions	Ensuring users accept your information and stay on your site or proceed to the next step	Emotion	Evokes emotion, whether it's a hedonic or utilitarian purchase (see Chapter 2)	

These researchers addressed the core attributes of web usability in different ways that are discussed in the following sections.

Instrumental – usability

This element of UX is to discourage the development of complex websites that are difficult to navigate and take too long to load and are more likely to be abandoned. Making websites easy to use is a key aspect of Google's algorithm which changes daily, according to Google (Sullivan, 2019, p. 1):

Each day, Google usually releases one or more changes designed to improve our search results. Most aren't noticeable but help us incrementally continue to improve.

Several times a year, we make significant, broad changes to our search algorithms and systems. We refer to these as 'core updates.' They're designed to ensure that overall, we're delivering on our mission to present relevant and authoritative content to searchers.

Part of the Google algorithm or formula considers 'whether the page loading times work well for users with slow Internet connections' (Google, 2020, p. 1).

A key aspect of usability is 'made for the medium' which considers whether the website adapts when it's being viewed on a desktop, tablet, mobile or other device. This has become a critical factor for search engines which are more likely to provide websites that have been adapted for different devices. Many companies adopt a 'mobile first' approach which means they design the websites for the smallest possible screen – your mobile phone – from the start.

Non-instrumental, aesthetics and pleasure

Website aesthetics consider if the content is pleasing to view. Research shows that if a website gains attention it is likely to be vivid and interactive, concepts accredited to Steuer (1992).

For Steuer, vividness was concerned with the richness of online sensory characteristics and how far technology could stimulate multiple senses. Vividness could be conveyed via features such as contrasting colours, images and sound. We are pulled towards a web page by the bright colours and imagery that we see.

Steuer classified interactivity as 'the extent to which users can participate in modifying the form and content of a mediated environment in real time' (p. 14). This interactivity has been demonstrated in the use of short videos, especially the duets in TikTok where users create their own interpretation of another video and run their piece side by side (see Case Example 4.1 – TikTok: The ultimate short-form content). Instagram is a good example of vividness and interactivity as the images are based on vivid contrasting colours and applying specific filters. The video stories add interactivity. As a result, many web pages have mimicked this design.

Affect and emotions

Websites are owned and controlled by the brand and they're trying to create some form of **engagement** (see Key Term), whether that's part of the customer journey or a response such as sharing a website with friends.

To achieve this response, web pages try to evoke emotion – using dramatic imagery or photos we can relate to that make us feel good or confirm we've made the right choice. The work by Venkatesh and Ramesh (2006) demonstrated that emotion was more important in some industries (e.g. travel and shopping) than in others (e.g. banking and news).

Usability as a concept has evolved. It's no longer just about websites, but also online tools including apps. There are official standards produced by the International Organization for Standardization (ISO) which focus on how websites can be understood, learned and appeal to users (see ISO 9241-11:2018) but the issue is whether organisations use these standards.

KEY TERM ENGAGEMENT

Consumer engagement is considered as a customer's psychological and emotional relationship with an organisation, defined as follows: 'Customer engagement (CE) is a psychological state that occurs by virtue of interactive, cocreative customer experiences with a focal agent/object (e.g., a brand) in focal service relationships' (Brodie et al., 2011, p. 261).

Activity 3.2 Analyse website usability

Select a sports or fashion website and analyse its usability, with Table 3.2 as your guide:

1. How relevant is the content? When was it last updated?
2. How easy is the website to use? What works well – and what doesn't?
3. Does the website evoke an emotion (good or bad)?
4. Is it made for the medium? How do the desktop and mobile websites compare?

CASE EXAMPLE 3.1 The failure of the track-and-trace app

During the pandemic in 2020, the UK government funded development of an app to track and trace people with the COVID-19 virus. The plan was that the app would enable people to check in easily at venues, such as restaurants or offices, and if there was an outbreak of the virus, the venue would be identified and all those who had visited could be alerted, tested and quarantined where needed. However, the app failed on several user experience aspects.

(Continued)

Before being launched across the UK, the app was piloted in one location, the Isle of Wight, but this trial failed. The app was found to have basic usability issues relating to *made for the medium* (see Table 3.2: Core attributes of web usability based on the components of UX). Some users could not download the app if they had an older mobile phone and others reported the app not working on most iPhones due to its configuration.

For apps to gain widespread adoption, they have to be usable on multiple platforms: Apple for iPhones, Google for Androids, but in the first trial it was found that the iPhone app only traced a small percentage of people, so didn't work.

The first version of the app was abandoned and a second was started, but other issues relating to functionality were highlighted. To work, the app needed low-powered Bluetooth to be switched on but there were reports that it didn't function if your phone was locked!

In addition to the instrumental usability, there were non-instrumental factors which removed the confidence of using the app due to the drain on battery life. Many users reported mobile phones losing battery fast and then removed the app which defeated the purpose totally.

More updates continued as the developers did more work to improve UX so that it worked on iPhones, didn't impact on battery life and worked on all types of device.

However, the app evoked negative emotion as people lacked trust in the system following so many reports of how it didn't work. There were further issues around the components of affect and emotions as individuals were concerned about government surveillance, so not everyone that could access the app downloaded it. An updated version assured users that data would be decentralised, so individuals would not be identified personally. This met with the guidelines from Apple and Google who did not want governments to be able to track individuals as this could have been used for harmful purposes in some parts of the world.

The UK wasn't alone in this as several other countries (e.g. Australia, Ireland) experienced similar difficulties with their track-and-trace app.

Case questions

- Which factors would you test before launching a new website or app?
- How would you recruit pilot testers to trial a new website or app?
- How would you persuade users to download a government-sponsored app?

3.4 SEARCH ENGINE OPTIMISATION (SEO)

Search engine optimisation is the practice of improving an organisation's place in the search engine results. Search engines automatically crawl through websites to generate a sophisticated database of content using 'robots' and 'spiders'. The content is stored and returned in microseconds when people search online. The pages which are shown to the person searching are called search engine results pages (SERPs) and usually show websites or specific web pages relating to the search, such as **landing pages** (see Key Term).

The words used by the person searching are called keywords or key phrases and these can extend to whole sentences, not just a few words. The process starts when you add words into a search engine as follows:

- I am hungry and want a takeaway curry, so I open a search engine:
- Step 1 – Broad search
  - *Vegan curry* – this generates thousands of pages of search results including recipes
- Step 2 – Modified broad search
  - *Vegan curry takeaway* – this generates many pages of results and many are too far away
- Step 3 – Phrase search using long-tail keywords
  - *Vegan curry takeaway near Cranfield* – this narrows down the results and there will be fewer pages containing this exact phrase but not all restaurants are open
- Step 4 – Exact search using long-tail keywords
  - *Vegan curry takeaway near Cranfield open now* – this narrows down the results even more and there will be fewer pages containing this exact phrase along with maps as I've added a place name

---

KEY TERM   LONG-TAIL KEYWORDS

A long-tail keyword (or key phrase) is a longer set of words. Instead of searching for a single word or phrase, we build what's called a longer tail – adding more words to our search string. For example, my search is likely to expand with each step.

Long-tail keywords are nearly a sentence and tend to be used more when the consumer is close to a point of purchase. Any website containing the searched-for phrase is more likely to appear at the top of the search engine results page (SERP).

Consumers have become more sophisticated in their personal search strategies and with so many searches taking place, organisations are keen to ensure that they feature higher up the page in the search results.

There are two main types of SEO that contribute to the search results: **on-page SEO and off-page SEO**.

3.4.1 ON-PAGE SEO

On-page SEO concerns the content on the web pages, the speed of delivery and the accessibility of the web page, whether viewed on a desktop, tablet or mobile device.

This is controlled by the organisation which can build short and long-tail keywords into its content.

On-page SEO is why the content on a page is so important. Web content comprises many different items, such as words, images, video, headings, as well as 'tags' and data. Tags are indicators of content importance and can incorporate searchable words. Most websites include space within a web page to add the tags. Tags can be considered as keywords, categories of content and words that help to index the page. **SEO data tags** include meta-descriptions, meta-tags and on-page headings. These can be added to the page and contribute to the way search engines index the pages.

HTML code

Websites are written in code that search engines can read and a popular code is HTML – hypertext mark-up language. Meta-descriptions are the snippets used by search engines in their results pages – the pieces of text displayed online. The HTML code sits behind all websites and includes indicators for the search engines to show the different data tags.

For example, the meta description code is placed in the head content of the relevant web page:

- <head> <meta name="description" content=" Building an Online Community. Discover how to build an online community through the four steps from identifying your goal to selecting the platform."> </head>

Meta tags are on-page headings arranged in priority order. Google ranks title tag as the most important and then heading 1 above heading 2. For example, the Title tag looks like this:

- <head> <title>Building an online community.</title> </head>

If you don't want to start programming, there are many website tools like Wordpress, Joomla, Magento or WooCommerce that automatically create the code for you.

3.4.2 OFF-PAGE SEO

Off-page SEO relates to methods of mentioning the web page in other places. This is not controlled by the organisation. Typically, this includes an organisation's social media pages, a Wikipedia page and any links on other web pages. The aim of these web links is to drive traffic back to the organisation's website. Search engines have considered pages with many links to have greater domain authority – to be more important than similar sites and more likely to be shown higher up in the search results.

So how does it work? You need to find relevant pages to add content, such as a directory or local web portal. It may be that social media pages, using the organisation name, are needed too. Just search for a company name and see what results appear.

Whilst other off-page SEO is achieved through adding links to the web page on relevant directories, these might be fashion directories, or gaining blog articles – stories – on other sites. For example, companies like Sweet Protection – a Norwegian personal safety company that sells goggles, helmets and technical clothing for snowboarders, cyclists and paddle boarding – may gain relevant links to athletes, enthusiasts or sporting clubs and ask them to share the website or specific blog posts.

3.4.3 WEAK PRACTICE IN SEO

However, because it is so important to be found in the search results, some companies adopt weak tactics. Their aim is to gain better positions within SERPs and this is known as Black Hat SEO (see Ethical Insights).

ETHICAL INSIGHTS Black hat SEO

This is weak practice to gain better search engine ranking and includes:

- Buying irrelevant links from link farms – the links connected to poor content that was often single-page websites with no connection to the subject
- Keyword stuffing – repeating the same keywords or key phrases on web pages
- Stealing content from better websites – stealing or plagiarising content to save writing similar material

These are all short-term gains as Google's updates often penalise these unethical SEO practices. Search engines flag these sites and they are less likely to be shown in search results unless the webmaster corrects the errors.

- Many companies seek links that aren't totally relevant, so how would you manage such requests if you were managing a brand web page?
- Some digital agencies still practise black hat techniques. How would you feel if you joined a new agency and your first task was to repeat the same keywords or key phrases on a client's web page?
- How do you feel about the idea of saving time by taking content from other websites?

Weak practice such as the use of link farms should be avoided. As companies realised that Google rewarded external links, many sought to gain as many links as possible. This resulted in the creation of 'link farms' where many single-page websites were established and companies were sold 100 links for just $25.

The issue was that many of these links were totally irrelevant and not a measure of website quality, just a count of the number of links they had achieved. When monitoring search engine behaviour, Google realised what was happening and stopped rewarding those showing irrelevant and spam links. This had a negative impact on many websites, which suddenly disappeared from Google's search results until they removed the irrelevant links.

DISCOVER MORE ON SEO

Google has created a Search Engine Optimization (SEO) Starter Guide which is available online; just search for 'google seo guide' and look for the Google developers page.

3.4.4 HOW SEARCH ENGINES RANK CONTENT

Search engines decide which pages to rank higher on the page based on a mathematical formula, or algorithm. These algorithms are closely guarded trade secrets and whilst there are companies that offer to 'get your business to the top of Google', this is not a realistic proposition as the Google algorithm is said to change incrementally, at least once a day.

What is known is that Google rewards content that is recent, relevant and made for the medium (see section 3.3). The concept of 'recent' considers the newness of the content, as older content is viewed as dated and less important. The notion of 'relevance' is based on how closely it matches the search terms. Search engines identify a series of relevance signals, such as matches to the search terms and keyword frequency as well as whether the terms feature in other parts of the web page, such as in images, headings and the main content. If it's mentioned many times on a page, the search engines believe the web page to be more relevant for the searcher. Google considers other aspects of usability such as how quickly (or slowly) a web page is presented to the viewer. You can analyse and compare website performance, including all SEO factors, using **website performance checkers** (see Digital Tool).

DIGITAL TOOL   Website performance checkers

There are tools to check website speed, performance and content, which contribute to the on-page SEO. To explore further, you could visit one of these sites, copy and paste a web address (its URL, which stands for Uniform Resource Locator) and watch the results! The number of free searches is limited and you may need to share your email address to gain access.
www.websitegrader.org
http://nibbler.silktide.com

3.4.5 HOW SEARCH IS CHANGING

However, the search landscape is evolving and some text-based search engines automatically complete the search terms, based on a combination of predictive text, your past search history and what other people are seeking.

Plus, in addition to the traditional search engines such as Google, Yahoo, Bing, Baidu and Yandex, we're seeing the growth of search via social media and voice devices:

- Social media search is available via: YouTube, Facebook, Pinterest, LinkedIn, Twitter, Instagram

- Voice search devices include: Amazon Alexa, Apple Siri, Google assistant, Huawei Celia Samsung Bixby, Tencent Xiaowei, Windows Cortana

Voice search (e.g. via an Alexa device) is an emerging area of research. Xing, Yu and Yuan (2019) examined all the academic papers on voice search since 2008 and found just 14 articles – compare that to 'brand marketing' where you'll find thousands. One researcher who has explored voice search in some detail is Alice Zoghaib (2017, 2019) and she provides a helpful background explaining the impact of speaker voice and how this can persuade the listener to take action. It's a complex blend of the pitch, brightness and roughness of the voice balanced with the gender of the speaker and listener.

It seems that voice assistants are mainly used for basic things such as simple questions and tasks (What's the weather today? Switch on the lights!), and that there is a still a lack of trust as well as a lack of consistency between devices (PwC, 2018).

Voice search is similar to the original text-based search engines where the results were nearly right or totally wrong. You continued to page 2, page 3, or even page 10 of Google, looking for the right result. With voice search, people might say the search terms once or twice and then revert to other search tools. One of the issues is the integration on the customer journey. If you ask Alexa to find a restaurant for a party, it might list nearby places, if they have correctly updated their Google My Business profiles, but it stops there. If you want to book a table, you might still need to go online. As a result, voice search is often part of the customer journey (see Chapter 2), but not the conversion.

DISCOVER MORE ON VOICE SEARCH

Read the article by Alice Zoghaib, 'Persuasion of voices: The effects of a speaker's voice characteristics and gender on consumers' responses', published in 2019 in the French Association of Marketing journal *Recherche et Applications en Marketing* (it's in English), as this explains what impacts and influences our voice search.

Activity 3.3   Evaluate an organisation's SEO

- Select a sports or fashion brand.
- Select a search engine of your choice.
- Type a description of the organisation without adding its name and see what results appear on the SERP.
- Do the results take you to the organisation's own web pages (on-page SEO)?
- Or do they take you to other pages (off-page SEO)? If yes, what types of pages and are there good links back to the organisation?
- Do this again, but select a competitor and compare the results of both organisations.

3.5 PAID SEARCH

Paid search, which is also known as 'pay per click' or 'price per click' marketing (PPC), is about bidding on search terms so that your website appears before others.

As search engines deliver organic results based on search terms, they also include adverts for organisations providing the searcher's request. One way to achieve a higher position on a Google page is to buy adverts.

The adverts are sold on an auction system, so the organisation that pays the most has a better chance of gaining the top place on the SERP. However, the price you pay for an advert today may change in seconds as these changes take place in real time and are based on the number of advertisers wanting to talk to your target audience at that moment.

The more in demand the keyword or key phrase or target audience is at that time, the more expensive the click, view or follow. Search engines consider other factors such as the quality of the content on the **landing page**, the importance of the organisations bidding for the keywords and the quality of the advert content.

Paid search includes promotional material placed on search engines, social media and audience networks. They all follow similar advertising models. Let's explore the main paid search options and how they work.

3.5.1 THE MAIN PAID SEARCH OPTIONS

Cost per thousand (CPM)

Called CPM – the M stands for 'mille', the Latin word for thousand, as CPM was initially used to measure radio listeners and television viewers. CPM was initially the main method of advertising and is often used for brand awareness campaigns. The downside of CPM is that your advert might be shown to the wrong audience who cannot afford the goods, or do not have the interest being promoted, but you are still paying when they see the ad.

Cost per click (CPC); pay per click (PPC)

CPC is one of the original methods of buying advertising online. CPC is the antidote to CPM, and although your ad is shown to a wide group of people, you only pay when they click on the advert. This allows you to automatically exclude the wrong target customers. This means that if you are promoting designer brands, you target those whose interests include luxury brand names and perhaps add in an approximate cost, to put off those where it is outside their budget.

Cost per action (CPA)

CPA is a results-orientated approach based on conversions and includes:

- A sale, i.e. a purchase added to a shopping cart or a donation on a charity site
- Providing email data for registration or an email list
- A video view
- A social share, like or follow

The CPA method works because you allow a piece of code called a **pixel** (see Key Term) to be placed on your website to confirm that the action took place.

KEY TERM PIXEL

A pixel is a tag or piece of code with a unique reference that is used to track conversions and collect data. This means that organisations can measure all results from an ad campaign to assess how well it has worked. Conversions are tracked from the clickable link, such as an image, advert or video, to the intended destination such as a **landing page**. The number of conversions are measured, often in a tag management system such as Google Tag Manager.

Pixels collect data, so when a customer visits a website page and then abandons the page to look at something else, such as a social media page, they might see an advert for the website following them – this is retargeting based on your behavioural data. Pixels or tracking code snippets are used in all paid search platforms.

Cost per view (CPV)

As the name indicates, cost per view is designed for video adverts where individuals view a video clip. How does it work? Your video ad is shown, which may be on platforms like YouTube, as well as being an in-game reward – you're playing your favourite computer game and to gain a life you watch a video. Before you see the video you want to watch, you are shown an ad, with the message that you can 'skip the ad in 5 seconds'.

To add value to the advertiser, typically the viewer has to:

- Watch at least 20 seconds of the video advert
- Or watch the whole advert if it's shorter than 20 seconds
- Or engage with your video, by clicking a call to action such as 'order now', 'learn more', 'visit website'

Video is omnipresent and is available on many platforms. Reasons for the growth of video are some generations watching only video instead of terrestrial TV and the worldwide usage of smartphones. Plus, newer social media networks have changed the way video is watched. Snapchat focused on vertical viewing, rather than having to tilt a phone, and TikTok prefers short videos.

In longer video platforms such as YouTube, Vimeo and Youku, video adverts require the addition of keywords, metadata, descriptions and more details.

Cost per follow (CPF)

Many organisations are focused on the number of fans, likes and followers they have. This is because it looks good! I'd call this a vanity metric (see Chapter 13); it's nice, but doesn't mean anything because your followers may not see your content – unless you use social media advertising.

To respond to this, social media platforms encourage organisations to buy followers. An existing piece of content, such as a post that has performed well, can be used as the advert. This means it looks less promotional and has been tested with an audience. The posts are shown to the target audience and you only pay when someone clicks on the 'follow' or 'like' button.

One disadvantage of the cost-per-follow system is that there is no refund if you lose followers and fans during the campaign.

Smartphone Sixty Seconds® – Find the most expensive keywords

- On your mobile phone, open a search engine – or use voice search.
- Search for 'the most expensive keywords'.
- What do you find?
- Why do you think these terms are so expensive?

3.5.2 PAID SEARCH PLACEMENT

Having considered the bidding options, let's explore where paid search ads can be placed.

Paid search via search engines

With over five billion searches on Google each day, Google remains the dominant search engine in Europe and the United States. In China, Baidu leads with over 1.5 billion daily searches.

Google Ads provides instant access to easy start ad campaigns. Like email marketing software, the platform uses a wizard to help. If the objective is to drive traffic to a website, after the URL is added, Google Ads will show potential keywords and their monthly volume. Based on this, it provides an indication of how much to bid.

Baidu, the dominant search engine programme in China, offers a wide range of paid search options. These tend to be aimed more at major brands as the costs involved are higher and the process is more complex. Baidu ads follow the traditional model of advertising sales and it's recommended that an ad agency navigates the set-up and manages ongoing ad campaigns.

DIGITAL TOOL Paid search help centres

Google provides a range of helpful videos and online tutorials which contain the latest best practice. Visit the Google Ads help centre (https://ads.google.com) which is a useful tool to understand paid search.

- See the Bing help site for ads (https://help.bingads.microsoft.com).

Paid search via social media

All social media networks use advertising to generate their income and this will continue. Back in 2005 when Facebook started introducing adverts, they provided an opportunity to proactively target people based on profile data. Previously, paid search targeted people *reactively* when searching for a specific term, whereas social media advertising allows organisations to *proactively* target people who might not have considered the product or service. For example, it is possible to create adverts for:

- People who have shopped at Nike, GymShark, Calvin Klein or Michael Kors
- Students attending your university
- People interested in Netflix

This is due to the volume of data that we share with the social media networks. You like brand pages, share recent purchases, change your settings to share your university journey, such as using hashtags, you change your home location to your university location and you share what you've watched on Netflix. You're expressing an interest about a brand and as soon as 5,000 others have expressed an interest, this becomes a social media audience that can be targeted.

As a result of this laser-focused targeting, many companies are moving from traditional print advertising in magazines to paid search, especially via social media.

Paid search via audience display networks

Audience networks are a collection of web pages who sell space on their websites to advertisers. These are often web pages (known as publishers) that are free to access, using advertising as an income stream. There are four parties involved:

- The merchant or network – the organisation managing the publisher and advertiser
- The publisher – that's the website, blog, video channel, game or app that sells space
- The advertiser – the brand that seeks promotion and pays to advertise
- The audience – the people seeing the adverts

The main audience networks are managed by Google, Facebook and Microsoft (which owns LinkedIn). Their lists of publishers are not publicly available, but advertisers can block some types of websites that may be inappropriate for their audience.

Audience networks often use artificial intelligence to connect the right audience to the right material. Examples of publishers include:

- Outlook – if you have free email, you may see ads appearing on your home page
- YouTube – if you don't pay for a subscription, you are shown ads
- Utility sites – which are free to access but gain their income by selling advertising space, e.g. PowerThesaurus.org
- Community sites – which are free to access and gain their income by selling advertising space, e.g. Freecycle.org

The publishers are paid commission which tends to be small and is only paid when there is a result, such as a click on a specific page – this is similar to cost per action and it is tracked via a tracking code or pixel.

The reason audience networks exist is that not everyone uses social media, but they may use other utility or community websites. As brands are keen to target users who may be elsewhere, the number has grown. Google's Display Network (GDN) is one of the largest, but there are many other affiliate networks that find and add merchants, such as Rakuten Affiliate Network and ShareASale who are members of the Performance Marketing Association (see https://thepma.org). They manage the process and provide the merchants with access to the **demand-side platform**. They make money via a commission which is shared with the affiliate.

Paid search via affiliate programs – performance marketing

Another method of paid search is via affiliate marketing, also known as performance marketing, which can be in the form of a banner ad, a review or other material. This is one method of marketing used by influencers (see Chapter 4).

To be successful, affiliate marketing requires three key components:

- The publisher – that's the blog, video channel, game or app
- The merchant or network – the organisation paying for the adverts
- The audience – the people seeing the adverts

The publisher is responsible for creating good-quality content that make people want to read and/or view it and return to the site for more.

As quality is important, if a blog is poorly written or simply focuses on selling products, it gains less traction and visitors might arrive at the site and leave quickly. If the game doesn't engage the audience to continue through the levels, the players won't return. If the app has little usefulness or benefit, it may be downloaded but not used. In these cases, this results in smaller audiences and less potential commission.

3.5.3 PROGRAMMATIC PAID SEARCH

Paid search adverts can be placed manually, where you create the advert, upload and select where the ads will be shown, whether that's via social media, audience display networks or affiliates. But there is another way of managing the process if you're a large advertiser, which is programmatic.

Programmatic ads are managed through artificial intelligence, using specific software programs. Karl Weaver, a media buying expert who has managed many major organisations, told me more about programmatic advertising. He commented that programmatic advertising works as web pages typically carry spaces for advertising and when you load a web page there is lots of information gathered about you and your web behaviour (see Key Term – **cookie**, Chapter 2 p. 49). This data is sent back to an ad exchange where the inventory on the site is auctioned off to the highest bidder. The ad that wins appears on the page as you load it. The auction takes milliseconds and the process is referred to as programmatic real-time bidding (RTB).

Programmatic is a delivery method, and there are unsurprisingly benefits of and downsides to programmatic advertising.

Benefits of programmatic advertising

- There are efficiency gains as the process is automated
- There is no need to research where to place the ad as it happens automatically
- What to pay is automatically calculated and marketers have pricing control and can decide whether or not to enter the auction
- There is a wider range of places to advertise
- There is access to digital performance data and analysis

Downsides to programmatic advertising

- It changes the nature of contracts between the organisation and the agency
- The type and number of people needed to deliver the work are reduced
- Data governance issues arise as there is less control as to where ads appear
- It could remove the need for creative people
- There is a risk of ad fraud

To work out what ad space to buy, advertisers will use a **demand-side platform** (see Key Term), which means that there is limited human intervention. The process allows ads to be targeted to groups of people accessible across a wide range of websites.

> **KEY TERM**   DEMAND-SIDE PLATFORM
>
> A demand-side platform (DSP) is automated software that bids on the space available through ad exchanges, allowing the advertiser to manage the whole ad process in one place. It's a tool that manages programmatic paid search and it is often managed by expert in-house teams or advertising agencies.
>
> There are many DSPs and the larger ones include Amazon, AppNexus, DoubleClick, Facebook Ads Manager.

Paid search is a complex process and to get the best results for the adverts requires dedication to assess what is and isn't working. This is why it is often managed by ad agencies, rather than in-house teams.

3.5.4 ADVANTAGES AND DISADVANTAGES OF PAID SEARCH

Paid search has advantages such as targeting the right people at the right time. Google ads target people – known as 'in-market audiences' – who are actively searching for an item and may be researching or comparing the options. Online adverts can be created quickly, enabling companies to react swiftly to changing situations. Facebook ads proactively target its users (on Facebook, Instagram, Messenger) by sharing brands they may not yet have discovered, but which may be relevant. The audience display networks reach wider audiences with specific interests.

One disadvantage is that users might not appreciate being targeted. To respond to this, Facebook enables users to manage which advertising messages they see from brands and has introduced the ability to 'hide messages like this'. When this is selected, Facebook asks users to 'help us understand what's happening' and probes with a further question 'why don't you want to see this?', which enables a tick box with options including:

- It's not relevant to me
- I keep seeing this
- It's offensive or inappropriate

This contributes towards a 'relevance score' for brands, so they can better understand what does and does not work within their targeted advertising on social media. In Adverts Manager, brands can look at their relevance score, on a 1 to 10 scale, with 1 being low. The lower the relevance score, the more expensive the adverts are likely to be as they are less appealing to users.

However, it is possible to upload your customer database and exclude current customers from advertising campaigns. This often takes place with email matching but be aware that this depends on the email address the customer has provided as many people have more than one email.

Other disadvantages include the lack of control as to where your adverts appear. By using the audience display networks, you can exclude being present on some types of sites (such as adult or mature) but you won't know exactly where the ads will appear until they're running. This means that the adverts may possibly target your existing customers. Imagine sending a special offer for an item to an existing customer who has just paid more for the same holiday by going direct to the company's website! When ads are running, if people hide the ads and feed back that they are not appropriate, Google includes these details in the company's relevance score. As with Facebook, in some cases this can mean that the lower the score, the more expensive the adverts.

Another factor is that some adverts can be spam and use clickbait to entice people to click and look at more information, sometimes with serious consequences (see Case Example 3.2: MoneySavingExpert and the fake ads).

CASE EXAMPLE 3.2   MoneySavingExpert and the fake ads

In the UK, a leading financial expert, Martin Lewis, who founded the MoneySavingExpert website, is a trusted individual. He does not get paid by companies to promote their goods. Products and services on the website are given a review, based on research and information from MoneySavingExpert fans.

Martin's face is recognisable to some people and has been used as clickbait – online adverts or posts that use attention-grabbing words or images. You've probably seen adverts saying 'This guy climbed to the top of the mountain and you won't believe what he saw' and when you click the link, the content is irrelevant. Clickbait is a false advert, a confidence trick to encourage you to click onto a page, so that the website owner can claim millions of daily visitors – even if they all leave in milliseconds – or even worse, to encourage you to invest, buy a product or a holiday that doesn't exist.

Martin Lewis's face was used as clickbait on adverts with content that suggested 'Safest way to invest' or 'Trust this recommended policy'. Yet Martin Lewis had not recommended any of these financial products and people lost money. He named these 'liar ads' and decided to take legal action against the scammers, where they could be identified. He has been successful in getting some such adverts removed and has persuaded the UK's Advertising Standards Authority (asa.org.uk) to launch a scam alert system, enabling individuals to report scams online so they can be investigated.

You can read more here about Martin Lewis at moneysavingexpert.com/shopping/fake-martin-lewis-ads and if you've seen a scam advertisement, you can report it at asa.org.uk/make-a-complaint/report-an-online-scam-ad.html. In other countries, scams, or fraud, are reported to the local police department.

Case questions

- Do you think Martin Lewis was right to complain or should he accept that this is part of being well known?
- How can you tell if an advert is fake or genuine?
- Who do you think should be responsible for fake adverts that trick people and lose them money?

JOURNAL OF NOTE

The *Australasian Marketing Journal* is an easy-to-read journal that covers a wide range of digital marketing subjects.

CASE STUDY

STRAVA'S APPROACH TO TRADITIONAL

DIGITAL MARKETING

This continues our long case study and you may find it helpful to read earlier parts in previous chapters.

Strava began in 2009 as a single activity app and, a decade later, it's become the leading activity tracking app used by athletes globally.

Strava's website (Strava, 2020, p. 1) explains its business focus: 'The Strava team is passionate about building the world's most engaged community of athletes. We are committed to our mission, our athletes, each other and our business.'

This change hasn't happened by accident, and there is a digital marketing plan underpinning these results that's evidenced through Strava's application of the digital marketing toolbox. The company has read the marketing textbooks and followed best practice. The information in this case is based on field research, the company's own website and reviews of online interviews.

Its website follows usability best practice. It is simply constructed with three main sections: 'About us', 'Subscription' and 'Careers'. The top right-hand corner includes 'Sign up' as a CTA. To ensure the website is easy to use and is fast to load from anywhere, Strava pays for the CDN Amazon CloudFront. The content features relevant material with vivid imagery using the brand colours, and evokes emotion by showing dramatic and happy images. Made for the medium, the website is mobile friendly and works on all devices.

Website software analyser tools show that Strava.com uses Google Analytics to track web statistics, Mailchimp for gathering email data and the Facebook tracking pixel (which applies to Instagram).

However, Strava has a separate business website that isn't displayed on the main page. Accessed via https://business.strava.com, this contains a different navigation bar that is focused on generating revenue. This second site describes how brands can connect with Strava, from creating clubs (which are free at the moment) to running challenges which 'start at $10,000 (USD) and scale based on duration, targeting and promotion. The maximum investment is $200' (Strava, 2019, p. 1). The FAQs include a note that charities still have to pay the entry fee for organising a challenge – there are no exceptions.

Partner brands are invited to 'Get in touch' and complete a form or sign up for the Mailchimp email newsletter.

The firm's blog is hosted externally via Medium (see https://medium.com/strava-culture) which creates another website to be managed. Strava has two other dedicated websites, one for projects (see https://labs.strava.com) and one for urban planning (see https://metro.strava.com).

At the time of writing, no paid search was found, although this can change in minutes. There is significant off-page SEO including a Wikipedia page, links to Google and Apple stores to download the app, reviews on blogs and videos. Effectively, Strava has created an ecosystem to promote its brand online.

CASE QUESTIONS

Imagine that you have just been appointed as digital marketing manager for Strava and you've been asked to make recommendations to improve its traditional digital marketing:

- How would you address the use of the websites – for users, brands and the blog? Discuss whether you would keep the different websites separated, or merge? You'll need to justify your decision.

- Looking at the Strava user website (Strava.com), what changes would you recommend to further improve usability?

- The idea of paid search has been discussed and you've been asked to prepare an outline proposal. This should suggest which option and why.

FURTHER EXERCISES

1. Review three promotional emails that you have received from commercial organisations and assess the email subject line, the contents and the CTAs. Which of these was most successful and why? Which was least successful and how might the sender have improved the content? Write a report to present your evaluation, findings and recommendations.

2. Compare and contrast the user experience for two websites in the sports goods or food sectors. Assess the components of UX and what works well and what doesn't.

3. Examine the search engine results used by a brand of your choice. Create a plan to enhance their SEO by using paid search and justify your response.

4. 'With so many websites online, it is impossible to get a new website noticed.' Evaluate this statement and present your views. You should support your arguments with evidence from textbooks and academic journal articles.

SUMMARY

This chapter has explored:

- The evolution of the digital marketing toolbox
- Types of email and their advantages and disadvantages

- Websites and the user experience (UX)
- The different elements of search engine optimisation
- Paid search and where adverts can be placed

GO ONLINE

Visit **study.sagepub.com/hanlon2e** to access links to interesting articles, websites and videos related to this chapter.

OVERVIEW
Chapter 4 covers all aspects of content marketing, starting with an evaluation, to types of stories and storytellers, concluding with content marketing strategy.

ACTIVITIES

Curate some content

Identify the characteristics of parasocial interaction

Calculate the engagement rate

KEY CONCEPTS

Paid, owned, shared, earned media

User-generated content

Influencers and opinion leaders

DIGITAL TOOLS

Use content audit templates

Manage social media content with Hootsuite

4

CONTENT MARKETING

PROFESSIONAL SKILLS

When you have worked through this chapter, you should be able to:

- Identify ideas for content creation and curation
- Create a content marketing strategy

4.1 INTRODUCTION TO CONTENT MARKETING

Content marketing is the cornerstone of all digital marketing. Words, photos, images, infographics, video, GIFs and memes are essential elements in digital marketing, and it is critical that organisations understand the strategic role of content. Content can increase brand visibility, drive traffic to websites, and help educate and convert customers. Valuable content can be charged for, used to gather data and is more likely to be shared.

Content marketing is not new as brands have been telling stories for centuries. For example, the agricultural machinery manufacturer John Deere has been using content marketing for over 120 years: educating farmers, telling stories and sharing best practice in over 15 countries.

Content marketing comprises different elements which are shown in Figure 4.1.

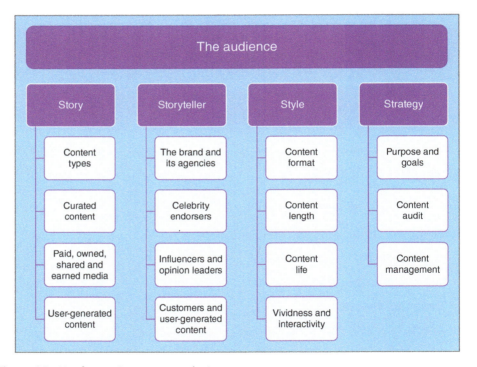

Figure 4.1　Key factors in content marketing

This chapter will discuss the different elements involved in creating a content marketing strategy. First, we'll explore the advantages and disadvantages of content marketing and then examine the key factors.

4.2 EVALUATION OF CONTENT MARKETING

4.2.1 ADVANTAGES OF CONTENT MARKETING

The benefits of content marketing include the following.

Content increases brand visibility

Instead of reading a sales pitch, consumers may be watching a video that provides advice or guidance, promoting the brand in different areas outside its corporate website or traditional locations.

Content helps create backlinks for search engine optimisation (SEO)

Good articles are often recycled by other people online. Have you ever quoted an article or added a link back to a page about a certain subject? By adding someone else's article to your web page, you are creating a backlink that search engines see and acknowledge that the original content must have value.

Content encourages conversion rate optimisation (CRO)

Clever content that provides help and advice such as buying guides and design ideas can convert browsers into buyers. For example, if you are visiting online retailers such as IKEA, they offer design tips and inspiration.

Content inspires social shares

Content can inspire social shares, especially where the content is vivid and interactive (see section 4.5.4). Digital tools make it easy to share content across social channels (see Digital Tool **Hootsuite**).

Content optimises the website for long-tail keywords

As our online search behaviour has become more complex, we seek more specific phrases. Content within blog articles, how-to guides or online reviews can build in these specific phrases, which are less likely to appear on other websites. A **long-tail keyword** (see Chapter 3) is a longer set of words.

Content generates new and retains consumers

Creative content can be found by new customers who are unaware of the organisation. It may be that someone searches for a specific phrase and finds the organisation for the first time. Imagine you've just started university and you're searching for 'reliable taxi firms'. You may find a list based on your location that includes firms you were unaware of.

DIGITAL TOOL   Hootsuite

Hootsuite is a digital publishing tool that allows you to find, share and publish content across different social platforms.

It has a free account as well as paid-for options and is an easy way to share content online. You will need to sign up to gain access.

- See hootsuite.com

4.2.2 DISADVANTAGES OF CONTENT MARKETING

There are downsides to content marketing too. Content can be fake, offensive and illegal.

Fake news has always existed, often during times of war and crisis, where it was better known as 'propaganda' or 'misinformation'.

During times of elections, many news stories emerge that are fake. Propaganda is often biased and politically motivated disinformation. The purpose is to discredit the other side and influence voters. But fake news can be shared quickly via social media and, as the stories can seem plausible, some people believe what they read. Table 4.1 shows types and examples of fake news.

Table 4.1   Types of fake news with examples

Type of fake news	What this is	Example
Parody	A spoof or satirical piece, often mocking a political leader	Political leader being portrayed as a hero or villain
Phony	Fake content often posted on social media with headlines that sound real	Worldwide shortage of toilet paper during lockdown!
Hoax	A prank that may be harmless and is commonplace online	Spaceships creating crop circles in fields
Conspiracy	A plot to discredit someone or an event	The moon landing never happened – it all took place in a Hollywood film studio
Clickbait	A piece of usually scandalous-sounding content that encourages you to click-through to a website	Five things your boss doesn't want you to know!
Misleading	A fake website that looks just like your usual one with similar branding	Fake banking websites where people log in and become victims of fraud
Manipulated or out of context	A real image used in a different setting	During COVID-19 images of coffins were used that were taken from earlier major disasters

Offensive content can create distress and damage lives. The main social media networks allow individuals to report malicious material that may be abusive, harmful, impersonating others or inappropriate, but it takes time for it to be removed.

One of the challenges with people sharing fake content is where the material is legally proven to be libellous, those sharing the material may be fined or their account deleted.

Smartphone Sixty Seconds® – Find fake news

- Using your mobile phone, go online and search for 'latest fake news'.
- What appears?
- Any stories you thought were true?
- What else appears when you search for fake news?

Another downside to content marketing is the need to appear at the top of search engines like Google. Search engines change their formula for ranking content on a regular basis and previously rewarded up-to-date or new content on websites. But some organisations started to gamify their content and used content farms to provide a steady stream of new content.

Content farms employ writers to create copy for search engine optimisation (SEO) purposes. Its aim is to be found and registered on search engines. The content is typically short (fewer than 350 words), generic and of low quality; however, it ticks the box for regular and recent content, but fails to retain the web visitors for long.

4.2.3 CONTENT AUDIT

If you're working in an organisation with lots of online content, you may need to evaluate the material with a content audit. A content audit or inventory means checking the organisation's content online and compiling it into a large list. This takes place to check that the brand is consistent across a range of platforms or for search engine optimisation analysis (see Chapter 3 for more on SEO).

DIGITAL TOOL Content audit template

Curata, a content marketing software company, shares its free content audit templates on its website along with a range of other content tools.

- Visit www.curata.com/blog/content-audit-template

Having evaluated the content, let's explore the key factors in content marketing, starting with the story.

4.3 STORY

All content starts with a story to be told – whether that's by using images, video or blog posts. Stories can be about the organisation, its products, or sharing knowledge and expertise. The story can be about the customers and others sharing information about the organisation from their perspective. These are different types of stories.

4.3.1 CONTENT TYPES

There are three specific types of content to consider: evergreen, planned and topical.

Evergreen content

This is also called 'flow' content that can be used at any moment because it is not time-sensitive. It can be planned and prepared months in advance, plus it can be recycled and used again. Examples include fashion retailers posting '5 things to consider when selecting a winter coat' or IT services companies sharing '3 ways to save money on IT infrastructure'.

Planned content

Planned content is prepared and developed in advance. It is often connected to scheduled events in the organisation's annual calendar, such as national days, seasonal events or product launches. For example, the fashion retailer can share 'what we discovered at Paris fashion week' and the IT services company may offer 'learn more about new privacy programmes'.

Topical content

Topical content covers newsworthy items, which are indicated as #breaking or #news on Twitter. These stories cannot be prepared in advance and require responses as they occur. There is a decision as to whether a response is relevant and right for their audience. Not all situations require a response and not all situations are relevant.

Whether it's evergreen, planned or topical content, Table 4.2 shows the Storybox Selection, with ideas for content creation for organisations.

4.3.2 CURATED CONTENT

Previously, we considered curation as something that happened in museums and art galleries, where expert curators constructed collections of items, built up artefacts and managed collections, to tell a story. Curators spend time researching, collecting and displaying objects.

Table 4.2 Storybox Selection

The organisation	Goods	Knowledge and expertise
• Organisational values • The heritage of the organisation • Corporate responsibility • Awards and achievements • Milestones and highlights • Quality assurance • The team's credentials • Customer stories	• The products, services • Original ideas or designs • How the product or service evolved • Behind the scenes • The processes • The market • Customer success • Educational stories	• Research and opinions • Surveys • Case studies • Forecasting the future • How to … • Online demos • Point of view • FAQs

Transferring curation to content has been described by researchers as 'finding, categorizing and organizing relevant online content on specific issues' (Fotopoulou and Couldry, 2015, p. 243). You need to consider the story, the storyteller and the style. Plus, it's not enough to repeat the content, as you need to add an angle; it should make the reader or viewer want to read, watch or listen.

Typical examples of curated content include weekly news rounds-ups or summaries; see, for example, Sparktoro (see https://sparktoro.com/trending) or Techcrunch (see https://techcrunch.com).

Activity 4.1   Curate some content

1. Select a piece of technology as a theme for a story.

2. Search online to gather different perspectives.

3. Based on your selection, make notes and curate some content.

4. Use your notes to write a 350-word blog post or create a two-minute video.

5. Make sure you don't repeat the existing content, but synthesise the ideas and add your opinion to make the story more interesting.

4.3.3 PAID, OWNED, SHARED AND EARNED MEDIA

One useful framework to consider the different types of content is the POEM model which describes three types of media, rather than content – named paid, owned and earned media (Corcoran, 2009).

In 2019 I adapted this to include *shared*, as companies never own their social media space, nor can they control exactly who sees what content. Social media platforms come and go – remember Bebo, Hyves, StumbleUpon, Vine and YikYak? This means brands don't own these platforms, they are always under the owner's control. They may be merged, rebranded, changed or closed – at any time. To reflect this,

I have re-framed the model as paid, owned, shared, earned (POSE) media, which is discussed next.

Paid – bought media

Paid media is defined as being where the 'brand pays to leverage a channel' (Corcoran, 2009, p. 1). This is content that the organisation has bought such as paid search (see Chapter 3), sponsored posts or promotional content. For example, if ASOS places brand adverts on Google, these are paid media.

Paid media has been created by the organisation who use it for promotional purposes. But it can be ignored by consumers using ad-blockers, or those that ignore corporate communications as they are seen as being less authentic.

Researchers (Wojdynski and Evans, 2020) observed a change in traditional paid advertising to 'covert advertising' (or native or stealth marketing) because it looks less like brand communications. You're looking through Instagram and spot a great story that's a paid ad. You see #ad in the caption, but continue to explore as it's useful content.

One issue is disclosure and whether brands follow legal and ethical guidelines, revealing that it's an ad. If brands don't disclose this, the audience may suspect, dismiss and abandon the content earlier.

Paid media includes content from influencers who are given rewards, such as payment or goods, in return for positive content about the organisation and its offers.

Owned – controlled media

When the content is controlled and managed directly by the organisation, such as its websites and email communications, this is owned media. Ironically, as the organisation owns and controls this media, it is considered less authentic by customers. For example, the ASOS website is owned media.

Shared – borrowed media

Where content is placed on third-party sites and social media platforms, organisations are sharing someone else's platform. This is a new addition to the model and is based on organisations adding content to social media sites. For example, the ASOS Instagram page is shared media.

Earned – won media

Earned media is content created by customers, fans and sometimes unhappy customers who are seeking resolution to a situation. Corcoran (2009, p. 1) suggested that earned media was 'when customers become the channel'.

At a basic level, earned media could be considered as positive content in the form of retweets and likes. This extends into longer-form content, such as parody videos and appreciation pages. For example, if you receive an ASOS delivery and record the process of opening the package and upload onto TikTok, this is earned media.

Earned media is often outside the control of organisations and is the content that users, whether customers, fans or detractors, prepare and share amongst their networks. This is often recognised under the alternative title of **user-generated content**, which is often abbreviated to UGC (see Key Term).

4.4 STORYTELLER

The storyteller or content creator is a changing area. Most content was traditionally developed by the brand for the brand where the brand had total control. Content within the digital marketing environment has become more complex, involving multiple storytellers, including customers, celebrities and influencers, as shown in Table 4.3.

Table 4.3 Types of storytellers, content and media

Storyteller	Type of content	Paid	Owned	Shared	Earned
The brand and its agencies	Branded content	X	X		
	Online PR				
	Product placement				
Celebrity endorsers	Online PR	X		X	X
	Product placement				
Influencers and opinion leaders	Online PR	X		X	
	Product placement				
Customers and users	User-generated content			X	X

Table 4.3 is a blended framework that includes the storytellers and content as well as applying POSE, so that you can easily see the role of the storyteller and examples of the types of content they may create.

A key aspect of the storyteller is how trustworthy we believe them to be. As we start to dismiss material from brands, we have placed more confidence in people we don't know – celebrities, influencers and other customers. This trust in the storyteller is known as **source credibility** (see Discover More) which explores how an individual views the communicator (see Hovland and Weiss, 1951). Source credibility categorises information sources as high or low credibility. Typically, high credibility sources were well-respected individuals or journals and low credibility might include politically biased commentators or websites specialising in gossip and rumour. The notion is that the higher the source credibility, the more trustworthy the material.

Although this is a model dating back to 1951, it has been developed and extended to include:

- **Expertise:** The knowledge that the source demonstrates adds greater credibility; for example, professors or medical professionals presenting data on a news programme are seen as more trustworthy than politicians providing information
- **Homophily:** People sharing similar demographics to me; for example, people of the same gender, age or background to me are more likely to understand my situation and I find their information more trustworthy

---

DISCOVER MORE ON SOURCE CREDIBILITY THEORY

Read 'The effect of characteristics of source credibility on consumer behaviour: A meta-analysis' published in the *Journal of Retailing and Consumer Services* (Ismagilova et al., 2020). This paper reviews findings from earlier studies and gives examples of where the model has been applied.

4.4.1 THE BRAND AND ITS AGENCIES

The brand may manage storytelling inside the organisation or use external companies such as PR, media or influencer agencies to tell their stories. Traditionally, branded content was used to promote goods, raise awareness of an activity or generate engagement from stakeholders. In the digital environment, we're witnessing **brand journalism** (see Key Term) as organisations tell and share stories that look less like promotional offers and more like editorial material, with greater value for the audience.

KEY TERM   BRAND JOURNALISM

Brand journalism is defined as 'a trend toward corporations employing journalistic means to engage audiences, either via news sites' native advertising nooks or distributed through content marketing platforms and schemes' (Serazio, 2020, p. 118).

Brand journalism has arisen as a result of low source credibility being attached to brands, the way we consume media, moving from traditional sources to online media and poor brand experiences. In this context, brand owners have to work harder and smarter to gain consumer awareness and engagement.

An extension to brand journalism is brand activism which is where companies speak out about political issues or causes. This is a form of political activism (Moorman, 2020) which involves using social media to raise political issues, using a related hashtag. If consumers agree, they might like or share the post, a practice described as clicktivism as, although the 'like' indicates some form of support, it may have little impact (George and Leidner, 2019).

After the American citizen George Floyd was killed by a police officer, witnessed on a bystander's mobile phone, the Black Lives Matter (#BLM) cause gained greater attention. Some companies were already engaged in the battle against injustice, such as Nike who understood and addressed the situation with authenticity across its owned and shared media.

But brand activism can go wrong. Some brands seem to be indulging in '**woke washing**' (see Discover More). On the one hand, they are attempting to demonstrate social awareness but, on the other, failing to be socially aware within their own companies. For example, cosmetics company L'Oréal jumped onto the #BLM bandwagon, saying it was important to speak out, but the company had fired its first transgender ambassador Munroe Bergdorf after she spoke out about racism. The president of L'Oréal Paris commented that they regretted the approach the brand had taken at the time and they later rehired Munroe to join a Diversity & Inclusion Advisory Board.

There is a need for organisations and individuals to be more educated about sensitive causes, but brands joining the conversation because they are missing out is similar to adding a trending hashtag that has no connection to the brand. Ultimately, this can result in loss of reputation and brand damage.

DISCOVER MORE ON WOKE WASHING

Read the article 'Brands taking a stand: authentic brand activism or woke washing?' by Jessica Vredenburg and colleagues, published in 2020 in the *Journal of Public Policy and Marketing*, which provides definitions and examples.

4.4.2 CELEBRITY ENDORSERS

Endorsing a product is a positive public statement to demonstrate a brand association. It connects the values of the brand and the endorser, confirms approval for others and provides a message which at a basic level states: 'I like this product, you should too.'

Celebrities are different from influencers, as they do not create regular content, because their primary role may involve acting, music, fashion, writing, sports, politics or business. According to Bennett et al. (2021, p. 1), 'celebrity endorsements have become a standard feature in marketing activation plans' and their study adds that they're used in between 15 and 60 per cent of all advertising campaigns in the USA, Europe and Asia Pacific.

Celebrity endorsement was an early form of influencer marketing, but the difference is that this is an act of endorsement that is usually carried out without payment. When payment is involved, the celebrity becomes a formal brand ambassador and should declare payment for promotional content, following local regulations.

This phenomenon has grown as consumers watch or see their favourite celebrities promoting products and feel the celebrity is speaking to them personally and that they are offering help in selecting products. This creates a feeling that the consumers know the celebrities intimately as they're sharing secrets or offering advice, speaking direct to them through the camera, even though they don't meet. This is known as **parasocial interaction** (Horton and Wohl, 1956) and 'despite being one-sided, these relationships can feel as real and intense as face-to-face interpersonal connections that encompass elements of friendship' (Aw and Labrecque, 2020, p. 896). **Parasocial interaction** (see Discover More) has been found to have 'a positive influence on customer–company relationship' (Haobin Ye et al., 2021, p. 1102) which means that companies benefit by using relevant celebrities to promote their products.

Activity 4.2   Identify the characteristics of parasocial interaction

- Find a celebrity in fashion, food or sports that you follow and feel you know well.
- Identify the characteristics that make you feel like you know them.
- How does the celebrity usually communicate with their fans?
- What do they do that makes them seem more real to you?
- Discuss the characteristics in class.

DISCOVER MORE ON PARASOCIAL INTERACTION

Read the article 'Extending the personal branding affordances typology to parasocial interaction with public figures on social media: Social presence and media multiplexity as mediators', by Andrew M. Ledbetter and Colten Meisner published in 2021 in the journal *Computers in Human Behavior*.

The **source credibility** model also applies to celebrity endorsements. We find the endorsement realistic based on the knowledge of the endorser (expertise), our belief that the content is true (trustworthiness) and because the message is from 'people like us' (homophily)

The central theme is that the celebrities are seen as credible, authentic sources and trusted more than the brands they're promoting.

4.4.3 INFLUENCERS AND OPINION LEADERS

Older research found that it was opinion leaders, not the media, that had the greatest influence on our judgement (Lazarsfeld et al., 1944). Although this was based on one piece of research, so it is not necessarily generalisable to other situations, this was an early idea of influencers.

Another theory, the Diffusion of Innovations (Rogers, 1962), generalised that the majority of early **opinion formers and opinion leaders** (see Key Term) were more cosmopolitan than their followers – they travelled more, had larger networks and were more open to innovation. One prescient observation was that opinion leaders needed access to mass media and had to be available. Think about those opinion leaders with mass followers on TikTok, Instagram, YouTube and Twitter – they meet these conditions.

KEY TERMS   OPINION FORMERS AND OPINION LEADERS

Opinion formers are formal experts. They work in this area, may be qualified or professionally trained and have significant specialist knowledge about the subject.
   Opinion leaders are informal experts or laypersons who know something about the topic and whose knowledge is valued amongst family, friends and followers.

According to several researchers (see Enke and Borchers, 2019), social media influencers (SMIs) are third parties with large networks who shape audience attitudes through their use of social media, which echoes the original concept of opinion leaders. They are also known as Key Opinion Leaders (KOLs).

Influencers are different from celebrities and Lou and Yuan (2019) suggested that this was because:

- Influencers generate regular social media updates in their specialist areas
- Influencer-generated posts offer their followers information about product alternatives or other informative content
- Influencers add their personality to posts as a sign of authenticity and to create entertainment or foster engagement

There are different types of influencers and, as Figure 4.2 shows, these are based on the size of the following and whether the influencer focuses on the role full-time or as a hobby.

Influencing as a hobby

Those whose hobby is creating content and posting online where they have a small following are artists. They are more concerned with the look and feel of the work, rather than the volume of content. Sometimes the hobby can become a job if they can increase their followers and maintain engagement.

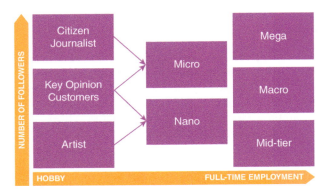

Figure 4.2   Types of influencers

Key opinion customers post for a hobby and may become opinion leaders or nano-influencers if they have around 1,000 to 10,000 followers.

Citizen journalists are those who like to post frequent content and have a larger following. They may be classed as micro-influencers with 10,000 to 50,000 followers. For example, Leal Alexander (@curlygallal) started documenting her hair-care journey just for fun and has built a following on Instagram. She is working with brands including Living Proof, Penhaligons and Faith in Nature as she has a great engagement rate.

Influencing as a full-time career

Figure 4.2 shows that those working full time as influencers include mid-tier with 50,000 to 500,000 followers, macro with 500,000 to 1,000,000, or the mega influencers with over 1 million followers.

For example, in the mid-tier is Tess Daly (tess.daly), not the BBC's *Strictly Come Dancing* host but an influencer with over 200,000 followers on Instagram. Passionate about fashion and beauty products, she has worked with fast-fashion brands Missguided and Pretty Little Thing. Her inspirational posts have greater credibility as Tess has spinal muscular atrophy (SMA) and shows her looks from her wheelchair.

A mega-influencer from China is Li Jiaqi who has nearly 30 million fans on Weibo and 40 million on the Chinese version of TikTok, Douyin. He adds entertainment and incredulity to the event as he once tried on 380 different lipsticks in an epic seven-hour live-streaming session.

How do you recruit an influencer?

If you're working for an organisation and are considering using an influencer to share your messages, the first element to consider is their values – that's what matters to them; it is their ethical compass and either steers them in a direction that aligns with your organisation, or doesn't. You'd need to review their earlier content to ensure they didn't infringe the core beliefs that are important to your organisation.

The next aspect to consider is the quality of the content. Does their content help the organisation? If it lacks interest, originality, authenticity or quality, it's unlikely that others will watch, read or share it.

The frequency of content should be considered. Some influencers publish content every one to three days. You'll be able to assess whether they're involved with creating the content themselves if they proactively respond to messages. If you DM (send a direct message) to an Instagram micro-influencer, how long do they take to reply? This is all part of the evaluation as to whether or not to select one influencer over another.

Engagement rate

A key metric for influencers is the engagement rate. The higher the better. According to Ethical Influencers (2020), the average engagement rate is between 1 and 3.5 per cent. Influencers with 3.5 to 6 per cent have a high engagement rate and above 6 per cent is considered to be excellent!

Lynette Sraha who works in influencer marketing told me that if the followers are high, but their engagement is less than 2.5 per cent, she would question their effectiveness.

Micro-influencers tend to gain higher engagement rates – they often have specialised audiences who are more interested in their content. For example, during the pandemic Salwa Rahman (urgalsal) developed her passion for make-up as a hobby and built a following showcasing her looks on Instagram. Her engagement rate is over 20 per cent and she works with cosmetic brands.

Activity 4.3   Calculate the engagement rate

The engagement rate equals the total number of engagements, divided by followers, multiplied by 100. If that sounds complicated, here's an example. @thesecountryroads has 23,900 followers and I looked at three posts:

A.   870 liked, 109 comments = 979 engagements, divided by 23,900 = 0.0409 x 100 = 4.09%

B.   1408 liked, 157 comments = 1565 engagements, divided by 23,900 = 0654 x 100 = 6.54%

C.   1360 liked, 150 comments = 1510 engagements, divided by 23,900 = 0.0631 x 100 = 6.31%

In this example, the engagement rate is between high and excellent.

- Select your favourite micro-influencer, then look at their three most recent posts.
- Add together the total number of likes and comments on a post.
- Divide this total by the influencers' number of followers.
- Multiply the result by 100 to get the percentage.
- Is it an average, good or excellent rate?

What do influencers earn?

Having identified potential influencers, the next question is to consider the fees involved. Influencers can be paid based on:

- The contribution they make; that's the post, story or material
- The number of clickthroughs from the post to the brand's **landing page** (see Key Term in Chapter 3)
- The amount of sales generated and payment per acquisition or action
- The size of their follower base
- Products from the brand owner

Professional influencers prefer to be paid for their time as it can be difficult to track the exact number of sales from a post. You might see the post and think about it, but a friend messages you so you abandon a possible visit and return at a later time. Being paid in products sounds great, but you may not need them!

Mega-influencers typically generate an income from their online following. Paid-for social media posts can be lucrative, but it depends on the social media platforms, the numbers of followers and the engagement rate.

For example, mega-influencers can earn $200,000 for a Facebook post or $150,000 for an Instagram post, or a YouTuber with 7 million subscribers or more can earn $300,000 with a brand contract. This is because an engagement rate of 6 per cent with 2 million followers means that a brand is communicating with 120,000 fans. But those earnings are rare rather than being usual.

At the other end of the scale, micro-influencers often work on payment per post. Some brands keep influencers on a retainer for three months for an agreed number of posts. Typically, micro-influencers are paid between £500 and £2,500 per post, enabling brands to assess the response. The Instagram account @influencerpaygap shares the reality of what is and isn't paid – the numbers may be lower than you think!

#notsponsored

A growing phenomenon is 'impartiality disclosure' (Stubb and Colliander, 2019, p. 210) where influencers add the hashtag #notsponsored. This is to:

- distinguish between commercial and non-commercial content
- add greater credibility to the post
- provide greater context and background before a sale may occur

There is legislation surrounding sponsorship and promoted content, although this seems to be less understood when working with influencers. The helpful guide *Best Practice Recommendation on Influencer Marketing* has been created (see European Advertising Standards Alliance, 2018). Taking a different approach, in 2020 the

Committee of Advertising Practice (CAP) published the 'Influencers' guide to making clear that ads are ads' which is aimed at influencers, not brands.

To avoid legal consequences, best practice is to disclose paid-for work by using labels such as #Ad or #Advert, with or without hashtags, to ensure that the labels can be easily understood by consumers.

ETHICAL INSIGHTS   Fake followers

Part of the rationale for working with an influencer is to speak to their fans and, whilst some seem to have large followings, they may include fakes.

Fake followers can be bought online and provide an artificial amplification of the influencer's following. They lack genuine engagement and comments may be automated (love it! want it!), instead of detailed comments with emojis. These fakes can damage the role of influencers, and companies may pay in the hope of genuine consumer conversations.

- What do you feel about fake influencers?
- How can you identify fake influencers?
- What action do you take when you find fake influencers?

4.4.4 CUSTOMERS AND USER-GENERATED CONTENT

Customer or user-generated content is recognised as being valuable as it's often freely created. In China, customers creating significant content, with a following, have been named 'key opinion customers' (KOCs). KOCs may demonstrate positive source credibility with greater homophily (real people with real issues) and trustworthiness by providing honest reviews with negative and positive comments. The main challenge is their expertise and how we decide if they are qualified to comment on the subject.

User-generated content has recognised advantages and disadvantages for organisations. Advantages of user-generated content for organisations include: it often costs nothing to create (Vanden Bergh et al., 2011); search engine results are often based on user-generated content (Petty, 2012); users' actions in social media are shared with their networks, as well as across the brand pages (Colicev et al., 2016); and other consumers identify blog articles created by other users as more credible (Kim and Hanssens, 2017).

Disadvantages of user-generated content for organisations arise as the content is outside the organisation's control (Vanden Bergh et al., 2011) and the content can be unpredictable – positive or negative (Kumar et al., 2016).

> **KEY TERM**　USER-GENERATED CONTENT
>
> User-generated content (UGC) or user-created content (UCC) has always existed. User-generated content has been described as 'a form of voluntary organisation' (Crowston and Fagnot, 2018, p. 90) with three key features:
>
> - Large numbers of distributed contributors, commensurate with the popularity of the activity, ranging from dozens to tens of thousands or more
> - Mostly unpaid contributions
> - Jointly focused activity, in which contributors collectively develop new content (e.g. text, images or software) of value to a larger audience

One area of UGC is reviews. From Amazon to TripAdvisor® we consume and believe reviews. The notion of source credibility and KOCs are factors in how we decode the content. Let's explore the source credibility elements applied to whether you trust a review on TripAdvisor®:

- **Expertise**: Is this highly qualified information? Are they knowledgeable or experienced? Are they a long-standing TripAdvisor® reviewer? Have they contributed many reviews?
- **Homophily**: Do we like the same things? Do we share the same beliefs? Is this person visiting the same locations as me?
- **Trustworthiness**: Do I trust this person? Are they genuine? Do the reviews contain real details?

We automatically process the content and decide if it's credible or not.

4.5 STYLE

4.5.1 CONTENT FORMAT

The critical factor to remember is that content is not all about words! Audio content has become increasingly important as Clubhouse started the first audio social media network. Plus, smart speakers from Alexa to Google home and Siri to Bixby search online for us. Content can be communicated in different ways, from words to images, from video to voice.

This means that it's no longer enough to be able to write good copy; marketers also need to be able to either create or commission images and video to bring their stories to life.

Blogs and vlogs

Blogs or vlogs (video blogs) are popular with brands and influencers. Blogs can be free to set up and you can create content immediately. The ongoing cost of blogs includes time to prepare and develop the content, licensing fees for images and time to promote the content.

Most organisations have a blog or 'news' area on their website. This is a strategic search marketing decision, as regular content within a blog brings specific benefits:

- Once the content has been created, it is always there
- More opportunities for keywords and key phrases to be included in posts
- Posts can be shared over and over and over
- Posts can be updated, which signals the strength of a specific post to search engines, such as Google, which can re-index or prioritise the post for searchers

The best-known example of a free blogging tool is Wordpress, which is said to be used as a website platform for over 15 per cent of websites worldwide. Other blogging tools include www.wix.com, medium.com and www.tumblr.com but Tumblr is often blocked as it permits unrestricted imagery such as content of an adult nature.

Vlogs require greater planning than blogs and vloggers use video distribution channels such as YouTube, Vimeo, Instagram and TikTok.

Podcasts

Audio social media is growing, with the global podcasting market predicted to reach $41.8 billion by 2026. The most popular subjects are crime, chat shows, news, sports and food. Podcasts grew during the pandemic as consumers explored new content and advertisers looked for alternative ways to connect with consumers. Plus, the first audio social media platform, Clubhouse, was launched in 2020, focused on talking and telling stories.

Over 125 million people listen to a podcast each month and 'podcast listeners have a median age of 34, younger than broadcast radio (47) and network television (57)' (Adgate, 2021, p. 1).

There are over 50 million podcast episodes available through Apple podcast, Spotify, Google Podcasts and other tools. Many businesses present podcasts; for example, Google has a chat show, 'This Week in Google', and mobile telecoms company Vodafone hosts 'Business Unusual', presented by radio personalities. This is an under-researched area and if the advertising revenues continue, it will become a hot topic in digital marketing.

4.5.2 CONTENT LENGTH

A key aspect of content format is the length of the content, whether short- or long-form. This is about the number of words in the article, the size of the image or the length of the video.

Short-form content has been described as twitterature, nanofiction (Rudin, 2011) and casual viewing (Snickars and Vonderau, 2009). This has been called 'quick break' or 'snackable' content (*Marketing Week*, 2016). It is driven by the growth of mobile phones, where many people consume video and short content, as well as the reduced cost in video and content production.

Long-form content, or in-depth content, includes blog articles, white papers, case studies, e-books and longer videos.

4.5.3 CONTENT LIFE

An emerging factor within a social media context is the life of the content. In traditional marketing, printed items such as brochures contained a date (e.g. the 2023–25 edition) and were replaced after 12 or 24 months – they had a shelf life.

Online content is more challenging, often with no expiry date. Website pages are uploaded and not removed, until a new website is created or when content is audited. Some social media networks automatically remove content after a set time, such as social media stories which can be described as short temporary pieces of content that typically disappear after 24 hours. Stories are popular as individuals share something briefly with friends.

Also favoured by influencers as the ephemeral nature of stories means that their fans need to constantly look at their social media, so they don't miss out! Yet for organisations, this is a lot of effort for a short time.

4.5.4 VIVIDNESS AND INTERACTIVITY

Successful content is more vivid and interactive (Gensler et al., 2013; Pletikosa-Cvijikj and Michahelles, 2013). So the more words in the item, the less likely it is to be shared, this is why we have seen the growth of image-based websites and short videos.

Facebook agrees and explains to advertisers: 'Your ad may not run. You may not reach your audience because there's too much text in the advert image.' Facebook prefers image-based adverts with little or no text. In website design, the concepts of vividness and interactivity (Steuer, 1992) are key factors and, according to the Content Marketing Institute, the top five types of interactive content used by marketers are: assessments, calculators, contests, quizzes, and interactive infographics (Walters and Rose, 2016). Figure 4.3 shows examples of content on the vividness to interactivity scale.

Smartphone Sixty Seconds® – Search for vividness and interactivity

- Select a brand of your choice online.
- Analyse the different content shared by the brand.
- Judge where it fits into the vividness to interactivity scale.
- What are your recommendations to improve or change the content?

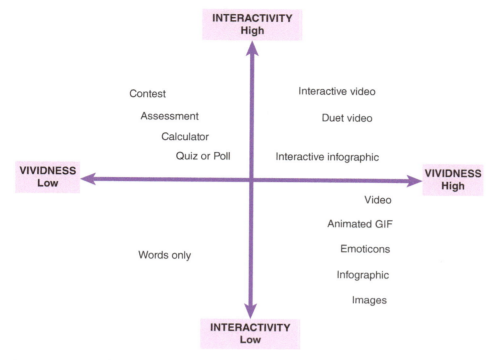

INTERACTIVITY High

Contest

Assessment

Calculator

Quiz or Poll

Interactive video

Duet video

Interactive infographic

VIVIDNESS Low

VIVIDNESS High

Video

Animated GIF

Emoticons

Words only

Infographic

Images

INTERACTIVITY Low

Figure 4.3   Examples on the vividness to interactivity scale

CASE EXAMPLE 4.1   TikTok: the ultimate short-form content

TikTok, known in China as Douyin, has positioned itself as 'the leading destination for short-form mobile video'. Although launched in 2017, it wasn't until the health pandemic of 2020 that it became an accepted technology (see **Technology Acceptance Model** in Chapter 2) as people had to stay at home and were looking for alternative entertainment. With short-form videos of 15 seconds, or connected clips of a maximum of 60 seconds, it's become a new social media tool which is intended for users aged 16 or older.

Popular content includes dance trends, lip-syncing, carrying out challenges and entertaining videos – successful content is often vivid and demonstrates interactivity as users copy earlier videos, mime to music videos or add music tracks to their voiceovers. The content formats offer creative effects such as adding animation, filters, stickers, time lapses or creating a 'duet' with a similar video.

TikTok has created a new group of wealthy influencers, known as creators, including the dancer Addison Rae Easterling and the singing D'Amelio sisters. Their income is based on sponsorships and selling branded merchandise.

(Continued)

TikTok is not the first short-form video platform but has been the most controversial as it has been banned in several countries. Vine was launched in 2013, offering seven-second videos but stopped in 2017. Periscope was launched and acquired by Twitter in 2015. Other social media such as Snapchat, Instagram and Facebook offer short video creation and distribution and have larger audiences.

Case questions

- TikTok is the latest in a series of short-form video platforms – why do you think it will last?
- How can platforms like TikTok make sure children don't see inappropriate content?
- How do you feel about well-known brands creating TikTok videos and using the platform as a marketing channel?

4.6 CONTENT MARKETING STRATEGY

Organisations may have business strategies, marketing strategies and product strategies. In a digital environment where content is such a valuable resource, a content marketing strategy takes a longer-term view of what's needed, for whom, why and how it will be evaluated.

There are fewer academic articles about content marketing strategy and the industry experts are the Content Marketing Institute (CMI), who created a Content Marketing Strategy Framework (Content Marketing Institute, 2017, p. 2), which is:

- **Purpose and goals**: Why are you creating content and what value will it provide?
- **Audience**: For whom are you creating content and how will they benefit?
- **Story**: What specific, unique and valuable ideas will you build your content assets around?
- **Process**: How will you structure and manage your operations to activate your plans?
- **Measurement**: How will you gauge performance and continually optimize your efforts?

4.6.1 CONTENT PURPOSE AND GOALS

Creating content for an organisation without a purpose or goal wastes time and effort. A content marketing roadmap should be underpinned by the 'BEST' principles (Pulizzi and Barrett, 2009):

- **Behavioural:** Does everything you communicate with customers have a purpose? What do you want them to do as a result of interacting with content?
- **Essential:** Deliver information that your best prospects need if they are to succeed at work or in life.

- **Strategic:** Your content marketing efforts must be an integral part of your overall business strategy.

- **Targeted:** You must target your content precisely so that it is truly relevant to your buyers. Different forms of content will need to be delivered through different social platforms.

To create a content strategy requires clear direction as to the different people involved, as well as the technology to support the content delivery as 'content marketing is an ongoing operation, not a short-term campaign' (Content Marketing Institute, 2017, p. 14).

4.6.2 CONTENT MANAGEMENT

Once a content audit has been conducted, you can agree how to manage content. This involves different roles such as those working inside the organisation and others outside the organisation. PR companies often provide a copywriting service (as do copywriters).

The aspects of content management process include:

- Agreeing the themes for the year
- Building a content calendar
- Sharing content guidelines
- Creating and editing
- Publishing or scheduling

Themes for the year

Annual themes can be focused on product launches and the organisation's own events as well as wider national or international events where relevant. Developing themes can take place by understanding persona needs or with keyword research using keyword tools (search online for free keyword research tools) and should be added to the **content calendar** (see Key Term).

Content calendar

Content creation is often planned and managed within a **content calendar** (see Key Term), which allows digital marketers to:

- Plan content around key events in the industry or important dates
- See where there are gaps in your content plan, with time to create more content
- Make sure the content is ready in good time

When working in an organisation, the further ahead you plan your digital content, the better placed you are to produce a consistent flow of content that builds the brand's perceived expertise in your chosen subject areas. Content can be planned on a daily, weekly, monthly or quarterly basis depending on the industry sector.

> **KEY TERM**   CONTENT CALENDAR
>
> A content calendar is a shareable resource that marketing teams can use to plan all content marketing activity. It is often in a spreadsheet, divided by month, which is shared in Google Docs or OneDrive, so that the latest version is always available. The benefit of using the calendar format is that you can visualise how your content is distributed throughout the year.

Content guidelines

Content guidelines include details about the editorial style and brand voice. Larger organisations have instructions on the use of abbreviations and grammatical norms, such as the use of active or passive voice and whether they use British or American English spellings. This may include templates to ensure everyone follows the guidelines.

Content creation and editing

Once content has been created, you can edit and include items such as links to earlier content, links to content outside the website, new or relevant information. When content is edited, Google sees this as a signal that the content is important enough to be revisited and reviewed. This indicates that it is quality content and it is often re-indexed after editing.

Publish or schedule

When the content is ready, you may decide to publish immediately or schedule for a later date. The benefit of a content calendar is that several key items can be prepared and scheduled in advance. This can be useful if the organisation has a time of year that's especially busy.

Plus, blogging tools such as Blogger or Wordpress incorporate 'publish now' or 'schedule later' functions.

4.6.3 MAXIMISE CONTENT DISTRIBUTION

Uploading a blog post, video or infographic is not enough to gain attention. The distribution needs to be carefully planned and maximise its potential to be seen. For example, if you conduct a survey you could transform this into eight pieces of content to maximise its distribution:

1. Write a white paper about the findings and add to your website, or make it downloadable from your blog

2. Create a summary of the survey in PowerPoint and add the slides to slideshare, bookmarking them

3. Write a blog article about the survey and post to your blog or refer to it in a guest post on another blog

4. Graphically illustrate the key points of the survey as an infographic and add to Pinterest, Instagram and/or Facebook

5. Summarise the highlights as a poster and share on your blog or professional social networks

6. Record an interview and publish as a podcast on your blog, as well as podcast libraries

7. Film one of the team talking about the key points from the survey and add to TikTok, Instagram, Pinterest, YouTube and/or Vimeo

8. Schedule and share bite-sized elements of the story via social media

Some distribution tools (see Digital Tool **Hootsuite**) can make achieving coverage across several social media platforms faster and easier.

4.6.4 CONTENT MANAGEMENT SYSTEMS

Websites often incorporate a content management system (CMS). Open Source blogging and website programs such as WordPress, Joomla and Drupal are forms of CMS and allow writers to add content, stores images, search posts and assign editors along with adding SEO elements.

When the content has been created, there is the question of who has access. Questions to consider are:

- Is the content available to all?
- Is it member- or subscriber-only content?
- Is it paid-for content?

Some organisations manage their content by **content-gating and paywalls** (see Key Terms) to encourage non-customers to sign up or at least to share their email address, so the organisation can start a conversation about their requirements.

Paywalls are familiar to researchers and students, as academic articles are often available on a pay-per-item basis, unless your institution has a subscription to access the content.

KEY TERMS   CONTENT GATING AND PAYWALLS

Paywalls and content gating involve hiding additional material behind a virtual wall, which is removed when the visitor has shared information, answered a question, paid a fee or signed up to a subscription. Examples of websites using content gates where you need to log in to access more material or add your own comments include TripAdvisor® and many news sites.

According to Olsen et al. (2020), there are mixed results to paywalls which can result in fewer visitors; however, those subscribing are more engaged (Wadbring and Bergström, 2021).

Having considered the content marketing framework, we need to consider the audience – who we are writing for; that's where we explore personas.

CASE EXAMPLE 4.2   ASOS Insiders

The world's number-one online shopping destination for fashion-loving 20-somethings – that's the clear vision for ASOS.

Launched in 2000, ASOS has had many online marketing challenges. From despatching orders with two left shoes, to the wrong dresses, to seemingly inaccurate online descriptions, customers in many countries have shared these #fails on Instagram. Just search #ASOS to see the amount of user-generated content about this brand.

ASOS is a highly automated business that understands its customers. The numbers of active customers has grown to over 23 million. When the business first started, the target customer was a range of young people aged 16–24 years. Since this time, the business has refined the age profile and seems to have clearly developed personas:

- Demographics – (a) those in the 18–21 age cohort and (b) those in the 22–25 age cohort. Financially, they are possibly on a budget and ASOS offers payment plan options
- Webographics – Use Instagram, shop on their mobiles
- Psychographics – Fashion lovers, enjoy going out and sharing their looks

ASOS has recognised that its customers want to be inspired. They want style tips and fashion advice, but from real people. The company aims to 'showcase our product through inspiring photography, video and live streams' (ASOS PLC, 2019, p. 17). It has a presence across many social media platforms and may be using a **COPE** content strategy to share and repeat content. But with over 85,000 products, there is a lot of content to create.

In this content-heavy and crowded retail fashion space, the ASOS team created a novel way to engage with customers. They had vivid content with many product shots and filters, but needed to add interactivity. Recognising that typical branded posts on Instagram gained a certain amount of engagement, they were seeking more.

To achieve this goal, they launched the ASOS Insider programme. This was a clever collaboration with the people representing their target personas who were storytellers with a following. They weren't aiming at mega-influencers, but micro-influencers, who included:

ASOS Syana who studied law and fashion. She started a blog about her love of fashion and joined ASOS Insiders in 2017 when she was 21 years old. Her Instagram account (asos_syana) shows she has around 52,000 followers.

ASOS Spencer joined in 2018 when he was 18 years old. He was part of a team that developed the clothing line COLLUSION. His Instagram account (asos_spencer) shows he has around 15,000 followers, so we may consider him as a micro-influencer, but his primary social media platform is YouTube where he has over 300,000 subscribers (Elmo Films).

The influencers gain ASOS products, and share style tips and fashion advice. Their bios include a link to an ASOS landing page. ASOS gains greater engagement from passionate shoppers who spend more.

This demonstrates the value of the storyteller and its benefit to business. Plus, ASOS has given a group of enthusiastic fashion fans who created content as a hobby the opportunity to turn an interest into a business.

Case questions

- Have you made a purchase based on recommendations from an influencer? How did this happen?
- How can the potential disadvantages of working with micro-influencers be managed?
- How do you feel about influencers when they move from micro to mega? Does their content improve or deteriorate?

4.6.5 CREATING SUCCESSFUL CONTENT

Successful content can include engaging material that gains responses, is sharable, is widely distributed and, more importantly, achieves its purpose and goals.

The easiest way to create content is to look inside the organisation and to write, talk or video others about the organisation's products or services. Why were they created? By whom and when?

Consider the individual interests, passion and expertise of those inside the organisation. It is essential to be authentic and better not to sell, but advise. Steps to creating successful content include the following:

- Explore your stories
  - Write, talk, illustrate, film stories about your:
  - Skills, service, people, success and differences
- Optimise your content
  - Re-write and add in more SEO with more keywords and long-tail key phrases
  - Build links to other assets
- Publish your content
  - Add to your own website or blog
  - Share with fans and advocates
  - Add as news item to your stories
- Promote your content
  - Add to email signatures
  - Talk about in your social spaces
  - Mention in other articles and build back links
- Harness fans and followers
  - Give them exclusive early access
  - Provide different imagery
  - Ask them to share

COPE: Create Once, Publish Everywhere

One of the key issues to consider when creating content is known as COPE, which stands for 'create once, publish everywhere' (Jacobson, 2009). The aim is to create content that can be used in different forms. This is also known as breaking apart content and is based on the premise that it takes time to create content, so it needs to work harder. It is possible to take one larger piece of content, such as a survey, research work or report, and divide it into eight separate pieces of content, as shown in section 4.6.3 'Maximise content distribution'.

Content is one of the critical elements of digital marketing. It's needed for email, websites, blogs, search engines, paid search and social media. Successful content requires careful planning and strategy that share a story from a relevant storyteller in a suitable style.

JOURNAL OF NOTE

Business Horizons is an easy-to-read journal with a focus on business management issues that often includes digital marketing subjects.

CASE STUDY

CONSTANTLY CREATING CONTENT AT STRAVA

This continues our long case study and you may find it helpful to read earlier parts in previous chapters.

Gabriel has had another late night. He was stressed about the blog as the visitor numbers have been declining for a while. He is the content manager for Strava and part of his role includes managing the blog (blog.strava.com), as well as podcasts and case studies.

Sports are in the spotlight. In the health pandemic, some governments allowed people to leave their home for a short time to exercise. The pandemic created many opportunities for 'Strava stories' which attracted a large following. But since the return to the new normal, the numbers keep dropping.

His team have tried lots of different posts. Topical content about specific athletes worked well as readers shared these stories with their friends. The team's evergreen content, with features about cycling in various countries, worked well in those locations. For a while they shared top photos, but this could be difficult as some people put themselves in danger to get a better photo. There could have been a dying for selfies incident, but fortunately this didn't happen.

His team are asking for guidance and he's not sure where to go next. You name it, he's tried it. He needs some sort of structure or framework to focus the branded content and to work on sharing the articles more when they're published.

From the start, Strava has created content, and the board of directors love content and want to see more. In addition to the blog, there's the podcasts, some from micro-influencers offering advice to rookie runners or amateur athletes. The user-generated content tends to lack depth and detail, and often only a few minutes that can be used, but not enough for a full podcast or post without a lot of work.

Gabriel is stuck; he doesn't know what he should do to retain the existing blog readers and gain more.

CASE QUESTIONS

- Conduct a content sample and audit Strava's content for one week. What are the gaps and opportunities?

- How can Gabriel identify areas of evergreen content for Strava?

- What advice would you give Gabriel to approach content management at Strava?

FURTHER EXERCISES

1. For an organisation of your choice, evaluate their use of evergreen, planned and topical content.

2. Using the Content Marketing Strategy Framework (see section 4.6 'Content marketing strategy'), create a content marketing strategy for an organisation of your choice.

3. For an organisation of your choice, create two pieces of long-form content, such as a blog post, a podcast or a vlog.

4. Content marketing is the only type of marketing in today's digital world. Discuss and present your views. You should support your argument with evidence from textbooks and academic journal articles.

SUMMARY

This chapter has explored:

- Types of content that can be shared
- Types of storytellers, content and media
- Brand journalism and brand activism
- The differences between celebrity endorsers, influencers and opinion leaders
- The Content Marketing Strategy Framework and BEST principles

GO ONLINE

Visit **study.sagepub.com/hanlon2e** to access links to interesting articles, websites and videos related to this chapter.

OVERVIEW
Chapter 5 provides the context as to the importance of social media and addresses social media marketing from the organisation's perceptive with a range of frameworks.

ACTIVITIES
Examine social media for marketing
Apply the honeycomb model
Analyse the sentiment

KEY CONCEPTS
Social presence theory
Social media network users
Stages of adoption

DIGITAL TOOLS
Explore the annual social media map
Assess whether the profiles are fake or real with Spot the Troll

5

SOCIAL MEDIA MARKETING

LEARNING OUTCOMES

When you have read this chapter, you will be able to:

Understand the key concepts in social media for individuals

Apply the honeycomb model

Analyse social media network selection within an organisation

Evaluate social media adoption

Create a strategic framework for social media in organisations

PROFESSIONAL SKILLS

When you have worked through this chapter, you should be able to:

- Recommend relevant social media networks for organisations
- Assess organisations' social media adoption

5.1 INTRODUCTION TO SOCIAL MEDIA MARKETING

There are many types of social media networks which are platforms that facilitate social networking, provide entertainment and showcase our profiles online, as well as enabling organisations to market to consumers. This chapter will make you more aware of the evolution and practices of social media marketing, so that you can better understand the context and how this has changed organisations.

Social media networks (SMNs) started in 1996 with a platform called SixDegrees that later closed due to lack of interest at the time (boyd and Ellison, 2007). According to Statista (2020), the most popular social networks worldwide, ranked by number of monthly active users, are:

- Facebook, YouTube and WhatsApp with over 2 billion monthly active users
- WeChat and Instagram with 1 to 2 billion users
- LinkedIn, TikTok, QQ and Qzone with between 500 million and 1 billion users
- Reddit, Kuaishou (also known as Kwai), Pinterest, Snapchat with between 250 and 500 million users
- Social networks with less than 250 million users include Bilibili, Twitter, Twitch and Clubhouse

The first of these to launch was LinkedIn in 2002, followed by Facebook in 2004, YouTube in 2005 and Twitter in 2006.

Instagram launched in 2010 and Snapchat followed in 2011, the same year that WeChat was launched in China. Douyin or TikTok launched in 2017 (although it has been intermittently banned in several countries) and Clubhouse launched in 2020.

Over time, social media networks have attracted the attention of organisations, because of the growth in the numbers of members and the ability of organisations to contact them and target advertising based on user profiles. Social media has become a powerful communication medium, where consumers can complain about poor service and get much faster responses. It's become a resource for developing new products, providing customer service, identifying customer segments, building brands and generating sales.

5.2 DEFINITIONS OF SOCIAL MEDIA

There is no agreed definition of 'social media' and whilst some researchers assume you know what this means, others use a variety of definitions and sometimes confuse social media, social media websites and social media networks.

By contrast, the definition of the earlier technical term Web 2.0, created by DiNucci (1999) as 'interactive content universally accessible through a standard interface' (p. 32), but largely accredited to O'Reilly (2005), has been debated, researched and agreed.

Sometimes 'social media' and 'Web 2.0' are mixed up, but there are clear differences. Web 2.0 focuses on technical tools (Tenopir et al., 2013), while social media usually concentrates on people.

An earlier definition of social media that was valid in the 1990s was 'a dynamic distributed network, potentially global in scope, together with associated hardware and software for accessing the network, which enables consumers and firms to (1) provide and interactively access hypermedia content (i.e., "machine interactivity") and (2) communicate through the medium (i.e., "person interactivity")' (Hoffman and Novak, 1996, p. 53). A later definition was 'social media is a group of Internet-based applications that build on the ideological and technological foundations of Web 2.0, and that allow the creation and exchange of User-Generated Content' (Kaplan and Haenlein, 2010, p. 61).

In this fast-moving environment, these definitions are soon out of date: it's no longer just consumer-to-firm interaction, it's also peer to peer – and we've moved beyond Web 2.0. In addition, many of these definitions are not easy to remember. I've created an alternative and more concise working definition of social media (not social media networks) which is future-proofed and includes all possible connections:

> Social media is the facilitation of interactive, connected, marketing purposes at organisational, peer-to-peer and personal levels.

It's easy to remember and demonstrates that social media is more than a communications channel, helping both individuals and organisations in many ways.

Activity 5.1 Examine social media for marketing

- Think about an organisation of your choice. Examine its use of social media for marketing purposes.
- Identify good examples that you believe are relevant for the social media network.
- Identify weak examples that are either repeated content across all networks, or perhaps are not relevant for the target audience.
- Justify your response.

5.3 THE ROLE OF SOCIAL MEDIA NETWORKS FOR MARKETING

For organisations to decide which social media platforms to select, it's important to understand more about the types of social media networks.

Earlier research considered four types of social media tools based on the functionality: wikis, social networking sites, microblogging sites and video-sharing sites (Argyris and Monu, 2015). Equally, Mills and Plangger (2015) grouped social media based on operational features: blogs/microblogs, social networks, picture sharing and video sharing. However, more recent work has moved away from the functionality of the platforms to the user benefits (Koukaras et al., 2020). Koukaras and colleagues developed a methodology to analyse 112 social media platforms and then categorise the social media types based on their utilities. This resulted in three primary social media types – social, entertainment and profiling networks – and they considered the utilities rather than functions, as summarised in Table 5.1.

Table 5.1   Social media network types and their utilities

Social media network type	Utilities	Examples of main and smaller platforms
Social	Connecting (Fans, Groups, Live Chat, Pokes, Gifts, Messaging, Explore), Multimedia (Photos, Videos, Text), Sharing (Post Text, Stories, Tweet, Retweet, Links, Hashtags, Sharing Content, Pins, Boards, Questions, Tags)	Facebook, YouTube, Instagram, Pinterest, Twitter, Snapchat, Reddit, PlentyofFish
Entertainment	Games, Shopping, Gaming, Art, Music, Culture, Travel, Luxury, Movies, Animes, Books, Comedy, Online Social Gaming, Gamers, Concerts, Fashion, Sports	Facebook, WeChat, Goodreads, Wayn, SoundCloud
Profile	Wall, Calendar, Embedded in Profile, Skills, Memories, Bookmarking, Goals, Career, Records, Professional Profiles, Profile, Journals, Diaries	LinkedIn, Snapchat, GoFundMe, 23andMe, Quora, QQ

This is a helpful way to classify the social media networks but it is difficult to simply add a social media network into one area, especially as many platforms continue to develop, adding further utilities to keep users engaged. We've seen this with LinkedIn which is a professional network, but adopting Facebook-type tactics such as 'liking' articles to generate greater engagement. Another observation is that based on Koukaras et al.'s research, Snapchat was mainly for profile use as well as social, offering multimedia utilities.

DIGITAL TOOL   Explore the annual social media map

- Search online for 'overdrive interactive map' and find the www.ovrdrv.com website.
- Open the map; you may need to register to download it.
- Explore the hundreds of social media networks.

The social media networks measure membership numbers in Daily Active Users (DAUs) or Monthly Active Users (MAUs). Those owned by shareholders produce quarterly updates and detailed annual reports. Social media networks are owned by shareholders or private funders and to deliver their services they mainly generate an income through advertising. There are some notable differences:

- WhatsApp is not monetised at present and so the volume of monthly users is not shared by its owners, Facebook
- LinkedIn (owned by Microsoft) earns additional revenue from membership and recruitment which is why it is a top site for job seekers
- WeChat and TikTok have mixed revenue models and also generate income through business registration fees and ecommerce

Smartphone Sixty Seconds® – Social media network users

- Search for the name of the social media network + 'investors'.
- Find their latest annual report
- Download it to learn more about their income, number of users and future plans

5.4 KEY CONCEPTS IN SOCIAL MEDIA FOR INDIVIDUALS

It is helpful to consider the key concepts of social media for individuals. This section considers constructs in social media, including uses and gratifications, the honeycomb model, social presence and media richness.

5.4.1 USES AND GRATIFICATIONS

Studies over the years into why individuals use social media contain common themes, with several researchers applying the concept of uses and gratifications. Uses and gratifications theory (UGT) considers the uses or motives for using something and the gratifications or needs that are fulfilled by the usage.

In traditional communications models, such as the two-step theory of communications (see Chapter 4), the audience is considered to be passive – leaning back rather than leaning forward. If you imagine a traditional scene in the home, the family in the same room and sharing one large screen – a television – while leaning back on the sofa, the media is being pushed towards them rather than individuals actively finding the media they want. Today, we have our own personal screens and we lean towards them. We're actively involved with the content, whether that's watching, sharing or posting. According to Katz, Blumler and Gurevitch (1973), with UGT the audience is considered active rather than passive as they're seeking the media for a specific goal. They also identified that need is connected to media choice – so you'd probably use LinkedIn to look for a new job, not TikTok, or use Instagram for inspiration rather than Twitter.

Another factor in UGT is that the media competes with other sources to fulfil your needs, so you might decide to look at Instagram instead of looking at Pinterest, or perhaps TikTok instead of YouTube. The growing number of social media platforms are competing for your attention. Katz and colleagues also found that individuals are self-aware and recognise why they use specific platforms. This echoes a critical factor in social media consumption for individuals, which is that we know why we look at certain platforms, whether that's to be entertained and watch videos on TikTok or YouTube, or research possible employers on LinkedIn.

Other research explored UGT to create a scale of uses and gratifications for using social media and identified the following ten factors (Whiting and Williams, 2013) which are shown in Table 5.2 along with examples found in their research.

Table 5.2   Uses and gratifications theory applied to individuals

Uses and gratifications for using social media	Examples of uses of social media	Examples of gratifications
Social interaction	To connect and keep in touch with family and friends	A place to interact and socialise with others
Information seeking	To find information about sales, deals or products	Help with self-education
To pass the time	When they have spare time or when bored and want something to do	It makes work (or class!) less boring
Entertainment	Playing games, listening to music and watching videos	It makes me laugh
Relaxation	To take my mind off things	Escape from reality and escape the stress of the real world
Expression of opinions	Commenting on updates and sharing comments	Opportunity to voice feelings on social media
Communication	Something to talk about with friends	Sharing stories with friends
Convenience utility	Because it is convenient and accessible anytime and anywhere	Convenience of being able to communicate with a lot of people at one time
Information sharing	Sharing personal information and building a positive reputation	Share information to market themselves
Surveillance	Watching people or things and watching what others are doing	Want to know what others are doing and try to keep up with others

One recurring area is using social media to have fun. This has been extended by several researchers who have defined a new industry, social media entertainment (SME), which includes the platforms, creators and subscribers (Stollfuß, 2020). This form of SME has been termed communitainment (Cunningham and Craig, 2016) and includes communication (such as a video or blog) that's shared with communities on social media platforms.

We're also keen to explore the latest entertainment experience, which explains why we jump from one social media platform to the newest or latest trend. When I wrote the first edition of this book, Snapchat was gathering momentum and was said to be the main social platform, but this never happened – it's declined in user numbers and is a niche platform. Who knows, will the same happen to TikTok and Clubhouse?

Social media has facilitated gaining knowledge, news or advice from many sources, and information is available 24/7. We can search LinkedIn to garner more details about companies, we can search Facebook for product reviews and Instagram for product information. One issue to consider is that some information may be fake (see Chapter 4 on fake news) or very one-sided because it is provided to us based on our filter bubble.

KEY TERM   FILTER BUBBLE

Defined by Eli Pariser, the filter bubble is an invisible force that removes content from your online searches. Based on your previous behaviour, it provides specific material to you. So if you support a particular political campaigner, it's likely you'll see more content that follows that theme. You don't even know you're in the filter bubble, so you believe the content to be true!

See Eli Pariser, *The Filter Bubble: What the Internet Is Hiding from You*, published by Penguin in 2012, for more.

5.4.2 THE HONEYCOMB MODEL

APPLIED TO INDIVIDUALS

Another way to consider social media is to consider how individuals use social media in its application to business. Kietzmann and colleagues (Kietzmann et al., 2011) explored aspects of social media and created a 'honeycomb model', named due to its shape. This model looks at uses, but not necessarily the benefits or gratifications. Figure 5.1 shows the honeycomb model of social media functionality applied to individuals.

Identity in social media

The central focus was identity and is concerned with the amount of personal identifiers or information that is shared by users. Imagine you're using Facebook. It knows your name, age, where you went to school, who your friends are and your birthday. Businesses could use this data with advertising around your birthday (hold your birthday celebration at our place! Or add this to your birthday wishlist!) or show adverts for films your friends have watched and liked. Suddenly, the data becomes useful and has a real value.

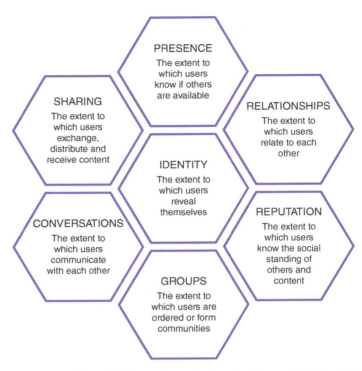

Figure 5.1   The honeycomb model of social media functionality applied to individuals

Source: Kietzmann et al. (2011, p. 243)

But some people use nicknames online, especially in Snapchat or Instagram, so you become harder to track. But in social media platforms like LinkedIn, you will use your real name, add your qualifications and your date of birth (even if that data isn't shared on the platform).

ETHICAL INSIGHTS   Selfie dysmorphia

A negative impact of social media identity is the desire to always look good. Filters provide unrealistic versions of the self, resulting in body dysmorphic disorder, yet many businesses still use models showing the perfect body on their social media pages.

'Snapchat dysmorphia' is recognised as a psychiatric disorder. An individual is preoccupied with 'one or more perceived defects or flaws in physical appearance that are not observable or appear slight to others' (Tremblay et al., 2021, p. 33). Also called 'selfitis' (Balakrishnan and Griffiths, 2018), the result is that younger people are seeking cosmetic surgery when it's not necessary.

- How do you feel about the idea of selfitis?
- What steps can brands take to reduce Snapchat dysmorphia?
- Cosmetic surgery is often a short-term solution and may need to be repeated many times but how can younger people be discouraged from taking such action?

Presence in social media

Presence concerns whether you decide to let others know you are online. Some secret social networks such as Whisper exist due to anonymity. Yet on other social networks, such as LinkedIn, displaying your real identity is essential.

Presence does not just mean letting people find you, it also means telling them you are online right now. Facebook Messenger shows if users are online at that moment and WhatsApp shows when you are active. Constantly sharing your presence status can result in the desire to be online 24/7, so that you don't miss out.

Relationships in social media

Our need to connect with others is an important construct of social networks. In the honeycomb model, 'relationships' considers how users are related to one another, whether by association, or through sharing of objects or as friends. There are different types of relationships: formal or informal; private or public; regulated or unstructured.

LinkedIn shows the relationships via their degrees of separation. There are two concepts here: **tie strength** (see Key Term) and degrees of separation, as within an online world it's difficult to be without presence. LinkedIn works on tie strength as people you have met once or perhaps twice might reach out for a request to help and, within a professional setting, many people will provide assistance. LinkedIn also exemplifies the concept of the six degrees of separation – if your teacher and I are connected, that's one degree of separation; if you're connected to your teacher, but I'm not, that's two degrees of separation. The good news is that you are most likely to be three degrees of separation away from your next boss!

> ### KEY TERM   TIE STRENGTH
>
> Research into offline rather than online 'social networks' discovered that people were more likely to help a contact they did not know that well (weak tie) than someone they knew well (strong tie), demonstrating the strength of weak ties and the benefit of a larger network (Granovetter, 1973).

Reputation in social media

In the honeycomb model, 'reputation' looks at how users can identify the social and professional status of others. LinkedIn has probably become the main reputation tool for professionals worldwide and this platform encourages users to explicitly demonstrate their professional standing by gaining recommendations and endorsements. If you are untruthful about a qualification, this can easily be verified by others who took the same qualification at the same time.

A study suggested that to monitor their online reputation, individuals look at themselves via Google, a practice known as vanity or ego surfing. This research also noted that the individuals were more aware of the consequences of weak online reputations and most damage occurred due to 'non-controlled communication by family members and friends' (Feher, 2021, p. 197). Managing our online selves is part of impression management, which is explored further in Chapter 6, 'Online Communities'.

In an online world, reputation must be monitored, managed and measured to ensure that the right content is being delivered and that relevant performance indicators are being met (see Chapter 13, 'Digital Marketing Metrics and Analytics').

Groups in social media

Being part of a group or a community is not a new idea (see Chapter 6, 'Online Communities') and McQuail's (1983) four motivations for media use included integration, which was about a sense of belonging or community involvement. Shao (2009) suggested that part of the uses and gratifications of social media was to be part of a community and potentially develop a group based on shared interests. There are many types of groups in social media that allow users to categorise their friends, fans and followers; for example:

- LinkedIn has hundreds of thousands of business groups. I suspect many are empty and I suggest there should be an auto-close function if a group hasn't been active for over two years
- Twitter allows users to create lists, making it easier to view content from specific types of other users
- Facebook lets individuals start groups for causes or for campaigning
- WhatsApp enables you to build family, friends and work groups. The only difficulty is sending the right message to the right group!

Conversations in social media

Around the edge of the honeycomb model, the next building block is conversations. Many researchers have identified social interaction as one of our primary uses of social media.

We chat, message and communicate with each other online, although how users communicate with other users varies between platforms. For example, on LinkedIn you are likely to be professional and courteous with work colleagues or potential employers, whereas on WhatsApp you could be as rude to your friends as you dare! When you are having a dialogue with businesses, you might be having discussions about their products or services, either positively or negatively.

However, it's not just a simple one-to-one conversation, it can be a one to many as we create closed groups using platforms such as WeChat and WhatsApp where we have private interactions, or participate in open groups in Facebook and LinkedIn where the communications are public.

There are concerns that 'our online interaction is becoming shorter and more quantified, for example, through actions such as liking and sharing' (Ditchfield, 2020, p. 928).

DISCOVER MORE ON CHANGING CONVERSATIONS IN
SOCIAL MEDIA

Read Hannah Ditchfield's article 'Behind the screen of Facebook: Identity construction in the rehearsal stage of online interaction', published in 2020 by *New Media and Society*, which explains how our online conversations are evolving.

Sharing in social media

Sharing is about how users share content. We all see funny memes (see Key Term **meme**) on Instagram and sometimes we share and sometimes we don't. Sharing builds our identity, shows our relationships, keeps us interacting and is a fundamental aspect of social media.

KEY TERM   MEME

The word meme was coined by Richard Dawkins in the book *The Selfish Gene* (Dawkins, 2006, p. 192). He described a 'new kind of replicator' as we are sharing more and more content. As a result, he sought a word to describe this 'cultural transmission' and started with the word 'mimeme', which was based on 'imitation'. However, he wanted a shorter word than that so he abbreviated it to 'meme', adding the comment 'it should be pronounced to rhyme with "cream"'.

Activity 5.2   Apply the honeycomb model

Identify how you use social media using the elements in Figure 5.1, 'The honeycomb model' and explore whether you have single or multiple identities online, if you talk about brands online and so on. Then on the opposite side, look at how businesses connect with or try to speak to you, using your social media channels.

This research demonstrates the importance of UGT to social media as well as identifying why individuals use social media. Extending the UGT work further, two key constructs that impact on how individuals use social media are social presence theory (the degree to which we are physically present) and media richness (which also echoes vividness and interactivity, which we considered in Chapter 4). Let's gain more understanding of these theories in the next section.

5.4.3 SOCIAL PRESENCE THEORY

Presence or sharing online identity is another recurring theme in social media and was included in both the honeycomb and the UGT scale and was used by Professors Andreas Kaplan and Michael Haenlein. They took four recognised theories to describe the features of social media: (1) self-presentation; (2) social presence; (3) media richness; and (4) self-disclosure. We will look at self-presentation and self-disclosure theories in Chapter 6, 'Online Communities'.

Social presence theory was first defined by John Short, Ederyn Williams and Bruce Christie as the 'degree of salience of the other person in the interaction and the consequent salience of the interpersonal relationships' (Short et al., 1976, p. 65). A simpler definition is: 'the degree to which a person is perceived as a "real person" in mediated communication' (Gunawardena, 1995, p. 151).

Social presence is influenced by two key factors:

- Intimacy – whether that's interpersonal (in person) or mediated (through a device)
- Immediacy – if it's asynchronous (pre-recorded) or synchronous (in real time)

Kaplan and Haenlein (2010) blended social presence and media richness and secondly self-presentation and self-disclosure on their classification axes. Let's investigate the classification further, but first we should look at the visual representation in Figure 5.2 that they created.

		Social presence/Media richness		
		Low	Medium	High
Self-presentation/ Self-disclosure	High	Blogs	Social networking sites (e.g. Facebook)	Virtual social worlds (e.g. Second Life)
	Low	Collaborative projects (e.g. Wikipedia)	Content communities (e.g. YouTube)	Virtual game worlds (e.g. World of Warfare)

Figure 5.2   Classification of social media by social presence/media richness and self-presentation/self-disclosure

Source: Kaplan and Haenlein (2010, p. 62)

Online content like Wikipedia is seen as low/low – low on media richness and presence and low on self-disclosure – after all, you never know the identity of the authors of the page and whether the content is accurate! At the other extreme, participating in a virtual world provides high levels of media richness and high levels of self-presentation.

During the health pandemic of 2020, the biggest issue concerned social presence – it was rarely allowed. Many communications had to be mediated through a device – mobiles, tablets, desktop computers. The words asynchronous and synchronous started to be used in education as teachers had to decide whether a class was pre-recorded or live. It may be obvious that social presence is often lower for mediated (e.g. via Teams, Zoom or an other online system) than interpersonal (e.g. face-to-face classes) and for asynchronous than synchronous communications. Effectively, if you are speaking to someone face to face it's a different experience to chatting online. So in a nutshell, the higher the social presence, the larger the social influence that the communication partners have on each other's behaviour. It's likely that this theory will be developed further as we've learned to live with mediated communications.

DISCOVER MORE ON SOCIAL PRESENCE THEORY

There is a useful article by Jason T. Bickle, Malar Hirudayaraj and Alaina Doyle in the *Journal of Advances in Developing Human Resources*: 'Social presence theory: Relevance for HRD/VHRD research and practice' (Bickle, Hirudayaraj and Doyle, 2019). This provides advice on how to best manage social presence for online instruction which could relate to your classes and if you need to deliver online content for an employer.

5.4.4 MEDIA RICHNESS THEORY

Writing in *Management Science*, Richard Daft and Robert Lengel examined why organisations processed information and concluded that this was based on the assumption that the goal of any communication is the resolution of ambiguity and the reduction of uncertainty (Daft and Lengel, 1986).

You could think of an email from your tutor with your end of year grades, confirming that you have passed. The purpose of the email is to let you know where you are. It reduces any ambiguity and uncertainty, especially if some grades were higher (or lower) than expected!

Considering that their work was created over three decades ago, Daft and Lengel (1986, p. 560) classified 'less rich' to 'rich media', with face-to-face being most rich and numerical documents less rich.

From studies into media richness, we know that the richer the medium, the more effective it is. This explains the effectiveness of social media sites that contain richer information, from text to images and from emoticons to live video.

5.4.5 CONSUMING, PARTICIPATING AND PRODUCING

UGT and the honeycomb model largely describe why individuals use social media, rather than how it's used. Social presence and media richness consider how the context and content influence our behaviour, but two other areas are participating and producing.

Participatory culture (Jenkins, 2008) concerns leaning forward and being actively engaged in the media, whilst production takes this one step further as we become the performer instead of the spectator. Levels of engagement are a useful frame to consider how social media is used and range from passive to planned.

Passive engagement, where we consume social media, is where the framework starts. Passive consumers are not contributing to the conversation; they simply watch or listen in the background and have been described as lurkers (Mathwick, 2002).

Consumers who are participating in conversations by adding comments and sharing feedback are actively engaged. Those with the greatest level of engagement are producing material to be shared. This material is usually planned and is shared for the individual's benefit, or to entertain friends, and is how some influencers started their career (see Chapter 4 for more on influencers). These individuals are producers and their work has been described as produsage which has been defined as 'the collaborative, iterative, and user-led production of content by participants in a hybrid user–producer, or produser role' (Bruns, 2006, p. 276).

Participation in social media can have benefits for students. Professor Santoveña-Casal (2019) conducted research with 1,960 students and found that those who participated gained better grades. Santoveña-Casal's paper 'The impact of social media participation on academic performance in undergraduate and postgraduate students', published in the *International Review of Research in Open and Distance Learning*, notes several caveats to the research – it may be that because it was teacher-led there was greater encouragement to participate and after the teacher was no longer involved, the communities did not continue.

Smartphone Sixty Seconds® – What's your engagement?

- On your mobile phone, go to your favourite social media platform.
- Find a post, image, story or video that you liked where you added emojis 👍☺
- Was this a one-off or a regular occurrence?
- Do you engage passively or actively?

5.5 KEY CONCEPTS IN SOCIAL MEDIA FOR ORGANISATIONS

Having considered key concepts in social media for individuals, the next factor is key concepts in social media for organisations.

Students tend to know how to use social media at a personal level and are often hired on the expectation that this knowledge will translate in the workplace where they will understand how to manage social media for a range of organisations. Let's examine how social media can be used at work, as there are differences in the application compared to individual usage.

5.5.1 CRITICAL BENEFITS OF SOCIAL MEDIA FOR ORGANISATIONS

Several researchers have called social media game-changing as it has altered the rules of communication and has delivered critical benefits for organisations. Considering the elements of UGT for individuals, we can identify specific benefits for organisations, as shown in Table 5.3.

Table 5.3 Critical benefits of social media for organisations

Usage	Benefit	How this helps organisations
Listening to **social interaction**, reviewing information sought, questions asked, joining **groups** about products or brands	Market and product research	To gain access to themed communities or difficult-to-reach targets and access to knowledge via online communities
Listening to **social interaction** and paying attention to customer **engagement** such as requests for new products	New product development	To generate new product ideas and gain insights by monitoring social media data
Monitoring **groups** and deciding if there is a specific segment	Customer segmentation	To monitor how customers self-segment by joining particular online communities
Monitoring brand **conversations** and responding where relevant	Brand building	To monitor brand awareness and promote content
Monitoring **conversations** mentioning the brand	Brand management	To witness how consumers discuss the brand; watching the artefacts and stories they share
Assessing positive reviews and rewarding customers and **sharing** these reviews with other, similar people	Sales cycle	To influence the consumer buying process by social media activities
Monitoring and responding to **conversations** and using **sentiment analysis** (see Key Term)	Customer service	To support customer service and the development of long-term relationships and manage online issues

KEY TERM   SENTIMENT ANALYSIS

Sentiment analysis is a review of the valence or tone of content. Typically, the tone is classified as negative, neutral, positive or mixed. Companies monitor mentions of their brand name, hashtags and specific products. Definitions of sentiment analysis include:

- 'Sentiment analysis attempts to identify and analyze opinions and emotions' (Abbasi et al., 2008).
- 'Sentiment Analysis enables us to manually or automatically classify tweets with regard to their emotionality, e.g. positive or negative' (Bruns and Stieglitz, 2013).

One of the challenges in identifying sentiment is that the analysis is often conducted by automated systems, which fail to understand the use of sarcasm, humour and irony. For more on the application of sentiment analysis, see Chapter 9.

Activity 5.3   Analyse the sentiment

- Use the website http://sentistrength.wlv.ac.uk and carry out a quick sentiment analysis test.
- Copy a comment from a consumer on a brand social media page.
- Paste this text into the box and analyse the results.
- Were the results positive, negative or neutral?
- Is this helpful or confusing? How do businesses manage these results?

5.5.2 THE HONEYCOMB MODEL APPLIED TO ORGANISATIONS

Section 5.4.2 introduced the honeycomb model (Kietzmann et al., 2011) and considered its application to individuals. This section considers its relevance in an organisational setting. Taking the building blocks, the implications for organisations are:

- Identity: Demographic, webographic and psychographic information about customers is available and can be used to better inform decisions
- Conversations: It's possible to listen to and monitor conversations and respond if needed, possibly conducting **sentiment analysis** (see Key Term)
- Sharing: It's necessary to understand the common social networks used by customers and to create content that is easy to share
- Presence: Location-based businesses may explore the relative importance of user availability and location, possibly providing offers to those on their website or social media pages
- Relationships: Understanding how to build and maintain relationships in social media
- Reputation: Demonstrating trust and authenticity to foster engagement and when organisations get this wrong, it may be shared on social media
- Groups: Facilitating communities in social media that organisations manage

The individual building blocks within the model are also areas to explore and this will vary depending on the organisation. It may be that several blocks are not relevant in some settings. As an example, sharing may be essential for an online food service, where individuals post images of delicious meals. This gives organisations opportunities to re-share and promote their business to a wider audience. However, sharing may not be relevant for banks or financial organisations as individuals may not want to share personal financial details and this could contravene local data protection legislation. Equally, the group's function may be important for online yoga classes, new students at a university or people moving to a new location, but this may be less relevant in a business-to-business setting where different organisations are competing against each other and unwilling to fully participate in the group. The important factor is ensuring that the context, situation and circumstances are appropriate for the different blocks.

5.5.3 STRATEGIC FRAMEWORK FOR SOCIAL ME-
DIA APPLICATION IN ORGANISATIONS

Having considered the key concepts in social media for organisations, the next issue is how organisations decide which platforms to select. This is based on the context – the type, size, location, customers and goals of the organisation. Sadly, many organisations follow the crowd and use the newest social media network, without considering their target audience or what's required to maintain the platform.

My research has explored how organisations select social media and I've created a model, the 'Strategic framework for social media application in organisations' (see Figure 5.3); it has nine steps, which I'll explain more here. The overarching notion is that specific steps are examined before starting to post material on a platform; this means that the social media platforms selected will be more relevant for the organisation and are less likely to waste resources.

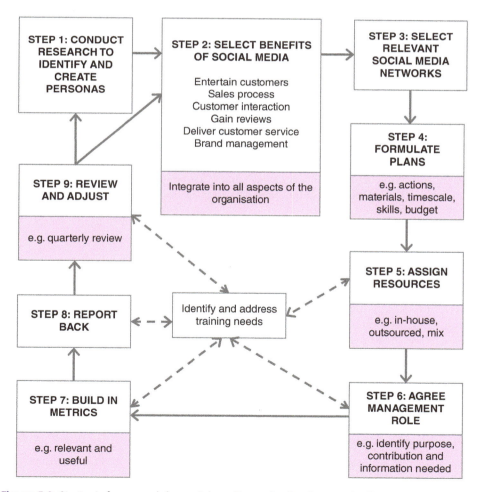

Figure 5.3 Strategic framework for social media application in organisations

Step 1: Conduct research to identify personas

To select a social media network and understand the benefits needed, you first need to understand the audience and should create personas (see Chapter 4). Some organisations are aware of their customers which is evident in their focused communications, but others, such as British brand Marks & Spencer, are less clear (see Case Example 5.1).

Step 2: Select benefits of social media

The required benefits to be gleaned from social media may include those shown in Table 5.3 ('Critical benefits of social media for organisations'). For example, entertainment may be less relevant for government organisations, but critical for retailers.

The sales cycle and customer service benefits will be important for many retailers and also for B2B organisations. A B2B business selling software may want its website to generate more leads. An online retailer may be seeking to increase direct sales.

Step 3: Select relevant social media networks

Based on the personas and the selected benefits, the relevant social media networks can be chosen. The aim is to ensure there is a synergy between the personas, the organisation and the social media networks.

Step 4: Formulate plans

The next step is to formulate plans that address the relevant activity on the social media networks, to meet the benefits. This will depend on the organisation, although the plans are likely to include actions, the materials needed such as imagery, content or software, timescales and budget (see Chapters 11 and 12).

Step 5: Assign resources

Assigning resources (see Chapter 12) involves deciding whether work is conducted in-house, or outsourced to an agency, or whether a mix of different approaches is needed. Marketing is an area where the **gig economy** (see Key Term in Chapter 12) is popular. This may be a factor for smaller organisations that cannot afford to recruit full-time permanent staff. Alternatively, existing staff could be re-trained to help manage social media.

Step 6: Agree management role

It's important to consider the role of management in the social media framework. This may be a discussion and agreement about how the management team is involved and whether there is a need to contribute specific guidelines or other useful information.

In my research, some members of senior teams were less involved or did not understand social media. So another factor is whether training is required for other members of the management team, such as board members or trustees.

Step 7: Build in metrics

It's important to include relevant and useful metrics to measure the results (see Chapter 13 for more on metrics). Metrics is another area where further training may be required, to establish benchmarks and to provide training for the management team or board of directors or trustees.

Step 8: Report back

Once the metrics have been agreed and are built into the strategic framework for social media application, step 8 involves reporting back. This could take the form of a dashboard, monthly report or verbal presentation via Zoom or Teams (see Chapter 12 for more on reporting). Regardless of the format, this step may also need training to both produce and interpret the results so that all members of the organisation are fluent in social media.

Step 9: Review and adjust

The loop continues as regular reviews should take place to evaluate whether the benefit is being gained. This review step is essential in social media management as the social media networks can change their terms and conditions which could result in the main benefit no longer being available or accessible. A quarterly review is helpful in a social media environment as the larger social media networks (e.g. Facebook, Twitter) provide four updates each year for shareholders and that's when most changes take place.

Not all organisations understand how to use social media, as you'll see in Case Example 5.1 which explores M&S and its use of social media.

CASE EXAMPLE 5.1   M&S and social media

The British retailer M&S (also known as Marks & Spencer) was established in 1884 and sells clothing, homeware and food in over 60 countries, with over 40 websites. Its total revenue is over £10 billion and it measures customer experience using the Net Promoter Score® (see Chapter 2) which is 57 for the main .com website and is considered to be a good score.

The business has lost its focus, trying to broaden its customer base, reinvigorate its clothing brands and transform its online presence. It is adopting 'digital first' behaviours to improve technology and invest in improvements to its app and websites, hoping this will encourage more of its core customers to shop online.

M&S is also cost saving and reducing the marketing budget. The actual budget is not published but is thought to be around £100 million or 10 per cent of revenue. Added to this,

(Continued)

the firm gains contributions for promotional activities from its suppliers, so if M&S decides to promote strawberries or carrots in the summer, the growers and farmers must contribute towards the cost.

The social media teams of around 100 people are located in several countries – the United Kingdom, India, Ireland, Australia, Greece and Romania. They use Conversocial as the social media management tool (see Chapter 12). In addition to this, they work with several photography agencies, there is an online content team and an offshore imagery team, as well as the online trading team and the marketing department.

The directors may not understand social media. Their annual report mentions social media but does not say which channels, however a search shows that they use Facebook, Instagram, LinkedIn and Twitter.

There is evidence of a lack of understanding of social media with their advertising. They run the same ads on Facebook and Instagram, without adapting the messaging to the different platforms. Some of the Facebook ads are less vivid with, for example, more text in some cases or white products on white backgrounds. Some adverts don't make sense. A Facebook advert included text promoting vegan food but the image showed a large piece of red meat. They seem to be at a crossroads, with the business, the target audience and in their use of social media.

In 2020, M&S attempted to use TikTok with one of its cartoon characters – Percy Pig, mainly used for confectionery and gifts – but the online feedback compared the short video to a psychological thriller. This was a strange choice of social media as over 50 per cent of its customers are aged 50-plus, whilst TikTok has a younger audience with 40 per cent aged between 16 and 24. Adding a TikTok account does not transform a traditional, dated retailer into a trendy ASOS hipster overnight!

This shows how some organisations are trying to keep up with others without fully considering their social media network selection which may waste time and money, as well as damaging the brand and alienating their core customers.

Case questions

- How would you promote a traditional brand like M&S on social media?
- What is the best approach to social media training in a large organisation? What factors would need to be considered to ensure all staff better understood the role of social media?
- Why do organisations employ people in different countries to manage their social media?

Having carefully considered the steps involved in strategic social media network selection, we can consider how organisations adopt social media and implement best practice.

5.6 SOCIAL MEDIA ADOPTION AND IMPLEMENTATION

Using social media within organisations varies enormously. It depends on the senior management team and their understanding, as well as their commitment to purposefully use the platforms, rather than following the crowd, where you hear the words 'we need TikTok because our competitors are using it', which is hardly a strategy, but is scarily commonplace.

Social media adoption and implementation are part of a journey. This often starts with some form of experiment and registration with one platform, say Twitter or Facebook. Then there is some understanding of how the platform works and the benefit to business, followed by a greater adoption and focus.

So how we do measure or pinpoint where an organisation is in terms of its social media journey? Two researchers based in Ireland, Aidan Duane and Philip O'Reilly, developed a stage model of social media adoption, showing the five stages that businesses step through until social media is fully integrated into the organisation. This is a strategic model and identifies the organisation's focus as well as the structure – if any – and the management involvement. Shown in Table 5.4, it is a useful tool to assess organisations' social media presence and to review their competitors. It provides a benchmark with a clear map of the next stage in the journey. If you are seeking a job interview with an organisation or working on a placement, you could identify their current stage and recommend a digital marketing plan to increase social media adoption!

Table 5.4 Stage model of social media adoption

Stage	Strategy	Focus	Structure	Management
1. Experimentation and Learning	It is experimental with every department doing their own thing	Posting some comments, images and videos, and providing some product/service information	Individual or departmental drive	None or very little involvement
2. Rapid Growth	It is coordinated across all departments by management, and a number of goals and objectives have been established	Consumer-centric focus. Efforts aimed at increasing internal and external awareness. Customers are encouraged to connect, follow, like, recommend and comment on products and its service	Bottom-up widespread user participation coupled with top-down management	Support and encouragement
3. Formalisation	It is formalised and controlled across the company, with a strategy aligned with the business plan. Staff adhere to an established set of rules	Planning, strategy, governance and alignment with overall business strategy	A more centralised, corporate-driven model to coordinate efforts	Controlled by management

(Continued)

Stage	Strategy	Focus	Structure	Management
4. Consolidation and Integration	It is very well integrated with key business processes across the company, and it is driving a fundamental change in how we do business	Optimisation of processes and creating scale. Fundamental business change. Pursue alignment with external partners/suppliers. Co-creation/ideation, crowdsourcing emerge	Extension of corporate model to integrate external partners, suppliers, customers, communities, experts, etc. Micro-outsourcing of activities may also occur	Shared by management/staff
5. Institutional Absorption	It is embedded into the core of what we do, and how we do it, from customers to suppliers, from internal partners to external partners	De facto application for key business tasks. Enterprise-wide social media technologies for the entire workforce Generate new/re-engineer existing business models	Aimed at customers, suppliers and partners, as business connectivity is transformed to establish wider business relationships	Shared by management/staff or decentralised

Source: Duane and O'Reilly (2016, p. 82)

CASE EXAMPLE 5.2   Gymshark's social media adoption

In 1992 the phrase 'surfing the internet' became popular, the Space Shuttle *Discovery* STS-42 was launched and Ben Francis was born.

In 2012 at the age of 20, Ben Francis founded Gymshark, a sports clothing brand. Initially, he hand sewed and hand made the clothing from his parents' house in the day and delivered pizza at night. Today the business is valued at £1 billion.

Gymshark was an early adopter of all social media. The online focus emanates from the founder's obsession with technology. Plus, the company has created its own influencers and sponsors 'Gymshark athletes' with the details shared on the blog gymshark.com/blogs/athletes.

Gymshark has over 5 million social media followers, using all channels, with customers in over 125 countries. The main social media account is Instagram @gymshark. It has three Twitter accounts, @Gymshark, @GymsharkCentral which shares news and updates, and @Gymshark_Help for customer service. The company also has TikTok, Snapchat, Facebook, YouTube, Pinterest and LinkedIn accounts, and uses a Spotify account for sharing playlists to work out and exercise.

Based in the UK, it has around 50 people looking after its social media in the United Kingdom, the United States, France and Germany. The company is going through a time of rapid growth: it has raised money from an investment group and is planning to compete directly with Nike and lululemon.

Case questions

- What tactics could Gymshark utilise to gain greater social media attention? What risks may be involved?
- As the business is growing rapidly, how does Gymshark ensure it is at the forefront of conversation? Not just as a one-off, but all the time.
- How might Gymshark stay up to date with the latest platforms and decide which ones to choose and which to ignore?

5.7 ADVANTAGES AND DISADVANTAGES OF SOCIAL MEDIA NETWORKS

In a positive way, social media allows old school friends to connect, older people to stay in touch with family members, and friends to plan and organise events. The main advantages of social media for individuals are consuming, participating and producing.

For example, staying in touch with family on Facebook may involve consuming content and looking at posts from others to see their activities. It may involve participating by adding comments and feedback, or producing, uploading and creating your own posts and content. Other platforms, such as Slideshare, may be for consumption only, to view slide decks.

During the pandemic, social media encouraged social distancing practices (Cato et al., 2021) and enabled families to stay in touch using Facetime, WhatsApp and WeChat. Local communities formed WhatsApp groups to check on elderly neighbours and share shopping trips. Effectively, social media networks became local community platforms, lifelines to keep people connected.

There are downsides to social media networks too. Researchers found that social media could help to spread disinformation and fake news during the pandemic (Cato et al., 2021), so much so that the World Health Organization and the United Nations stated that they were 'fighting an infodemic in the same way as we are fighting a pandemic', adding that 'an infodemic is defined as a tsunami of information—some accurate, some not—that spreads alongside an epidemic' (World Health Organization, 2020, p. 1). This was evidenced where the panic buying of toilet rolls, rice and pasta took place as shortages were predicted, even though all governments confirmed there were no supply issues.

Individuals can use social media for negative purposes and exhibit online antisocial behaviour to bully others and troll communities. Negative application of social media manifests in different forms, including celebrity abuse on Twitter and hate speech on Facebook, as well as cyber bullying and trolling. Researchers have defined cyber bullying as 'a deliberate, repetitive and permanent behavior pattern against a defenseless victim mostly by an unknown group or individual through electronic environments such as text messages, picture/video clips, phone calls, emails, chat-rooms, instant messages and websites' (Sari and Camadan, 2016).

Likewise, the act of trolling has been defined as being 'a negative online behaviour intended to disrupt online communications, aggravate internet users and draw individuals into fruitless debate' (Coles and West, 2016, p. 44). Early research provided three criteria for troll behaviour (Herring et al., 2002, p. 375):

- Messages from a sender who appears outwardly sincere
- Messages designed to attract predictable responses or flames
- Messages that waste a group's time by provoking futile argument

Do you recognise anyone exhibiting this behaviour? Someone you know? Or perhaps someone famous?

DISCOVER MORE ON TYPES OF TROLLS

Read the article 'Who would respond to a troll? A social network analysis of reactions to trolls in online communities' by Qiusi Sun and Cuihua Shen, published in 2021 in the journal *Computers in Human Behavior*.

There is advice on how to tackle this unacceptable behaviour on these websites:

- www.bullying.co.uk/cyberbullying
- www.internetmatters.org/issues/cyberbullying

DIGITAL TOOL   Can you spot the troll?

- Visit the website https://spotthetroll.org and take the quiz (it works better on laptops than mobiles)
- Did you spot the troll?
- Any surprises?

As social media is the facilitation of interactive, connected, marketing purposes at organisational, peer-to-peer and personal levels, what goes online, stays online. An inappropriate comment today can have consequences many years later.

Social media will continue to be used as we have so many life events and connections in these networks. What's likely is that we will learn to better manage our online presence and the platforms will improve how they address unacceptable behaviour.

JOURNAL OF NOTE

The journal *Social Media + Society* focuses on social media. It has an international editorial board and is an open access journal, so if you don't have access to a university library, you can still download the articles.

CASE STUDY

STRAVA THE NEW SOCIAL NETWORK

This continues our long case study and you may find it helpful to read earlier parts in previous chapters.

'Strava is the social network for athletes', claims Strava's blog, clearly positioning the company as not just a running or cycling app, but a social network.

Strava uses other social networks, including:

- Facebook: www.facebook.com/Strava
- Instagram: www.instagram.com/strava
- Twitter: https://twitter.com/strava
- LinkedIn: www.linkedin.com/company/strava-inc
- There is also a YouTube page: www.youtube.com/user/StravaInc which isn't widely promoted and has fewer than 50,000 subscribers.

The Facebook page has nearly 900,000 likes but is only updated when there is specific news, rather than on a regular basis. The team seem to ignore complaints and negative comments from users. The Facebook page name has been changed several times from Strava Cycling to Strava. The page is managed by 23 people, of whom 14 are in the United States, 5 in the United Kingdom, 2 in Indonesia, 1 in France and 1 in Japan. It's likely that this team also manage the other social media pages.

The Instagram page has nearly 1 million likes and runs adverts that are managed using Facebook Ads Manager. The page is updated more than the other social networks and generates about 5,000 likes and comments, which is an **engagement rate** of 0.5 per cent and is lower than average (see Chapter 4 for more on engagement rate).

The Twitter page is maintained more regularly and the person managing this uses the Twitter website to respond to comments from fans and add new material. The tweets use emojis which bring more humour to the posts. There is a secondary Twitter support account (@stravasupport) which has fewer than 15,000 follows. The landing page included in the bio is 'How do I contact Strava Support?'

The LinkedIn page shows details of the employees and has a link to Strava career opportunities. There are few posts and a low **engagement rate** (0.3 per cent).

The bios vary on each page, indicating a lack of consistency and possibly different team managers managing different platforms:

- Facebook: Millions of runners and cyclists use Strava to record their activities, compare performance over time, compete with their community, and share the photos, stories and highlights of their activities with friends.
- Instagram: Your goal is our mission.
- Twitter: The #1 app for runners and cyclists.
- YouTube: Strava is a global community of millions of runners, cyclists and triathletes, united by the camaraderie of sport. Our website and mobile apps bring athletes together from all walks of life and inspire them to unlock their potential – both as individuals and as communities. From Olympians to weekend warriors, we're out there on the road and trail, all over the world, day after day. Join us at Strava.com, the App Store or Google Play.
- LinkedIn: A passionate and committed team, unified by our mission to build the most engaged community of athletes in the world.

Strava has claimed its brand name on several other networks too, including Medium (medium.com/@strava) and Reddit (reddit.com/r/Strava). These pages have little content, so it's assumed that the brand manager took the names so someone else couldn't use them and try to re-sell to Strava at a later time.

Strava's social media is managed using Khoros software which provides social listening and enables social media managers to allocate specific tasks to different team members. This type of software typically costs around £100,000 per year.

Strava is clearly listening to its users' comments online but fails to respond to all. There is inconsistency in the frequency of posting across the social media platforms and engagement is low.

CASE QUESTIONS

- Discuss why the engagement on Strava's Instagram and Twitter pages is so low

- Why does consistency matter to a brand? Should Strava introduce greater consistency to its social media bios?

- Should Strava respond to negative comments online? If so, how should this happen across its different social media networks?

FURTHER EXERCISES

1. Identify and justify the benefits of using social media, for either a fashion retailer, a games company or a sports organisation.

2. Discuss the risks of using social media for an organisation of your choice and provide recommendations on how these risks might be mitigated.

3. Apply the strategic framework for social media application to an organisation of your choice, making recommendations to adapt where needed.

4. Social media was invented for people, not organisations. Discuss and justify your response.

SUMMARY

This chapter has explored:

- Key concepts in social media for individuals
- Social presence and media richness theory
- The benefits of social media
- The strategic framework for social media application in organisations
- Key factors in social media adoption

GO ONLINE

Visit **study.sagepub.com/hanlon2e** to access links to interesting articles, websites and videos related to this chapter.

OVERVIEW
Chapter 6 introduces and develops the theme of online communities, explaining why they matter, how they developed and why organisations start brand communities.

ACTIVITIES

Explore your privacy paradox

Identify your communities

Recommend approaches to establish an online community

KEY CONCEPTS

Social capital

Community life stages

Key factors in online community management

DIGITAL TOOLS

Create a Facebook Fan Page

Examine an online comment moderation tool

6

ONLINE COMMUNITIES

LEARNING OUTCOMES

When you have read this chapter, you will be able to:

Understand the types of online communities

Apply the concepts of self-presentation and self-disclosure

Analyse community lifestages

Evaluate the rules of engagement required for your organisation

Create a plan to build a community that is engaging and thriving

PROFESSIONAL SKILLS

When you have worked through this chapter, you should be able to:

- Identify and recommend relevant online communities for organisations to explore
- Plan, create and manage a successful online community

6.1 INTRODUCTION TO ONLINE COMMUNITIES

The notion of community has always existed and traditionally communities were associated with a particular place and the people that lived there. We are aware of farming communities, rural neighbourhoods and social groups, all promoting an idyll or pastoral myth of belonging, being part of a group that is often associated with connections that were created and nurtured over many generations.

A wider community or group of people could be described as a society, or an ordered community. Societies have existed for centuries, such as community-based groups, religious assemblies and professional guilds. These organisations may be formal communities where people meet like-minded people, often with a commercial or practice-based focus.

Community and society are recurring themes in academic literature. In 1887 German sociologist Tönnies distinguished between the idea of community (*gemeinschaft*) and society (*gesellschaft*). He suggested that community was based on an *emotional* feeling that followed traditions or shared rituals, whereas society was founded on a *rational* aim, acting together for the common good. He identified a connection between community and society. In an online setting, the concepts of community and society can blur and the boundaries become less clear.

KEY TERM   ONLINE OR VIRTUAL COMMUNITIES

Online or virtual communities are 'a group of people who may or may not meet one another face to face, and who exchange words and ideas through … computer … networks' (Rheingold, 1987, p. 78). A study by Yao et al. (2021, p. 2) described online communities as places that 'allow people to gather in a virtual environment without restrictions stemming from geographic distance or temporal availability, offering them a platform to share experiences, ask questions, and receive and provide social support'.

You probably recognise online communities better as Facebook, Instagram, TikTok or WeChat. Plus, during the COVID-19 pandemic, online communities grew. Online groups used enterprise social networks that were designed for business, such as Microsoft Teams, Slack and WebEx.

The World Health Organization (WHO) recognised that WhatsApp was used more by communities during the pandemic. So to communicate with wide groups of people quickly and glocally, WHO launched a free multilingual global health chatbot that could be shared by communities locally. It met the criteria for technology acceptance (see TAM in Chapter 2) as it was easy to use (just type 'hi' in your language to access the facts) and was useful, providing the latest health news.

This chapter will explain the benefits of being part of a community and unravel the types of groups. You will learn more about self-presentation theory and see why you should be careful about what's shared online. The role of the organisation in online communities is explored, plus how to respond to community feedback – including complaints, before they become a crisis.

6.2 WHY COMMUNITIES MATTER

Communities are powerful spaces and can change society. In a marketing context, brands have benefited from direct contact with their consumers, providing insights into how their products are consumed and understanding deeper feelings attached to their brand. The idea of 'brand community' was established by Muñiz and O'Guinn (2001) who explored types of consumption communities, noting that these could meet online as well as offline. There are three elements to a community (Muñiz and O'Guinn, 2001):

- The sense of belonging
- The presence of shared rituals and traditions
- The sense of duty or obligation to the community

Within an online setting, the sense of belonging concerns more than being part of a group; it involves *feeling* like you're part of the group. Belonging in online groups extends beyond geographical locations, so the sense of place is less relevant. For example, an online community may promote topics such as #MentalHealthAwareness used on TikTok, Twitter and Instagram. In this example, the feeling of belonging emanates from shared consciousness concerning mental health.

The presence of shared rituals and traditions is seen in religious or faith groups. These may be centred around events, weekly services or annual festivals. Online rituals include using memes or hashtags such as #happy or sharing information, such as 'empathy rituals' which Brownlie and Shaw (2019, p. 104) uncovered when exploring the emotional elements of online conversations. They identified one-to-one sharing of feelings in Twitter and demonstrated how the wider community tried to support those in distress. This is part of the sense of duty to the community, even though it may not be a formally recognised group.

6.2.1 STRENGTH OF WEAK TIES

One aspect of being in a community is helping others, perhaps those we haven't met face to face. A study analysed social networks within offline communities (see Key Term **Tie Strength** in Chapter 5) and how they functioned (Granovetter, 1973). This study is nearly a blueprint for how LinkedIn works as it demonstrated the benefits of being connected.

Strong ties include family members, relatives, close friends and people you know well. Weak ties are those you consider an acquaintance, formal connections through work, a friend of a friend or someone your friends follow. These ties are connected to your different network types. You may use WhatsApp for strong ties and Microsoft Teams for weak ties. If you're seeking a new job, assessing your strong and weak ties may help with introductions or company knowledge for interviews.

Granovetter argued that these interpersonal ties were founded on four interconnected elements, discussed here.

Time in the group

The time given to the group and how often you participate related to stronger ties which were higher maintenance and required more effort. So if you're sharing content with close friends (strong ties) you may carefully craft the content before sharing. If it's someone you don't know, or a friend of a friend (weak ties), perhaps less time and effort is needed, so it may be faster responses; for example, reviewing and liking content, adding comments and emojis.

Emotional intensity

The emotional intensity where individuals share personal stories and feelings on Twitter (Brownlie and Shaw, 2019) can be episodic and occur when needed. For example, during the pandemic some people struggled to cope and shared their innermost feelings on public social networks. Random strangers posted messages of support. These individuals have been described as 'digital Samaritans' (Brownlie, 2018, p. 66).

For example, LinkedIn is enabling emotional intensity by supporting people looking for work and has created badges for profile photos displaying #OpenToWork or #Hiring for organisations with vacancies.

A study by Lin and Chu (2021) noted that supportive emotional behaviour included demonstrating care or understanding. Facebook recognised this and created emoticons to show care (face holding a heart) or sadness (crying face), as it seemed strange to add a thumbs up or 'like' when someone had bad news.

Intimacy

Intimacy relates to people you know well or are familiar with such as family members, relatives, close friends. With close friends, there is familiarity and mutual confiding where secrets are shared.

This can include playfulness or in-group comments that are meaningless to others, as part of a community code. Kaplan (2021, p. 608) describes public intimacy in social media as a 'staged display of interpersonal ties between two or more actors in front of a third party'. The familiarity excludes those not in the group.

Reciprocity

Reciprocity is helping each other – you help me, so I'll help you. This is a key factor in social networks as being connected to a community provides benefits. You may have heard the expression 'it's not what you know but who you know' or relationship marketing, which in China is termed 'guanxi' and 'wasta' in the Gulf region. This describes how participation in a group can provide mutual help.

People on social media networks such as Instagram and Twitter gain follows and likes in return for their posts which is another form of reciprocity – I like what you say, so I'll follow you and share your content. Reciprocity works with both strong and weak ties and, although strong ties may help you to find a job through their connections, weak ties can help to pass on information.

Social capital

Online ties build 'social capital', through the number of connections and how one can help another (see Key Term **social capital**). Some social media networks were established specifically to enable members to increase and improve their connections, such as LinkedIn.

KEY TERM   SOCIAL CAPITAL

Social capital was originally proposed by Pierre Bourdieu (1986) as the value of the collection of interactions between two or more people. Capital as an idea represented the value or collection of assets. 'Social' capital is the value of relationships within a network, which leads to social obligations or material benefits. Having social capital enables you to use your personal networks to make things happen.

Your social capital – your networks and who you know – reflects the benefits you gain and resources you can access. For example, if you're seeking a job in accountancy and your parents or other friends work in this field, it's easier for you to hear of job openings and potentially gain internships. But it's important to look after your social capital and not just make contact when you need something. Nurturing your online communities contributes to your social capital (Lin and Chu, 2021). Social capital guides what's acceptable to you or not and can encourage positive (or negative) behaviour. If your friends find smoking unacceptable, it's unlikely you would start smoking.

Researchers have identified two main types of social capital: bonding and bridging. Bonding social capital takes place *within* groups, with those you already know, and is based on strong ties.

Bridging social capital is *between* groups. For example, a friend on WhatsApp asks if you know any logo designers, so you might look at your LinkedIn contacts and find a designer. You might not know the designer well – you've met at a virtual event and seen their work, but you don't know their birthday or where they live. This is a weak tie. However, you act as a bridge between your friend and the designer. You link the two groups by helping your friend solve a problem and by helping the designer gain work.

In a digital marketing context, LinkedIn acts as a bridge between our personal social networks. In your LinkedIn network, some ties are strong – people you have known for some time; yet others may be weak – they taught you for one semester, so the emotional intensity and familiarity may not exist. However, the strength of weak ties explains why you may help an acquaintance in your LinkedIn network, because of their links to your other connections and to nurture your social capital.

Figure 6.1 shows an example of building social capital in communities. Let's imagine that Community 1 is a professional site such as LinkedIn. You may have been a member for some years and share content such as job updates or new qualifications. This is part of the emotional intensity and intimacy, which relates to self-disclosure and self-presentation covered later in this chapter. You may have helped others in this community as part of your obligation to your LinkedIn connections. This all contributes to bonding your social capital. At the same time, you belong to more than one community. Community 2 may be a WhatsApp friends group. A friend may ask a favour and you bridge your social capital between one community and the other.

Figure 6.1 shows the relationship between the community elements (Muñiz and O'Guinn, 2001), tie strength (Granovetter, 1973) and social capital (Bourdieu, 1986).

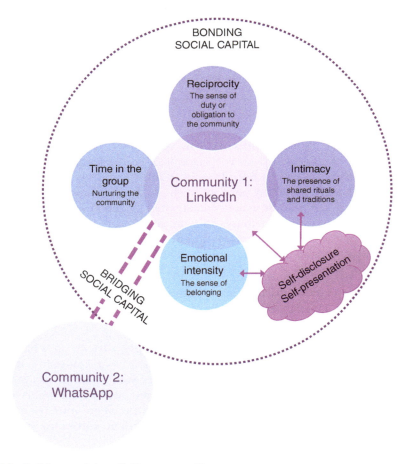

Figure 6.1 Building social capital in communities

Smartphone Sixty Seconds® – Your strong ties

- On your mobile phone, log into the social media network you use most.
- How many friends or connections do you have?
- How many of these are strong ties?

6.3 THE DEVELOPMENT OF ONLINE COMMUNITIES

In a digital environment, we have been forced to rethink the traditional concept of 'community'. The internet has facilitated the rapid growth of online populations, from social media networks to interest groups; and from support forums to brand communities. Online communities can be public open spaces, such as a company TikTok account or Twitter page. Or they can be closed communities or private groups in WhatsApp or Snapchat.

The first online community is considered to be Usenet, formed in 1980 as a forum for online discussions. In 1985 an early version of social networks, the WELL (Whole Earth 'Lectronic Link), an online bulletin board, enabled members to message one another. Then in 2004 LinkedIn created groups to facilitate conversations between people who were not connected. Facebook followed in 2006.

Most social media networks enable users to create groups and they share these characteristics:

- Recognised or classified as groups
- Personalisation options with the ability to select a name and add imagery such as logos
- Privacy options to share the group publicly or remain a closed community
- Membership approval may be required
- Admin and other roles are present
- Content approval to ensure posts meet community guidelines
- Group insights to monitor engagement are available

Other social media networks may not offer formal group functionality and a collection of people following a hashtag or meme can represent a group. People attending festivals, conferences or other events can follow each other and participate in conversations based on a hashtag created for that time.

The reason that many social media networks host a forum or space for online groups is to keep people within the social network ecosystem. However, hosting a community via a social media network creates a challenge for organisations:

- The organisation doesn't ultimately control who sees the content.

- As the terms and conditions change on a regular basis, the risk is that the organisation could create a large online community and discover that the social media network has decided to remove it.

- Online communities can be created by fans or foes, and unless they are breaking the law (e.g. making incorrect comments – libel, or using your registered logo – breach of copyright) it's difficult to take any action to close a community that the brand or organisation doesn't favour.

6.3.1 DIFFERENCES BETWEEN TRADITIONAL AND ONLINE COMMUNITIES

A study investigated social network principles in online communities (Ganley and Lampe, 2009). This work identified differences between traditional and online communities, which included:

- Less structure guiding the online community
- Less at stake for online participants as they can leave and may never contact other community participants again
- Less transparency as many online communities enable the use of pseudonyms or facilitate anonymity
- An informal agreement rather than a formal hierarchy is in place within online communities

In some places, these differences are obvious; for example, in online communities it is possible to join and leave the community at will. Whilst Ganley and Lampe consider this as meaning there is 'less at stake' (p. 267), this suggests there is less commitment, which may lead to community decline.

If you are a member of a traditional offline community that meets weekly, say an exercise class in a community centre, someone might message you if you miss a meeting or two. If you miss a few meetings, you may feel you are letting the group down, yet online you can vanish overnight and no one may notice.

The use of pseudonyms and forms of anonymity have been discussed within research into online communities. One level of anonymity is used to commit malicious acts such as cyberbullying, trolling, fraud and hate crime. At another, anonymity is in place to protect the individual's personal data.

In situations where there is some data, such as a personal profile, or bio, the information is often limited and may not present a total picture. Researchers have considered perception in social media profiles and suggested that the lack of detail forces us to 'fill in the gaps' (Bacev-Giles and Haji, 2017, p. 50). Thinking back to the exercise class, you may not know all the details about all the members, but you know approximately where they live, whether they drive or walk, their preferred classes and if they are beginners or experts.

Online groups can exist in a 24/7 environment, with many 'registered' members but few participating, so it doesn't matter if you join and never turn up again. No one will chase or castigate you for lack of attendance. On the other hand, in an online community you can share as much or as little about yourself as you want. This is part of **self-presentation** and **self-disclosure theory** and one challenge is that sometimes you can unwittingly reveal a little too much detail.

Self-presentation theory and your online self

In 1956 Canadian sociologist Erving Goffman explored how people presented themselves to others, consciously and unconsciously. Goffman noted that we control the impression we give like actors, to influence the behaviour of others, because they may treat us better if they perceive a certain status.

Goffman proposed a theory of self which has become known as **self-presentation theory** (Goffman, 1956) or 'impression management'. Self-presentation theory is a critical factor in how we represent ourselves in our online communities and how we use 'sign vehicles' (Goffman, 1956, p. 1) to convey the desired impression in the part being played. So, in our online communities, whether these are work related, connected to our university or family members, the sign vehicles that differentiate our roles include our profile photo and the posts we add.

This has been extended to self-enhancement theory where individuals work 'to increase the positivity and reduce the negativity of one's self-views' (Zheng et al., 2020, p. 290). Effectively we focus on our good points, rather than dwelling on the negatives.

Goffman suggested that we wear masks for different situations, which have been called 'social personalities' that relate to our different online characters in social media (Horky et al., 2020, p. 2). Research suggests that our behaviour changes on different social media networks because they serve different audiences, both our strong and weak ties. The notion of masks can be seen in social media communities as our online self-presentation has evolved with the use of filters (see Chapter 5, 'Ethical Insights: Selfie dysmorphia') that present an unrealistic self, as well as individuals using pseudonyms to remain anonymous or having fake accounts, such as a 'finsta' on Instagram (Zheng et al., 2020).

One of the challenges with social networks as online communities is that we may post and share much more than we mean to. This is known as self-disclosure theory.

Self-disclosure theory

Self-disclosure is any information you share about yourself to another person and this often centres around wanting to impress the group with activities or skills we possess. You may have one representation of yourself on a university hall's Facebook page, a different one on Instagram and your WhatsApp self may be different again. You're building a patchwork or collage of your identity online which is generally OK, unless it all comes together and shares too much detail.

We are in a time of change and a study by Nabity-Grover and colleagues (2020) suggests that the pandemic has changed self-disclosure behaviour. People used to discuss socialising or share images when meeting friends, but these actions were considered unacceptable during lockdowns. If such images were seen, it could be met with anger from others. As a result, individuals started disclosing more intimate details, such as revealing a vulnerability that made them eligible to gain vaccinations before others.

DISCOVER MORE ON SELF-DISCLOSURE THEORY

Read Hamutal Kreiner and Yossi Levi-Belz's (2019) article 'Self-disclosure here and now: Combining retrospective perceived assessment with dynamic behavioral measures', which was published in the journal *Frontiers in Psychology* and examines different self-disclosure questionnaires and assessment tools.

The privacy paradox

One of the challenges with self-disclosure is known as the 'privacy paradox' (Barth and de Jong, 2017), where users post and share significant amounts of information online but are either consciously or subconsciously concerned about their online privacy.

The privacy paradox suggests that there is a gulf between actual behaviour and attitudes towards privacy. The challenge is managing the amount of disclosure. However, individuals appear to 'more aggressively self-monitor their pandemic-related self-disclosures' (Nabity-Grover et al., 2020, p. 3).

Activity 6.1   Analyse your privacy paradox

1. Analyse your online profile to explore your online shared data, saying where the data exists (i.e. Instagram, Snapchat, Twitter, etc.)

2. How much do you reveal?

3. Do you have to log in to see the data or is it available publicly for anyone to see?

4. How do you feel about this?

With the development of so many social media platforms and so much self-disclosure, a new business has emerged – social media cleaning tools identify negative content such as: inappropriate and questionable content, sexually explicit content and materials containing alcoholic beverages. One example is DigitalOx (digitalox.co.uk), which checks for potentially damaging content and is popular with recent graduates before they meet employers who might peek at their social media pages!

Researching online communities

Online communities have been the subject of much research as they provide rich sources of ready-made data. Rob Kozinets has spent years researching online communities to the extent that he evolved the concept of ethnographic research (studying subjects in their natural habitat) which he named 'netnography' (Kozinets, 2002).

Online communities provide easy access to data and observing groups using netnographic methods provides researchers with sources of significant amounts of behavioural information. However, there are ethical and legal arguments about gathering data via social media without permission (see Quinton and Reynolds, 2018).

DISCOVER MORE ON NETNOGRAPHY

Read *Netnography: The Essential Guide to Qualitative Social Media Research* by Robert Kozinets, published by Sage in 2009.

6.4 A TYPOLOGY OF ONLINE COMMUNITIES

The earliest online communities were member-to-member support groups, sharing information, thoughts and opinions. The use of online communities could be divided into two purposes for both organisations and individuals:

- Hedonic: for fun, entertainment, communication, support
- Utilitarian: for a reason, information, education, contacts

It may be that I am a member of an online group on LinkedIn for utilitarian purposes, to gain information and network with like-minded people. Within WhatsApp, a group might be for fun; it might have a hedonic focus.

Whether hedonic or utilitarian, there are many formats of online communities. They can be open or closed, public or private, official or unofficial. Private communities or invite-only groups are growing. Clubhouse launched as an invite-only platform, requiring users to explore strong or weak ties to find someone to share an invitation. From the beginning, Clubhouse was founded based on your ties or connections.

Private groups came to attention during the presidential handover in the USA in 2021. There appeared to have been many conversations taking place in closed groups which contained hate speech and incited violence. One platform hosting private groups was Parler which was removed from the app stores after it appeared to disregard the terms of service.

Looking at individuals, they may join online communities that are based on special interest, mutual benefit or consumption. Let explore types of online communities.

6.4.1 COMMUNITIES OF PRACTICE

Communities of practice are groups interested in specific topics. They were developed by Jean Lave (1991), who explored different styles of learning. Those engaged in these communities are active practitioners, work in this area or are subject experts.

For example, researchers can share their work on researchgate.net which describes itself as 'a leading platform where the world's scientists share their research and expertise, collaborate on projects, and engage with the best scientific content'. Another example is Stack Overflow (stackoverflow.com) which is a community for developers to learn and share information related to software programming.

During the COVID-19 pandemic, many online communities developed within workplaces using tools such as Microsoft Teams and Slack, enabling team members to send messages, share information and work on projects. As these are related to their work, they are communities of practice.

Some communities of practice can be less structured than formal groups, such as Researchgate – there is no hierarchy as members join and add their own content. Yet others, such as Slack, may have defined structures with different levels of access to material and varied team roles depending on their job functions.

6.4.2 COMMUNITIES OF INTEREST

Communities of interest differ from communities of practice as those involved are curious, but have no expert knowledge. Communities of interest may be demographically different, living in different environments, and the thread that surrounds the community is a common passion.

For example, the niche social networking platform Pinterest is a good example of communities of interest, as individuals share images based on themes such as food, fashion or travel.

Another example of a community of interest is The Student Room (thestudentroom.co.uk), which claims to be 'The UK's biggest student community'. While this could also be considered a community of practice, its members are seeking advice about student issues, rather than being experts about students. Its most popular forums are: relationships, video games, fashion, uni applications and uni student life. Its equivalent in the United States is known as College Confidential (talk.collegeconfidential.com). What is interesting is that although these two communities are separated by thousands of miles, the topics are similar, focusing on student life, achieving good grades and getting into the right place.

6.4.3 COMMUNITIES OF TRANSACTION

Communities of transaction enable the 'buying and selling of products' (Armstrong and Hagel, 1996, p. 135). They are not about a specific practice or interest; instead, they allow individuals to be either a buyer, a seller or both.

Transaction communities have become the online answer to traditional local newspapers and, whilst both facilitate transactions between individuals, the differences with the online community include the following:

- A much wider market can be targeted, beyond the typical reach of a local newspaper advertisement
- Interested people can monitor results and decide whether to sell a similar product
- Individuals can bid via an auction system rather than paying a fixed price

However, in this situation neither party is technically a retailer; they don't have an endless supply of chairs or desks.

One of the largest communities of transaction is eBay, which describes itself as 'the world's online marketplace; a place for buyers and sellers to come together and buy or sell almost anything!'

There's less regulation in these member-to-member sales organisations. eBay and others have introduced feedback and star rating systems, along with a comprehensive help guide for what action to take when things go wrong, including a dedicated resolution centre which aims to settle issues.

6.4.4 COMMUNITIES OF RELATIONSHIP

Communities of relationship are often constructed around life events to provide emotional/psychological support (Armstrong and Hagel, 1996). These may be better named as communities of support as that's their main purpose.

These include Mumsnet, a community aimed at mothers looking for help and advice, as well as health-related groups such as those providing support for rare diseases.

6.4.5 COMMUNITIES OF FANTASY

Escapism online often occurs via online games where individual users are identified by an alter ego or avatar. To support game playing and improve practice, there are hundreds of forums for players of games such as *Call of Duty*, *Minecraft* and others. To protect their online identity, participants create an alter ego using names such as BULLET_PROOF111, ShadowCat, CAMANDERWULF and destroyer1725.

ETHICAL INSIGHTS   Dating deception

One community where strategic self-presentation and deception are prevalent is dating sites, as the goal is to gain as many romantic opportunities as possible.

Exaggeration, fabrication of characteristics and portrayal of a better 'ideal self' are commonplace in online dating and have been explored significantly by many researchers. Interestingly, research has discovered that greater numbers of men lie and change their characteristics in online dating sites than women (Guadagno et al., 2012). So be careful who you're connecting with online!

- Have you ever engaged in catfishing (deliberately changed your self-presentation in an online community)? Do you feel like you are deceiving people?
- Why do people exaggerate or fabricate their characteristics and portray themselves differently online?
- Have you ever discovered someone's real identity to be very different and ghosted them as a result?

6.4.6 CONSUMPTION COMMUNITIES

Consumption communities have been defined as 'a virtual platform for "a community of interests" which forms groups of people who have similar interests regarding a product or service, and through these communities consumers can obtain information regarding consumption, maintain connections and participate in related groups of activities' (Le, 2018, p. 161–2).

Business support groups can be both consumption communities and brand communities. For example, Apple shares details of its online communities which are often based on the device owned and your location. They share similar goals even though their web appearance is totally different. Within consumption communities, the structure can be formal or informal.

6.4.7 BRAND COMMUNITIES

Professors Muñiz, Jr. and O'Guinn coined the phrase 'brand community' as 'a specialized, non-geographically bound community, based on a structured set of social relationships among admirers of a brand' (2001, p. 412). Brand communities can be brand-owned or fan-owned, and 'brand communities offer effective means to achieve favorable brand outcomes, such as enhanced consumer brand loyalty' (Relling et al., 2016, p. 107).

There can be a brand community for almost anything, from cars to toys, from film-star fan clubs to pop groups. The challenge is that not everyone behaves well inside communities and they can be used as a place to complain (see section 6.6.3 'Responding to community feedback') and troll other members. However, engagement levels vary in brand communities:

- Passive engagement is sitting in the background and monitoring
- Active engagement is commenting on new posts, or planned engagement where members carefully construct content to share in the community

One challenge brand communities have is trying to make consumers feel value so they belong to the group, but this can be difficult when many people use these groups to register their unhappiness with brand products.

CASE EXAMPLE 6.1   Wikipedia: the largest online community of practice

Wikipedia is a free online encyclopaedia. It was initially called Nupedia and designed to be a space where teachers would create and upload material, free of charge.

The creators soon realised this would not work and opened up the platform so anyone could register and add content. Thus, in 2001 the version we recognise today was launched and now has over 125,000 active contributors. Some contribute a single article, whilst others add much more.

The name 'Wikipedia' is a portmanteau of the words wiki (a technology for creating collaborative websites, from the Hawaiian word wiki, meaning 'quick') and encyclopedia. (Wikipedia, 2018)

Wikipedia is recognised as a community of practice. Whilst it may be considered a useful resource at times, there are arguments for and against the platform. Those who believe it is useful have stated 'Wikipedia has become the main platform for the public communication of science' (Minguillón et al., 2017, p. 996).

Those against the platform have observed that 'the "anyone-can-edit" policy of Wikipedia has created many problems such as trolling, vandalism, controversies, and doubts about the content and reliability of the information provided due to non-expert involvement' (Jhandir et al., 2017, p. 581). There is vandalism on Wikipedia and a page defining the types – see wikidata.org/wiki/Wikidata:Vandalism. Plus, there's a dedicated project to counter incorrect changes, the WikiProject Counter-Vandalism: wikidata.org/wiki/Wikidata:WikiProject_Counter-Vandalism. As a result of this, some pages (such as those on presidents and prime ministers) are locked so that they cannot be vandalised.

Another issue to consider is representation. There are fewer women represented on the platform than men (see https://en.wikipedia.org/wiki/Gender_bias_on_Wikipedia) and fewer people of colour (see https://en.wikipedia.org/wiki/Racial_bias_on_Wikipedia), meaning it's easier for a white male professor than a female professor or a professor of colour to gain a page on Wikipedia.

According to its own page (en.wikipedia.org/wiki/Wikipedia:Statistics), Wikipedia is said to have over 6 million articles, 55 million pages, over 40 million registered users, yet only 330,000 active users. According to Similar Web (2020), the Wikipedia website is ranked 7 in the world with over 5 billion visits a day.

Similar sites include Quora.com (see quora.com/about), which has fewer visitors than Wikipedia and generates an income from advertising.

The co-founder of Wikipedia, Jimmy Wales, is said to have a net worth of $1 million. He regularly asks visitors to the page to contribute towards the ongoing work of the website and on a job advert website it is claimed: 'We receive financial support from millions of individuals around the world, with an average donation of about $15. We also receive donations through institutional grants and gifts' (Greenhouse, 2020, p. 1). The website is hosted by the Wikimedia Foundation which, according to the 2019–2020 financial statements (Wikimedia Foundation Inc., 2020), gained donations of $120 million in 2020 and $110 million in 2019. Its total expenses in 2020 were $112 million, of which $55 million were salaries.

This seems like a cash-rich, non-profit organisation with the overall community in decline, especially as online searches indicate that only 1 per cent of the editors contribute content.

Case questions

- What actions could Wikipedia take to gain greater engagement from the community?
- Wikipedia is currently free for users and, unlike many social media platforms, does not use advertising to gain a revenue, instead relying on donations. Discuss whether this should continue or change and explain why.
- How might Wikipedia change the balance of its web content and represent greater diversity?

6.5 THE LIFE CYCLES OF COMMUNITIES

Whether you are building or starting a community, it is useful to note that communities move through different stages, not dissimilar to the concept of a product life cycle, as shown in Figure 6.2.

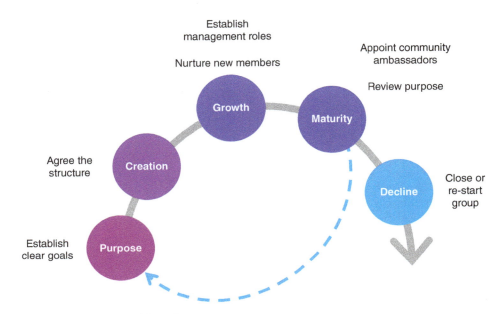

Figure 6.2   Community life cycle

The following sections explore each of these stages.

6.5.1 PURPOSE

It is critical to define the purpose, goals and membership profile of the community. With clear goals and membership criteria, it is easier to grow. If there is no focus and the group is open to 'everyone', it is harder to encourage people to join.

Instagram introduced pods as groups, but these focus on engagement rather than community or group belonging. Pods adopt gamification to gain more likes and follows for each other – like all my posts and I'll like yours! These pods lack a strong purpose, with conversations often taking place outside Instagram in messaging apps such as Telegram.

6.5.2 CREATION

Community creation depends on the context; for example, whether this is a structured or unstructured group, if members use real names or pseudonyms and if it surrounds a single event or an ongoing situation. For example, a group that focuses on a one-off festival that takes place over one weekend may not last for five years, but for five months: the build-up beforehand, the event, the conversations and shared memories afterwards.

Structured groups need agreement about who is involved, which technology platform will be used, or not, and how the group is managed. Social media networks such as Facebook facilitate the creation of structured groups, making it easy to set up the community, add people and develop roles for different members. As a result, many structured online communities are situated in social media networks such as Facebook, WhatsApp or Reddit.

On the other hand, they may have less structure and involve group chat such as on TikTok, or be connected to a hashtag on Twitter or Instagram. The difference in the less structured groups is that following or commenting on a hashtag is open to everyone – whether they support the community or not.

6.5.3 GROWTH

Growing a community involves nurturing new members, making sure that they feel welcome and will return, and encouraging interaction between members. This connects back to tie strength (see section 6.2 'Why communities matter') where you encourage time spent in the group and foster familiarity between members to ensure that the community thrives.

As the community grows, you may need to develop tools for members to recruit others. It can be easier for members to find new members.

For a community to thrive, you may need some structure, to identify a leadership team with roles to share the workload, as well as ensuring that some members are emotionally engaged and spend time in the group. At the growth stage, the primary group management roles may need to be established and include administrators (admins), with the power to add or remove members, and moderators who can add, edit or remove content.

Dr Ezgi Akar and colleagues investigated different types of roles in online communities and concluded that there were four primary roles, as shown in Table 6.1. As these are typical roles in online communities (which you may recognise), the ideal situation is to achieve balanced numbers with these roles. Without the socialisers and content generators, there is a lot more work for the group admins!

6.5.4 MATURITY

Once the community is working well with the desired initial number of members, you will need more managers and community ambassadors to respond to queries and provide information.

Big groups are challenging and often lead to sub-groups and smaller groups splitting away. The group identity may be diluted and it is important to develop a succession plan for the future of the group. This starts by reviewing the community goals and deciding what works and what needs changing.

Table 6.1 Summary of user roles and contribution behaviour

User role	Contribution behaviour
Socialisers	• Create most of the content and inspire others to add comments • Frequent visitor • Socially interactive approach with other community members
Content generators	• Add to existing content, rather than starting new pieces and generate lots of material • Often visit and essential members of the community
Visitors	• Regular visitors but create less content
Passive members	• Sit in the background and visit less frequently than the other users, rarely adding content

Source: Adapted from Akar et al. (2019)

The content will need to engage and bring members back to the community, so more interactive content will be needed (see Chapter 4, 'Content Marketing') or support for members may need to be introduced (e.g. messaging or email).

6.5.5 DECLINE

Communities decline. There are said to be over two million groups on LinkedIn, yet many are barely attended and are either dormant or dying. For example, you may have used one social media network when you were younger that you have since abandoned.

Communities decline for many reasons: the members find somewhere else to go, life changes and people are too busy to contribute, the content declines and there is less participation. Yao and colleagues suggested that 'retaining members is a key challenge faced by many types of online communities' (2021, p. 2). Their work indicates that the community is based on individuals' life stages who may have gained the support or help needed and moved on. So sometimes a group needs to be closed or deleted.

Smartphone Sixty Seconds® – Too many groups

- On your mobile phone, log into LinkedIn.
- In the search bar at the top of your LinkedIn homepage, enter a keyword such as 'marketing' or 'business'.
- Select the option 'in groups'.
- The list of groups will appear – how many are available?
- How might you decide which ones may be suitable for you to join?

6.6 WHY ORGANISATIONS START ONLINE COMMUNITIES

With over 65 million companies using online brand communities (Herhausen et al., 2019), there are many benefits for organisations.

They are easy to create as business-to-business social media platforms, such as LinkedIn, have ready-to-use groups which have been popular spaces for companies to establish online communities. Microblogging platforms such as Twitter work well as a customer service system, as long as there are sufficient trained staff to respond.

One of the reasons to harness these ready-made social communities is because company-moderated websites or company-owned media are trusted less. At the other extreme, personal social media platforms such as Facebook do not always welcome large brands moving into private space, as it can be intrusive (see Key Term **the uninvited brand**) and impacts on the user experience.

KEY TERM   THE UNINVITED BRAND

A critical matter is whether an organisation should establish an online community in a social networking space. Susan Fournier and Jill Avery (2011) conducted work on the concept of the uninvited brand, where an organisation jumps into your personal community when you are least expecting it. As Fournier and Avery said:

> Brands rushed into social media, viewing social networks, video sharing, online communities, and microblogging sites as the panacea to diminishing returns for traditional brand building routes. But as more branding activity moves to the Web, marketers are confronted with the stark realization that social media was made for people, not for brands. (p. 193)

This raised the question of brands staying out of social media communities and whether brands should be interrupting conversations, or embedding themselves into communities, to provide advice and support where relevant.

Facebook has recognised the notion of the uninvited brand and has reduced the amount of branded content shown to users. Typically, it's less than 5 per cent of the brand's audience. This means that if brands want to share their content with more fans, they need to pay for advertising (see Chapter 3) and, even then, the fans can mute or block the communications.

However, every organisation wants to start its own community. It's not easy and establishing an online community requires a clear purpose and ongoing maintenance. This requires dedicated resources and there may be alternative solutions, such as participating in pre-existing ready-made communities or doing something totally different.

Having considered why communities matter to individuals and the diverse types of groups, we need to understand the main motivation for organisations to create and participate in online communities.

6.6.1 PRODUCT DISCUSSIONS

Ensuring your product or service is positively promoted is a key factor in brand awareness. The ability to gain product discussions within an online community where customers promote the product is valuable and more authentic than the company doing this. This is referred to as online brand community engagement (OBCE) or social media engagement behaviours (SMEB) and is mainly positive.

However, as researchers have witnessed, 'online brand communities have changed the way consumers complain by providing a space for them to easily and quickly voice their discontent towards the brand's product and service failure' (Yuan et al., 2020, p. 44). The downside is that product discussions can become negative; the worst ones are referred to as firestorms such as '#deleteUber and United Airlines' passenger removal incidents' (Herhausen et al., 2019, p. 1). Firestorms can result in damaged business reputations, loss of business and boycotting of products or services.

This is why organisations need to carefully monitor content across online communities and identify when negative discussions are taking place. For how to respond, see section 6.7.4 'Responding to community feedback'.

6.6.2 SOCIAL SELLING

The role of online communities is changing and in some cases they are becoming sales channels, which has been described as social selling.

Social selling has been defined as 'a selling approach, which leverages social and digital channels for understanding, connecting with, and engaging influencers, prospects and existing customers at relevant customer purchasing journey touchpoints for building valuable business relationships' (Ancillai et al., 2019, p. 303).

CASE EXAMPLE 6.2   Lego® Ideas Community

LEGO® toy bricks have been made in Denmark for nearly 100 years. They encourage creativity in children who have to build their own toys using the blocks. The results include a range of creations such as buildings, pianos, ships and dragons – it can be totally random! They're often handed down from one generation to the next, so they are recycled many times.

In 1987 LEGO launched the *BRICK KICKS* magazine to motivate children (and their parents) to share the best LEGO creations and be inspired by others to make new items. This was digitised and moved online to become the Lego® Ideas Community. The website (ideas. lego.com) explains the community's purpose:

Love getting imaginative with LEGO bricks? Fancy yourself as a LEGO master builder? Well, this is the place to be. Share your cool creations and creativity, enter prize competitions, showcase your proposals for new LEGO Ideas sets and vote for awesome models dreamt up by your fellow fan designers.

This is a community of interest with a sense of belonging and it's based on seeing new creations. If you're a keen LEGO user, the competitions are an incentive to showcase your skills. Plus, it's not just for children as there are worldwide architectural competitions where teams are invited to build LEGO models of their favourite buildings or structures.

On average, the website gains over 3 million visitors worldwide every year. The growth of the community will vary as some children stop using LEGO and others discover the toy bricks for the first time. Adding competitors and getting schools involved are a clever way to nurture the group and encourage more time to be spent there.

Case questions

- What are the benefits of the LEGO Ideas Community for the LEGO brand?
- This community has been established for some years – how can the community managers ensure it does not decline?
- What rules of engagement would be useful on this website?

Activity 6.2   Identify your communities

1. Find two communities that you belong to. They may be a community of practice, interest, transaction, relationship, fantasy, consumption or brand.

2. For each community, identify its key elements:

    - What is it called?

    - Where is it based?

    - Is it platform-specific, such as only on Instagram?

    - What's the topic or area of interest and is this an official or unofficial group?

    - Is it a public group open to anyone or is it a private group?

3. Which of these communities do you go to most often and is this due to:

    - The sense of belonging?

    - The presence of shared rituals and traditions?

    - The sense of duty or obligation to the community?

Let's investigate the critical factors to consider before establishing an online community and what's involved in managing such a community.

6.7 ESTABLISHING AND MANAGING ONLINE COMMUNITIES

6.7.1 ESSENTIAL QUESTIONS IN ESTABLISHING AN ONLINE COMMUNITY

Having evaluated the role of online communities for organisations, before establishing an online community, essential questions need to be addressed, including:

- What is the aim or purpose of the online community?
    - What are its specific objectives?
    - Have any key performance indicators (KPIs) for the online community been agreed?
    - Where will the community be based (i.e. in a specific location such as Facebook or LinkedIn)?
- What will the community be named?
- Is the preferred name available in the relevant social media networks?
- What does the community cover, in terms of focus or subject?
    - What is not included in the community?
    - What will be the benefits of the community?
- Who will join the community? Existing or potential customers or both?
    - Why will they join this community?
    - What will make the community members participate?
    - What will make the community members continue to return after joining?
- Who will create the content for the community?
- What are the competitors to this community?

You may find that you are working in an organisation that has decided to create an online group. To successfully develop and manage an online community, you need to answer these questions. The organisation needs to commit to a long-term strategy and provides resources. It's worth involving others in Activity 6.3 to test whether or not the online community will be successful.

Activity 6.3   Recommend approaches to establish an online community

Imagine you've just started working for a local sports organisation and you've been asked to create its first online community. Review the essential questions in 6.7.1 and provide a response. If some questions don't have an answer, this indicates either that there are knowledge gaps or that the community is unlikely to be successful. Based on this information, recommend an approach to create this online community.

One of the arguments for establishing an online brand community is that customers have established their own group representing the organisation. It is often better for a brand to create an official space and support the unofficial groups.

Alternatives to creating your own organisation's group include the formal endorsement of fan or customer groups, providing supporting information and cultivating brand ambassadors.

DIGITAL TOOL   Create a Facebook fan or brand page

- Think about a favourite film star, singer, brand or other entity
- Log in to Facebook (or possibly join!)
- Go to www.facebook.com/pages/create
- Follow the steps online and create a Facebook fan page
- What content do you need to make this a great page?
- What knowledge gaps has this shown you about your chosen favourite?

And don't worry! You don't need to publish until you're ready – you can save it as a draft and delete later. It's a great way to experiment with building a community page and understand the content required.

6.7.2 MANAGING AN ONLINE COMMUNITY

If you already have an online community or have decided to establish one, the next stage is managing it. Managing the community doesn't mean controlling it, but responding to queries, providing information and supporting any brand ambassadors. This requires resources: people, time, technology and finances.

One query to be addressed from the start is whether to have real people and real names as the community managers, or whether to have pseudonyms or nicknames. Pseudonyms are common amongst social media users although this lacks authenticity and should be avoided where possible.

The key factors in online community management include:

- Understanding customers' needs
- Opportunity for co-creating new products
- Launching new products
- Listening to customers' feedback
- Sharing news
- Managing issues
- Co-creation of content
- Monitoring your brand
- Responding to customers

One way of managing comments is by using a moderation tool (see Digital Tool **Disqus.com**) which alerts admins when new content is posted. These tools allow community managers to share the management of comments with team members and to respond swiftly.

DIGITAL TOOL   Disqus.com

Disqus is a web plugin tool that allows you to monitor comments from the community and respond. It can be added to a website or blog, where there is community engagement. It's popular as it blends into the look and feel of your site and allows real-time comments.
The program has a free option (with adverts) and paid-for options.

6.7.3 RULES OF ENGAGEMENT

When managing an online community, rules of engagement allow the members to understand how the community works. Rules of engagement may include those shown in Table 6.2, although your organisation may only need one or two of these rules, as many may not be relevant.

Table 6.2   Rules of engagement examples

Rule	Example
Legal or moral restrictions	Age limits may be required with topics around alcohol and gambling.
Definition of 'troll' activity and how you will manage it	We won't tolerate abusive or offensive behaviour.
Use of profanity or hate language	We'll block posts containing sexist or racist language.
	Although we don't want to censor any conversations within our YouTube community, as part of the overall YouTube policy any offensive posts to other users, or using expletives, will be deleted by our YouTube team.
Handling promotion of competitors or solicitation	If you'd like to sell products or services, please email details to (name).
Criminal activity	Be aware this is a public space and avoid fraudulent, libellous statements.
Inappropriate content	Inappropriate content such as pornography or violence will be blocked and users will be banned.
Spam, link baiting or propagation of viruses or malware	Any spam or malicious content will be removed and reported to the relevant authorities.
Rules around being nice to staff	Please be nice as we're real people trying to help!
Managing expectations around response times	We're here from 8am until 8pm and aim to respond on the same day.
Contact details to redirect serious or private issues	Never share personal order numbers or address details. Message us and we'll respond.

Typically, organisations share rules of engagement in obvious places; for example:

- Microblogging platforms: in the bio
- Social network and video platforms: on the profile photo or 'about us' or 'description' or 'community rules'
- On blogs and websites: as an occasional post or in 'guidelines'

In addition to providing rules of engagement, when building a community, guidelines around content management (see Chapter 4) will need to be developed, so that the organisation is speaking with the same voice and conveying the same messages, across all platforms. Plus, the guidelines should address whether the organisation standardises processes; for example:

- How frequently postings are created
- How frequently postings from the community are read and responses provided
- Whether individuals are named as community managers or if all posts are issued by 'the organisation'
- If posts are moderated
- Whom to contact if help is needed (e.g. to report inappropriate content)

6.7.4 RESPONDING TO COMMUNITY FEEDBACK

Online communities provide a forum for community members and others, to share feedback about the organisation in public. This can include compliments and complaints. Online community managers need to know how to respond – and whether to respond – to both positive and negative comments in the community.

Most communities are open for membership and viewing, which means that it may be the easiest place to complain. Gregoire et al. (2015) explored the role of social media as a community in the customer complaining process. They started by considering the customer complaining process based on an initial service failure – that's when something goes wrong – that occasionally then enters the realm of 'double deviation', where it goes wrong again. Figure 6.3 shows the types of behaviour based on these situations.

It is useful to understand why people complain, especially across social media, and this study included a typology of social media complaints, which are outlined here, with an explanation of the issue and ways to respond.

Directness

This is directly contacting the company online, through the company's social media pages, to constructively request resolution of a service failure:

- Respond quickly!
- Acknowledge within one hour

- Basic issues: try to solve online
- Complex issues: use a private channel

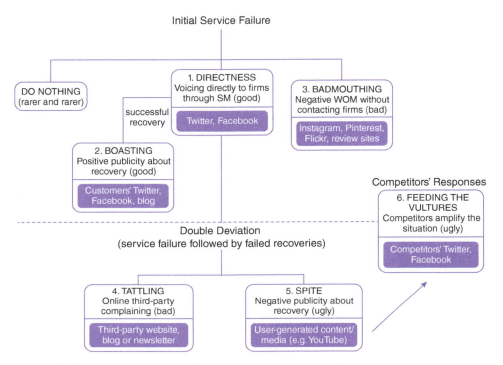

Figure 6.3   The place of social media in the customer complaining process

Source: Gregoire et al. (2015, p. 174)

Boasting

Spreading good word and positive publicity via social media about how well the firm resolved the complaint:

- Thank the customer
- Retweet and share – not too much

Badmouthing

After the first service failure, spreading negative word-of-mouth through your own social media pages – all without ever contacting the firm:

- Be proactive and acknowledge
- Try to move to private channel
- Publicly present the solution

Tattling

Complaining to a third-party website, blog or newsletter:

- Try to resolve
- Expensive and late are better than viral and legal
- Consider sharing circumstances/provide context

Spite

After the firm botches its response to the initial service failure and complaint, thus failing the customer twice, the customer spreads negative word-of-mouth with a heated vengeance via user-generated content shared on social media:

- VIRAL WARNING!
- Publicly acknowledge
- Try to negotiate and compensate in person

Feeding the vultures

A competitor not only takes joy in the firm's mishandling of the complaint, but uses social media to amplify the mistake to steal more of the firm's customers:

- Be gracious in defeat – not much else you can do

Complaining online will grow. Online community managers need to recognise the types of complaint and respond accordingly.

Communities will continue to evolve, whether public or private groups. However, there is a move towards more closed interest groups with platforms such as Are.na, which is similar to Instagram and Pinterest, but offers more private posts and enables greater linkage of the ideas – you could say it's identifying the tie strength between posts.

We're likely to see more local communities developing. As the pandemic enabled groups to stay in touch, regardless of their location, many local community groups formed, with individuals learning more about their neighbours for the first time. The emotional intensity and sense of belonging in a neighbourhood motivated the creation of such groups as people struggled to manage the virus.

For example, the Locals app (see locals.org) allows people to meet close to their home. The app uses Muñiz and O'Guinn's (2001) principles of the sense of belonging and Granovetter's (1973) reciprocity in tie strength, with individuals joining together and organising activities.

Communities will come and go. They will always exist in different formats and they're more likely to be successful if they adopt Muñiz and O'Guinn's guidance.

> ## DISCOVER MORE ON CRISIS COMMUNICATION
>
> From time to time, things go badly wrong and an issue becomes a crisis. For this you need expert help and can discover more with this textbook: *Ongoing Crisis Communication: Planning, Managing, and Responding* by William Timothy Coombs (Sage, 2011).

JOURNAL OF NOTE

The journal *Sociology* is the official journal of the British Sociological Association and contains research about social media and groups, as well as new developments in consumer behaviour.

CASE STUDY

THE RISE OF THE STRAVANS

This continues our long case study and you may find it helpful to read earlier parts in previous chapters.

Communities are forms of clubs where some people are included and others are not. Aimed at the 70 million Strava members, the Strava club is promoted as 'a community of athletes'.

This is a hedonic community that exists to share information with like-minded people and could be described as a community of interest and a brand community. As a brand community, there is a clear sense of belonging and the presence of shared rituals and traditions is evident as these community members have their own name – Stravans or sometimes Stravarians.

All members need to log in at the website (strava.com/clubs) which enables Strava to track which members are active most frequently and their online behaviour – whether they watch, like or comment and how they react to specific posts.

There is evidence of self-disclosure theory as Stravans use their own names, rather than pseudonyms, and can share their running or other exercise routes for others to follow. Within the context of the privacy paradox, many runners are pleased to share their achievements publicly. However, there have been incidents where security services have accidently shared their running routes which could be useful for terrorists. There have been situations where individuals could be stalked for running the same route every day and Strava has had to address some of the publicly available data by creating privacy zones, ensuring the details are unavailable publicly. The club's purpose is:

A place to discover remarkable activities, athletes and stories from around the world. To enable members to discover these remarkable activities, Strava encourages users to share their findings in a section named 'highlights from our community' – if you see something outstanding, let us know.

This must be working as it's said to be a growing community with new members joining each month. Plus, Strava is busy recruiting local community managers and on Strava job posts they explain that Strava's community managers are challenged thus: 'forging relationships with key individuals, local clubs, shops and partners you'll help amplify community word of mouth and ultimately drive growth'. The company recruits those actively engaged with athletics – whether that's running, cycling or something else, as well as being social animals – those with good offline connections that can be moved online. These local community managers can build the momentum, in the role of socialisers, individuals who create material and inspire others to add content too.

Whilst interactivity is positively encouraged, Strava has rules of engagement – called Community Standards (see strava.com/community-standards) – that focus on respecting yourself, others and the community.

Strava has taken its online community to the next level as it's sharing it with its advertisers too. The benefit for members is that, as subscribers, they gain access to perks, such as discounts off sports watches, insurance, clothing, personal coaching plans and nutrition.

The clever part of the Strava club is that it enables the company to connect with its fans, start conversations, see what works and build a larger community. It's recognised that building communities engages and retains fans. They become part of the business, they share new product ideas, they share information with friends and they make repeat purchases, whether that's renewing the app subscription or buying add-on products. The challenge is engaging members and ensuring they return.

CASE QUESTIONS

- The Strava community appears to be in the growth stage – how does it ensure this does not fall into the decline stage as it becomes much larger?

- Imagine you're a regular runner or cyclist. How do you feel about sharing your route with others? Are there any safety precautions you should consider?

- Strava has started to monetise its community by offering perks to members. How might the company evaluate what is and isn't appropriate for its club?

FURTHER EXERCISES

1. Using self-presentation theory, examine the social media content shared by a well-known individual. Consider the enhancement strategies being used and the amount of self-disclosure taking place.

2. Find a brand that you admire and select one of its online communities. Identify whether there are complaints in these communities and evaluate good and weak

practice of how these are managed. Make recommendations to improve the responses where relevant.

3. To what extent is it essential to establish an online community? Analyse the advantages and disadvantages of creating an online community for (a) a sports group, (b) a clothing brand, or (c) a music organisation, which is engaging and thriving.

4. Discuss whether a hashtag constitutes an online community. Provide evidence for and against your arguments.

SUMMARY

This chapter has explored:

- Why communities matter
- The development and typology of online communities
- The life cycles of communities
- Why organisations create online communities
- How to establish and manage online communities

GO ONLINE

Visit **study.sagepub.com/hanlon2e** to access links to interesting articles, websites and videos related to this chapter.

OVERVIEW
Chapter 7 addresses the key issues in mobile marketing, exploring the role of mobile and wearables in marketing, then delving into types of mobile apps and methods of promotion.

ACTIVITIES

Assess whether apps are locational, temporal or personal

Create a wireframe for a university club

Evaluate mobile promotion

KEY CONCEPTS

The 5Ps framework for personalised mobile marketing

Native, hybrid and web apps

Characterisation of push notifications

DIGITAL TOOLS

Find out how much it costs to build an app

Discover how many apps have been downloaded

7

MOBILE MARKETING

LEARNING OUTCOMES

When you have read this chapter, you will be able to:

Understand the factors in mobile marketing

Apply the 5Ps framework for personalised mobile marketing

Analyse the downsides of wearable technology

Evaluate locational, temporal or personal notifications

Create a wireframe for an app

PROFESSIONAL SKILLS

When you have worked through this chapter, you should be able to:

- Estimate the costs to build an app
- Use wireframe tools

7.1 INTRODUCTION TO MOBILE MARKETING

There are more mobile devices in the world than people. There are forecast to be nearly 18 billion mobile devices worldwide by 2024, in a population of 8 billion (O'Dea, 2021). Whilst the numbers don't seem to add up, some people have two phones with the second for work or have a connected wearable such as a smartwatch.

Mobile has moved from the first generation of mobile phones (1G) in the early 1980s where the 'mobile' was more like a small box that weighed in at 10 kilogrammes, to the second generation (2G) in the 1990s and 3G in the new millennium. Many countries are using the fourth generation (4G), but with so many users and the need for faster data, our mobile signals can be poor and WiFi is not always stable. These challenges are solved by the next generation – 5G. 5G delivers faster data, easier streaming, speedier gaming, and removes unstable WiFi signals as many devices will be able to connect at the same time. When we hear the word mobile, we often think of phones, but portable devices are also wearable and implantable. Wearable technology is 'advanced sensor and computing technologies that a person can wear on their body during daily activity to generate, store, and transmit data' (Jacobs et al., 2019, p. 148). This is a growing market, with the volume of smartwatch sales having increased from 325 million in 2016 to over 1 billion in 2020.

Implantables are more complex and require explicit permission from health regulation bodies to ensure they are safe to use at many levels. There are issues to consider including:

- Could they generate adverse effects and make people unwell?
- Are they secure or could others hack into the device and harm the user?
- What data may be generated?
- How and where might this data be stored and used?

One longstanding piece of implantable technology is the pacemaker which is typically half the size of a small mobile phone. Implanted next to the heart, a pacemaker provides a small pulse that maintains a regular heartbeat. One of the largest manufacturers of pacemakers, Medtronic, has an app – MyCareLink Heart – which allows patients to monitor their device. So, instead of visiting a medical professional to check the battery and assess recent heart performance, the patient can check their own situation and if there is a critical care issue, their health provider is automatically contacted.

Moving beyond implantables, Microsoft has been exploring 'smart skin' as part of smart tattoo technology. In 2020 the Museum of Science and Industry in Chicago hosted a Wired to Wear event that showcased wearable tech embedded into clothing which included smart tattoos to control your mobiles.

At this stage, these are prototypes and need more research to understand how they can be used as well as to gain approval to be used at a commercial level, but it's a fascinating glimpse into the future. What we don't yet know is whether there are marketing applications for these devices. Will future pacemaker apps contain adverts for healthy food, local gyms or paid-for health services?

As this book is about digital marketing, the focus of this chapter is to provide the context of the mobile-phone ecosystem, starting by briefly exploring individual usage of mobile devices; then we'll examine the types of mobile devices, so that you understand that mobile is no longer only about phones, followed by an investigation of the different types of mobile apps, mobile marketing and an area specific to mobiles – SMS text messages. Finally, the chapter discusses the challenges facing consumers.

Smartphone Sixty Seconds® – Your screen time

- On your mobile phone, find your screen time (if you can't find it, ask Apple Siri, Google assistant, Huawei Celia Samsung Bixby, Tencent Xiaowei, Windows Cortana)
- How many hours was your screen time last week?
- How much of this was not for work or uni?
- How do you feel about this?

7.2 THE ROLE OF MOBILE AND WEARABLES IN MARKETING

We use mobile phones for communication, shopping, taking photos, creating video, listening to music, connecting on social networks, sending documents, gaming and streaming movies. These digital devices contain most of our life – our databases of friends, our wallet, event reminders, tickets and our personal media library. Mobile devices are unique as the content is personal to each of us. They are near us most of the time, from when we wake up until we close our eyes, and this device proximity and dependence provide digital marketing opportunities.

Mobile marketing is disrupting traditional marketing efforts because it:

- Delivers ubiquitous computing, sharing direct access to technology at any time and place
- Provides instant access to software, whether that's an app, voice search or online space
- Permits the ability to check prices, compare online and offline, on the spot
- Enables easier processes to order food, book transport, secure accommodation and buy tickets in real time
- Incorporates a digital wallet, a means of paying by phone

Mobile commerce adds time and location to the offer, providing instant access to conversations with brands, potentially when consumers are in locations near to the brands, such as physical stores. This is supported by other work which explains that mobile marketing is different because of its 'hyper-context personalized targeting' (Tong et al., 2020, p. 64) as you can reach an individual via their mobile phone, wearable device and shared devices, wherever they are.

For organisations, the features and benefits include:

- **Locational**: Can target users in specific physical locations (e.g. Uber sending users a notification offering taxi services near their location)
- **Temporal**: Can send time-limited messages or offers (e.g. Strava sending users a notification to record their daily activity)
- **Personal**: Messages can be personalised using push notifications (e.g. individual offers based on browsing history)

Activity 7.1   Assess locational, temporal or personal notifications

- Look at your mobile phone and select one of your apps.
- Identify whether you gain notifications from this app based on where you are (locational), or at specific times (temporal), or perhaps individual messages (personal), or even a mix of these.
- Assess why this is and the purpose of the notifications.
- Evaluate the notifications and consider which are useful for you or could be improved.

The next section explores other ways that brands can use mobile marketing.

7.2.1 THE 5PS FRAMEWORK FOR PERSONALISED MOBILE MARKETING

There are differences around mobile marketing and to address this Dr Tong and colleagues developed the 5Ps framework for personalised mobile marketing which is shown in Figure 7.1. You'll notice that this is an extended version of McCarthy's 4Ps (1964).

Section 7.3 explores mobile products and section 7.5 examines mobile promotion in more depth. This section summarises the key factors in mobile price, place and prediction.

Figure 7.1   The 5Ps framework for personalised mobile marketing

Source: Adapted from Tong et al. (2020)

Mobile price

Mobile pricing is part of a wider pricing strategy and is addressed in traditional marketing textbooks. So in brief, pricing in mobile contexts offers greater flexibility. As Uber and Airbnb have demonstrated, it has dynamism and can be instantly changed based on demand. The nature of dynamic or flexible pricing makes the mobile environment more competitive as the number of users seeking services in certain locations, at specific times, can be identified. It also removes the concept of a single fixed price.

One example is Uber's surge pricing model which increases rates at peak times when there is short supply due to too many people needing a taxi in that location at that time (Eckhardt et al., 2019) or as Tong, Luo and Xu (2020, p. 72) described it: 'flexible pricing strategies in the competition for geo-conquesting'.

However, increasing rates and adopting surge pricing can go wrong. Kalaignanam et al. (2021) found that Uber could suffer negative customer reaction if the surge pricing was seen as being too opportunistic and they raised their rates to take advantage of an unfortunate situation, such as transport strikes. Another study found that Uber drivers understood how surge pricing worked and gamified the system; they would 'turn off their Uber apps just as a large flight was arriving to the airport' so fewer taxis were available, resulting in more demand and creating a surge pricing situation where drivers could charge higher fees (Wells et al., 2021, p. 325).

So the concept of flexible pricing needs careful consideration within the organisation and with other stakeholders.

Flexible pricing strategies can move both ways. As well as rates increasing, they can also decrease with discounts being offered. This can be used to encourage consumers to order services or buy goods at less busy times.

Mobile place

The study recognised that the mobile was not in a fixed location but in a dynamic place. This also applies when consumers are travelling.

One example of where the promotion focuses on the place is with a home improvement retailer in the United States (Home Depot). Home Depot 'designs the content of app push notifications for in-store promotions based on the app users' present in-app product search behaviors' (Tong et al., 2020, p. 72).

Mobile prediction

Mobile prediction concerns examining user data to understand if consumers are exhibiting patterns of behaviour which can be addressed. Whether that's a group of people wishing to take public transport at the same time with the app indicating that the service is busy right now, try in 20 minutes time, or spotting a regular journey and making suggestions en route.

During the pandemic many contact tracing apps worked based on accumulated location-based data. Consumers were invited to scan QR codes to enter buildings, so if an outbreak of the COVID-19 virus occurred, all those at risk could be identified. However this is subject to users downloading the app and permitting it to access their location. One of the challenges with the virus contact tracing was concern for digital surveillance which gathered data from 'citizens' personal smart devices to synthesise their digital and physical footprints in the name of contact tracing' (Yang et al., 2021, p. 184).

7.3 MOBILE PRODUCTS

Mobile products are considered to be apps within the device as well as mobile payment methods such as Apple Pay. We'll explore apps in more detail in section 7.4.

While we're aware of marketing potential on our mobile phones from advertising, messaging, in-app purchases, there is potential for marketing applications with wearable technology. According to researchers in Poland, 'wearables are a great combination of sport and finance technologies that bring a novel service quality to the consumer' (Borowski-Beszta and Polasik, 2020, p. 1083). This unique position brings marketing opportunities for brands. Table 7.1 shows the use of wearables for marketing, with examples.

Table 7.1 Use of wearables for marketing

Device	Sector/Company	Example	Issues
Wristbands (Nike Fuel)	Insurance/Esurance	Offers free wristbands in return for sharing health data	• Close monitoring of personal health data, exercise records
Wristbands	Leisure/Disney	The Magic Band – facilitates hotel room access, ability to unlock additional experiences	• Can track all activity around the theme park and direct to less busy areas • Can upsell additional activities
Watch	Airlines/Various	Boarding passes on watch	• Opportunities to add promotional messages near the gate • Can't board the plane if your battery runs out!
Watch	Insurance/Vitality	Offers free iWatch in return for sharing health data	• Free watch but close monitoring of personal health data, exercise records • What happens when the exercise stops? Do the premiums increase?

ETHICAL INSIGHTS   Wearables as customer conversion tools

Wearables are being offered as free goods by health and insurance companies as a promotional device to convert new customers. It is not clear whether these companies will increase the premium for those who exercise less, or will they find ways to nudge some individuals to encourage greater activity?

The offers include reduced costs on an Apple watch when you buy a qualifying plan. It seems like a great way to get new tech at a discount and is ideal if you're keen on sports.

- A discounted desirable piece of tech sounds like a great idea, but what are the downsides of such an arrangement with a health company?
- What ethical issues should companies offering free wearables consider?
- Do you use wearables? If yes, how do they make you feel?

7.3.1 MOBILE WALLETS

Mobile wallets are considered as mobile products. The ability to create a mobile wallet or mobile payment system, whether you have added a credit card or pay as you go, means that the only device needed when you leave home is your mobile.

As to whether consumers decide to adopt mobile payment methods, this depends on trust signals which Hossain et al. (2020) confirmed as: company awareness, design and interface, transaction security, personalisation, and navigation functionality.

Mobile payment types and examples of the different applications include:

- **Mobile wallet** which re-charges a credit card, such as Google Wallet, Apple Pay, Samsung Pay, WeChat Pay and Microsoft Wallet
- **Mobile peer-to-peer payment** system with services like Venmo, Facebook Messenger, Paym
- **Pre-loaded credit cards**, typically used for convenience apps such as travel – to access buses and trains, or food – to buy tea and coffee on the move
- **Text to pay**, which is often used for fund-raising where the user is invited to 'text £5 to XXXX'

The advantages of mobile wallets are that they provide a fast checkout which can involve a simple one-click payment system. This makes them convenient, with less effort required to make the payment. It removes the need to carry cash.

The disadvantages are potential losses from malware as you might download a virus or be hacked and your wallet could be compromised. Other risks are to your personal privacy and the loss of data.

There may be a temptation to spend more and, according to Manshad and Brannon (2021), a way to discourage over-spending with mobile technology is via haptic feedback, a small vibration of the phone to encourage the user to think again before spending. Imagine your wrist buzzing every time your mobile thinks you're about to over-spend!

7.4 MOBILE APPS

The app market has grown dramatically from just 500 apps in 2008, when the Apple store was launched, to millions of apps today. According to App Annie (a global provider of mobile data and analytics), consumers have downloaded over 200 billion apps. Each mobile phone we buy has more data storage, to cope with our love of apps.

Apps are created in three formats: native, hybrid and web. These are summarised here along with their advantages and disadvantages.

7.4.1 NATIVE APPS

These are developed for use on a specific platform, such as iOS or Android, and to work offline. For example, Strava, Instagram and Shazam are all native apps. Advantages include:

- Being compatible with the software and hardware of individual devices
- Use of **geofencing** (see Key Term) so you can track consumers in stores or other locations

- Access to customer actions
- Being fast loading
- Creating a good user experience

The disadvantages are that they are often more expensive as separate coding skills are required for each device type.

7.4.2 PROGRESSIVE WEB APPS (PWAS)

PWAs are web apps that look and function like a native app such as Trip Advisor® or ecommerce sites. Advantages include:

- Use of device features such as camera and microphone
- Being fast to load
- there being no need to install as access is via a web browser

The disadvantages are that they are internet-enabled and need a browser to run. They're not listed in the app stores so can be harder to find. Plus, there are examples of these apps needing more battery power. The main issue is that unless someone is logged in to their Trip Advisor® or ecommerce account, they lack access to consumer data.

7.4.3 HYBRID APPS

These apps work across different platforms and are part native app and part web app. For example, Evernote, Twitter and Gmail are hybrid apps. Plus, an organisation may not need a product catalogue but just the ability to operate online and access their email. Advantages include being:

- Distributed via app stores
- Lower in development costs
- Faster to develop
- Easy to add new features

Disadvantages are that as a cut-down version of a website they may not work offline and sometimes they may have limited visual design options.

While there are differences, there is no right or wrong answer as to the type of app to develop, as it depends on the context.

If you're managing a large ecommerce site, a progressive web app (PWA) may be more suitable as it can be saved to the device's home screen, there is no need for installation and it can be updated quickly. PWAs load quickly and can link to all products in a catalogue. If the website catalogue is changed, this immediately updates the PWA, saving time and money.

However, if you need customer data to see behaviour and respond to customer actions, such as Strava, a native app may be a better solution. Developers have to follow the coding guidelines for each device and submit separate apps to each store. This is why you sometimes see the message 'not available for Windows phones'.

In some cases, an organisation might not need an app, but a better mobile website. For example, one approach to integrating websites and mobile sites is to adopt a mobile-first approach. This is a practice encouraged by Google as it indexes a mobile site in its search engine before the traditional website (Google Developers, 2021). However, Google also adds PWAs to its search results.

See Digital Tool **Sensor Tower** to assess your favourite app.

KEY TERM   GEOFENCING

Geofencing means creating geographical boundaries using technology. In researching wearables to protect children, Dr James Gilmore (2020, p. 1335) described geofencing as 'a location-based feature that allows parents to create virtual "fences" in its smartphone application'. Gilmore adds that geofencing was first used in logistics where goods could be tracked on their journeys, and in retail where stores could capture data about their consumers.

DIGITAL TOOL   Sensor Tower

See how well your favourite app is performing! This is a free tool to encourage you to sign up for more – as an app developer.

- Go to Sensor Tower (https://sensortower.com)
- Add in the app name
- Select whether you want the Apple iTunes or Google Android version
- See the total number of downloads

7.4.4 COSTS OF DEVELOPING APPS

Apps can be expensive to develop and the pricing depends on the purpose of the app and the functionality (see Digital Tool **How much does it cost to build an app?**).

DIGITAL TOOL How much does it cost to build an app?

The website http://howmuchtomakeanapp.com provides an indication of costs involved in building an app, based on the type of app and your requirements.

There are three price groups; free, freemium or paid-for. Free apps tend to gain revenue by selling advertising.

Aydin Gökgöz and colleagues (2021, p. 423) noted that a 'free app encourages trial and promotes the paid version'. For example, Zoom has a free mobile app but adding more people or spending more time in the call requires a premium subscription.

Although app pricing rates are controlled by the developers who can schedule adjustments to pricing in app stores, Aydin Gökgöz and colleagues (2021) found that price sensitivity is a factor in whether or not consumers download apps. This is why app developers might list an app with a launch price and increase or decrease this over time.

7.4.5 UNDERSTANDING THE APP DEVELOPMENT PROCESS

As marketers, you may not be coding and developing new apps, although you need to understand the process as you may be responsible for briefing developers.

Many apps never make it into the app marketplace because they fail the basic requirements, ignore the design guidelines and are rejected (see Discover More on App Marketplace Design Guidelines). So some organisations spend millions of dollars on wasted apps. The initial questions before developing an app include:

Purpose

Why is the app needed? The purpose of the app may include:

- To entertain
- To provide functionality and make tasks easier
- To deliver efficiency and save time and money
- To gain user data
- To increase sales by simplifying the customer journey
- To generate income from advertising

Target audience

Who is the main audience? This will impact how and where the app is listed in directories:

- Children or parents?
- Students or older adults?

DISCOVER MORE ON APP MARKETPLACE DESIGN GUIDELINES

Explore the design guidelines from app marketplaces:

- https://developer.apple.com/design/human-interface-guidelines
- https://developer.android.com/design

App design

When designing an app, developers often start with wireframes which are online sketches of the functional elements in a web page or app. It is important to visualise these as the person creating the brief might have a long list of requirements for in-app functions and a wireframe shows the reality of how this looks. Seeing the design means that functions that are not critical can be removed, which contributes towards a more positive user experience.

Wireframes facilitate the customer journey (see Chapter 2, 'The Digital Consumer') as you can look at each stage through the app. Wireframes are useful to content creators so they can plan the material for each page.

Activity 7.2   Create a wireframe

There are free online tools that you can use and experiment with to gain greater understanding of wireframes:

- In groups create a mock-up of an app for a university club, whether that's a social gathering or an activity-based group.
- Consider what the app will be used for and the functions needed.
- Go online to this digital wireframe tool: https://ninjamock.com (to use online) or www.mockplus.com/free-wireframing-tool (to download).
- You may need to register for a free account and perhaps begin with the quick tour.

- Create a new project for an iPhone or Android.
- Drag and drop the different elements needed onto the mock-up page, such as the header, links, text and buttons.
- When you've created your mock-up, compare with classmates and discuss what you discovered.

DEVELOPMENT

Only after the purpose is clear, the audience has been agreed, the wireframes planned and the design considered does the development begin.

The development phase may include:

- Coding which depends on the type of app being created
- User management, especially if there are lite and pro versions
- Customisation or personalisation
- Data integration so that any data or push notification functionality can be built in from the start

It is necessary to explore how to synchronise data. If you think about tourism apps with hotels being added and possibly removed, on a regular basis, there should be a way to keep the app up to date.

User interface design and development

The next stage is user interface design and development. When the 'back-end' coding is done, what does the user see? Does it work? Is it as originally planned?

One app that failed on the user interface design was LinkedIn. The desktop app functioned well but the mobile app could be dangerous as you might explore someone's profile and connect without intending to!

Testing

There should be at least two rounds of testing – the initial testing then beta testing, and then more testing, all of which should lead to improvements.

Deployment

When the app is ready to go, it's time to add to the app marketplaces. Factors to consider at this stage include:

- Timing – are you submitting an app a month before major holidays such as Thanksgiving in the United States, Christmas in the UK or other festivals for your target audience? If the answer is yes, you will have to fight to get noticed as so many apps are released at these times. It is better to release before or after major events to gain greater visibility in the app stores.

- Reviews – these are critical to the success of an app so it may be shared with fans at an early stage to gain positive feedback.

- App store optimisation – ensuring that the app looks attractive to potential users when they explore the app marketplaces.

Promotion

As a marketer, you will probably be responsible for the app promotion. This is often easier if you were involved in the initial design process (see section 7.5 'Mobile promotion').

Updates

One factor that keeps apps at the top of the charts is updates. When apps are updated, they are relisted as new in the charts. Plan in advance the optimum timing for the updates. Apps that are not updated eventually stop working as they no longer function due to software updates on devices.

Measuring results

App analytics are similar to Google Analytics (see Chapter 13, 'Digital Marketing Metrics and Analytics') and, for example, the data shows you:

- Session length – how long a user spends using the app

- Time in app – the total time in app over a specific period of time such as a week or a month

- Source of users – where they found out about the app and downloaded it; this could be via the app marketplaces, social media or elsewhere

- Retention – this is a big issue as many users download an app, use once and never again; and retention shows the percentage of visitors who return after their first visit

- Lifetime value – how much you might generate from individual users – assuming that it's paid-for, or has in-app purchases or sells advertising

The longest-established provider of app metrics is Yahoo Flurry. There are others, such as localytics.com and App Annie, but Yahoo Flurry has significant longitudinal data to see how your app compares to others in the same sector.

The challenge for business is readiness to adopt the technology (for more on this, see Figure 8.1 Technology Readiness Scale). The issue may be that mobile marketing strategies are not yet in place.

CASE EXAMPLE 7.1   FatSecret

Rodney Moses qualified as a medical doctor and later took a master's degree in information technology. His brother, Lenny Moses studied economics and finance and later took a master's in law. Together, they founded an app to help users track food and nutrition intake and help people lose weight. Based on the idea of 'my big fat secret', they created FatSecret which is one of Australia's most successful apps.

The app has been downloaded over 50 million times worldwide and has gained many awards. There's a free version and a subscription offer from $7 per month. It integrates with Google and Apple health so that users can connect their food intake with their exercise regime.

It's a competitive market with many apps available, from MyFitnessPal to CalorieCount, Noom and Fooducate. There are said to be nearly 50,000 health and wellness apps available worldwide.

Similar to other food and nutrition apps, the FatSecret app contains the nutrition details of thousands of food brands and supermarkets. So if you have a salad, sandwich or soup at lunch time, it shows a list of supermarkets and their typical offers, to make it easy to add to the app. So when a user wants to register their breakfast, lunch or dinner, they open the app, search for the brand and add the item, which automatically calculates the nutritional intake. It is mainly based on calorie counting and shows the nutritional components such as salt and sugar.

You're invited to join the app community and share how you're feeling. Users can take photos of their food and share recipes. These extra features mean that it's more than a regular calorie-counting app because it offers community chat to support those in their nutrition journey.

FatSecret allows other organisations to use its content. On another website (platform. fatsecret.com/api), the company explains how it shares its food and nutrition database. Over 10,000 developers in over 50 countries can access this database. A basic version of the **API** (see Key Term) is free for non-profits and start-ups. There is a charge for enterprise businesses that allows them to add all FatSecret data, under their own brand name. So if you started a new exercise or health plan business and wanted to add in food content, your company could subscribe and access this data, instead of having to calculate the contents of hundreds of thousands of different food products for yourselves.

The company's Instagram page shows fabulous food and contains some 'before and after' photos. The hashtag #FatSecretapp is used across several social media platforms.

Facebook and Twitter have policies and guidelines on adverts containing sensitive content, including health, nutrition and weight loss. For example, Facebook's Business Help Centre states 'Ads must not contain "before-and-after" images or images that contain unexpected or unlikely results. Ad content must not imply or attempt to generate negative self-perception in order to promote diet, weight loss or other health-related products.' As Instagram is owned by Facebook, the same policies apply.

Twitter's policies vary according to the region, so different rules may apply in individual countries. Hence, separate social media accounts may need to be created for each geographical area and local certificates of product authorisation from health ministries

(Continued)

may be required. TikTok has a similar approach and prohibits advertisements 'promoting weight loss/management fasting products or services'. TikTok has additional country rules and in some locations adverts for healthcare are permitted to those aged over 18 years.

YouTube's Community Guidelines are governed by its owner, Google, which has a long list of banned keywords and follows a similar approach to Twitter, which means adverts are reviewed on a case-by-case basis.

While these policies and guidelines ban exaggerated material, inaccurate content and adverts that create negative reactions about body image, it means that legitimate advertisers who are promoting a balanced or helpful approach to diet, may be less able to share their content because they are in the same category.

Case questions

- The app's name could be considered as being offensive which may make it a challenge for marketing – what are your thoughts on this?
- What do you consider to be FatSecret's main challenges in gaining more app users?
- How might genuine food and nutrition companies promote their apps on social media?

KEY TERM   API

An API is an application programming interface, which is a piece of software that allows two applications to talk to each other. For example, Google Maps has an open API so that if you're developing a website, you can add a map, via Google Maps. So your map is always up to date as the content is pulled from Google, rather than your own development team.

7.5 MOBILE PROMOTION

As a channel, mobile offers different delivery options from SMS to in-app messages and push notifications. Early research focused on screen size as an issue, but this has changed and grown, with some mobile phones increasing screen size (e.g. Apple iPhone Max versions or Galaxy Ultras). Regardless of screen size, consumers are spending more time on their mobiles and surveys indicate that this may be between four and six hours per day.

7.5.1 MOBILE ADVERTISING

There are a range of mobile advertising options, as shown in Table 7.2.

Table 7.2 Mobile advertising options

Advertising format	Explanation	Advantages
Text messaging	SMS messages with offers	Easy to deliver
Push notifications	Alert message with an offer	Alerts are managed by consumers
Mobile display ads	Banners on web pages and in apps	More effective for **utilitarian** purchases, recognised brands and higher involvement
Native mobile ads in-feed social	Looks like a regular piece of content although it must contain the word 'ad', 'promoted' or 'sponsored'	Behaves like an ordinary piece of content so easier to engage
Native mobile ads in-feed content	Within editorial feeds and on news walls	Matches site content
Native mobile ads in-feed commerce	Retail product listings on site such as Amazon, Etsy	Same functionality as other product listings and can prioritise specific product listings
Native mobile ads in-map	Ads that appear when you look at a map and see the nearest coffee shop or takeaway restaurant	Users are less familiar with the location and may be actively seeking services such as food or drink
Native mobile ads in-game	Often used in games and free software, can work on a rewards or points basis	Captures users in the moment
Native mobile ads paid search	Typically these appear in search engines such as Google, Bing and Yahoo	Users often searching with intent and need the item at that time, so can result in higher conversion rates
Native mobile ads recommendation widgets	'Recommended for you' or 'You may like' widgets often appear at the end of some content	Can drive traffic to specific content
Native mobile ads custom	A more expensive option as these are often custom ads created by brands and can be editorial, apps, games or videos which work well with location data	Useful for brand awareness

Chapter 3 explored paid search in more detail, so this section provides an overview of what makes mobile advertising effective, then we'll explore text messages and push notifications which are unique to mobile.

Professor Dhruv Grewal and colleagues (2016) explored mobile advertising and created an effectiveness framework, which is shown in Figure 7.2, which identifies the potential challenges and disadvantages of mobile advertising.

Exploring the different elements in Figure 7.2, the first is *context*, which concerns the situation where the user receives the ad; we could call this mobile place as part of the 5Ps. *Consumer* relates to the customer journey (see Chapter 2, 'The Digital Consumer'). Once the context has been understood, the next stage is the *ad goal*. What is the purpose of the advert? The difficulty is that the metrics are not standardised, which creates issues when measuring mobile.

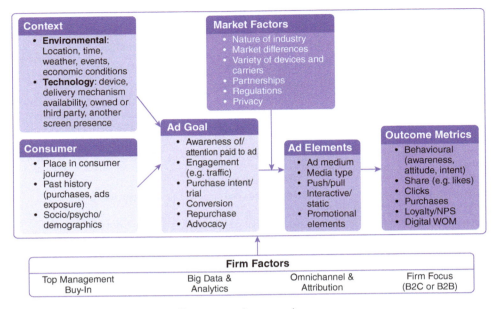

Figure 7.2   Mobile advertising effectiveness framework

Source: Grewal et al. (2016, p. 4)

Market factors addresses different issues such as the industry and the opportunities available. Home Depot can use reminders when consumers are walking around in store, whereas a clothing brand may not be able to achieve this as easily as it may be online only or sold via other retailers with less access to consumer data.

Market differences vary based on the location, their mobile networks and whether people have pre-paid or regular contracts and the same mobile number. Technology may be an issue, with so many diverse devices offering different options. One solution may be to develop partnerships with local intermediaries to process the adverts as they will be aware of local regulations (see data protection in Chapter 1). The last part of this element is privacy, also connected to data protection.

Ad elements are about the channel, whether that's in your mobile social media feed or mobile website. *Outcome metrics* relate back to the ad goal and what the desired results should or could be. Grewal and the team suggested different types of metrics from awareness to word of mouth (WOM), and from clicks to the goal most organisations have – purchase in the customer journey.

7.5.2 TEXT MESSAGES

Short message services (SMS) or text messages have been available since the early 1990s when the Global System for Mobile Communications (GSM) network – that's the 2G – was the standard technology. The first SMS messages were limited by the technology, which permitted 160 characters and were designed to be short.

The main advantage of SMS text notifications is that you don't need a smartphone – a regular analogue phone can receive these messages. Organisations can use SMS for:

- Booking confirmations – from taxi firms
- Service appointment reminders – from your dentist or hairdresser
- Healthcare appointment reminders – for clinic visits, vaccination dates
- Transaction notifications – from your bank
- Verification codes – from software companies

If we consider the role of mobile place, perhaps not in a marketing context, but for critical communications, SMS can be used in healthcare for disease prevention. Researchers have monitored how real-time, location-based messages about outbreaks of viruses might be sent to individuals, using tracking technology (Yin et al., 2020) to warn them of potential dangers. This could also apply to other situations such as natural disasters or localised emergencies.

SMS is useful for delivering communications to specific audiences; for example, providing support messages related to healthcare at all levels, from smoking cessation to weight loss, from diet to mental health.

In 4G and 5G networks, basic SMS messages have become more sophisticated with the development of multimedia message service (MMS) which includes images and video. However, we've moved beyond MMS to rich communications services messaging (RCS) which allows companies to interact and integrate the chat messages into business systems. RCS is used by many types of organisations including:

- **Delivery companies:** to advise you when a package has been shipped – you can track and manage your package and watch its journey on a map that's embedded into the message functionality
- **Online shopping:** to confirm your order
- **Telecoms companies:** to ask about your customer service experience, allowing you to rate or review staff
- **Political parties:** to conduct opinion polls
- **Brands:** to gather customer feedback in questionnaires

There are downsides as users can ignore these messages, delete them or block future texts by sending the word STOP to the sender. In some locations, the mobile signal may be weak and text messages may appear too late.

Plus, not everyone has a mobile phone – this is more likely in elderly or socioeconomically disadvantaged groups as part of the digital divide (see Chapter 1).

CASE EXAMPLE 7.2   #TextForHumanity

As mobile phones are often used for negative purposes, Swedish telecoms company Sinch partnered with Mental Health America to create the world's first texting switchboard, #TextForHumanity, allowing anyone to send and receive a positive text from a stranger.

Mental Health America was founded in 1909 and its website states that it is 'dedicated to addressing the needs of those living with mental illness and promoting the overall mental health of all' (Mental Health America Inc., 2021, p. 1).

Sinch has grown from six people in Stockholm in 2008 to a company that manages around 150 billion engagements every year. It has turned text messaging into mobile marketing for companies such as Toyota, Nespresso and Clarins.

There is growing evidence of negative content being shared via mobiles. The digital detox is emerging as people seek an escape from hate speech and online negativity. This has an impact on people's mental health and well-being. It is heightened on one of the most depressing days of the year which is said to be 'Blue Monday' – the third Monday in January – when people are back to work or college after the holidays and feel unhappy.

Mental Health America has conducted a number of community outreach programmes but this one focused on placing the mobile at the centre of the activity. So #TextForHumanity was launched a week before Blue Monday.

The service quickly gained media attention with celebrities sharing the link. #TextForHumanity connected strangers, anonymously enabling one person to send a positive message to another and receive a message back from someone else.

Sinch's technology enabled it to take a basic text message and transform it into a small artwork to be shared across social media. The messages were curated so only positive texts were shared. Nearly 100,000 messages have been sent and received across 85 countries, with over 50,000 shares via social media.

Since launching the service, Sinch has gained 300 per cent in business enquiries from other companies wishing to work with them. What started as a way to make mobile use more positive has become a mobile marketing campaign generating more business.

Case questions

- Why do you feel the #TextForHumanity mobile marketing campaign was successful?
- How else could #TextForHumanity be developed?
- What are your thoughts about using simple text messages, rather than video or animated adverts as digital communications tools?

7.5.3 PUSH NOTIFICATIONS

Push notifications are powerful mobile marketing tools as they are designed to interrupt and promote content to the reader which can have benefits; to gain the notifications, authorisation is required from the user who controls these based on how they have configured their settings.

Push notifications are different to SMS, for example:

- They look like a text notification but are only available in smartphones and appear as a pop-up on your screen
- SMS requires a mobile phone signal, whereas push notifications need internet access
- SMS can be sent to a wide group of people in an area, while push notifications can only be sent to users of the app sending the message

Writing in *The SAGE Handbook of Digital Marketing*, Professor Diana Gavilan characterised push notifications, as shown in Figure 7.3.

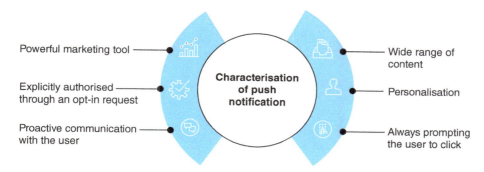

Figure 7.3   Characterisation of push notifications

Source: Gavilan (2022)

There is proactive communication with the user based on their location and the context. For example, notifications can encourage users to re-use an app, which in turn contributes to the app's success and creates opportunities for more feedback and better ratings.

The content format of notifications varies, from simple text message to more complex video content. The content can be personalised with time-limited offers and can bring shoppers back to the cart to complete a purchase.

Most importantly, notifications always require an action from the user to click to open or swipe and ignore. This enables marketers to assess the number of notifications that have been opened and acted upon.

DISCOVER MORE ON PUSH NOTIFICATIONS

Read the full chapter on 'The role of push notifications' by Diana Gavilan in *The SAGE Handbook of Digital Marketing* (2022).

However, although we enable push notifications it doesn't mean we always want the information. Push notifications may have contributed to **doomscrolling** (see Key Term) as they are often used for news alerts and can appear on locked screens, encouraging the user to open the message and read more. So 'push notifications represent an in-between form of exposure that is in some ways purposeful—people have downloaded an app and enabled notifications—and in some ways incidental—notifications appear whenever news breaks, as opposed to when the user has decided to consume news' (Stroud et al., 2020, p. 32).

As marketers, we need to be aware that text messages are personal communications and when used by organisations without permission, they are seen as intrusive and may contravene privacy legislation (see Chapter 1).

Smartphone Sixty Seconds® – Your notifications

- Check your phone to explore your notifications.
- How many notifications have you had today?
- What topics do these cover?
- How many have you switched off?

Activity 7.3   Evaluate mobile promotion

- Evaluate a recent mobile promotion campaign of your choice.
- Explore which aspects of mobile promotion were included.
- What worked well and where are the opportunities for improvement?

7.6 MOBILE COMMERCE

Mobile commerce is important in digital marketing as it 'helps in building long term relationship with customers' (Sarkar et al., 2020, p. 294). Mobile commerce, or m-commerce, or m-retail, has been defined as 'the second generation of e-commerce and involves the use of mobile devices to conduct electronic transactions' (Chou and Shao, 2020, p. 1).

However, not all consumers use mobile devices for shopping and they have been used for browsing rather than shopping (Tong et al., 2020). Research by Wohllebe and Dirrler (2020) found that they are sometimes used as a digital shopping assistant inside retail stores.

7.6.1 UBIQUITY OF SERVICES

The mobile phone has truly created ubiquitous computing where we are always connected to the internet and can download an app or visit a website from any place at any time.

Shopping via a mobile site removes spatial constraints, such as needing to be in the store to access the goods. It takes away any temporal challenges and is not based on time-critical factors, such as discovering the shop has limited opening hours. The mobile site is open 24/7 from any location. This notion of ubiquity is a reason why consumers use mobile websites (Chopdar and Balakrishnan, 2020).

However, a loss of internet access, such as poor connectivity, reduces the ubiquity. Although this is outside the organisation's control, it can lead to customer frustration (Sarkar et al., 2020).

7.6.2 WEBSITE DESIGN

As noted in Chapter 3, website design, whether desktop or mobile, needs to be easy to use for shopping purposes. The practical benefits of a mobile site or its usefulness have been identified as factors in whether consumers decide to shop using their mobile (Wohllebe and Dirrler, 2020). The concepts of ease of use and usefulness echo back to the Technology Acceptance Model referred to in Chapter 2.

While the mobile website design may meet the criteria, the screen size may be too small to see the item and there may be less information available on the mobile site, which could result in the customer making less accurate decisions (Papismedov and Fink, 2019).

7.6.3 FULFILMENT

Consumers need to see that placing an order via a mobile device provides delivery of the products within a suitable time. This can include real-time updates to encourage a purchase (Chopdar and Balakrishnan, 2020) which often include messages such as 'FREE delivery: Tomorrow. Order within 2 hrs 42 mins'. Organisations can also offer mobile-only deals to entice consumers to buy using their phones.

7.6.4 CUSTOMER SERVICE

The ability to respond to consumers' needs via the mobile website is a consideration in mobile service quality. The challenge is again screen size as if **chatbots** (see Key Term in Chapter 9) are used they can cover the whole screen when a consumer is looking at an item and asking questions. If a customer has many questions, they're more likely to browse on their mobile and buy on their desktop.

7.6.5 SECURITY AND PRIVACY

Security and privacy are trust issues, so ensuring that consumers' personal information and payment details are protected is a key factor in persuading consumers to use mobile websites (Hossain et al., 2020; Sarkar et al., 2020). But if consumers are aware of the brand and trust has been established, they are more likely to use the mobile site (Wohllebe and Dirrler, 2020).

An extension of m-commerce is mobile social commerce. This is different because it is a less-directed activity which combines social media with shopping. The user may be looking at social media pages such as YouTube, WeChat or Instagram when they see a product that captures their interest and they click and buy. Shopping via social media is the main form of social commerce, although this has developed and different types are shown in Table 7.3.

Table 7.3 Types of social commerce

Type of social commerce	Explanation	Examples
Social shopping	Shopping via social media sites which may include adverts or direct links to buy goods instantly	Instagram, Pinterest
Live streaming	Live video product demonstrations and displays in social media sites	Facebook, Taobao
Group buying and daily deals	The website negotiates deals in advance which are offered to people who have signed up to receive notifications	Groupon, Letsdeal
Pick list sites	Websites that select items from a range of brands and curate collections or create special edits that relate to the time of year, specific colours or other themes	FarFetch, The Lyst, gothelist.com
Platforms for peer-to-peer sales	Websites where the content is created by many users selling new or used goods	Etsy, eBay, ASOS marketplace
User review websites	Reading reviews about accommodation and destinations and making bookings through the review site	TripAdvisor®

7.6.6 QR CODES

Quick Response (QR) codes are small dots or pixels on a page, usually printed in a square shape. They are similar to barcodes and the main difference is that barcodes are restricted to 20 numbers, whereas QR codes can store large amounts of data which means that when they are scanned, they show additional content such as: website details (URLs); contact information including business cards; and specific information or small videos about the product or location.

Since the global health pandemic, QR codes have become widely used:

- **Checking into venues:** contact tracing in health epidemics
- **In education:** verifying students, especially for exams
- **On some CVs:** adding value with an 'introduction to me' video!
- **In healthcare:** delivering additional patient information for medics
- **In tourist attraction:** providing background or information about the exhibit
- **On product packaging:** giving more details about the product

There has been further marketing application of QR codes in social media with Snapchat, where you create your Snapcode that can be shared. Some virtual reality glasses include a QR code that takes the user through to a VR application (see Chapter 8 for more on virtual reality).

7.6.7 LOCATION-BASED OR PROXIMITY MARKETING

Location-based or proximity marketing was seen as a way to instantly connect with customers as they were in-store, but it never quite worked. Using mobile phone technology as you entered a store, a signal would ping from the beacon and indicate your presence, enabling retailers to send immediate offers to your mobile. Beauty business Sephora trialled the use of beacons but ran into challenges as people walked too fast from one department to another, plus mobiles are often inside pockets or handbags, so they didn't get promotional messages until it was too late.

Although beacons were heralded as a new form of hyper-local marketing or 'beacon mania', they failed for three reasons: scalability, exclusivity and visibility (Nicholas and Shapiro, 2020, p. 11).

Scalability was an issue as Apple and Google could not agree the Bluetooth standard required which created infrastructure issues. Google's own Project Beacon platform, to encourage beacon installation throughout large chain stores, was closed in April 2021. Plus, there were concerns about whether the data was a commodity – data that could be re-sold to others – or an asset – generating sales growth following the investment in beacon technology. Consequently, critical mass was never achieved.

However, the COVID-19 pandemic created a resurgence in proximity notifications to help local health departments advise individuals where they have been in the same location as someone with a virus. Yet the distrust remains and not everyone wants to be tracked.

7.7 CHALLENGES WITH MOBILE MARKETING FOR CONSUMERS

Whether it's in your pocket, handbag or on your desk, mobiles are the one item we carry with us at all times. So, you might feel concerned if you leave your mobile phone at home which is becoming a real issue as mobile phone dependence is escalating. Our relationship with mobile phones is changing our behaviour and a new mobile language has evolved reflecting our actions. We prioritise phone usage even when with friends and family: 'phubbing' or phone snubbing, looking at the phone rather than having a conversation with those next to you (Ivanova et al., 2020).

We have witnessed smartphone zombies – smombies (Langenscheidt, 2015) – people who are so addicted to their devices that they can't put them down, even when walking on busy pavements and crossing the road, resulting in people bumping into other people or creating traffic accidents.

During the pandemic, another form of mobile phone addiction emerged – **doom-scrolling** (see Key Term).

KEY TERM DOOMSCROLLING

This is compulsive news-checking, scrolling your news feed and desperately trying to find the latest news. Worldwide news outlets have commented that reading a constant stream of disaster stories has a negative impact on mental health.

7.7.1 NOMOPHOBIA

There are studies that suggest a connection between overuse of mobile phones and our mental health. Researchers have recognised that students who become over-dependent on their phone show signs of both 'behavioral and technological addictions' which can lead to 'lower academic performance' (Zhong et al., 2020).

To test the extent of groups' addiction to their mobile phones, a Mobile Phone Dependence Questionnaire was developed (Leung, 2017) which considers three key elements:

- **Mobile phone behaviour** – number of messages sent and from where, at home, travelling or in class
- **Usage of mobile phone** – average time making and taking calls in different locations and times, amount of app usage
- **Feelings towards the mobile** – concern about losing the phone or being in areas where there is a weak signal

Within this, aspects of compulsive behaviour were identified which demonstrate excessive usage – more than six hours a day.

Connected to this is nomophobia or fear of having no mobile phone where individuals are very uncomfortable without being able to communicate or connect to others, concerned when they cannot access information or are deprived of the convenience that a smartphone provides (Yildirim and Correia, 2015).

7.7.2 DIGITAL DETOX

We look at our mobile devices many times an hour. These devices can be the first thing we check in the morning.

This may be why mobile devices offer reports to show weekly screen time or digital well-being, so that users can moderate the time spent online (see Smartphone Sixty Seconds® – Your screen time). Additional functionality includes parents being able to limit the amount of time available to their children on mobile devices. Whilst this may seem like a form of excessive control, other researchers have identified the growth of digital addiction in younger children playing online games for 8 to 12 hours per week (Keya et al., 2020).

As a result of our increased dependence, some people are taking a digital detox which 'is defined as efforts to disconnect from online or social media, or efforts to reduce involvement in digital media and restrict the use of digital devices' (Jiang and Balaji, 2021, p. 4). Jiang and Balaji (2021) propose the idea of a 'digital detox holiday' to escape all access to the internet to have a break. Perhaps this is an area we should all explore further.

DISCOVER MORE ON DIGITAL DETOX

Read these two articles on the digital detox:

- 'Getting unwired: What drives travellers to take a digital detox holiday?' by Yangyang Jiang & M. S. Balaji (2021), published in *Tourism Recreation Research*.
- Focusing on how students feel when they walk away from their devices: 'Unplugged: Digital detox enhances student learning' by Natalie T. Wood and Caroline Muñoz (2021), published in the *Marketing Education Review*.

JOURNAL OF NOTE

Mobile Media & Communication is a specialist journal that explores the relationships between mobile communications, the users and technology.

CASE STUDY

This continues our long case study and you may find it helpful to read earlier parts in previous chapters.

STRAVA INC. – BORN FOR MOBILE

Strava was born for mobile. With apps for all phone types, Strava has over 70 million users. It wasn't the first social-fitness app and it's not the largest – this is probably MyFitnessPal (part of Under Armour) with over 180 million users.

It's a competitive field with many other apps in this market, including: Cadence Trainer, Codoon, Couch to 5K, Endomondo, Garmin, miCoach, Nike+, Run with Map My Run, Runkeeper, Runtastic, Sports Tracker and Under Armour.

Claire has used Strava for just over two years. She used to have Garmin but that only logged her activities and lacked the connection with her friends. She feels that the difference with the Strava app is that it gained knowledge and understanding from earlier apps, taking their best features and adding more. One of these is the leaderboard where every athlete can add their personal records which are ranked by comparison to others on the same route. The fastest man and woman on a specific route are awarded star status as King or Queen of the Mountain (KoM, QoM) and they can store their crowns in their profile page.

She read that one of the reasons that Strava was established was to share achievements. Runners don't get KoM status, but do get CRs (course records).

One of her friends who cycles has gained QoM, although that's only been once, after an especially tough race. But who doesn't love being QoM – there's even a dedicated club named the Strava QoM Hunters!

Strava enables ordinary people to compete against each other as well as professional sportspeople, adding entertainment and gamification to the app. This is more than a fitness app as users can explore routes, add challenges, create training goals and record their own activity. Consequently, nomophobia is an issue with many exercise apps as if it's not recorded, it didn't happen!

The app works on smartwatches and fitness trackers too. Claire has linked her app to her Samsung watch. She thinks that in the future it's likely that Strava would be available on smart clothing and wearable glasses, making tracking easier. As a lifestyle app, it encourages additional usage with push notifications as reminders to connect her address book, follow friends and try new activities.

When running alone, Claire and her friends often start their run by setting the 'beacon' which shows parents or flatmates where they are. This was Strava's first safety feature and is part of the premium package.

There are other benefits to Strava. The app augments the gamification with the addition of regular challenges. For athletes seeking something new, the monthly challenge is something to look forward to, which Claire and her friends instantly share on WhatsApp.

CASE QUESTION

1. How can companies like Strava stay ahead with mobile technology and wearable devices?
2. Claire started using Garmin but dropped this in favour of Strava. What should Strava do to ensure their premium subscribers continue using Strava?
3. What steps could Strava take to convert Garmin or Nike+ users, to switch to Strava?

FURTHER EXERCISES

1. What are the advantages and disadvantages of wearable technology for students?

2. Apply the 5Ps framework for personalised mobile marketing to an organisation of your choice.

3. Write a brief for a mobile app. Identify its purpose and target audience. Support your proposal with research evidence.

4. Tracking apps have benefits for personal safety and have been used to solve crimes. Discuss and justify whether these apps are a benefit or a threat to our personal liberty.

SUMMARY

This chapter has explored:

*   The role of mobiles and wearables in marketing
*   How to apply the 5Ps framework for personalised mobile marketing
*   Factors to consider with mobile products
*   Mobile marketing implications for organisations
*   Challenges with mobile marketing for consumers

GO ONLINE

Visit **study.sagepub.com/hanlon2e** to access links to interesting articles, websites and videos related to this chapter.

ACTIVITIES

Apply the Technology Readiness Scale

Analyse experiential value

Create your AR business card

OVERVIEW
Chapter 8 addresses augmented, virtual and mixed reality within a marketing context, starting by explaining the different realities with examples of their application in practice.

Typology of experiential values

KEY CONCEPTS

The ethical issue of deepfakes

Dimensions of interactivity

DIGITAL TOOLS

Augmented Reality Live Patent Search

360Cities

8

AUGMENTED, VIRTUAL AND MIXED REALITY

LEARNING OUTCOMES

When you have read this chapter, you will be able to:

Understand the different types of realities

Apply the Technology Readiness Scale

Analyse experiential value

Evaluate the dimensions of interactivity

Create an AR experience

PROFESSIONAL SKILLS

When you have worked through this chapter, you should be able to:

- Evaluate the realities for organisations
- Create an AR business card

8.1 INTRODUCTION TO AUGMENTED, VIRTUAL AND MIXED REALITY

Augmented, virtual and mixed realities are being used in retail, education and training, tourism and travel, manufacturing and industry, property and construction, medicine and healthcare, as well as games and entertainment. The realities provide 'interactive digital environments' (Bec et al., 2021, p. 2) and interest has increased since the COVID-19 pandemic when travel was reduced and retail stores were closed.

The concept of **virtual reality** has existed for decades. Technology is often founded in science fiction and VR is no exception. Whilst early sci-fi writers imagined virtual environments, research labs have been working on VR goggles, which were initially termed 'Head Mounted Displays' (HMDs) and resembled a clumsy type of SCUBA mask for more than 50 years.

There were many concepts presenting opportunities for brands to engage consumers further, or alter product design, but it took years for this to happen. VR started to become more accessible in the 1980s when technologies such as electronic miniaturisation and computer graphics developed further (Rheingold, 1992).

Yet it wasn't until 2019 that VR headsets as we know them started to change. It had taken decades from the early prototypes to get to the commercially available Samsung Gear, Oculus Rift and Microsoft's first HoloLens, as technology has become smaller, cheaper and easier to use. For example, Microsoft's HoloLens 2 is a mixed-reality, head-mounted display that integrates into the environment which means that it can be worn with spectacles or a hard hat if you're on a construction site. The idea has turned into a practical business application offering marketing and sales opportunities as well as a tool to be used in the working environment.

This chapter explains the different types of realities as well as providing real-world case examples to see how organisations are using these in their digital marketing mix.

8.2 THE DIFFERENT REALITIES

Let's start by exploring the differences as there is some confusion between the types of realities. The different realities are:

- **Augmented**: The consumer is in the physical world and this enhances the real environment where you're located. The equipment needed is a mobile phone.
- **Virtual**: The consumer is in a digital world and this offers exploration of another environment. The equipment needed is a headset.
- **Mixed**: This reality is merged between the physical and digital worlds. It enables consumers to see into a digital environment whilst in a physical location. The equipment needed is a headset or display system.

Let's explore each of these realities further.

8.2.1 VIRTUAL REALITY

Virtual reality (VR) was defined as 'a real or simulated environment in which a perceiver experiences telepresence' (Steuer, 1992, pp. 76–7). Virtual reality (VR) has also been described as 'a computer-generated simulation of an environment' (Bec et al., 2021, p. 2). The focus with VR is all about the environment where the user is present, based on using technology.

Six dimensions of presence in the virtual environment

Researchers have identified six dimensions of presence in virtual environments (Lombard and Ditton, 1997):

1. **Presence as social richness** which provides intimacy and immediacy (e.g. bringing the consumer closer to the brand)

2. **Presence as realism** considers how the medium can produce realistic representations and seem real (e.g. showing the intricate detail of certain products or for travel)

3. **Presence as transportation** makes you feel like you are there, transported to the actual place (e.g. making the consumer feel as if they are in the specific environment, often used in the travel sector)

4. **Presence as immersion** by using goggles, gloves or other smart clothing to be immersed in the situation (e.g. consumers are totally engaged with the experience)

5. **Presence as social actor** within the medium with the user responding to social cues (e.g. 'Can I take you there now?' and responding to the situation, such as making comments)

6. **Presence as medium as social actor** with the user responding to the external devices, such as goggles, which become part of the individual (e.g. using haptic signals to encourage consumers to take specific actions)

These dimensions are factors to consider when considering whether to create a VR experience as they focus on what the organisation wants to achieve. Studies demonstrate that VR provides a greater sense of presence than a traditional blog post, providing richness and realism, transporting the user away from their current situation into another world (Kim et al., 2020; Lo and Cheng, 2020).

This is why the technology has been so popular in games – taking consumers into another world that feels real. However, the concept of richness works in retail. The luxury brand Burberry uses AR so consumers gain more product information in a traditional store which makes them more likely to complete the purchase.

The degree of immersion was unsurprisingly dependent on the devices being used. When participants used basic goggles, such as Google Cardboard, the impact was reduced, further demonstrating that the development of the device technology has increased social richness. Before the pandemic, Thomas Cook, a travel company, was experimenting with immersion rooms, where consumers booked a 15-minute experience, wore VR googles and travelled to places on their bucket list before deciding where to go. However, Thomas Cook closed after sustaining too many losses during the pandemic.

The role of presence as the social actor demonstrated that consumers would move from VR to real world. For example, consumers in the study were more likely to book a stay with the hotels providing a VR experience, partly as they concluded the hotel was of a higher quality due to the use of VR (Kim et al., 2020). Another factor with tourism is that hotels or destinations should ensure the VR content is authentic and provides unique experiences that might not be available from other sources; for example, behind-the-scenes visits to 'boost the emotional factors of enjoyment, emotional involvement, and flow state with animations' (Kim et al., 2020, p. 85). See also **flow experience** in Chapter 7.

The last dimension, presence as medium as social actor, is defined by Lombard and Ditton as the computer responding to the individuals. At a basic level, this is already here with haptic signs, such as your smartwatch vibrating if you've been at your desk for too long and haven't stood up for a while. Some vehicles already act as the medium where they monitor signs of fatigue and suggest the driver takes a break. Perhaps in the future, these breaks could be sponsored by refreshment venues along the route.

8.2.2 AUGMENTED REALITY

Augmented reality (AR) was first considered as 'a variation of virtual reality' which 'supplements reality, rather than completely replacing it' (Azuma, 1997, p. 356). Definitions focus on adding a digital coating or a giant filter that alters the world or environment where we are based, making the experience richer. For example, Alexandra Bec and colleagues suggested that AR is 'a type of mixed reality where the real environment is overlayed in a digital context' (Bec et al., 2021, p. 2).

AR can boost engagement as it brings 'richer, more immersive content, enhancing interaction with, and perceptions of the world around us' (Cranmer et al., 2020, p. 2). This improved engagement and pleasure create **hedonic consumption** (see Key Terms) due to the multisensory experience as AR combines positive feelings of excitement and pleasure. If you use Snapchat, you've already used AR. The lenses and filters that are super-imposed onto images are a form of AR.

> ### KEY TERMS   HEDONIC AND UTILITARIAN CONSUMPTION
>
> The Greek goddess Hedone represented pleasure and enjoyment and is the origin of the word hedonism. Describing consumption as hedonic indicates that it provides delight. Hedonic consumption is defined as: 'designat[ing] those facets of consumer behavior that relate to the multi-sensory, fantasy, and emotive aspects of one's

experience with products' (Hirschman and Holbrook, 1982, p. 92). A hedonic consumer is thus a consumer who gains happiness from the customer journey process.

The opposite of hedonic consumption is utilitarian. Utilitarian benefits have been described as the functional, instrumental and practical attributes of the item (Chitturi et al., 2008). You buy the item because you need it, not because you want it.

From a marketing perspective, AR enhances user experiences and can help move the consumer along the customer journey (see Chapter 2). The use of AR is popular in several sectors, including tourism, which can take consumers from consideration to conversion, by accessing greater detail. For example, imagine if you're considering whether or not to visit somewhere, being able to explore before booking can help the decision-making process. As a result, AR has been used by organisations such as the luxury travel brand Kuoni as well as several cruise line companies (Cranmer et al., 2020).

DIGITAL TOOL   Augmented reality live patent search

To explore the latest technology developments in AR, look at some current patents published on www.augmentedreality.org/ar-patents, which shows you the future plans for AR.

DISCOVER MORE ON COMMERCIAL RESEARCH INTO AUGMENTED REALITY

AugmentedReality.org publishes research into augmented reality and its application commercially. See www.augmentedreality.org/ar-market-research.

8.2.3 MIXED OR CROSS REALITY

Mixed reality blends virtual and augmented reality and has been described as presenting 'the co-existence of the real and virtual worlds' (Bec et al., 2021, p. 2).

Practitioners have also called this cross reality (XR) which incorporates all technologies including augmented and mixed reality, but that's just another way of describing mixed reality. Others suggest this is extended reality which is another way of describing an immersive mixed-reality experience that uses gloves, other smart clothing (see Chapter 7) or haptic devices – yet this describes the original concept created by Krueger where the user was immersed in the space.

KEY TERM   MIXED REALITY (MR)

The main definition used comes from researchers Paul Milgram and Fumio Kishino, who worked on a taxonomy of mixed-reality virtual displays in 1994. They suggested mixed reality was 'the merging of real and virtual worlds' (Milgram and Kishino, 1994, p. 1322).

8.3 APPLICATION OF DIFFERENT REALITIES FOR MARKETING

The application of virtual reality started in space and science. Initially it was clunky, and the **Technology Readiness Scale** was developed to assess technology.

Since 1989 NASA has run a dedicated 'VR applications program' and uses VR in hardware development, operations development, support and missions operation training (Hale, 1995). It is cheaper and safer to train astronauts on the ground before they embark on a mission into deep space. This is important background information because we've found that many innovations start in space and translate into everyday use. Your laptop, wireless headset and even the cameras in our mobile phones all started with space missions!

However, not all organisations are ready for the technology.

8.3.1 TECHNOLOGY READINESS LEVELS

The notion of a technology that *enables* a function is a critical concept in manufacturing. NASA, the United Nations, the European Union and others use the Technology Readiness Level (TRL), which is described as a 'measurement system used to assess the maturity level of a particular technology' (NASA, 2012a).

New technology projects are checked against agreed criteria and then rated on a scale from 1 to 9 that indicates their Technology Readiness. TRL 1 is the lowest level where some form of scientific knowledge has underpinned the concept. TRL 9 is the highest level where the system has worked in an operational environment (NASA, 2012b). Figure 8.1 shows the Technology Readiness Scale.

If we think about VR goggles, they were at TRL 1, 2, 3 and 4 in 1960 with the work at the University of North Carolina. TRL 5, 6 and 7 were achieved in 1965 when Ivan Sutherland created the first goggles, but it wasn't until 2014 with the launch of Google Cardboard that VR goggles were complete and available – TRL 8 and proven with user feedback at TRL 9. It took nearly 50 years for the technology to be fully ready.

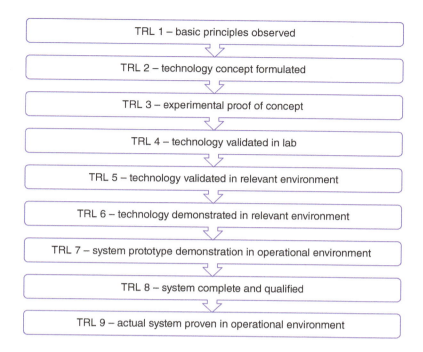

Figure 8.1 Technology Readiness Scale

You may consider TRL to apply only in areas of science or space, but the United Nations assesses the TRL of countries that need to engage with action on climate change, as part of their 2030 Agenda for Sustainable Development.

During the pandemic, several retailers re-assessed how ready they were for technology, with winners and losers. For example, ASOS was a clear winner as it was well prepared as an online-only organisation, yet many traditional high street retailers worldwide ended up closing as they weren't ready to consider or use technology.

Activity 8.1   Apply the Technology Readiness Scale

- Using the Technology Readiness Scale, apply this to a technology of your choice. It could be a piece of very new equipment or an older device.
- Plot out when the technology reached each stage.
- If it is not yet at TRL 9, explain why.

Considering that it has taken over 50 years of ideas for the different realities to reach a point where the hardware and software are readily available, they are now used in many sectors. This section explores how and where the realities have been used for marketing purposes. Examples of sectors adopting VR and AR for marketing purposes include:

- Retail
- Home products
- Tourism

8.3.2 RETAIL BRANDS USING AR

Retailers have been keen to adopt the realities as they can see the application assisting with the customer journey (see Chapter 2). The application of AR helps customers to move beyond consideration towards making the purchase decision.

Luxury fashion brands

Luxury fashion has always focused on the hedonic experience of acquiring and owning the goods. One luxury brand, Burberry, sees AR as part of its commitment to digital innovation and its 2019/2020 annual report stated that AR is a means of engaging consumers.

Burberry experimented with an in-store 'Digital Runway Nail Bar' that was placed in beauty concept stores to enable consumers to virtually try on nail colours using AR – holding the phone over their nails to see the colours and decide which nail polish to buy. But it has extended the use of AR beyond simple product try-on functions to provide more information to consumers – building the story. The pandemic impacted on the business with stores being closed globally, but Burberry continues to use AR. The marketing application uses AR in the retail outlets as this 'transforms the product discovery-and-search phase by blurring the lines between online shopping and the in-store experience' (Burberry, 2020).

Another luxury brand, Gucci, has created an AR app that enables consumers to try on sneakers, hats and sunglasses and buy them from the app. It's a fun way to try on new shoes.

The company that owns Gucci has noted that 'luxury consumers are seeking a creative and differentiated product offering, together with a customer experience that is both personalized and integrated across physical and digital distribution channels' (Kering, 2020, p. 52). To address these requirements, luxury brands are using AR as part of a hedonic customer journey to provide greater immersion and engagement in retail stores. Where traditional stores are closing, AR gives consumers greater reasons to visit for a total experience, rather than a simple shopping trip.

Clothing retailers

The development costs involved in augmented reality often mean that only luxury brands or those selling millions of products can afford to explore AR. For example, ASOS, a global retailer with over 80 million orders placed in a year, 85,000 products available online and 23 million active customers, is using AR. The ASOS

'See My Fit' app allows consumers to see how an item of clothing will look on them, based on their height. Instead of developing this app in-house, ASOS has partnered with specialist developer Zeekit (see Case Example 8.1) with its greater expertise in technology.

Since the pandemic, ASOS has increased its use of the app and aims to add hundreds of new products each week. This AR tool enables consumers to see how the item looks without leaving home and should reduce the number of returns.

Clothing retailers with smaller sales and less expensive goods may explore the use of tools created by specialist technology companies such as Zeekit.

CASE EXAMPLE 8.1   Zeekit, the virtual fitting room

Zeekit is a specialist start-up technology firm (acquired by Walmart in May 2021) who want to change the way you look at clothes online. Using ordinary people as its models, the company has a library of diverse shapes and sizes, giving fashion consumers the option to try on clothing in a virtual setting, using a model that best reflects their body.

Retailers pay for the technology to use on their websites or apps. There are two parts involved: firstly the models, which include thousands of real people with many different body shapes, sizes and heights; and secondly the clothing, which is plotted out. When the two are combined, using artificial intelligence, consumers can select a relevant body shape and try on shirts, coats or pairs of trousers, to see how the garment would look on someone like them.

Used by ASOS for its See My Fit app, consumers can select the model that they most identify with so the app image looks more like a real photo, rather than a standard catalogue picture. Also used by Adidas and Tommy Hilfiger, the concept of real-life and real-size models brings greater authenticity to fashion. The Zeekit website states: 'Combining fashion and technology, Zeekit has developed the first dynamic virtual fitting room, giving every person the chance to see themselves in any item of clothing found on-line.' Zeekit's own app allows individuals to upload a photo of themselves and try on selected ranges of clothing from a range of brands.

The benefits of Zeekit are that consumers can try on clothing without placing an order, without visiting the store and without spending a lot of time in a changing room. The process happens from the consumers' own homes and they can snap and share with friends before deciding what to purchase.

Case questions

- Do you feel using a model that has a similar shape and size would help to buy clothing or be off-putting?
- In what ways can AR or VR technology further improve shopping online?
- What apps have you downloaded that have provided a similar service?

Beauty retailers

AR has demonstrated its advantages for beauty retailers and one example is from Benefit cosmetics that has an online web-based facility to sample different eyebrow types with their 'Brow Try-on' tool. Consumers can upload an image or use a web cam to see different possibilities and buy the products needed to create the look in real life. Interviewing Cindy Shen, VP of e-commerce and CRM, Amanda Lim (2021, p. 1) reported that the brand had seen a '43% increase in daily usage of the Brow Try-On Experience on our websites'; as a result, using AR will become 'even more important in the customer journey with the shift towards online shopping'.

The hair brand Wella introduced a Smart Mirror that allows consumers to try different hair colours with 360-degree video capture to view the hair at every angle. The company partnered with The YouCam Makeup: Selfie Editor which, instead of focusing on a single beauty or haircare range, includes many different brands, from the Japanese brand Coffret D'or to the US brand Aveda.

The YouCam Makeup: Selfie Editor has been downloaded nearly 1 billion times and has positive ratings. This may mean that instead of brands such as Rimmel trying to create their own AR apps, they add their products to YouCam where consumers can experiment with many different products. This is likely to be why Rimmel London stopped updating its own app and at this stage it is probably gone from the app stores.

YouCam integrates with Instagram, enabling consumers to create and share their looks. It is owned by Perfect Corp, whose aims are to 'transform the beauty game by marrying the highest level of augmented reality ("AR") and artificial intelligence ("AI") technology with the ultimate shopping experience, completely reinventing the online-to-offline ("O2O") consumer beauty journey' (Perfect Corp, 2021, p. 1). It's clearly working for Perfect Corp as it raised $50 million from investors to further develop its use of AR and technology. The company's customers are reporting higher conversion rates after virtual try-ons.

Automotive retail

The automotive sector embraced VR and AR at an early stage. Intelligent windscreens using embedded Head-Up Displays (HUDs) have been available in luxury car brands for some years and are available on many vehicles, allowing drivers to see information such as their speed, weather conditions and traffic, projected directly on to the windshield.

In car showrooms, some automotive companies are using AR to help buyers change the car colour or add extras. For example, Audi has experimented with virtual showrooms where no actual cars were present, instead giant screens controlled by iPads to build the car and see it being created. This use of AR contributes to moving the consumer along the customer journey, from considering in the pre-purchase stage towards the purchase stage.

Augmented reality has a role in retail, both physical and digital. It enhances the customer journey experience and reduces potential shopping errors and returns.

AR in this context creates enjoyment and makes shopping a more holistic and hedonic experience.

8.3.3 HOMEWARE BRANDS USING AR AND VR

Augmented and virtual reality tools are well suited to visualising environments such as room settings. As a result, manufacturers and sellers of furniture, paint and even radiators have adopted these realities. For example, the paint company Dulux has created a visualiser which allows consumers to see how colours look on a wall in their home. You can change the shade, save in a favourites board and gain ideas before buying. With over half a million downloads, it's inspiring home decorators in several countries.

Over the years, IKEA has experimented with augmented and virtual reality and its VR kitchen app allowed home-owners to plan their new kitchen, but this is no longer being updated, so we assume it was less successful than intended.

A less complex AR app is IKEA Place, which enables consumers to point their mobile phone into one of their rooms, select a piece of IKEA furniture and see how it fits. It's fun to use and see what works in the room. There's a clear marketing benefit too as the company is less likely to have goods returned, because they are too big or don't fit, which has been recognised as a business benefit (Dacko, 2016). There is an element of consumer return on investment as they can make decisions based on their own space, rather than buying the wrong products. Plus, consumers may save time by deciding what they want to buy in their own environment.

Smartphone Sixty Seconds® –Use the IKEA Place app

- Take out your mobile phone and go into the app store and search for the IKEA Place app (Augmented Reality Furnishing).
- Hold the app up to a wall.
- Select an item of furniture, such as a lamp, chair or table.
- Add into the setting.
- You may need to adjust the item and move it into position.
- How does it look?

8.3.4 TOURISM AND TRAVEL ORGANISATIONS USING AR AND VR

Virtual reality is an important aspect of tourism marketing as it enables potential visitors to explore places and discover more without leaving home. Virtual reality is used to promote destinations, venues, attractions and events. Researchers have acknowledged that with the ability to share content via social media, virtual reality and tourism become a powerful combination for destination marketing.

Examples of how the travel and tourism sector has used VR for promotion include:

- Hotels promoting their venue or special events: Marriott Hotels promote the honeymoon package offered at hotels in London and Hawaii
- Airlines promoting activities at the destination: Qantas cabins allowing passengers to experience the Great Barrier Reef
- Technology companies such as Google Earth enabling travel to destinations worldwide
- Non-profit companies sharing travel under the world's oceans: The Hydrous Team offers a 360-degree tour of the world's oceans

DIGITAL TOOL   360Cities

Netherlands-based 360Cities is a photo library with 360-degree images from across the globe. Visit the website to virtually visit the cities or if you have them, put on VR goggles and watch in VR (www.360cities.net).

In addition to using VR as a promotional tool, some resorts are using VR in the hotel offer. One example is the luxury hotel brand, the Four Seasons, which introduced a mixed-reality experience to help people relax in its egg-shaped pod 'The Vessel'.

Another way of using VR is in person. For example, Flyview Paris is targeting tourists who want to have the experience of flying over the city in a jetpack. Paying visitors are given goggles and step onto a device in the VR room and the sensation of flying over Paris is created. This provides a different approach to the usual city tour where you hop on and off a bus for the day. It enables visitors without much time to experience the city and could be extended so that you don't even need to visit Paris to take a tour.

It is impossible to consider VR and tourism without addressing the COVID-19 pandemic. The Secretary-General of the United Nations World Tourism Organization (UNWTO) stated that 'Tourism is one of the world's major economic sectors. It is the third-largest export category' (UNWTO Secretary-General Zurab Pololikashvili, 2021, p. 1). He added that the health crisis had a major impact on tourism, with a 98 per cent drop in bookings at the height of the pandemic.

As news sources indicate that tourism will not return to pre-pandemic levels until 2024, one response to the pandemic was the German national tourist board who launched a campaign #DiscoverGermanyFromHome. This encouraged people to use their imagination and dream of places to travel – in Germany and showcased different parts of the country, its arts and culture. The tourist board's focus was planning for the future and being top of the list when people started feeling safe to travel again. The board recognised that VR was not a substitute for actual travel and this VR experience could enable future visitors to explore and plan, by gaining more knowledge of the different areas before leaving home.

A study by Eleanor Cranmer and colleagues (2020) found that AR enables travel and tourism companies to increase consumer spending as travellers can experience the tours before arriving and add more activities to their holiday. Their research indicated that AR could 'enhance their marketing efforts, reduce marketing costs and provide richer, more accurate and engaging information' (p. 6).

Virtual reality is likely to grow in travel and tourism, with more destinations providing authentic pre-visit and in-visit experiences.

8.3.5 EDUCATION USING AR AND VR

Virtual reality, augmented reality and mixed reality have been used in the education sector, as teaching tools, from primary school to university (Tzima et al., 2019). Benefits of using the realities in teaching include more motivated students, improved performance and greater critical thinking being encouraged.

In addition to employing them in the classroom, VR and AR are used as marketing tools for educational establishments. The main area is campus tours, which is discussed in Case Example 8.2: YouVisit.

CASE EXAMPLE 8.2   YouVisit

When students are deciding where to study, they often visit the campus in person. But sometimes that's not possible if they're overseas or when locations are closed.

YouVisit is a virtual tour guide, specialising in campus visits in the USA. You visit the app store, download the app and sit back and watch a tour of where you're thinking of studying.

It is owned by EAB who claim on their website (EAB, 2021, p. 1):

Interactive digital exploration converts your visitors' interest into intent. Our tours prompt students to take action—to register, schedule a visit, or apply—based on their engagement level so you can more effectively recruit them. Our progressive Conversational Inquiry Form leads to a 2x conversion rate compared to traditional web forms.

YouVisit uses a simple model: either the college or university can record their own tour using the YouVisit tool, or they can pay YouVisit to carry out the filming which can be helpful as VR is not the same as 360-degree video, and may need to be filmed using high-quality cameras that can read images in 3D – some newer smartphones do this. When the work is done, it's uploaded to the YouVisit app which means that one college sits next to another one which may be a competitor, presenting both opportunities as well as threats.

There is no custom branding available and for this reason some educational establishments create their own tours. However, it's considered cost-effective at around $10,000 for a virtual tour. Once the tour is created, it can be used for several years.

(Continued)

There are clear marketing benefits with this type of augmented reality. All viewers need to register to access the details, providing their name, email address, the course they are considering and the date they're looking to start. This information can be shared with the universities who can contact the student to discuss further. The app shows the different buildings and the surroundings, and adds in images of happy students in those locations, explaining how the space is used.

Another advantage is that when students visit the universities in person, they can use the app in different buildings to discover more.

YouVisit is one example of an AR tour system, although there may be changes ahead since it was acquired by EAB. There are many similar tour apps showcasing universities to students and this is a business that will continue to grow.

Case questions

- Have you used a tour app such as YouVisit? What was your experience?
- What are the downsides of these apps, what's missing – other than physically being there?
- How can AR tour apps enhance the experience further?

8.3.6 GAMES

The main area where all forms of reality – virtual, augmented and mixed – have seen major developments is in gaming. Whilst AR can be used for gaming and there are nearly 350 million mobile AR apps worldwide, VR gaming is still being developed. The high entry cost of headsets limits the number of people who can access the market.

VR games make money with in-game advertising, in-game purchases (extra lives, more weapons) and subscriptions. The games are available from VR storefronts which include the headset manufacturers' stores (PlayStation Network, Oculus Rift, Microsoft) as well as the specialist Steam and their competitors. According to Tipatat Chennavasin, the co-founder of the Venture Reality Fund (an organisation which invests in games' developers), over 100 VR games have generated incomes of more than $1 million.

Pokémon Go explained to many people how augmented reality works, and Professor Philipp Rauschnabel and colleagues (2017) created a conceptual model for an adoption framework for mobile augmented reality games, which is shown in Figure 8.2.

The model was created due to a lack of theories that explained consumers' reactions to augmented reality. Rauschnabel acknowledges that the model was based on earlier theories such as uses and gratification (see Chapter 5), which suggested that the users' reactions and intended behaviours are based on their evaluation and perceptions of various benefits, risks and social influences. This is shown in the first two parts of the model. The next element is the users' reactions, which looks at their attitude and behavioural intention – this takes us back once again to the Technology Acceptance Model (see Chapter 2, 'The Digital Consumer').

Rauschnabel's research involved a survey of 642 respondents in Germany who had installed Pokémon Go on a mobile device and who were paid to participate. The results indicated 'that consumers' attitudes toward playing mobile AR games are mostly driven by the level of enjoyment they receive and the image that playing a particular game conveys to other people' (Rauschnabel et al., 2017). So, there may be other issues with the research, as Pokémon Go players in Germany might behave differently to players in the UK, the United States or China. However, this model is a useful place to start in considering the adoption of VR games, to assess how likely they are to succeed.

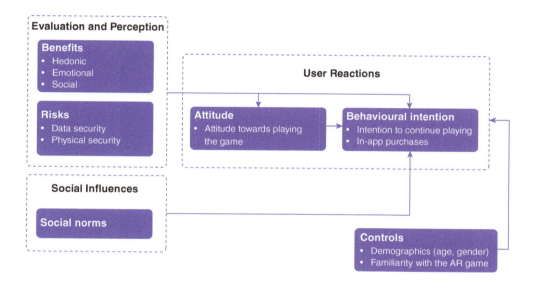

Figure 8.2   Conceptual model for an adoption framework for mobile augmented reality games

Source: Rauschnabel et al. (2017, p. 278)

8.4 KEY CONCEPTS IN THE REALITIES

Our relationship with the realities is founded in different research studies, including experiential values and dimensions of interactivity, which are discussed in this section.

8.4.1 TYPOLOGY OF EXPERIENTIAL VALUES

Before the pandemic, retail was already changing as consumers had greater choice between online and offline stores. This was recognised by researchers who created a typology of experiential values, which was based on two axes: (a) intrinsic and extrinsic; and (b) active and reactive (Mathwick et al., 2001). The typology is shown as a matrix in Figure 8.3.

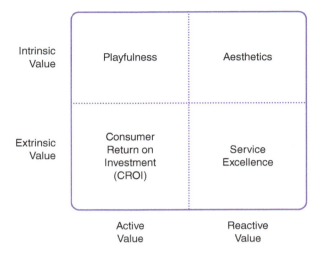

Figure 8.3 Typology of experiential value

Source: Mathwick et al. (2001, p. 42)

The four quadrants signify different approaches to the experience, influenced by internal and external factors:

- **Playfulness** (intrinsic and active): the enjoyment and hedonic benefit of shopping (see Key Terms)
- **Aesthetics** (intrinsic and reactive): how the consumer sees the retail environment, the photography and layout of the digital space
- **Consumer return on investment** (extrinsic and active): this concerns the **utilitarian** benefit where the consumer actively invests their money (see Key Terms)
- **Service excellence** (extrinsic and reactive): the consumer makes quality judgements against the service

---

KEY TERMS   INTRINSIC AND EXTRINSIC VALUES

Intrinsic and extrinsic usually relate to our motivations. We may be strongly driven to do something for our own benefit; that's internal or intrinsic motivation. Or we may be rewarded with a better career or pay rise from an achievement; that's external or extrinsic motivation.

In the typology of experiential value, intrinsic relates to values from within, where personal satisfaction is gained from the playfulness or the aesthetics of an item. Extrinsic concerns the external factors which are gained, such as the return on investment or excellent service.

One example that demonstrates the elements of playfulness, aesthetics, consumer return on investment and service excellence is Adidas. The sports retailer installed immersive fitting rooms in a flagship store in London's Oxford Street. This allows consumers to see what the products look like in real life as the changing room mirror becomes a digital screen. This brings playfulness into the shopping experience as it's fun to try on many different products. In terms of the aesthetics, this was part of a total store redesign, so the overall environment is well presented and aesthetically pleasing.

Consumers gain a return on the time investment by being in control of the whole experience through the Adidas app. This allows consumers to request products to be brought to them in the fitting room or wherever they are in the store! Adidas has transformed the process of finding in-store assistants and trying on clothing into a multi-sensory experience in store, enabling consumers to try on clothing and request different options from the mirror which helps the customer journey. This wasn't a one-off as, post-pandemic, Adidas opened a new store in Dubai in the UAE, blurring the lines of digital and physical touchpoints, again adding in the immersive fitting rooms to the store.

Activity 8.2   Analyse experiential value

- Find a virtual reality or augmented reality shopping app (search online or ask friends).
- Using the typology of experiential value as a framework, review the app and its functionality.
- Conduct an analysis into what works well and where improvements would be helpful.

8.4.2 DIMENSIONS OF INTERACTIVITY

There are said to be dimensions of interactivity (Heeter, 1989) which demonstrate the difference between new technology and the user's involvement, which are shown in Table 8.1. It is critical to understand these dimensions when creating an AR or a VR app for an organisation.

Applying this to different realities, the first dimension of interactivity about *choice* applies to the tools needed to access the different realities which is about the devices (such as headsets) and the programs (such as games or other apps). In general, an external headset is needed to access VR and the choice is limited and expensive. Augmented reality may require an app or a game to be downloaded and a mobile device. AR can function via mobile apps and companies like Blippar are working on 'augmented reality digital placement', which allows users to tap and see the AR features in adverts.

Dimension two, *the effort users must exert*, still exists as it's necessary to load the application, or use external headsets. However, the effort is being reduced with voice recognition, the development of better devices with longer battery life and improved network speed as we access 5G.

Table 8.1   Dimensions of interactivity

Dimensions of interactivity	What this means	Application to virtual reality	Application to augmented reality	Application to marketing
Complexity of choice available	When more choice is available, the audience is smaller and users need to interact to decide which medium to choose	Deciding which headset to select	Deciding which app to select	If devices such as headsets are needed, there will be fewer users which is why many companies focus on AR rather than VR in marketing
Effort users must exert	The amount of effort that users make to access information	The ease of use of tools such as headsets, screen size, battery performance, network speed		Access to the apps must be easy
Responsiveness to user	How real the medium is for the user	Whether the content is realistic and provides a full picture of the situation	How well the AR effects work in the app	If the apps don't work or provide an enhanced experience, they will be abandoned with negative feedback left online
Monitoring information use	New technology provides greater tracking of information accessed	All activities in the environment can be tracked		Organisations must follow local data protection guidelines
Ease of adding information	Users acting as the information source or content provider	Users can add their own content to VR apps	AR apps often have stickers or filters that can be created by users	The app must be easy to use, such as IKEA Place, where you click to select and add e.g. a chair into a room setting
Facilitation of interpersonal communication	Users can message and communicate with other users	Connected technology enables communication with others	Easy to share content with friends	Apps such as YouCam are trying to encourage users to follow others, but we don't know how successful this will be

Source: Adapted from Heeter (1989)

The third dimension, *responsiveness to user*, is the one area that's fast developing and has greatest impact on industrial contexts. For example, better headsets provide an increased field of view, improved graphics and the ability to use voice commands, and are more responsive than before. When the headsets are paired with connected clothing – gloves or smart wearables (see Chapter 7) which detect body movements – the user responsiveness increases and this enables greater functionality. Equally, the YouCam technology maps the face so closely that it provides 'hyper-realistic makeovers powered by revolutionary 3D face AR technology' (Perfect Corp, 2021, p. 1), which means it is responsive to the individual user and is one of the reasons this AR app has been so successful.

Monitoring information use, the fourth dimension, was originally considered by Heeter as having the ability to gain feedback and assess what worked where. Tracking is ubiquitous as all devices are tracked from the moment they are switched on. Privacy and data collection are a recurring theme in digital marketing and this is an area governed by legislation in all countries (see Chapter 1). In addition to the legislation, the large technology companies such as Microsoft publish their privacy principles to explain what data is collected, where and how. YouVisit monitors all visits and allows universities to see which other educational establishments the students are considering.

The next dimension, *ease of adding information*, depends on the application. Previously, this was considered as being how users contribute to product development through feedback. However, users are now creating content for both VR and AR apps. Sports coaches can add content, such as a tennis game, so the player and coach can work together to improve future performance. In Snapchat, users can create filters and stickers to share with friends, because, as digital consumers, the user has become the producer (see Chapter 2, 'The Digital Consumer'). The ease of performing a task relates back to one of the main factors in the Technology Acceptance Model (see Chapter 2).

Finally, the sixth dimension, *facilitation of interpersonal communication*, exists across the realities as individuals, whether playing games or using industrial applications, can interact with one another. But sometimes users may not want interaction and may ignore this function.

Having understood the key concepts, the next section will evaluate the realities.

ETHICAL INSIGHTS Deepfakes

As well as using AR and VR for a positive purpose, they've been used in negative ways, one of which is deepfakes. A person's image is mapped onto someone else and they are shown performing actions that never happened in real life. For example, in the USA a politician was shown to be slurring their words as if they had consumed too much alcohol. This was someone else with the politician's image added to make it seem as if it was real. Another example is movie stars being shown in film clips that they never made, which may damage their reputation.

- There are face-swapping apps which can be used to fake a situation – when is this OK?
- If we're in an age where deepfakes are everywhere, how can we tell if it's a real person or a fake?
- Is it the role of governments to create legislation or should technology companies manage these issues?

Smartphone Sixty Seconds® –Search for deepfakes

- Take out your mobile phone and search for deepfakes.
- What can you find?
- What are the main issues?
- How would you feel if your face was used in this way?

8.5 EVALUATION OF THE REALITIES

While games are for entertainment and some retail apps are for brand building or customer experience, when creating a VR, AR or MR application for business use, there should be a specific problem to solve. For example, IKEA's use of AR enabled consumers to place a piece of furniture in their home, to see if it fitted or not. This solved two problems: first, it removed a hurdle for a potential sale; and, second, it removed a potential return when the consumer is unable to fit the new table, bookcase or chair into their home.

8.5.1 BENEFITS OF REALITIES

We have seen how industry gains benefits such as saving time and money, and improving the customer experience. These are tangible benefits that are easy to quantify when justifying further expenditure in this area. Brands using VR claim benefits which include those discussed here.

VR and AR contribute to the customer journey

In Chapter 2, we considered the customer journey, and both VR and AR are recognised as having a role to play in moving consumers along this journey. For example, holidays often require planning, especially for far-away destinations. AR enables consumers to plan the trip before leaving home and can enhance the overall experience (Bec et al., 2021; Cranmer et al., 2020).

VR and AR add rich information to a setting

Richness of information is one of the six dimensions of presence in virtual environments. If the consumers are tourists who already travel with smartphones and often view a location through the smartphone, AR can provide more information (Cranmer et al., 2020).

Brands have also noted that engagement is higher in VR than web-based experience due to the immersion and richness of the experience.

VR and AR provide good data

As consumers use apps or download experiences, each one can be tracked, unlike a physical visit to a retail store, where it's unlikely your details would be gathered unless you made a purchase. These apps can capture significant user data, as well as the frequency and type of usage.

Equally, for students using YouView campus tours, greater data insights are provided than a physical tour with parents. Universities can assess their main competitors and which elements the students focus on most.

VR and AR provide environmental benefits

In travel and tourism, a study by Alexandra Bec and colleagues (2021) noted that virtual reality can protect or preserve a physical cultural heritage site. They noted that this may be useful where destinations are suffering deterioration or destruction as a result of too many visitors damaging the local ecosystem. Whilst not strictly a marketing benefit, their study suggested that 'virtual and mixed reality mediums can offer an alternative form of destination consumption to accommodate for the trends of social distancing and reduced movement' (p. 3).

Plus, there is a potential marketing benefit! These mini-tours could be chargeable, with consumers staying at home, visiting locations they've always dreamed of and contributing to the maintenance of heritage sites at risk.

8.5.2 CHALLENGES WITH THE REALITIES

The challenge of individual users is that all the realities need devices, whether that's the latest mobile phone with the capacity to run a high-memory game, a headset or other gaming device.

Access to equipment

Companies creating VR apps depend on consumers to have access to equipment such as headsets or cameras, although most smartphones have built-in cameras that work with AR.

Pricing is still a factor as to whether or not consumers gain access to the best VR experience. Although the better-quality headsets such as HoloLens are still outside most people's budgets, Samsung Gear and Oculus Rift headsets are now less than $300, with refurbished models under $50, bringing VR closer to more people. Snap's decision to invest in Spectacles, its AR glasses, may make this reality more readily available, but it's thought it will only work using Snap products such as Snapchat.

The cost of reality

The budget for building AR and VR apps should be considered. According to the BBC (2020, p. 1), budgets vary from low to high depending on the aim of the experience in virtual reality:

- £20K – low budget: Short experiences on mobile, perhaps using 2D assets in a 3D environment and viewed with Google Cardboard, Google Daydream or Samsung Gear VR

- £80K – medium budget: Short experiences with Google Cardboard, Google Daydream or Samsung Gear VR but with more scripting, character design, spatial audio and interactivity

- £150K+ – high budget: Scripted experiences with game-like production for high-end headsets such as HTC Vive and Oculus Rift in which the user can explore the environment

These are indications of the initial development costs, before any form of promotion or distribution. Plus, budgets increase when more features and functions are required.

Yet many organisations are adopting the realities, not just for marketing purposes, but also to improve business performance and save resources, in manufacturing and other sectors. The companies behind the technology who are making these industrial AR and VR applications are generating annual sales revenues of over $50 million (e.g. Iflexion, OTR, iTechArt). This indicates that it's a growing market.

Plus, Google, Microsoft, Facebook, Sony, Samsung and HTC have invested in this technology. Some tech companies share their software development kits to enable more companies to use and apply the realities. Microsoft has gone even further and has appointed mixed-reality business partners – these are firms with staff trained in mixed reality who can help other businesses wanting to adopt the realities.

We rarely learn about the apps or technology that didn't quite work. For example, Rimmel London hasn't removed its Get The Look app, although there is no mention of it on the company's website and perhaps it failed – we don't know. Another example on the technology side is Magic Leap, an alternative headset which was originally priced at over $2,000 but is less well known and it is not yet possible to predict its future. With Snap's Spectacles priced at under $350, the cost of the equipment may be decreasing.

Having developed an AR or a VR app, the next issue is whether it will be accepted by the target market. This takes us back to the Technology Acceptance Model (TAM) in Chapter 2. Consumers need to see the usefulness of the app which must be easy to use. Plus, any related hardware, such as headsets, needs to be affordable for a large enough audience to gain traction.

8.6 CREATING YOUR REALITIES

Before creating either a virtual or an augmented reality experience, you need to reflect on the earlier factors in this chapter as well as practical considerations which we'll explore here.

Purpose of the VR or AR experience

The purpose of the experience is the first element to consider. The experience has to add value for the consumer, as Mathwick et al. (2001) identified. This may include playfulness as a fun experience, or beauty as an aesthetic experience. The consumer needs to gain a benefit from downloading the app which is termed return on investment (Mathwick et al., 2001). The app must work to provide service excellence; if not, it gains poor reviews on the app store and may be abandoned.

As well as the experiential value, the purpose should address the six dimensions of presence to ascertain whether the purpose concerns richness, that is bringing the consumer closer to the brand, as the luxury brand Burberry offers with its in-store AR experiences. It could be realism, where specific parts of a product or location are to be showcased, or transportation, taking the consumer to somewhere else, enabling an escape from the present. If it's VR rather than AR, immersion should be considered where the purpose is to engage consumers fully in the experience.

Audience for the VR or AR experience

Who is the audience? Do they have access to smartphones or how will they see the experience? It's important to create personas (see Chapter 2) from the start and to understand the webographics profile of the audience. This involves reflecting on the dimensions of interactivity (Heeter, 1989) so the experience isn't complicated, is easy to use and responds to the consumer.

Focus of the VR or AR experience

What's the focus of the experience? For example, the brand Burberry uses handbags, Taco Bell, the food chain uses images of food, and a museum might focus on a painting. These companies use AR to move the consumer along the customer journey, from considering a purchase or a visit to making a purchase or booking. It's important to consider the focus before starting.

Materials needed for the VR or AR experience

What materials are available? You may need some images in advance of the items featuring in your realities. These need to be good quality, not glossy as they reflect too much light. You need to ensure you own the copyright to the images (see Chapter 4).

When you've decided on the purpose, the audience, the focus with some materials ready, you're set to create an experience. Explore Activity 8.3 to create your own AR business card.

It's worth noting that virtual reality is more complex to create than augmented reality as it requires coding knowledge along with specialist software.

DISCOVER MORE ON THE DIFFERENT TYPES OF AR

Read the blog on Hubspot that explains the different types of AR that can be created, with examples:

- https://blog.hubspot.com/marketing/augmented-reality-ar

Activity 8.3   Create your AR business card

To create an AR business card, you need to prepare your materials. Think about the contents of a traditional business card, such as your name, email or other contact details.

- For an AR business card, you'll need to prepare an image showing your contact details and perhaps a line about your skills.

(Continued)

- You can either record a short video introducing yourself – no more than 10 seconds – or use some emoticons or call-outs, such as arrows pointing to your email to 'contact me here'.
- Select a tool to create the AR experience, e.g. Overly (see overlyapp.com) or BlippBuilder (see blippar.com and search for education). Sign up for a free account and follow the on-screen instructions.
- When you're happy with your AR business card, you can save and publish it. Download the app to view your AR business card.

The future of reality

The realities are being used in many sectors to communicate key information, enhance the customer experience, build brand awareness or generate sales. Larger retail brands like Nike and Adidas are leading the field in moving this to the next stage where the consumer doesn't need other equipment, such as in their virtual fitting rooms. Where one brand leads, others are likely to follow.

Applications for the realities will grow as:

- Headsets become more comfortable to wear, being smaller and lighter
- Tethered headsets become less common as wireless connections are adopted, enabling greater freedom to move
- The cost of the equipment reduces
- Mobile systems improve, with easy connectivity to 5G, bringing faster download speeds

Skin electronics

In the future, we may not need equipment to access VR or AR – we could become our own devices! Thinking of the external equipment needed to process the realities, one solution considered by Dr Jae Joon Kim and colleagues from the University of Tokyo (2021) is skin electronics. Soft electronic materials would be stuck onto the skin, as wearable devices.

This takes the idea of a wearable watch or wristband to the next level, miniaturising it and making it more like a Band-Aid or adhesive plaster. Figure 8.4 shows an example of the differences between conventional and skin electronic VR/AR devices.

Conventional VR/AR Devices:
- Rigid and Thick
- Heavy
- High Wearing Discomfort
- Limited Skin Sensing
- Limited User Physiology

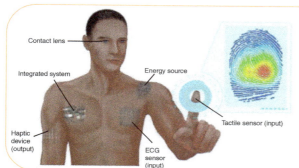

Skin Electronic VR/AR Devices:
- Flexible and Thin
- Lightweight
- Low Wearing Discomfort
- Less-limited Skin Sensing
- Less-limited User Physiology

Figure 8.4 The differences between conventional and skin electronic VR/AR devices

Source: Kim et al. (2021, p. 2)

DISCOVER MORE ABOUT THE FUTURE OF AR AND VR

Professor Philipp A. Rauschnabel writes about AR and VR in an article published in the *International Journal of Information Management* entitled 'Augmented reality is eating the real-world! The substitution of physical products by holograms' (2021). It explains more about the future of the realties, such as how we will be streaming Netflix via an app, onto a wall, without the need for a TV screen.

A further factor to consider is that as the pandemic led to many people working from home, it is likely that this trend will continue. Many people will travel to the office less frequently. This means we will see the growth of shared reality, where teams wear headsets, as if they are in the same room, accessing the same materials or co-designing products.

In addition to sharing, remote assistance will be easier to access, as technical experts will be able to see where the difficulties exist and solve these faster or before we've realised that they've become issues.

JOURNAL OF NOTE

Exploring the use of computers from a psychological perspective, the journal *Computers in Human Behavior* contains several articles on the different realities and technology.

CASE STUDY

SHOULD STRAVA ADOPT AR?

This continues our long case study and you may find it helpful to read earlier parts in previous chapters.

Gabriel has just finished a management meeting on Zoom. The big conversation was all about improving reality. During the COVID-19 pandemic, as people went into lockdown worldwide, the number of Strava users increased as people were allowed to exercise outdoors, but there was then a decline as the winter months made outdoor running less appealing. Who'd want to get up for an 8 a.m. run when it's minus 2 and icy underfoot?

One of the management team shared information about an online conference she'd attended which was all about augmented reality fitness apps. Not everyone is a runner and as Strava has added more activities to its app, the audience is changing. Families went out for brisk walks around the park but those with younger children needed greater incentives to keep moving. Some schools tried to add gamification to outdoor activities, using AR to get children moving by chasing monsters as part of the exercise program.

In the meeting, Gabriel saw some heated conversations as those who had worked at Strava for many years weren't keen on any part of this, saying it wasn't what Strava was designed for. Others thought it may be a great way to connect with totally different audiences and argued that it's possible that families may continue with park walks.

Gabriel thought that some of the team may have found an interesting way around this by connecting other apps to Strava, such as overlaying their activities and seeing them in AR. Fitness AR seemed like an interesting tool, but was bought by Mapbox some years ago. But the real opportunity was the increase in use of static machines. With gyms being closed, the specialist interactive exercise technology company Peleton watched as its sales skyrocketed during the pandemic, with wealthier individuals purchasing immersive bikes at over $1,500 each and treadmills at over $2,000. These bikes and treadmills need run routes and Veloreality offered a range of exciting places from around the world to run or cycle to – from your own home and in cinema quality.

While Gabriel's role is managing content, there was a request for more on how the app can be used with AR to enhance the experience. Users wouldn't need googles, but they might need some expensive home gym kit for this to work. Gabriel has two days to come up with some ideas for how best to include more content about VR and AR in the content they create.

CASE QUESTIONS

- Imagine you're in Gabriel's role and managing content at Strava. What are the first stories you would create on AR and VR and how would you pitch them to the management team?

- What is your experience of AR or VR in an exercise or fitness context – something you have used or not yet? Discuss how the future of AR or VR may develop in this sector.

- Have we become more digital as a result of the pandemic and has this changed our relationship with the real world?

FURTHER EXERCISES

1. What application do you see for group AR or VR experiences within organisations? What might be the advantages and disadvantages?

2. Imagine that you are working as a marketing manager in an organisation of your choice and several members of the management team are keen on the idea of VR or AR. You have been asked to evaluate the realities and make recommendations as to whether they should develop an AR or a VR app.

3. Although VR or AR can be used positively to enhance the customer journey, what are the potential downsides for organisations?

4. AR and VR are already present in our world and we will continue to use these tools in different formats. Discuss whether those who are not ready to do so will be left behind. Provide examples in your arguments.

SUMMARY

This chapter has explored:

- The different realities and what these mean
- The Technology Readiness Scale
- Application of different realities for marketing
- Typology of experiential values
- Benefits and challenges with realities

GO ONLINE

Visit **study.sagepub.com/hanlon2e** to access links to interesting articles, websites and videos related to this chapter.

PART 3

DIGITAL MARKETING STRATEGY AND PLANNING

CONTENTS

9 Digital Marketing Audit   241
10 Digital Marketing Strategy and Objectives   269
11 Building the Digital Marketing Plan   299

Apply social listening skills

Evaluate competitors

Market sensing

ACTIVITIES

OVERVIEW
Chapter 9 explains the benefits and practicalities in conducting a digital marketing audit. From understanding the marketing to assessing customer needs and how to gather data for analysis.

Conduct sentiment analysis

KEY CONCEPTS

DIGITAL TOOLS

Capability and competence

Chatbots

Discover how to extract competitor customer comments

Explore online tools being used with twdocs.com

9

DIGITAL MARKETING AUDIT

PROFESSIONAL SKILLS

When you have worked through this chapter, you should be able to:

- Use social listening skills
- Construct a digital marketing audit

9.1 INTRODUCTION TO DIGITAL MARKETING AUDITS

To stay relevant organisations need to understand the market in which they operate. Those that fail to see and respond to these changes often close and disappear as their customers have already moved on.

To assess a market, you can conduct a digital marketing audit (sometimes called a situational analysis), where you analyse the overall circumstances of the organisation. The key factor here is not just gathering the data but making sense of what it means to the organisation and responding accordingly. This has been better described as 'market sensing', attributed to Professor George Day (1994), which is 'a business's ability to acutely understand and have an insight of the macromarket environment or the operating ecosystem and its potential impact on competitors, customers, and other stakeholders' (Bayighomog Likoum et al., 2020, p. 596). Therefore, the aptitude to conduct an audit is an essential skill for marketers.

A digital marketing audit provides a solid foundation on which to build your digital strategy. It ensures you have a full understanding of the critical internal and external factors covering all aspects of the organisation before building a strategy and developing a plan.

This chapter shares the essential elements for creating a digital marketing audit. You will learn how to discover threats and opportunities before they emerge, with useful frameworks to structure your analysis.

9.2 WHY DIGITAL MARKETING AUDITS ARE ESSENTIAL

There is a temptation to launch tactics such as advertising on social media, building a website, developing an email campaign or making major decisions such as moving into a new market, but without real evidence.

Without a review before you start, the social media campaign might miss the right audience, the website may not speak to your real target customers and the email campaign may render negative results.

A digital marketing audit provides a clear picture of the landscape in which you are operating, whether it's a juice bar or a software business. It highlights competitors, key issues in the sector and makes the team think about the worst-case scenarios, being prepared for external events which could damage the organisation – what could happen if ...?

Some marketers believe an audit is a waste of time and think that as change happens so quickly, it's better to learn to adapt instead. Yet, when carried out well, advance planning can predict potential changes and enable organisations to cope better when change happens.

An essential aspect of a digital marketing audit is the use of the models and frameworks that provide a structured approach to gathering data, reviewing, analysing and comparing information, to arrive at effective recommendations. This is not a one-off and is a cyclical process; the audit takes place before the strategy is created and long before the plan or tactical campaigns are launched.

9.3 MARKET SENSING IN A DIGITAL CONTEXT

Market sensing (Day, 1994) is a deep ability to assess a market, its environment, emerging or future trends, and to analyse why this information matters to organisations. It moves beyond market research and the process of gathering data, by adding expertise to assess and interpret what this means and how it may disrupt the situation. You could describe this as making sense of the context in which the organisation is situated, whether it's a non-profit, community, government, consumer brand or commercial structure.

An example of market sensing was the process adopted by the UK's Oxford vaccine team, led by Professor Sarah Gilbert, who had been preparing for a lethal and unknown strain of the SARS virus which they named 'Disease X'. As part of their work towards defeating new viruses, they had been scanning the environment and preparing responses for several years. Their deep knowledge and research into understanding how viruses are transmitted, combined with the ability to make sense of global diseases, ensured that they were able to introduce a new product and deliver a stable coronavirus vaccine in record time.

Market sensing starts with information gathering, progresses to information analysis and concludes by using the information or responding to the situation, as shown in Figure 9.1. I've adapted the model for a digital marketing audit as market sensing includes assessing customer value; in this version, we're looking at an overview of assessing customers, as Chapter 13 explores customer value.

The following sections investigate each of these stages.

9.4 UNDERSTANDING THE MARKET

Understanding the market is the first stage in market sensing and this is sub-divided into two parts: the micro- and macro-environment analysis.

There are debates about what constitutes the micro- and macro-environment, as well as the internal and external environment. Typically, the internal environment relates to the organisation and its staff, whereas the micro-environment also includes others directly connected to the internal environment such as competitors, customers, suppliers and other stakeholders.

The macro-environment includes wider stakeholders, foreign competitors and PESTLE factors. In a digital setting, all competitors, whether foreign or local, are competitors, as we can order online from Amazon, Alibaba, eBay or Instagram without considering where the supplier is located. So, in this digital setting, the micro-environment – or the smaller space where we have some control – includes the organisation, plus its supply chain, and the macro environment includes PESTLE factors.

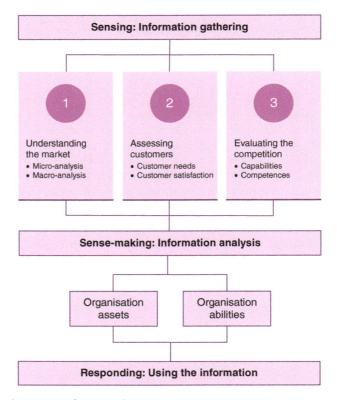

Figure 9.1 Market sensing framework

In market sensing, the competitors are often considered separately as they may not be typical product rivals. For example, many hoteliers initially dismissed the idea of Airbnb, claiming that it would never replace a hotel room. While that may be correct, sometimes people don't *need* a hotel room, they *want* an experience, such as to stay in a tree house, on a boat, or in an aeroplane apartment. This indicates that although it's not a typical or direct competitor, it's competing for a share of the customer wallet, which makes it a competitor.

The other difference in market sensing is to consider customers as a distinct area, rather than adding to the micro-environment.

It's necessary to include both the micro- and macro-analysis elements because an audit that only considers internal factors may miss major external factors and vice versa. For example, taxi-cabs worldwide only considered their own business, rather than the wider environment, which provided opportunities for Uber to use digital methods to enter well-established traditional market sectors. The response – which came too late – was to try to use legal means to stop Uber in different locations, which worked in some places, but failed in many others as the app is now available in over

10,000 cities worldwide. Perhaps taxi firms conducted a micro-analysis and looked at their local competitors but ignored overseas entrants that accessed the market using digital tools. Early market sensing may have resulted in a different outcome, such as enabling taxi firms to adapt their business approach and create more digital barriers to market entry.

9.4.1 MICRO-ENVIRONMENT ANALYSIS

To conduct a micro-environment analysis and assess the organisation, it is useful to apply a framework, so that we can compare with competitors in the next stage of market sensing. As an example, I've used the original 7Ps (Booms and Bitner, 1980) in a digital setting. The reason for choosing the 7Ps as a framework is that the 'Ps' are all within the control of the organisation and they can turn the weaknesses into strengths where needed.

Let's explore an overview of where the digital strengths and weaknesses of an organisation can be found for an online retailer. For more on the 7Ps in a digital context, refer back to Chapter 1 which considers digital products, places, payments and processes.

Digital place

Place is the location and in a digital context refers to digital spaces where the customer journey (see Chapter 2) can happen.

In online retail, the primary place is the organisation's own website as it's their owned media (see Chapter 4) that they control. Digital strengths include the pre-purchase and the purchase stages taking place via other locations too, such as social media or via intermediaries.

In a digital context, the idea of place is dynamic. For example, the website can expand with dedicated URL extensions for other countries, such as: .com, .co.uk, .ie, as a further strength is being able to see where consumers are located as they share their address details for delivery. So, if there were many consumers from Norway or Australia, the company may decide to establish a dedicated .no or .au extension to adapt the content and reflect the local language. So the website data helps the process of identifying new markets.

Digital weaknesses will occur when the website is not working.

Digital people

In a digital context, we often consider the digital skills of the staff. Chapter 12 considers digital capabilities, roles and responsibilities in more depth. As an example, some online retailers may have a planned approach where staff undertake digital training or award-bearing courses to upskill their knowledge. A weakness would occur if the training was less organised and lacked structure.

Another area which is both a strength and weakness is the levels of technology adoption or readiness. Chapter 2 considered the Technology Acceptance Model and Chapter 8 explored Technology Readiness Levels. Some organisations may embrace new technology and encourage and support their staff to do the same. Others may only do what's necessary which can lead to falling behind.

Responding to consumers' questions via live chat is part of the digital people role. Where there are frequently asked questions, these can be managed by **chatbots**. They provide a front-line service for consumers, but are based on text-based programmes that look for the keywords and respond. Sometimes they get this wrong which is when real people take over in a live chat session.

KEY TERM   CHATBOTS

Chatbots provide human–machine interaction. The name comes from chatter + robot and chatbots are also called conversational agents, conversational tools or voicebots. Often found on websites or apps, they have existed since 2000. The first was named ALICE (Artificial Linguistic Internet Computer Entity).

We are seeing newer forms of chatbots including woebots, where people share anxiety with these automated systems (Lee et al., 2020).

Digital processes

For online retailers, there are many processes including order management, logistics and delivery, as well as data protection.

Strengths include a digitally integrated and automated supply chain process. This requires several steps from the ecommerce website to delivery to consumers. So when an online order is placed, the item is checked out of the inventory or warehouse, with an automatic order processing system. Weaknesses might be manual processes (e.g. individually printed shipping labels), and this is where things can go wrong if orders are mixed up. Although it seems like this is about logistics rather than marketing, ensuring smooth delivery is a key factor in customer reviews.

Managing data is another digital process. Data protection policies and procedures (see Chapter 1) are often in place throughout online stores as there are severe penalties if these guidelines are ignored.

During the pandemic, online stores with digitally enabled business infrastructures were instantly able to move to remote working. With cloud-based systems in place, they did not need to visit their warehouses. So, they could continue delivering products and maintain levels of customer service.

Digital (physical) evidence

In online retail, physical evidence includes factors such as the usability of the website and the user experience (see Chapter 3). When selling products online, companies often use web security seals (search online for examples) which can help in providing trust signals to consumers.

Another issue concerns transparency from suppliers. Information showing the materials used which is added to product descriptions, has become more important for consumers as part of the 'information quality' that is required (Tzeng et al., 2021, p. 519).

Digital products

Digital application of the products in the 7Ps can include the innovation and development of new products, especially for online retailers. Online stores are more easily able to create or adopt new products based on customer demand. The web team can see where product sales are declining or increasing.

The search terms that consumers are using within the website can be monitored to assess where there is demand for specific items. In addition, the worst-selling products can be offered at reduced rates and removed from the website in the future.

Digital pricing

Pricing in a digital setting can be dynamic and automated, having the ability to change based on external factors, such as reduced supply. Online retailers can offer time-limited discount codes and assess the number of consumers who respond to the deals.

A weakness may include fixed or rigid pricing systems that remain the same, even when competitors change their prices.

Digital promotion

Earlier chapters consider promotion in more detail (see Chapters 3, 4, 5, 6), so this section outlines the key strengths and weaknesses for online retail.

For online retailers, gathering marketing data to inform promotion campaigns is easier in a digital setting. There is an instant ability to gather the number of web visits, the top website landing and exit pages, and to decide where to focus marketing promotion activities.

When the consumer data has been gathered, it can be used for dynamic and personalised online promotion, such as finding similar consumers on social media.

This is an example of how to apply the 7Ps in a digital context. It doesn't address all the offline elements which may be involved. And don't get tied up about which model to use! You can use any framework that works for you, as long as you are consistent and use the same tool for comparative analysis. Plus, you can adapt models to suit your needs, by adding and removing elements to better fit the context of your organisation.

9.4.2 MACRO-ENVIRONMENT ANALYSIS

A macro-environment analysis considers issues outside the organisation, which in theory are beyond the organisation's control and are located within the wider market.

The best-known frameworks are probably PEST or PESTLE, which are mnemonics for political, economic, social, technological, legal and environmental. If the 4Ps are dead, perhaps so too is the PESTLE model! In 2006 George Burt and colleagues reviewed PESTLE (also called PEST, STEEP – it all depends on your tutor) and suggested that there were limitations to using the model, not least of which was trying to define the environment (Burt et al., 2006). If you consider the global pandemic of 2020, how many organisations had accounted for this within a PESTLE? But in the absence of other models that consider macro-factors it's a useful notion, which we will explore.

Rather than listing the PESTLE factors, Case Example 9.1 shows the digital PESTLE for a well-known Norwegian brand, Helly Hansen. A digital PESTLE is often presented in a table structure, but that often lacks depth, so I've approached this by using separate paragraphs which enable further discussion, as well as the inclusion of further academic underpinning.

CASE EXAMPLE 9.1   Helly Hansen's digital PESTLE

Helly Hansen is recognised as a quality brand in many countries. It was started in Norway in 1877 by a sea captain named Helly Juell Hansen who was looking for a better way to stay warm and dry in the harsh seas around Norway and the North Atlantic Ocean.

For a business that has existed for over 145 years, the product offer includes skiing, sailing and outdoor clothing for professional sportspeople, explorers and workers. Its clothing is used by lifeboat crews, Olympic athletes and rescue services across the world. However, the company has made mistakes at times by targeting the wrong customers, but ultimately managed to return to its core values and regain customers.

Using the PESTLE framework, we can evaluate Helly Hansen's digital threats and opportunities.

Political factors

The majority of Helly Hansen clothing is made in China, Bangladesh and Vietnam. Digital threats may emerge due to the **country of origin (COO) effect** (see Discover More) which concerns consumer perception about where the goods were manufactured, regardless of where they are actually made. As a Norwegian brand, it may be assumed the clothing is locally made. Knowing that goods are produced in other countries may negatively impact on the brand. This happens when consumers feel animosity towards any of the countries of origin, or if political or economic issues arise, such as trade wars or increased taxes on products from specific countries (Huang and Wang, 2020).

However, Helly Hansen adopts a transparent approach and shares the detail on its website, even naming the individual factories where the goods are made. So digital opportunities may arise due to this transparency which mitigates potential threats concerning non-disclosure and COO.

Helly Hansen has strong codes of ethics displayed online which show its approach to suppliers. There may be further digital opportunities to demonstrate the benefits of global trading with online interviews of overseas workers. This could further enhance the online authenticity of the brand.

Economic factors

When consumers are aware of a brand name, they may search online and buy at the cheapest price which may turn the brand into a commodity. Another economic digital threat for Helly Hansen is the possibility of fakes being sold in online auctions, reducing the value of genuine products.

There are digital storytelling opportunities (see Chapter 4) to explain the differences between fake and genuine goods, because global counterfeiting grows each year, resulting in company losses, reduction in taxes to governments and ownership of poor-quality products. Yet consumers are unaware of this impact (Harun et al., 2020).

Social factors

The rise of **consumer ethnocentrism** (see Key Term) where people believe that it is immoral to buy foreign-made goods and should focus on locally manufactured items, for reasons such as better quality, or fewer airmiles, are factors for organisations like Helly Hansen to consider (Huaman-Ramirez et al., 2019). The move away from globalisation towards localisation may be an issue that Helly Hansen has to consider, especially if activists launch an online campaign.

However, other Norwegian brands known for technical clothing, such as Sweet Protection, also manufacture overseas. It may be that it is accepted that it is too expensive to manufacture clothing in Norway, but this is not entirely clear.

Technological factors

The main digital threats to professional clothing may be the introduction of smart elements, such as those discussed in Chapter 8, as competitors could offer smart clothing for harsh environment workplaces.

The oilskin-type jackets used by lifeboat crews could include trackers and other devices to alert the land stations if there is a problem at sea. There may be other opportunities to promote the technical capabilities in the existing clothing, using video or user-generated content, showing how it's made and where it's used.

Legal factors

A potential legal issue is the misuse or loss of data. Many major brands, such as British Airways, have been hacked and lost customer data which damages the company's reputation.

Another example is a misguided employee creating fake reviews to improve their employer's online ranking; its distribution chain, including hundreds of online stores, may take legal action against the brand.

(Continued)

To counter these issues, Helly Hansen should share guidelines and policies so that weak behaviour, such as generating fake content, does not occur. Additionally, the firm might create a data management plan, especially for staff working from home, so that personal devices cannot be compromised by family members.

Environmental factors

The rise of fast fashion is having a major impact on our environment, with millions of litres of water used in clothing production, as well as harsh chemicals. It seems that Helly Hansen is ahead of the curve as its website contains a section on sustainability, explaining how it is reducing its environmental impact. The website recommends that customers should repair the clothing rather than rebuy, using the repair kits provided with some products. There are opportunities to showcase this approach across the company's social media, using hashtags such as #repair or #reuse.

Since 2008, the company has been a member of bluesign®, an independent system to ensure that products are produced with responsibility towards the environment and pose no health hazards. However, it still has some products that are not up to this standard. Helly Hansen is very aware of this so is less likely to encounter threats from negative social media comments.

Consumers have greater awareness now of the move from 'fast fashion' to more sustainable goods and the website contains guidance on re-use of the goods, whether donating to a charity shop or re-selling online. This is a recurring theme and Helly Hansen will need to monitor this closely.

Case questions

- What is missing from this evaluation? Can you add further threats and turn them into opportunities for Helly Hansen?
- Which of the many digital opportunities should Helly Hansen address first? Explain which elements should be prioritised and why.
- How do you feel about fake products? Is it acceptable for companies to copy long-established brands?

Having better understood the market, the next stage is to assess value for the customer.

KEY TERM CONSUMER ETHNOCENTRISM

Consumer ethnocentrism (CE) was originally 'described as a belief or attitude concerning the appropriateness and morality of purchasing foreign products' (Sun et al., 2021, p. 565), where consumers prefer products or services from their home country rather than others. However, it's now seen as more than an attitude and can be due to national pride.

> ### DISCOVER MORE ON COUNTRY OF ORIGIN (COO) EFFECT
>
> Country of origin (COO) effect is a country bias where consumers believe goods from some countries are better than others. The article 'Country-of-origin effects in celebrity endorsements: the case of China' by Xiao Tong and Jin Su, published in the *International Journal of Fashion Design, Technology and Education* (2021), explains how COO impacts consumers' brand decisions.

9.5 ASSESSING DIGITAL CUSTOMERS

Having understood the market, it's time to assess how customers feel, which is at the heart of marketing. This considers what the customer is seeking, whether your organisation can provide this and customer satisfaction.

9.5.1 ASSESSING CUSTOMER NEEDS ONLINE

Understanding the customer is the essence of a successful organisation, although not all organisations bother to find out! When a customer initiates contact, the question is, what are they seeking? Other than complaining (see how to manage different types of online complaints in Chapter 6), the main reasons why customers make contact with organisations are to seek information, request advice, register or subscribe, or make a purchase.

Organisations can assess customer needs through data from web analytics software, such as website searches, pages visited and baskets abandoned. Online surveys can provide insights and are popular because they are fast and inexpensive. In addition, free tools such as crowdsignal.com and surveymonkey.com can capture the data. These appear as a website pop-up request as visitors arrive at, or leave, a web page.

The growth in **chatbots** (see Key Term), encouraging customers to 'chat now' and say what they need, with automated instant responses, also feeds into the data to assess customer value. All transcripts from chatbots and human chat sessions can be reviewed to understand why help is needed.

9.5.2 SOCIAL LISTENING

One way of assessing customer needs is by watching and listening to them. This is a form of social media monitoring which was defined as 'an active process of attending to, observing, interpreting, and responding to a variety of stimuli through mediated, electronic, and social channels' (Stewart and Arnold, 2018, p. 86). The critical factor is that this is an active rather than accidental process.

A study by LaTour and Brant examined a luxury hotel brand, the Dorchester Collection, and how it used social listening. They found that due to social listening, the hotel group 'changed its usage of social media from focusing on communications to experience management' (2021, p. 1). They explain how the brand gave responsibility for social listening to the customer experience team. To ensure they had the **competence** (see Key Terms) to respond, the team trained its staff in how to read guests' content. The customer experience team has been given the **capability** (see Key Terms) to respond, by following the process shown in Figure 9.2 and being empowered to make decisions.

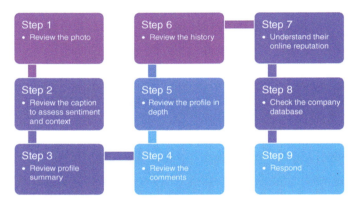

Figure 9.2   Manual social listening process

Source: Adapted from LaTour and Brant (2021, pp. 6–7)

Figure 9.2 is a manual social listening process that starts when guests tag the Dorchester in their Instagram feed. In step 1, customer experience team members check the photo to ensure it's appropriate and has a connection to the hotel. At step 2, they read the caption to check the language is acceptable and assess the sentiment (see Key Term in Chapter 5). If it's positive, they generally respond because the user already loves the brand; if it's negative, they send a direct message to take the conversation offline. If the post is neutral, they watch and wait.

In step 3, team members briefly review the guest's profile summary to learn more. In step 4, they examine the feedback from friends and check the sentiment. If those steps are positive, they continue to steps 5, 6 and 7 where they closely review the guest's profile, check older posts and Google their name to explore their online reputation. Step 8 checks if the guest has stayed before, or with other hotels in the group. Finally, they respond.

This takes time and effort. As the Dorchester Collection is a super-luxury brand, it can afford to do this. There are fewer guests, but they spend more. At the other extreme, an online retailer selling thousands of products each day at lower prices can't spend this much time and effort on listening to consumers. So, it would use social media listening tools such as Hootsuite (see Case Example 13.2 in Chapter 13).

KEY TERMS   CAPABILITY AND COMPETENCE

Capability is having the ability or processes in place to do something. For example, a small business website may have a bandwidth that's capable of managing 5,000 visitors over a month, whereas a major online retailer's website may need the capability to manage 50,000 visitors. If the small business received 50,000 visitors, the website would probably crash due to the smaller data hosting package as it lacks the capability to manage such volume.

Competence is having the skill or knowledge to perform a task. For example, at work people are often measured on their expertise to carry out certain pieces of work, such as creating online adverts, planning content schedules or managing an online community. Whilst studying, you're building your competency levels.

Activity 9.1   Apply social listening skills

Select an organisation of your choice or somewhere you are working:

- Select one of your chosen organisation's social media pages.
- Look at comments from customers.
- Apply social listening skills using steps 1 to 7 shown in Figure 9.2.
- Identify opportunities to respond to the customers.

Smartphone Sixty Seconds® – Social listening tools

- Take out your mobile and search for *social listening tools*.
- How many can you find?
- Look again and this time search for *social listening tools free* and you'll see that the list decreases.
- Explore what the different tools offer and how they vary.

9.5.3 CAPTURING CUSTOMER SATISFACTION

Customer satisfaction is described as a comparative assessment of a customer's post-purchase experience based on their expected understanding – did you receive what you expected? Was it better or worse? Researchers (Amangala and Wali, 2020) have identified two main types of customer satisfaction:

- **Transaction-specific satisfaction**: A customer's evaluation of their experience on a particular exchange or service encounter
- **Cumulative satisfaction**: The customer's overall and accumulated evaluation of exchanges or encounters with a specific product or service provider over a period of time

According to researchers (Farah and Ramadan, 2020), customer satisfaction is essential for brands as it has a positive impact on customer loyalty. It is recognised as a critical aspect of creating positive online comments, inspiring existing customers to return and new customers to come on board.

One company that assesses its customer value is the Winning Group (see Case Example 9.2) who regularly gather customer feedback.

CASE EXAMPLE 9.2   The Winning Group – we say YES
in a no world

Winning Group in Australia sells kitchens, washing machines, barbeques – every home product you could consider. They have physical stores and a website. A family business that started over 100 years ago, its focus is on helping the customer with its expert knowledge, excellent service and a range of exclusive brands.

The Group's mission is 'to provide the best shopping experience in the world'. A Net Promoter Score® (see Key Term **Net Promoter Score®** in Chapter 2) of over 85 in one week where they made over 3,500 deliveries (Bencic, 2020, p. 1) is impressive. A score over 40 is fairly good, over 50 is good, over 60 is very good, but 85 is amazing and indicates the customers are very happy with the service.

You may think that this successful company does not need to conduct a digital marketing audit but its website explains the focus on digital marketing (Winning Group, 2021): 'From using machine learning to measure the results of advertising, to automating and personalising the marketing experience to individual visitors, our digital marketing is all about data-driven creativity.' This data-driven approach ensures that the website continues to deliver what's needed. Working with the chief strategist, the user experience (UX) team analyses the data for greater insights, being able to review which pages work best, where customers leave the website and the time it takes to return.

Although the name of the brand comes from the founder's last name, the company clearly is winning, with new awards every year in categories including online retail, online customer excellence and internet retail. The business seems to be based on a passion for customer excellence that's supported by data.

Case questions

- The Winning Group uses NPS® – what other methods could the company use to gather more in-depth consumer insights online?
- How might the Winning Group use online reviews for market sensing?
- Why do consumers spend time participating in online surveys or creating online reviews?

9.6 MONITORING THE DIGITAL COMPETITION

All organisations have competitors! If you work in the third sector, within a charity or government department, it may appear that there are no competitors. However, all those organisations competing for a share of the wallet are competitors. If you operate in the same sector with the same target consumers, these are direct competitors; if a possible donor is considering your organisation or another that is completely different, this is an indirect competitor.

Even those working in the public sector, in government to consumer roles, have competitors. Typically, governments allocate budgets based on a range of political and economic factors. So, if your government department or public sector body has experienced budget cuts, it's because others have taken your share.

A competitor review provides a benchmark of how others are performing. This stage of the digital marketing audit involves asking:

- What are the key digital strengths and weaknesses of the key competitors' capabilities?
- What are the key digital strengths and weaknesses of the key competitors' competences?

Some organisations may have the **capability** to do something but lack staff with the **competence** (see Key Terms) to make it happen, so they may need to recruit skilled staff. In other situations, the staff may be competent, but the organisation's infrastructure lacks the capabilities needed, such as older technology which frequently fails. In these cases, staff may leave due to frustration and not being able to perform their tasks more easily.

We can use a framework to evaluate the competitors and compare like with like, which provides more objectivity and highlights potential gaps.

9.6.1 THE DIGITAL 7CS FOR COMPETITOR EVALUATION

The 'Ten Cs of marketing for the modern economy' was created as a 'useful framework for marketers assessing for the modern digital marketscape from both an internal and external perspective' (Gay et al., 2007, p. 12). However, in a digital context there is duplication and I have adapted and removed (a) creative content, which incorporates online communications, (b) control, as it's difficult to assess how competitors measure their results, (c) coordination, which sits within consistency, and swapped (d) the positions of customer and competitor – as this is being used as a tool to evaluate competitors, they are placed in the centre. This results in a revised model which I call the digital 7Cs for competitor evaluation and is shown in Figure 9.3 and explored further in this section.

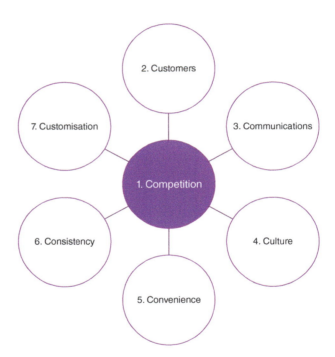

Figure 9.3   The digital 7Cs for competitor evaluation

Source: Adapted from Gay et al. (2007)

Let's examine each element of the digital 7Cs for competitor evaluation.

1 Competition

One challenge most businesses face is disruptive marketing, where competitors who were previously unknown suddenly appear, as if from nowhere, changing the rules of that market. Disruption was originally defined as 'a process whereby a smaller company with fewer resources is able to successfully challenge established incumbent businesses' (Christensen et al., 2015, p. 46). Disruption was classified as a process where companies target the edges of a market or the areas that are not well served, rather than the mainstream. For example, Zipcar is an online alternative to car ownership or long-term rental (join online and hire a car by the hour or day). It is aimed at those who don't have, need or want a car, such as those living in cities where parking is complicated and expensive, but sometimes need a vehicle to collect or transport things. This market wasn't served by traditional rental companies who seek a minimum rental period with a fairly complex process to access and return the car.

The process used to disrupt a market often relates to technology which could be introducing an app, offering additional functionality (find me now, pay now), or reintermediation – reintroducing intermediaries to manage a process, such as the Danish company Just Eat, as a bridge between customers and smaller food outlets.

However, not all disruptive efforts succeed, but they have a different approach to business. Shyp (pronounced 'ship') was an on-demand delivery app to make logistics easier. Using your mobile, you took a photo and added it to the app, then the goods were collected and delivered. This sounded like a disrupter to the logistics market but failed as the cost was too low – just $5 – and the customers were mainly individuals who didn't use the service often enough for it to succeed.

2 Customers

The framework starts by understanding the target audience or personas (see Chapter 4) that the competitors are seeking.

Some competitors are not interested in your customers because their capabilities are managing companies of a certain size, or those with specific needs or certain situations. For example, the digital company Conversion Rate Experts (see conversion-rate-experts.com) promotes its capabilities to larger companies, by stating on its website: 'Note that we can work with your company only if it generates over $250,000 or the equivalent in your local currency.' So if you're working for a smaller agency, but providing similar services, you are not aiming for the same customers. Different processes or capabilities are needed to manage larger organisations.

The online fashion retailer ASOS's main competence is creating relevant products for customers who are 'fashion-loving 20-somethings'. Its capability is creating social media posts which engage the audience and the company has recruited ASOS-Insiders (see Chapter 4) to generate relevant content and to enhance this skill.

3 Communications

Social media has changed brand communications from the typical monologue and dialogue to a trialogue. Research has examined relationships between consumers and brands through the use of social media brand pages – such as the company's Facebook, Instagram or other social media pages. One study identified that consumers gain social benefits where they feel connected to others or they gain special treatment with rewards or discounts (Tsimonis et al., 2020).

As social media brand pages are open to anyone, these pages provide rich data sources for research. However, there are ethical issues about gathering data without consent (see Ethical Insights: Posting for fun not research). In a digital marketing audit, reviewing competitors involves examining what's being said and where, and how this presents opportunities or threats for the organisation. Studying an organisation's responses to customers on social media demonstrates their brand voice, so you can assess whether this is formal or informal, fun or serious (see Digital Tool **Extracting competitor customer comments**). You can examine how these responses meet the needs of the customers and assess whether they solve their issues.

DIGITAL TOOL   Extracting competitor customer comments

There are several tools which allow you to go to a web page and extract the data, which makes the analysis much easier. Free tools, which have limited access at a basic level, include:

- octoparse.com
- parsehub.com
- data-miner.io

These tools allow you to visit a web page and download content from a website to an Excel-type file.

Based on company processes, some organisations reply to comments personally whilst others use the brand name. This depends on the number of staff managing the online communications and on company policies. Many organisations have increased their capability by using tools such as Hootsuite or Sprout Social which allow them to assign responses to different people to better manage communications. You can see which tools are being used with **twdocs.com** (see Digital Tool).

DIGITAL TOOL   twdocs.com

The Twitter tool twdocs.com allows you to freely download ten elements of Twitter data from an organisation which shows the communications tools they may use to manage their social media. You'll need a Twitter account to access the data. Visit twdocs.com and follow the on-screen instructions to download, for example, the latest ten tweets from your chosen company. You'll be given an Excel document to open and the last column shows the social media management tools being used.

ETHICAL INSIGHTS   Posting for fun not research

Individuals post content on social media brand pages for many reasons, including entertainment, seeking responses to questions or sharing content with friends. However, they may not be consciously creating content for research purposes and might not give consent to their data being used for research, even if they are aware of this. Ackland (2013) has identified three main concerns about social media research:

Informed consent. Do the participants know the research is taking place? And from whom? Informed consent may be difficult to obtain from all group members, companies using the social media platform and those who respond to the posts.

Distinction between public and private. Individuals may not be aware that their online contributions, as text, images and video, whilst in the public domain, are being used for research as technically their content is public, but they may consider it to be private.

Participant anonymity. Should anonymity be granted to social media users? If they publicly complain to an organisation, is it appropriate to anonymise their details? There are examples of where this has taken place, usually involving complex political situations where lives may be at risk.

- How is informed consent obtained? Is it practical to let all members of the forum know?
- Would you be happy if your data, such as images or posts, were used for research purposes?
- Other than political situations, what harm might come from using social media data for research?

DISCOVER MORE ON MARKETING ETHICS

The SAGE Handbook of Marketing Ethics published in 2020, edited by Lynne Eagle and colleagues, provides a comprehensive overview of research into ethical issues in marketing.

4 Culture

Culture is about the organisation's personality, what's acceptable and what's not, and its core values inside and outside the business. Some company cultures value skills and encourage staff to enhance their expertise and competencies. Others recruit those with the desired competencies, rather than training existing staff. Explore job adverts on a chosen organisation's careers page to find out their approach.

Corporate culture is especially visible online, where announcements of CEOs resigning, influencers being dropped or staff being fired, as a result of an inappropriate post, text or other online error, are swiftly shared across social media. The challenge today is that 'Even in their private roles as individuals, consumers, or citizens, employees thus may function as part of the organization's workforce' (Schaarschmidt and Walsh, 2020, p. 718), which means that outside work someone may post something that could be connected to their organisation with negative impact. This is why many people add the words 'views mine' in their online bios.

Authenticity and transparency have become the digital indicators of corporate culture where brands can be exposed if bad news is being hidden (McCorkindale and DiStaso, 2014) and the key traits within transparency have been identified as integrity, openness and respect (Rawlins, 2008, p. 95), yet weak corporate behaviour still occurs. A study investigating major corporate scandals involving managerial errors, product or consumer deception, and financial misdoings found that social media amplified the bad news, even if only for a short time (Barkemeyer et al., 2020).

Since 2001 Edelman, a public relations firm, has conducted an annual survey of trust which is known as the Edelman Trust Barometer, sharing insights into feelings about trust in business, government and media. The findings are shared on its website. Scandals stay online as a Google search for brand names and terms such as #fail, #scandal or #disaster indicates.

Smartphone Sixty Seconds® – Search for trust

- Use your mobile phone to search for the *Edelman Trust Barometer*.
- What's the state of trust within business, government, NGOs and media?
- How has this changed in the last two years?
- Why do you feel this has changed?

5 Convenience

Convenience is the ease with which a customer can make a purchase or complete a conversion action; for example, how easy it is to:

- Access previous orders
- Sign in to your account
- Download or upload a document
- Register for a webinar or an open day
- Fill in a form
- Request support

This can be assessed by exploring competitors' websites and trying to sign up, download or register for more details. Convenience usually relates to capability rather than competence as this is about functionality. This is mainly found in larger rather than smaller organisations.

For example, Amazon focused its business on customer convenience with the development of the one-click purchase and Prime delivery options. You may find the product you want on the brand's own website, with three to five days' delivery, but you choose to buy the same item from Amazon at the same price, with faster delivery. This provides convenience for the customer and some convenience for the supplier. Amazon competes with its suppliers on convenience as its logistics capabilities outperform its suppliers. While this reduces the income for suppliers as they pay commission to Amazon, suppliers gain the convenience of faster sales via Amazon.

6 Consistency

A key feature in branding, consistency is ensuring that the same service, the same message, the same tone of voice and the same use of imagery are demonstrated across all online and offline platforms. In a digital environment, this can be a challenge where:

- Online staff are aware of an offer that wasn't shared with the offline teams
- Organisations with multiple sites (e.g. supermarkets, cafes, cinemas, hairdressers) have entrepreneurial local managers who create their own content.

These issues are about capability and processes and it may be that the competitors have not ensured that all teams, online and offline, in all locations, always have access to all messages and material.

When examining competitors, you will be able to assess the amount of coordination by checking the brand online, its website and social media spaces to see if the key messages are the same or different. If they are different, this may be because they are managed by teams in various locations or they have separate managers who adopt their own processes, rather than a consistent approach.

DISCOVER MORE ON CHATBOTS

For more on chatbots, see 'The chatbot revolution: Companies and consumers in a new digital age' in *The SAGE Handbook of Digital Marketing* by Shaalan, Tourky and Ibrahim (2022) which may be available in your university library.

7 Customisation

Customisation encompasses the degree of personalisation that websites offer.

As websites contain hundreds of pages, it can be difficult to find what's needed. So consumers may arrive at the website, have a quick look and leave, seeking the item elsewhere. This is the rationale behind web personalisation and customisation, to show consumers what they might be seeking. For example, Amazon shows products related to your purchase history and Netflix suggests movies based on your previous choices.

Data on the user's interest, such as how they navigated the site and when, is available via cookies (see Key Term **Cookie** p. 49) in Chapter 2. Google Analytics and other packages provide a real-time view, which means that marketers can see who is on the website right now and where they are visiting.

A study by Professor Benlian (2015, p. 253) demonstrated that 'content and design personalization cues can increase users' attachment to a website'. If you consider the websites you frequently visit, they may remember your purchase history and your preferences, including delivery location. Customising your experience makes it a simplified shopping experience.

When examining competitors' websites, you can assess the extent to which they offer customisation as this is mainly utilised by larger companies with greater budgets for enhanced capabilities, such as Amazon and Netflix. Customisation techniques include: analysis of past transactions, sample suggestions, content filtering and product recommendations.

Although I've used the digital 7Cs to evaluate competitors, this framework can be applied to an organisation you are studying or to make comparisons between organisations.

Activity 9.2   Evaluate competitors

Based on an organisation of your choice, use the digital 7Cs for competitor evaluation and evaluate some competitors to your chosen organisation. If any aspect of this model doesn't work for you, adapt it!

9.7 INFORMATION ANALYSIS

Having gathered the data, we need to make sense of the information. This involves analysing the data to understand what it means. This depends on the organisation's assets and its abilities, whether the abilities or skills are in-house and if they have the tools or assets needed.

Typically, an organisation's assets are its systems, but this extends to its people, leadership, the brand name and reputation. Digital assets include the website, automated ordering or fulfilment processes, online profiles and online brand communities.

The challenge is that just having the assets doesn't always mean they are used or managed well! That's where the organisation's potential abilities are crucial and these organisational capabilities are described as 'the glue that brings these assets together and enables them to be deployed advantageously' (Day, 1994, p. 38). We could describe digital abilities as having digital marketing skills or knowing people who can help.

One of the challenges is that conducting a digital marketing audit may result in many types of data, such as content from blogs, social media pages, discussion boards, forums, online communities, shopping and review sites.

Data from social media can be explored by looking at the text for different elements such as the content, sentiment, opinion or tone of voice (see Key Term **Sentiment analysis** in Chapter 5).

Activity 9.3   Conduct sentiment analysis

In a group of three to five, find a Twitter or Instagram account, for a food, games or fashion company:

- Look at the last 25 posts and replies, and ideally copy and paste them into an Excel or numbers sheet.

- Create five columns for negative, neutral, mixed, positive and 'not sure'.

- Classify these posts into negative, neutral, mixed or positive sentiment analysis.

- If you were not sure and unable to classify some data, discuss further in the group.

- How did you define negative or positive content?

- Were there any ironic or sarcastic posts?

- What volume of negative or positive posts existed?

To conclude, digital marketing audits may be triggered by a surprising situation or a disaster when organisations need to re-think their business model. Being informed at an early stage can help organisations to adapt and manage market changes. Furthermore, providing an audit to inform the strategy saves time by focusing on what matters. This means that decisions are based on evidence.

Although many aspects of digital marketing audits can be conducted automatically, such as using social listening tools and downloading data, we need real people to make sense of the data and apply it to the individual organisation's context.

JOURNAL OF NOTE

The *Journal of Business Research* applies theory to business situations and covers a range of topics including digital marketing.

CASE STUDY

STRAVA'S WATCHING THE COMPETITION

This continues our long case study and you may find it helpful to read earlier parts in previous chapters.

Gabriel has been reviewing the content from various competitors but just looking at their websites doesn't provide a clear overview of the key differences. He's decided to use the digital 7Cs for competitor evaluation as a structure to assess the largest competitor, which is said to be Runkeeper.

CULTURE

Gabriel is aware that Runkeeper was founded in 2008 in Boston and then bought by the Japanese company ASICS in 2016. It seems that ASICS planned to use the app to drive footwear sales. This acquisition provided a strong basis for Runkeeper, with many opportunities to upsell additional products, as well as gaining user feedback on running shoes.

Gabriel thinks the culture is traditional and formal which is evidenced by looking at Glassdoor, a recruiting website which includes company reviews. It's a mixed picture – several staff comment on the micro-management and old-fashioned management approaches at ASICS, yet others love working there. The corporate website states that the company was founded by Mr Onitsuka in 1949 who wanted to make 'athletic shoes with the aim of nurturing healthy young people through sports' but this initial passion is not demonstrated on Glassdoor.

CONVENIENCE

There seem to be more weaknesses in the area of convenience. Although the Runkeeper app is straightforward to download, a robotic woman's voice loudly confirms when the activity is starting (so you'd need to remember to wear earbuds before starting an early morning run or it would wake everyone in the household). The 7Cs model concerns 'the ease with which a customer can make a purchase' and Runkeeper does not facilitate any immediate sales, but this may change in time.

When recording an activity, users are encouraged to add an image and their thoughts about the run, neither of which add convenience. However, there is another section where users note the running shoes worn for the activity – the brand, model and nickname. This is a strength and enables Runkeeper to notify the user when it's time to buy a new pair of running shoes, potentially adding an area of convenience.

COMPETITION

Runkeeper was an online-only digital business from the USA whereas ASICS was a traditional company founded in Japan. When ASICS bought Runkeeper in

2016, it aimed to enhance the user's sporting lifestyle with better use of digital technology.

Runkeeper uses digital marketing to convert customers through its app. Once downloaded, users are invited to upgrade to premium membership – Runkeeper Go, which is around $30 a year. Gabriel believes this is neither a strength nor a weakness as it's the same for all fitness apps.

COMMUNICATIONS

When joining Runkeeper, the app provides a message: 'Welcome to the team! You're joining millions of active runners who have chosen Runkeeper™ as their digital coach.' This positions the app as an instructor more than a community. This concept is echoed as the app is endorsed by the tennis champion Novak Djokovic.

Its social media brand communications are strongest on Facebook, with nearly 300,000 likes. There is evidence of dialogues and trialogues, where customers jump into conversations. Although the posts are mainly offers or events, the six staff in the USA who manage the page don't respond to spam posts – people promoting 'get rich quick' schemes. In some cases, they respond to user complaints.

The Twitter account has over 80,000 followers but little engagement, other than occasional messages from users about issues with emails and offer codes being out of date. Instagram has 50,000 followers with more engagement. Gabriel concludes that the company's social media lacks depth of personality and does not feel like it is part of a community. The responses on social media have a corporate tone and are signed off by 'ASICS Runkeeper' rather than named individuals.

Gabriel thinks that Runkeeper's communications are weak as the blog content lacks depth and consists mainly of 'how to' articles or generic guides.

CONSISTENCY

The Runkeeper logo has been adapted to include a stylized 'A' from ASICS, but the brand messaging lacks consistency. Although it is known as Runkeeper, its social media is named ASICS Runkeeper to demonstrate that it's part of a larger brand.

The social media pages lack consistency. The Twitter page describes the company as 'a mobile app designed to help you reach your running goals, one step at a time. Support: @RKSupport' and the Facebook page is similar, but directs users to a website (support.runkeeper.com).

The Instagram bio is different and states 'ASICS Runkeeper™ – We're on a mission to help you reach your #running goals. Use #Runkeeper or #TrainwithRunkeeper so we can celebrate your journey together.' It may be that the focus is different here as Instagram is about sharing images.

The YouTube bio is once again different, stating 'Runkeeper is a mobile app obsessed with helping people get out the door and reach your fitness goals, one step at a time. Everyone. Every Run. #Runkeeper.'

Gabriel is aware that consistency is a key feature in branding, ensuring that the same service, the same message, the same tone of voice and the same use of imagery are demonstrated across all online and offline platforms. Yet Runkeeper lacks coordination.

CUSTOMISATION

Unsurprisingly the app is customisable. Users can add their profile details: name, date of birth, gender, weight and height. When activities are completed, these show the distance, pace and achievements over the week, month or year.

Similar to Strava, there is a social login, enabling users to log in via Facebook.

CASE QUESTIONS

- What other aspects of a digital marketing audit could Gabriel have included in his assessment of Runkeeper?
- Imagine you're working for Runkeeper in the social media team. How would you address the issues that Gabriel has found?
- Why should companies deliver consistent content and messages? Does it matter?

FURTHER EXERCISES

1. Using a framework, conduct a micro-analysis of a games, food or fashion company and draw conclusions as to their digital strengths and weaknesses.

2. Select an organisation of your choice and conduct a digital macro-environment analysis and make recommendations based on the findings.

3. Using the digital tools in this chapter, download content from an organisation of your choice and assess the content.

4. Discuss how you feel about companies or researchers using your public posts, photos or videos for research purposes. Consider what steps could be taken to mitigate potential harm to those being researched.

SUMMARY

This chapter has explored:

- The rationale and benefits of a digital marketing audit
- How to apply market sensing in a digital context
- How to use the 7Ps and PESTLE for a digital marketing audit
- Methods of assessing customer needs online
- The digital 7Cs for competitor evaluation

GO ONLINE

Visit **study.sagepub.com/hanlon2e** to access links to interesting articles, websites and videos related to this chapter.

OVERVIEW
Chapter 10 introduces strategy and objectives, explains the differences and shows how to apply different frameworks.

ACTIVITIES

Create the TOWS matrix

Apply digital marketing strategy framework

Evaluate objectives using the REAN framework

Digital marketing strategy framework

KEY CONCEPTS

Hierarchy of objectives

Greenwashing

DIGITAL TOOLS

Share the workload with Trello

Discover news about products and companies in The Conversation

10

DIGITAL MARKETING STRATEGY AND OBJECTIVES

LEARNING OUTCOMES

When you have read this chapter, you will be able to:

Understand the difference between corporate, business and functional strategies

Apply the TOWS matrix

Analyse the organisation's digital marketing strategy

Evaluate objectives using the REAN framework

Create a digital marketing strategy

PROFESSIONAL SKILLS

When you have worked through this chapter, you should be able to:

- Create a digital marketing strategy for an organisation
- Develop digital marketing objectives for an organisation

10.1 INTRODUCTION TO DIGITAL MARKETING STRATEGY AND OBJECTIVES

You may wonder why you need a digital marketing strategy rather than just a marketing strategy. Making it digital encourages organisations to address opportunities for moving their business online (not just selling a few products via Amazon), to enable staff to connect with customers, regardless of location, and to process orders using automation rather than manual intervention.

A digital marketing strategy places the customer at the centre of the process (see personas in Chapter 2), instead of the products or service, and moves the culture within the organisation to think differently. In an environment where online access to information, products, services and systems is considered a routine process, organisations that don't provide this are deemed to be behind the times or out of date and may suffer as a result of not being able to digitally compete with their competitors.

In the future, it's likely that the digital marketing strategy will simply be part of the marketing strategy. Until then, as we're still in a world where many businesses have not yet embraced elements of digital, we need to have a clearly defined digital marketing strategy.

One challenge is that digital marketing strategy can seem complex and very much focused on tactics. Often interpreted by organisations and agencies as a Facebook campaign or blog creation, a digital marketing strategy is so much more than this. A successful strategy is based on evidence and in Chapter 9 you will have conducted a digital marketing audit, making sense of the market, analysing the impact and evaluating the competitors.

It's a long-standing discussion between academics and practitioners as to which goes first, the objectives and then the strategy, or the strategy followed by the objectives. In fact, some frameworks suggest objectives are first. Having worked as a practitioner for many years with hundreds of organisations, I believe it's sensible to create the strategy first and then the objectives. If you create a list of objectives before the strategy, it's like deciding what to wear before you know where you're going!

In this chapter, we will explore core concepts, followed by the different approaches including digital marketing strategy models, plus details on the hierarchy of objectives.

At the end of the chapter, you will better understand what's needed to create an effective digital marketing strategy.

10.2 CORE CONCEPTS

10.2.1 THE DIFFERENCES BETWEEN STRATEGY AND TACTICS

Strategy and tactics are often confused. You will hear someone saying their strategy is 'advertising on Instagram'. That's absolutely not a strategy. It's a single tactic.

Digital marketing strategy is not just tactics and lists of actions. Strategies require a clear and strong vision. They set the direction for the organisation and are often designed to be in place for several years. A strategy that's changed every six months causes confusion, wastes money and sends out the wrong messages to the target audience. It is not uncommon for organisations to confuse strategy, objectives and tactics (see Key Term **Strategy**).

- **Strategy** is a plan or programme to achieve your aim or vision.
- **Objectives** are detailed SMART (specific, measurable, achievable, realistic and timed) goals.
- **Tactics** are actions to achieve the objectives.

KEY TERM   STRATEGY

Definitions of strategy are similar to an overarching plan. Marketing leaders from the past suggested:

- 'The marketing strategy is the set of decision rules, or program that adjusts (product price, advertising budget, distribution budget) from period T to period T + 1, for all T' (Kotler, 1965, p. 104).
- 'A formal corporate strategy provides a coherent model for all business units and ensures that all those involved in strategic planning and its implementation are following common goals' (Porter, 1997, p. 12).
- 'Strategy is a plan' (Mintzberg, 1987, p. 11).

In this textbook, a digital marketing strategy is a plan to address digital marketing within an organisation.

10.2.2 CORPORATE, BUSINESS AND FUNCTIONAL STRATEGIES

Strategies can be confusing because an organisation may have more than one. These are often in hierarchical order, as shown in Figure 10.1, which includes the link between strategy and the **hierarchy of objectives** (see Key Term).

Figure 10.1   The link between strategy and the hierarchy of objectives

KEY TERM   HIERARCHY OF OBJECTIVES

An objective has been defined as 'an aim or end of action' (Granger, 1964, p. 63). An order was suggested so that business objectives could be grouped. There is a ranking where the corporate objective is at the top, followed by key objectives in the business, then sub-objectives for individual departments. The hierarchy of objectives means the sequence from the main company goal to individual department aims.

Corporate strategy

At the top is the corporate strategy which mainly exists in major organisations with multiple brands. For example, Estée Lauder, a global manufacturer of skincare, make-up, fragrance and haircare products, owns many other brands (e.g. AVEDA, Bobbi Brown, Jo Malone, MAC Cosmetics and Origins). The company has a corporate strategy that guides the individual brands and addresses larger issues such as its management of resources, its approach to sustainability and its ethical codes.

Unsurprisingly, small businesses are unlikely to have a corporate strategy and may start the process with a business strategy.

Business strategy

The middle level looks at the individual business strategies. Brands inside the business have their own business strategies which address overarching aims, including company structure, staffing, accountability, legal issues, finances, logistics, marketing and product development.

For example, within Estée Lauder, the individual business units such as AVEDA and MAC Cosmetics have their own methods of recruitment, product development and marketing. They may share legal services with their corporate brand, but they manage their business according to their own policies.

Functional strategies

The lower level considers the operational strategies which relate to specific functions or departments, such as marketing or digital marketing, sales and product development.

For example, the marketing team at MAC Cosmetics has a different digital marketing strategy to the Origins team. Their products and pricing are different, their target audience is different and their messaging and adverts are different. It's also possible that customers do not associate plant-based ingredient brands such as AVEDA and Origins with the brand owner, Estée Lauder. The purpose of the functional strategies is to deliver the aims of the business strategy.

It would be too complicated to have a single strategy that comprised the corporate, business and functional levels which is why they are broken into distinct elements. However, there is a link between each element as the corporate strategy informs and guides the individual business strategies which guide the functional strategies.

10.3 TRADITIONAL STRATEGY MODELS

Strategy, along with many marketing concepts, is founded on military theory. Armies and their generals need clear and decisive strategies to go to war; if not, with hundreds of soldiers walking around with weapons, there would be total chaos.

Historically, the focus of marketing was very much on making and selling products on the basis that if you made it, you could sell it. Consequently, strategy focused on leadership or share within markets, competition and product offers. It wasn't about the customer, it was about beating the competition and gaining maximum market share.

DISCOVER MORE ON TRADITIONAL STRATEGY MODELS

There are many textbooks that include traditional models, such as:

- *Marketing: An Introduction* by Masterson, Phillips and Pickton, published by SAGE (4th edn, 2017)
- *Marketing* by Baines, Fill, Rosengren and Antonetti, published by Oxford University Press (5th edn, 2019)

Smartphone Sixty Seconds® – Search for strategy

- On your mobile phone, search for 'NYSE top companies' or 'FTSE top companies' (the *Financial Times* top 100 companies list).
- Select and search for the investor's website for one of these companies, to find the annual report.
- Look at the report and identify their strategy.
- Is the strategy clear?
- What model or framework are they using?

Today, strategies can be more consumer-centric, although some companies adopt weak practices, such as **greenwashing** (see Key Term and Discover More), so that they look more impressive to their stakeholders. But as so many companies publish their strategies online, they're easy to access and analyse.

KEY TERM   GREENWASHING

Greenwashing is a strategy adopted by some companies which researchers have classified as deceiving stakeholders actively or passively (Gatti et al., 2021). Active greenwashing is where false information is provided or deceptive practices adopted to manipulate the situation. Passive greenwashing is where the corporation selectively promotes specific activities, to draw attention away from other important factors.

DISCOVER MORE ON GREENWASHING

The article 'Perceived greenwashing: The effects of green marketing on environmental and product perceptions' by Szerena Szabo and Jane Webster (2020), published in the *Journal of Business Ethics*, looks at the background to greenwashing and how this is presented in websites.

ETHICAL INSIGHTS   Greenwashing

Strategy can be negative as well as positive and large corporations may commit to environmental and sustainability strategies, with many objectives to demonstrate their green credentials. However, when this is simply ticking a box, with no substance or support behind the objectives, this is greenwashing.

Research indicates that consumers will pay more for sustainable products. This has led to some companies making claims that they are environmentally friendly or saving the planet.

Also called green sheen or green lies, this can often be detected where the packaging includes images such as sunshine, leaves, plants, animals or happy families, but does not explain how it is certified or eco-friendly.

For example, Quorn Foods promoted its Thai Wondergrains (meat-free pieces with mixed rice and green peppers in a coconut and lemongrass sauce) as helping to combat climate change. Several people complained and the UK's Advertising Standards Authority launched an investigation. It found that the advert was misleading. This is one example of greenwashing, but there are many more from fossil fuel as well as fast-fashion companies.

- If you buy products that are labelled as being eco-friendly, what does this mean to you?
- When do you feel it is relevant for companies to develop environmental strategies in their approach to marketing?
- How do we balance the desire from consumers to buy more things with the need to adopt earth-friendly marketing strategies?

10.3.1 IDENTIFYING STRATEGIC OPTIONS WITH THE TOWS MATRIX

When creating a strategy, it is useful to understand the options available. This should be evidence based and built on the audit (see Chapter 9, 'Digital Marketing Audit'). Once the audit has identified the current situation, it is easier to consider the future direction of the organisation.

The **TOWS matrix** takes the material captured in your audit, plots this into the matrix and extracts your strategic marketing options. This framework provides 'a systematic analysis that facilitates matching the external threats and opportunities with the internal weaknesses and strengths of the organization' (Weihrich, 1982, p. 59). You might have noticed that TOWS is 'SWOT' spelled back to front (for an example of how this looks, see Table 10.1: Orange Money Africa TOWS framework). Let's explore the elements.

SO: 'maxi-maxi' strategy

Strengths and Opportunities: This is a strong position and it's about using the organisation's strengths to maximise opportunities. Described as the aggressive strategy, it often involves expansion and diversification.

WO: 'mini-maxi' strategy

Weaknesses and Opportunities: Where weaknesses have been identified, they should be minimised by taking advantage of opportunities. This could be described as a competitive strategy.

ST: 'maxi-mini' strategy

Strengths and Threats: This strategy utilises the organisation's strengths to minimise threats. This is often seen as a conservative strategy.

WT: 'mini-mini' strategy

Weaknesses and Threats: The WT strategy aims to minimise weaknesses and avoid threats and if this is the only strategy available to the organisation, it may be that a complete review is required to see if the organisation is still viable. This has been called a defensive strategy as it's about protecting the organisation.

Case Example 10.1 explores each of these TOWS strategic options in more detail, applying the TOWS matrix and showing how this is interpreted.

CASE EXAMPLE 10.1   Orange Money Africa

Access to a bank account to manage money, receive wages, pay bills and organise savings is something many of us take for granted. However, this is not universally available and there are many people excluded from the traditional banking system. One solution is access to a bank via your mobile which provides greater inclusion and enables individuals to protect their families and their income, and reduces their insecurity (Ky et al., 2021).

Across Africa, a well-known mobile-first banking system is Orange Money Africa, which enables people without bank accounts to take and make payments using their mobile phones, without the need for a conventional bank account. This is useful in situations where individuals have informal employment contracts and lack the required paperwork, making it difficult to open a bank account.

The mobile app was launched in Kenya and rolled out in other countries including the Ivory Coast. Orange Money is part of the French Orange mobile telephone network, with nearly 150,000 employees and over 260 million customers worldwide. Orange provides connectivity – telephone networks and internet access including 5G, business IT support services, cybersecurity – as well as financial services which includes Orange Bank and Orange Money.

Orange Money has nearly 20 million active customers and allows them to pay utility bills, share payments and transfer funds through the app or via text message. For example, in the Ivory Coast, the app is used to pay school enrolment fees. Consequently, Orange Money has gained the trust of people in Africa and is recognised as a reliable and safe mobile banking system. Trust is a major issue as mobile money needs to be protected and the products sold should be relevant to and appropriate for the customers (Okello Candiya Bongomin and Ntayi, 2020).

Orange is committed to technology and has declared that it is 'investing heavily in digital tools' (Orange, 2019, p. 96).

Its strategic approach is evidenced by its forward-looking 2025 strategic plan, which reveals many of the company's strengths and weaknesses, opportunities and threats, which have been added into the TOWS framework in Table 10.1. While many of these elements apply to the whole of the Orange business, they are also relevant to Orange Money Africa as the app requires connectivity to function.

As part of its 2025 strategy, Orange is using all of the TOWS strategies, as shown in Table 10.1. Part of the focus is addressing social and environmental responsibility (S3). While the

Table 10.1   Orange Money Africa TOWS framework

	Internal Strengths (S)	Internal Weaknesses (W)
	S1. Trust by stakeholders	W1. Major investment required to expand into new countries such as the Ivory Coast
	S2. Talented team of people	
	S3. Focus on social and environmental responsibility	W2. Growing carbon footprint with the sustainability of devices
External Opportunities (O)	**SO 'Maxi-Maxi' Strategy**	**WO 'Mini-Maxi' Strategy**
O1. Enhanced connectivity with 5G	S1, O1. Partner with stakeholders to offer 5G	W1, O1. Launch 5G in key cities
O2. Growing online markets	O2, S3, S2. Open an Orange Digital Center	W2, O2. Launch a mobile loan or rental plan along with a pre-owned phone range
External Threats (T)	**ST 'Maxi-Mini' Strategy**	**WT 'Mini-Mini' Strategy**
T1. Social accessibility of 5G	T1, S3. Launch 5G where it is needed most	W1, T3. Minimise product cost in market expansion by expanding the range of affordable smartphones
T2. Skills gaps	T2, S2. Set up a Foundation in operating countries and coordinate outreach programmes to build skills	
T3. Affordability of devices		T3, W2. Collect old telephones to recycle

(Continued)

company has a talented team of people (S2), there will be future skills gaps (T3) and one solution Orange has identified in its maxi-mini strategy is to set up a foundation in every operating country and coordinate outreach programmes. This foundation provides training in digital production for vulnerable groups so that they can access jobs in the digital economy, as well as providing a future talent pool.

Mobile phone ownership and the access mobiles provide to the internet is considered a basic utility in many countries. The challenge can be the affordability of the devices (T3); at the same time, companies like Orange need to consider the sustainability of devices (W2) and how to provide opportunities for low-income households. The mini-mini strategy is to expand the range of affordable smartphones and is connected to the mini-maxi strategy which involves launching mobile loan or rental plans with a pre-owned phone range. This makes mobiles more affordable and reduces the carbon footprint.

Combined with the maxi-maxi strategy, as part of its social responsibility (S3) Orange is opening digital centres in Senegal which is a growing market (O2), training young people in digital technology and contributing to its future team (S2).

Mobile money has the power to change lives and transform nations. The long-term approach adopted by Orange involves being part of the community and positively contributing to the country's individuals, both from a technology and a societal perspective.

Case questions

- Look at the TOWS matrix in Table 10.1 – what other options may be available?
- How can Orange Money Africa avoid potential greenwashing?
- How can online-only financial providers build trust and remove potential concerns about not having a physical presence?

Activity 10.1   Create your TOWS matrix

1. Look back at a digital marketing audit you have conducted for an organisation of your choice.

2. From this, extract the strengths, weaknesses, opportunities and threats, and place them into the outer boxes.

3. Make sure all elements are numbered.

4. If you have too many in one area, such as strengths or weaknesses, identify whether there is duplication and group items. This should be a focused list.

5. When the outer boxes have been completed, look first at the SO: 'maxi–maxi' strategy box and identify which strengths can maximise opportunities. Turn this into a short sentence, numbering the relevant strength and opportunity, so if presented to the organisation, staff can see your thought process.

6. Repeat for the remaining three strategy options.

7. If possible, reorganise each box and prioritise which strategic options will be addressed first.

8. Support the TOWS with a few paragraphs that justify your recommended options.

10.4 DIGITAL STRATEGY MODELS

Digital strategy models are led by practitioners rather than researchers. This section explains three digital strategy frameworks.

These digital marketing strategy models follow a similar three-step route from pre-purchase, to purchase and post-purchase, recognising that this may all happen simultaneously. For example, you may see an app, download it and review it within an hour of purchase. Although these may seem like funnel models, it is more complex than that as there may be many elements within the different stages (look back at Chapter 2, Figure 2.2: Example of a customer journey map, for an example) and they all focus on growth of awareness, conversion or enthusiasm.

Let's compare some digital and traditional approaches to marketing strategy to better understand the differences.

10.4.1 COMPARING DIGITAL AND TRADITIONAL APPROACHES TO MARKETING STRATEGY

Traditional models such as Ansoff's growth strategies (see Discover More on Traditional Strategy Models) focus on the product, whether it's encouraging existing customers to purchase existing products (market penetration), making existing customers aware of new products (product development) or encouraging new customers to purchase existing products (market development).

In a pre-internet era, these growth strategies made sense as customers had less access to information about new products and depended on information from newspapers or magazines, but subscriptions are declining and publications are closing.

Past consumers may have visited an exhibition, but these are becoming less and less popular. For example, in 1958 over 1.3 million people attended the Ideal Home Show in London to learn about new household gadgets, yet in 2015 this had dropped to 230,000 and due to the global pandemic was cancelled in 2020 and 2021.

Today we may become aware of new products by seeing someone online wearing or using the item, or when it appears in our news feed as a result of an online article. It's less about direct promotion and more about awareness in a social setting.

DIGITAL TOOL   The Conversation

The Conversation is an independent online news network that started in Australia and shares the latest research-based information. It covers topics from business and the economy to strategy and the environment. When companies adopt weak strategies, The Conversation authors often provide background to the topic.

- Visit https://theconversation.com

The digital models contain other differences as the main measured action is conversion, which is facilitated using technology. We can see whether someone who downloaded a document has read it, if they looked at an awareness video, how many seconds they watched, if they shared an image and how many times. In a traditional environment, we never know if the brochure sent through the post was read, we don't know if they mentioned the new products to friends and family and we're not sure what they did with the discount code we sent to them. Adding digital tracking mechanisms makes measurement of our digital marketing activities easier to understand, along with what works well (see Chapter 13, Digital Marketing Metrics and Analytics).

Moreover, digital marketing continues beyond conversion. The end goal for Ansoff's growth strategy is conversion, yet in the digital marketing strategy models another step is included, post-purchase. This encourages co-creation, with customers promoting the product to friends, family and strangers via social media. It encourages businesses to improve product quality as reviews are shared publicly and it provides valuable data for companies considering new product opportunities as they collate customer feedback.

Figure 10.2 shows the differences between the digital and traditional approaches to strategy. The product focus model is based on Ansoff's growth strategies (1957) whereas the newer model is a blend of the digital strategy frameworks.

The fundamental changes are the move from a product focus to a consideration of taking the customer on a journey. The traditional product focus viewed the sale as the end of the journey – thank you and goodbye! The customer journey considers the sale to be a step in the journey, but not the end – thank you, would you leave us a review?

This is a reflection about the loss of control that organisations have in a digital environment as the power has moved from the companies to the consumers and onwards to their communities. Many companies don't manage this well and the details can be shared by staff and consumers.

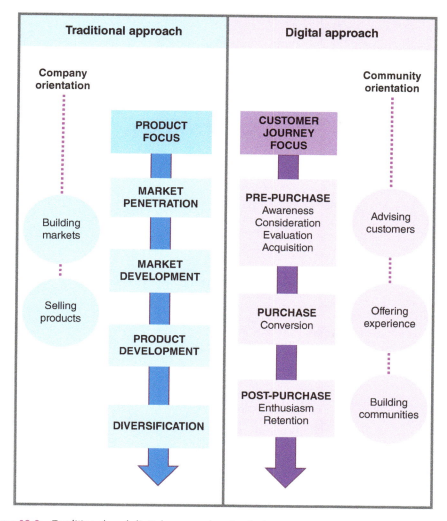

Figure 10.2 Traditional and digital approaches to strategy

The digital strategy models recognise that not all companies have products to sell but may act as intermediaries for peer providers and peer users. For example, Airbnb has no hotels, Uber does not own vehicles and neither eBay nor AliBaba stock products. However, these companies have emerged as a result of the digital environment which has facilitated online trading and peer-to-peer exchanges. We could say that the orientation of digital-first companies, such as Airbnb, Uber and eBay, is focused on the community rather than the company. They provide advice, offer experiences and facilitate collaboration, as shown in Figure 10.2.

Having considered the differences between traditional and digital frameworks, the next section discusses the digital strategy models.

10.4.2 THE DIGITAL MARKETING STRATEGY FRAMEWORK

Social media companies ask organisations to identify their strategy when advertising. They offer three choices: awareness, consideration and conversion. As these strategic options were found in social media, I originally called this the *social media strategy framework* although this can be used beyond social media to encompass all elements of digital strategy, so I have adapted its name. Figure 10.3 shows the different steps in this framework with examples.

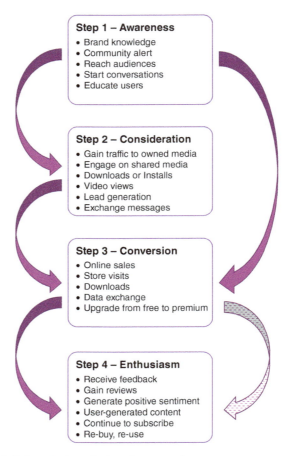

Step 1 – Awareness
- Brand knowledge
- Community alert
- Reach audiences
- Start conversations
- Educate users

Step 2 – Consideration
- Gain traffic to owned media
- Engage on shared media
- Downloads or Installs
- Video views
- Lead generation
- Exchange messages

Step 3 – Conversion
- Online sales
- Store visits
- Downloads
- Data exchange
- Upgrade from free to premium

Step 4 – Enthusiasm
- Receive feedback
- Gain reviews
- Generate positive sentiment
- User-generated content
- Continue to subscribe
- Re-buy, re-use

Figure 10.3   The digital marketing strategy framework

The digital marketing strategy framework has four steps and the notion is that customers will move from step 1 to 2, 3 and 4. But the customer journey is rarely linear and customers or community members may stop and start, never progressing through to the next stage, or they move backwards and forwards. Have you ever been about to 'click to buy' when a friend messaged you and the sale stopped? This is how digital marketing works. Let's explore the framework in more detail.

Awareness

Step 1 in the digital marketing strategy framework is awareness, whether that's about the brand, the community, the activity or a product. In a digital space, awareness can take place faster than in the offline environment as we may see something on Instagram or TikTok and click through or search to gather more details or make a purchase in minutes.

The purpose of the awareness stage is sharing knowledge and understanding of the product or brand, perhaps alerting people to a new community, or reaching audiences with specific messages. This may include starting conversations or educating existing or new customers, and the purpose of awareness is to encourage people to move towards conversion. Depending on the type of product, customers may go via the next step, consideration, or direct to conversion, or stop and never move forward. They're aware and the strategy has succeeded or they don't want or need the item at this time.

Consideration

Step 2 is consideration and within the digital marketing strategy framework this stage may be bypassed if consumers move from awareness straight to conversion. Or they may reach this step and never progress further, having evaluated the offer, perhaps dismissing it in favour of another offer.

Potential consumers may be evaluating your brand which may result in visits to the website, or they may talk about the brand online in communities, or engage in another way to learn more.

Apps may gain downloads or installations, videos may be watched, leads generated or messages sent to your organisation. It might also involve finding out more information such as registering for an app or undertaking a free trial.

For example, you consider a change of behaviour, such as a move to online registration for government services, or find out about giving up smoking on health websites, or register for a company newsletter to gain more insights into the organisation.

As well as evaluating the product or message, consideration can encourage those who have discovered the product to move towards conversion.

Conversion

Although conversion is step 3, in a digital environment this can take place immediately after awareness. You watch an influencer on YouTube talking about a specific product, search for it and buy it instantly. The speed between the steps is one of the major differences in digital marketing.

It is also possible that once a product or service has been considered (whether that's in minutes or months), you move to conversion. It's important to remember that conversion is not simply a sale as this can mean different concepts for different organisations. For example:

- For online stores, conversion focuses on goods being added to the shopping basket and a checkout.

- For physical stores, online conversion may include making a booking or visiting in person, for example with a local restaurant or take-away service.

- In business-to-business situations, conversion can be about sharing data – providing your mobile number or email address in exchange for information such as a report.

- For government services, conversion may represent online registration or down-loading documents, such as a guide to help stop smoking or lose weight.

- For software companies with freemium pricing strategies, conversion may be upgrading from free to premium, such as moving from Basic Zoom to the Pro package.

In the traditional marketing models, conversion is often the last step, but in the digital marketing strategy framework, conversion isn't the end.

Enthusiasm

Organisations want digital consumers to do more, whether that's re-subscribing and recommending friends (Dropbox), buying additional products (Apple) or renewing Prime and leaving reviews (Amazon). Therefore in this framework, the final step is enthusiasm.

Enthusiasm here is passion for the company and the desire to return and rebuy or to share with others.

For example, re-subscribing to an app means companies need to justify why consumers should continue spending their time or money with them. Some people have an auto-subscribe and don't even think about this step, it just happens. If they weigh up the options of staying with the company, it may be that they are already committed as they have stored too much data to downgrade to a basic account. Imagine all the photos and memories you've saved in iCloud or in OneDrive but you've reached the limit of your storage plan. Do you delete some photos or pay to upgrade your storage plan?

Enthusiasm means promoting the organisation to others via positive online reviews or feedback; or better still, other forms of user-generated content, such as unboxing the product, providing a case study or explaining why you chose that organisation.

The Digital Marketing Strategy Framework can be applied to organisations who want to grow awareness, gain new customers or share new products, with a focus on the customer journey rather than trying to gain conversion for products that the target personas have not yet discovered.

CASE EXAMPLE 10.2   Just Eat Takeaway.com

In Denmark in 2001, an online food delivery service was launched by five entrepreneurs, one of whom, Jesper Buch, wanted a late-night pizza and couldn't get it delivered. As a result, Just Eat was launched. One year earlier, a parallel situation occurred in the Netherlands when Jitse Groen couldn't get a takeaway delivered for a family event outside the city centre. With a group of entrepreneurs, Takeaway.com was established, offering a food delivery service.

In 2020 the two firms merged to create Just Eat Takeaway.com (JET), one of the largest delivery platforms in over 25 countries. They initially raised €700 million from investors to focus on future growth and represent one of the largest meal delivery companies in Europe. Due to the pandemic, sales skyrocketed by over 50 per cent in 2020. In the first three months of 2021, they had a 79 per cent increase on the first quarter of 2020.

Like Uber and Netflix, these two businesses started as the result of their owners identifying problems and seeking solutions. Their strategy wasn't making and selling products, but innovating and launching something new. Just Eat may be the largest food community in the world, but it doesn't own any restaurants or employ any chefs (at the moment).

Accessed via the app, the combined company offers takeaway, restaurant and food businesses the opportunity to be listed on the Just Eat app for a payment.

Let's see how the Digital Marketing Strategy Framework applies to Just Eat Takeaway. com. Traditional strategy elements are noted in brackets.

Step 1 – Awareness

The company initially focused on major cities where there were more restaurants and more people, especially students, which enabled the company to gain critical mass (7Ps – place; Ansoff – market development).

There are two customer groups in the Just Eat strategy: hungry customers seeking food and local restaurants wanting to increase sales. Sales teams identified local restaurants and made contact to offer opportunities to target more customers. Just Eat pay for the advertising, whilst the local restaurants pay commission based on results when they gain orders (7Ps – processes and pricing; Ansoff – product development).

Awareness is less of an issue for the brand which has become well known, with over 25 million active users and over 250 million food orders placed per year.

Step 2 – Consideration

This step involves encouraging non-customers to download the app and bringing more local restaurants into the system. However, the company is gaining traffic to its website with over 16 million visitors a month (7Ps – product; Ansoff – market development).

The app is easy to find, download and use, so it's thought consideration is more about restaurant choice and availability. But in 2020 Just Eat agreed a partnership with the international

(Continued)

food brand McDonald's, increasing its potential customer base (7Ps – product; Ansoff – product development).

Step 3 – Conversion

There is a dedicated page which includes a quick response form on its website that states: 'Restaurants on Just Eat take 4,000 orders a year on average. We'll put your restaurant in front of more potential customers than anyone else' (Just Eat, 2021, p. 1). The company has made the sign-up process very simple and this includes a video from another takeaway explaining the benefits they've gained and demonstrating social proof (7Ps – processes, physical evidence; Ansoff – market development).

Step 4 – Enthusiasm

The post-purchase step for Just Eat Takeway.com is on two levels: to hold onto the restaurant partners and to motivate happy customers to share reviews. This encourages the customer to re-use the app (7Ps – processes; Ansoff – market penetration).

Consumer reviews generate sales (Prabowo and Alversia, 2020) but the challenge is that it's often those with the strongest opinions who leave feedback (Han and Anderson, 2020). Just Eat Takeaway.com encourages positive reviews from customers which is essential in the food and beverage market. Just Eat explains:

> Leaving a review helps other people find great places to order from on Just Eat. It's also a chance for you to tell the place you ordered from what they did well and where they could improve. Remember to be constructive and don't get personal. (Just Eat, 2021, p. 1)

However, some reviews may be negative due to the cuisine, rather than the role of the intermediary. This can lead to fake reviews as the restaurants seek to improve their online profiles, but Just Eat is aware of this:

> Just Eat has a system in place that helps us identify and remove fake reviews. We believe these could have been placed by someone closely related to the restaurant, with the aim of boosting that restaurant's rating on Just Eat. We do this to ensure that our review system remains honest – that's why we need to remove them as quickly as possible. (Just Eat, 2021, p. 1)

Just Eat Takeaway.com is a digital-first business and has embraced digital marketing strategy, using each part of the framework and ensuring the customer journey – for both their restaurant partners and consumers – is effortless.

Case questions

- What are the strongest parts of the Just Eat Takeaway.com digital marketing strategy and why is this?
- As Just Eat Takeaway.com has grown to become the largest food delivery service in Europe and other parts of the world, what will be the main challenges in maintaining its digital marketing strategy?
- What are the advantages or disadvantages of using the 7Ps or the Ansoff matrix in this case study?

10.4.3 THE ACQUISITION, CONVERSION, RETENTION FRAMEWORK

The acquisition, conversion, retention (ACR) framework is displayed as a circular rather than a linear model, as the organisation acquires, converts and retains customers. Whilst this framework has existed for some time, it is largely credited to the consultancy firm Econsultancy (2009). As with the awareness, consideration, conversion framework, this is another purely digital model considering *online* customer acquisition, conversion and retention.

The notion of customers taking an online journey from acquisition to conversion and retention includes three steps. As with the Digital Marketing Strategy Framework, acquisition and conversion may take place within minutes. It's a self-explanatory and simplistic model which may be why Econsultancy no longer includes this on its website. However, as an online-first model, it works well as a framework for how organisations can better harness digital marketing.

10.4.4 MCKINSEY'S CONSUMER DECISION JOURNEY

A digital strategy model created by the consulting firm McKinsey & Company proposed another loop model instead of the traditional linear approach. This was justified by an extensive study that found 'consumers are changing the way they research and buy products' (Court et al., 2009, p. 2).

The study authors explained that this model was why Amazon offered recommendations to customers who were exploring products online and ready to buy. Shown in Figure 10.4, the model is more sophisticated than traditional strategy models.

Whilst this is technically a map of a consumer journey (see also Chapter 2), it is a digital strategy model because it considers the plan an organisation should make. It

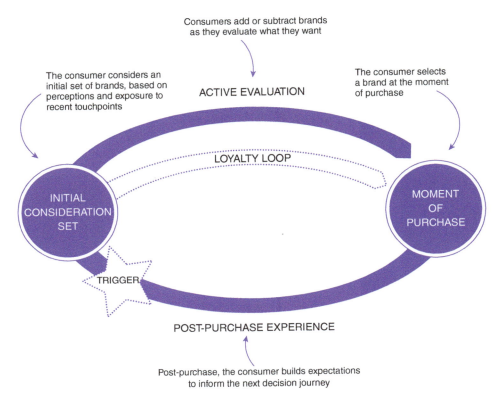

Figure 10.4 The McKinsey consumer decision journey

Source: Exhibit from 'The consumer decision journey', June 2009, McKinsey Quarterly, www.mckinsey.com. Copyright (c) 2021 McKinsey & Company. All rights reserved. Reprinted by permission.

worked as a strategy model for Amazon, which is recognised as one of the world's leading brands.

The McKinsey consumer decision journey comprises four phases: (a) initial consideration set; (b) active evaluation; (c) moment of purchase; and (d) post-purchase experience. Let's explore how the consumer decision journey applies to strategy in the case of a student seeking a university:

- Consideration: If thinking about attending university, students may have one in mind at the start

- Evaluation: Searching for reviews about the university, students start to actively evaluate it against other similar or different places and they may message friends and family

- Purchase: This is when the sale takes place – the students register for a place and the critical factor is that this is no longer the last stage in the sales funnel

- Post-purchase: After the place has been confirmed (based on results), students check to see what others have said about the university and they may share feedback

Activity 10.2   Apply Digital Marketing Strategy frameworks

Based on the digital strategy models in this chapter, select one of these frameworks and apply it to an organisation of your choice.

You're looking for examples of how they build awareness, encourage consideration, support conversion and gain enthusiasm. Remember that they might not use each element of the framework and you'll need to consider why that is.

Whilst strategy is an intended plan, it can change due to disruptions in the marketplace that were not predicted or were ignored (see Chapter 1, digital disruption). It is essential for marketing professionals to be able to adapt the models and frameworks. One of the challenges is that students often stick rigidly to every single aspect of a model, even when not appropriate. If it's not relevant, remove or adapt the element and explain why. And if the market changes, don't stick to the same strategy: review and adapt too!

The key is to have a strategy – a clear vision for the future which is shared with staff. The strategy may not contain all the detail as it is the overarching focus and more information may be included in the final plan. The key components in a strategy are that it is:

- A short statement
- Based on a strategy model of your choice
- Not timed
- An overview rather than detail
- Usually brave!

For example, Strava's strategy is 'to build the most engaged community of athletes in the world'. For more on creating a strategy, see *The Digital Marketing Planner: Your Step-by-Step Guide* (Hanlon, 2022).

10.5 HIERARCHY OF OBJECTIVES

When the strategy has been agreed, the next stage in the digital marketing process is to create objectives, but first let's reflect on how these fit into the strategy.

We looked at the structure of the different types of strategy in Figure 10.1 which started with the corporate strategy, then moved to the business strategy and finally the functional strategies which include the marketing department. This demonstrated the link between strategy and the **hierarchy of objectives** (see Key Term).

At the business strategy level, there will be strategic business objectives which are often framed around growth, regardless of organisation type. This can be more customers, increased sales, larger communities, more positive sentiment, or in business to government, the growth of people completing activities online.

Companies with shareholders need to demonstrate how they will provide a return on investment for those shareholders which again focuses on growth. How the growth will be achieved may not be specified – that's down to the individual departments at a functional level.

These individual departments include marketing and others such as information technology, research and development, finance, human resources, supply chain, legal, customer services and communications.

Therefore, the marketing department's objectives stem from the strategic business objectives.

At the functional level within the marketing department, we need to address the digital marketing strategy which will in turn generate (a) digital marketing objectives, (b) digital marketing mix objectives and (c) digital marketing campaign objectives, which is known as the hierarchy of objectives, shown in Figure 10.1.

For example, Strava's corporate strategy (see Case Study) may be to build the world's largest community of athletes. This is devolved into business strategy for the business units that include the Strava App or Strava Metro. The business strategy is translated into a digital marketing strategy which results in digital marketing objectives. A suggested digital marketing objective is 'To gain 20 million new members by December'. The question is: how will this be achieved? This is why the next level of objectives for the digital marketing mix are needed. In turn, they are developed into digital campaign objectives.

10.5.1 DIGITAL MARKETING MIX OBJECTIVES

The digital, extended marketing mix or the 7Ps (Booms and Bitner, 1980) is often used by marketers to ensure all aspects of marketing are covered. The digital marketing mix should address all 7Ps and even if there is no objective for an element, this should be noted to demonstrate your understanding and to ensure none of the 7Ps are missing. However, it is not possible to make all products digital, so it's exploring the elements that can be made digital. Table 10.2 shows examples of how digital factors can be applied to the 7Ps and includes examples of digital marketing mix objectives.

Table 10.2   Digital marketing mix objectives

Digital Marketing Mix	Digital application	Examples of Digital Marketing Mix objectives
Product	Adapting products to introduce digital elements such as digital gift cards for physical products, downloadable or cloud-based items, developing apps to collect data	To add five digital products to the product offer by September
Price	Alternative pricing models such as dynamic pricing, crowdfunding or participative pricing	To pilot one crowdfunding project in July

Digital Marketing Mix	Digital application	Examples of Digital Marketing Mix objectives
Place	Online access to the products via websites or social selling through social media (see Chapters 3 and 5)	To enable social shopping on two platforms by October
Promotion	Online-only promotion and proactive targeting of specific groups (see Chapters 3, 4 and 5)	To generate 100 sales from persona group 1 during August
People	Staff roles changing as many are involved with customer services and managing communities (see Chapter 6)	To improve positive feedback by 10% in our community within 12 months
Physical evidence	The online user experience (see Chapter 3)	To recruit 25 customers to test the website user experience during July
Processes	The customer journey (see Chapter 2)	To reduce the customer journey by two steps in the next six months

These digital marketing mix objectives indicate what needs to be done and demonstrate how the 7Ps can be used in a digital context.

DISCOVER MORE ON PARTICIPATIVE PRICING

Participative pricing mechanisms include Pay-What-You-Want (PWYW) and you may be more familiar with this in auctions where you can name your own price (NYOP). To discover more, read the article 'Assessing customers' moral disengagement from reciprocity concerns in participative pricing' by Narwal, Nayak and Rai in *the Journal of Business Ethics* (2021).

With Strava, there are no separate objectives for the *product* (the app) as this is managed by the app team. Some promotional *pricing* may be required to encourage downloads, which links to *place* and access to the app. *Promotion* will need to be considered and while at a digital marketing mix level this is an overview, full details will be provided at a campaign level. *Physical evidence* needs to be considered as relevant local imagery will be required. *Processes* are less relevant for Strava as the main factor involved is downloading the app which has been demonstrated as being straightforward. Finally, *people* may involve engaging with well-known athletes in Australia who are already using the app. So the hierarchy of objectives is applied to Strava, as follows:

- Corporate strategy: Build community
- Business unit: Strava App
- Strategic business objective: Growth – to grow the Strava community by 28 per cent by December
- Digital marketing objective: To gain 20 million new members by December

- Digital marketing mix objectives

  o Pricing: To offer 50 per cent discount for premium access during the Australian Outback and Great Ocean Road Marathons in the next 12 months
  o Place: To offer 50 per cent discount in Australia in the next 12 months
  o Promotion: To organise a social media campaign that generates 100,000 downloads in six months
  o Physical evidence: To photograph the top 25 landmarks in Australia within three months
  o People: To recruit the top 50 athletes in Australia using the app within six months

- Digital marketing campaign objectives: To start a social media campaign aimed at key personas

These objectives are all SMART – specific, measurable, achievable, realistic and timed – and written as a simple sentence, rather than a long paragraph, and focused on one element, to ensure they are specific. They can be measured as they include a quantifiable element, they are achievable within the timescales, realistic in relation to the corporate plan and all include a timescale.

Another factor to note is that the objectives focus on *what* not *how*. How they will be achieved is unravelled in the tactics and is addressed in Chapter 11, 'Building the Digital Marketing Plan'.

10.6 FRAMEWORKS FOR CREATING DIGITAL MARKETING OBJECTIVES

To make it easier to create objectives, we can use a framework. This section will explore two frameworks for creating objectives: REAN and the 5Ss.

10.6.1 REACH, ENGAGE, ACTIVATE, NURTURE (REAN)

In 2006 two consultants developed a model to use with clients which they named Reach, Engage, Activate, Nurture, shortened to REAN (Jackson, 2009).

They had considered older models of marketing communication, such as AIDA (Awareness, Interest, Desire, Action), but there were challenges. First, what is 'interest'? Does it mean a web visitor, someone who has downloaded a document or something else? It was vague and lacked clarity. Then there was desire and how this is measured online. How do you know when desire has been reached?

In a digital world, they needed a digital model and so they created REAN. REAN follows a customer journey model, similar to ACR and the digital strategy framework; for example:

- Reach: Activities to generate awareness that can be measured, such as attracting traffic to owned media
- Engage: Customers' conversations or activities before conversion, such as watching videos, liking the brand on social media

- Activate: Similar to conversion and centred around the sale, such as downloading an app or buying online

- Nurture: Looking after the customer, encouraging them to return, such as opening emails, re-subscribing to online services.

Another difference with the REAN model is that Blanc and Kokko suggested that the REAN elements could be applied to different departments, not just the digital marketing team:

- Reach: To reach 5,000 new customers before December (marketing promotion team)

- Engage: To engage with 30 per cent of all web visitors in quarter 2 (communications team)

- Activate: To activate sales from 10 per cent of all web visitors over the next six months (sales team)

- Nurture: To nurture 80 per cent of all customers by July (customer services team)

In the same way, the ACR and the digital strategy framework could also be applied to different departments, to share the workload and to ensure the activities are matched to the right skills.

Activity 10.3　Evaluate objectives using the REAN framework

For an organisation of your choice, create and then evaluate your objectives using the REAN framework.

DIGITAL TOOL　Trello

To share the workload, a free online productivity tool you can try is Trello. It uses a card-sorting system where you place cards or actions into columns that address: to do, doing and done. You drag and drop moving the cards as the actions progress.

It's useful when creating objectives and developing digital marketing plans as you can tag other team members with activities in order to share the workload.

- Visit https://trello.com

10.6.2 SELL, SERVE, SPEAK, SAVE, SIZZLE – 5SS

Another tool to create objectives is the alliterative 5Ss model, originally created by Dave Chaffey and P.R. (Paul) Smith in their book *eMarketing Excellence* (Chaffey and Smith, 2008).

This model was originally intended to be a rubric to assess website effectiveness; it wasn't designed as a tool for developing objectives. As an early adopter of websites, I found this a useful tool and soon realised it would work well as a structure for developing objectives in organisations, so I started to use it when creating digital plans and the idea developed.

You may find that when creating objectives it is difficult to find one for each of the elements of the 5Ss, such as sizzle.

Smartphone Sixty Seconds® – Identify the objectives

- On your mobile phone, go online and find a brand you have visited before.
- Based on their web content, judge what are the company's top three digital marketing objectives.

5S – Sell

This is a traditional objective that looks at sales growth and is about the numbers – the volume of sales or 'conversion activities' such as newsletter registrations, downloads and other relevant activities. Sales objectives may also be created within strategic business objectives.

5S – Serve

Customer service objectives ensure organisations strive to improve and develop the service. It is the one area where smaller businesses can compete with large businesses, who may struggle to consistently deliver fabulous service with thousands of staff.

5S – Speak

Speak is staying in contact with customers and planning communication. Some organisations send you daily emails, some weekly and some every now and then. Speak is also evolving with live chat where people can instantly speak to company representatives online. This may involve the communications, marketing or web teams.

5S – Save

Organisations are under constant pressure to improve processes and this is where saving time and hassle, for the organisation or the customer, has become an important factor in business management.

The best-known example of saving time is probably Amazon's one-click ordering system. About 25 years ago, the United States Patent and Trademark Office (USPTO) issued Amazon.com with a patent for the one-click order system. The objective was to save customers' time when placing an order and remove the hassle of re-entering their name, address, delivery location and payment information. However, you could say this was less about saving time and more about improving the customer journey.

Amazon's one click to order was both save and sizzle, which introduces another challenge: some objectives can achieve two elements in one. What you have to remember is to focus on the primary objective.

5S – Sizzle

The toughest objective to develop! A famous marketing slogan from the last century, attributed to Elmer Wheeler, head of the Tested Selling Institute, was 'Don't sell the steak – sell the sizzle' (Wheeler, 1937). This was re-phrased in the UK as 'Sell the sizzle not the sausage'.

Sizzle is the magic, the factor that makes a difference to a product or service, and adding something so different to the product, promotion or other part of the digital marketing mix, that it stands out and customers and competitors alike say, 'Wow, that's amazing'.

Sizzle needs a bit of thought. It's often not seen within the organisation and can be developed with the help of customers. The key is to ask customers, 'If we could wave a magic wand and change one thing, what would it be?'

Examples of digital marketing objectives using the 5Ss include:

- Sell: To increase sales via our Instagram page to 5 per cent in the next quarter
- Serve: To add messaging functionality to Twitter to automatically respond to FAQs, by June
- Speak: To add live video chat to the website within 12 months
- Save: To analyse frequently asked questions and add to live chat by December
- Sizzle: To create a how-to video channel to explain our FAQs by the year end

The stronger and clearer the objectives, the easier it is to build a digital marketing plan. It's worth spending time to ensure the digital marketing objectives are easy to understand so that more people will agree to them, especially if you're on a placement!

Finally, don't have too many objectives. If you create a list of 30 or more, the plan will be never-ending and nothing will be achieved.

JOURNAL OF NOTE

The *MIT Sloan Management Review* looks at management insights and how this impacts on strategy. Aimed at practitioners, this is an easy-to-read and useful journal.

CASE STUDY

STRAVA'S GROWTH STRATEGY

This continues our long case study and you may find it helpful to read earlier parts in previous chapters.

Strava's website explains its mission: 'We're a passionate and committed team, unified by our mission to build the most engaged community of athletes in the world.'

A mission is an overall focus, similar to a vision, and it doesn't provide detail or share secrets with competitors. Having considered the mission 'to build the most engaged community of athletes in the world', the next step is the strategy – the overall plan (but not the tactics). Strava is adopting a growth strategy focused on customer conversion. With 70 million members in 195 countries, it is growing, yet at the same time it needs to consider the retention of existing members, as well as upgrading free members to the paid-for premium account.

To contextualise these figures, the world population is approaching 8 billion, so Strava members represent just less than 1 per cent of the world's population. Data from the European Cycling Federation indicates that around 1 per cent of people cycle in the capital cities of Romania and Portugal, rising to 10 per cent in Ireland and Croatia, and 11 per cent in the UK. In the Netherlands, known for its cycling culture, cities such as Amsterdam claim 35 per cent, but the leader is Copenhagen in Denmark with 49 per cent of the city population cycling. The Cycling Action Network in New Zealand claims that around 30 per cent of people ride bikes, whilst in Australia, the government transport agency Austroads (which also represents New Zealand) suggests that it's 13 per cent, with, unsurprisingly, greater use in larger cities.

Other countries, such as Norway, the Netherlands and China, are ahead in another area of cycling with bike-sharing schemes, although it may be harder to track this data as it's not about the number of bicycles, but the number of cyclists. Plus, in some locations, a bike may simply be a means of transport, rather than a hobby, where there is no requirement for a fitness app.

With around 225 countries in the world, having an active membership in 195 is very strong and similar to well-established social networks such as LinkedIn which is present in about 200 countries.

Based on the online information, Strava's hierarchy of objectives, which leads to the digital marketing objectives, may include:

- Corporate strategy: Build world's largest community of athletes
- Business unit: Strava app
- Business strategy: Growth

- Digital marketing strategy: Conversion
  - Digital marketing objective (a): To gain 20 million new members by December
  - Digital marketing objective (b): To convert 20 per cent of free members to the premium account by December

These are ambitious targets as it has taken over ten years to grow to 70 million users, but it may be that many more people take up cycling in the next ten years.

CASE QUESTIONS

- Create digital marketing mix objectives for Strava's digital marketing objective 'To gain 20 million new members by December'.

- How might Strava encourage free users to become paying members? Create digital marketing campaign objectives to show what's involved.

- Why do you think Strava decided to launch its Strava Metro service free of charge?

FURTHER EXERCISES

1. Select an organisation of your choice and analyse its digital marketing strategy to identify whether there is a clear framework or whether the organisation lacks structure. Based on your assessment, make recommendations for improvement.

2. Create a digital marketing strategy for an organisation of your choice, based on the business unit. This should include personas (see Chapter 2).

3. Imagine you're working for a government organisation and need to encourage citizens to adopt healthy eating. Consider which strategy model is most relevant and justify your decision.

4. Digital marketing strategy is a waste of time as the world changes too quickly. Organisations should simply adapt on a day-to-day basis. Discuss.

SUMMARY

This chapter has explored:

- The core concepts involved in digital strategy
- The usefulness of the TOWS matrix to develop strategic options
- Digital marketing strategy models
- The different elements in the hierarchy of objectives
- Frameworks for creating digital marketing objectives

GO ONLINE

Visit **study.sagepub.com/hanlon2e** to access links to interesting articles, websites and videos related to this chapter.

Build your stakeholder map

Transform objectives into tactics

ACTIVITIES

Stakeholders

Propose the creative offer and messaging

OVERVIEW
Chapter 11 takes students through the process of digital marketing planning from applying the digital marketing mix and creating a digital marketing campaign.

KEY CONCEPTS

DIGITAL TOOLS

A/B and multivariate testing

Crowdfunding

Create online designs using Canva.com

Find free images with Pixabay.com

11

BUILDING THE DIGITAL MARKETING PLAN

PROFESSIONAL SKILLS

When you have worked through this chapter, you should be able to:

- Build a digital marketing plan
- Create a digital marketing campaign

11.1 INTRODUCTION TO BUILDING THE DIGITAL MARKETING PLAN

A plan provides a roadmap, an agreed set of steps, and enables organisations to save resources. Having a plan ensures you are prepared for what might happen as well as agreeing the organisation's future direction. This chapter explains how you bring together different elements to build and present a digital marketing plan. You will discover how to engage stakeholders and comprehend the requirements for constructing a budget.

A lack of planning may impact on the organisation in many ways, including:

- Confusion as no one is sure what's happening
- Working in silos as no information is shared and there's a lack of integration
- Lack of skills as no one may be available internally to carry out the work and the organisation may need to spend more on external consultants or agency staff
- Difficulty measuring effectiveness as if no plans are in place, no one will know whether the goals have been achieved
- In a complex and changing external environment, the wrong decisions being taken based on lack of information
- Short-term decisions being made based on immediate rather than long-term requirements and could be wrong

Having identified issues with a lack of a plan, this still occurs. Yet making a plan prepares organisations and people for things that might happen, rather than ignoring the situation and assuming it will all be OK. With an understanding about the challenges due to a lack of planning, it's time to identify some tactics to achieve your strategy and objectives, though if you haven't finished your objectives, you can't create the plan!

There are different ways to create a digital marketing plan, which largely depend on the organisation or the brief you have been given and typically follow the steps shown in Figure 11.1.

Figure 11.1 shows what's involved in building the digital marketing plan along with why the steps are needed and examples of how to present the different steps. And as you will notice, the plan won't work unless you have already developed the personas, strategy and objectives. This is an iterative approach that starts by adding earlier work (personas, strategy, objectives) and then considers potential tactics. Once agreed, detailed tactics are added and the skills required identified. You can then evaluate the resources and the budget. The resources element in Step 5 and the review element in Step 6 we will consider in Chapter 12, 'Managing Resources and Reporting', which also includes budgeting.

Before we construct the plan, let's consider who's involved.

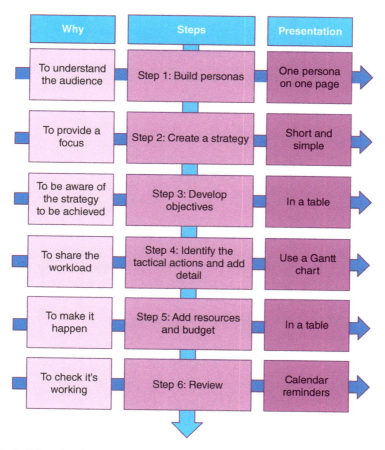

Figure 11.1 Building the digital marketing plan

11.2 UNDERSTANDING THE ROLE OF STAKEHOLDERS IN PLANNING

Planning is about people and processes. We need to first address the people or the stakeholders that are involved in the processes. Getting the stakeholders involved means it has more chance of success. If we create a plan without them, they may abandon, boycott or discredit the brand.

Stakeholders were initially defined as 'any group or individual who can affect or is affected by the achievement of the organization's objectives' (Freeman, 1984, p. 46), yet in a digital world stakeholders can be expanded to include other interested groups or friends of those groups, which is why they need to be identified before the plan starts.

Stakeholder theory is about 'The Principle of Who or What Really Counts' (He et al., 2020), and stakeholders are said to have power and interest (Mendelow, 1981), legitimacy, urgency and salience (Mitchell et al., 1997). In a digital context, we can describe salience as influence. Let's explore the main characteristics of stakeholders, with explanations and examples.

11.2.1 CHARACTERISTICS OF STAKEHOLDERS

The characteristics of stakeholders include power, interest or relationship, legitimacy and authority, urgency and salience or influence.

Stakeholder power types

These can be:

- Coercive which is achieved by force or threat – for example, online hackers holding websites to ransom, such as the Health Service Executive (HSE) in Ireland which was attacked when the COVID-19 vaccination programme started
- Utilitarian from material or financial impact such as Amazon delisting products with many negative reviews
- Normative based on normal behaviours or standards – for example, ASOS and other retailers removed Boohoo products from their websites after allegations of modern slavery

Interest or relationship

This involves those with an interest in or relationship with the organisation such as consumers, employees and shareholders. For example, the oil company ExxonMobil witnessed power from interest when two shareholders gained seats on the board to force the company to adopt a greener strategy.

Legitimacy and authority

This is where the actions are justified based on local laws, beliefs or values. For example, the clothing retailer H&M was fined €35,258,707.95 after data breaches in Germany.

Urgency

This concerns the degree to which stakeholders can call for action and it can involve time-sensitive issues. For example, COVID-19 vaccines were approved, then withdrawn from use and reintroduced in different countries due to new reports.

Salience or influence

This power is about the priority assigned to the claim based on prominence such as network size. For example, Ben & Jerry's ice cream joined the #StopHateForProfit campaign to make social media networks address hate speech.

11.2.3 STAKEHOLDER MAPPING

Once you've identified your stakeholders, it's useful to visually map them, so you can see everyone that may need to be consulted in the digital marketing plan.

This can be done by assessing their characteristics, their levels of power, their interest or relationship with the organisation, their legitimacy and authority, the urgency and their salience or influence. You can decide how you evaluate who is most and least important; for example, using a scale of 1 to 10 or simply classifying as high, medium or low.

Activity 11.1   Build your stakeholder map

- Identify the stakeholders for a food, games or fashion organisation of your choice.
- Create a mind map or diagram to visually show who the stakeholders may be.
- The next step is to assess their characteristics. You could do this using a table, or by adapting your diagram, perhaps colour-coding from green to orange and then red for those with greatest power.

DISCOVER MORE ON STAKEHOLDER MAPPING

The article 'The value of stakeholder mapping to enhance co-creation in citizen science initiatives', led by Artemis Skarlatidou and colleagues, provides examples of the process of stakeholder mapping, with sample questions and different approaches (Skarlatidou et al., 2019).

11.3 DIGITAL APPLICATION OF THE MARKETING MIX

The 7Ps, also known as the extended or digital marketing mix (Booms and Bitner, 1980), has been used as a planning model as its focus can be tactical as well as strategic. In Chapter 10, we considered digital marketing mix objectives – this was *what* we will do, whereas the tactics in building the plan are *how* we will achieve these objectives.

11.3.1 DIGITAL PRODUCTS

Digital products include items that are downloadable or available online, as well as those available offline. When selling physical products, digital alternatives include gift cards, but this applies mainly in a retail business-to-consumer (B2C) setting. In a business-to-business (B2B) context, it depends on the product as this could include tools for manufacturing cars, machinery to manage forests, shipping containers to transport goods – none of which can be digital.

However with some B2B purchases, some elements can become digital. For example, software and IT services can be provided remotely and although buying IT equipment still requires physical products, it may be that online training can be offered as digital goods. Chapter 1 also considers digital products.

11.3.2 DIGITAL PRICING

Traditional pricing models have fixed prices and discounts or offer codes. Digital pricing includes more options:

- Subscription pricing
- Pay what you want (participative pricing)
- Buy now pay later (BNPL)
- Group buying
- Crowdfunding

Subscription pricing

Subscription pricing is understood in traditional settings, such as paying for access to a health club or being part of a membership group. This notion of a monthly pay-as-you-go subscription pricing model has gained wide spread adoption in the digital world.

Instead of persuading individuals to pay a larger amount of money up front, it's just a small recurring charge. Subscription pricing facilitates growth for companies who simply need to increase the audience base and convert users to increase sales, such as the example with Strava. You can subscribe to films (Netflix), delivery services (Amazon Prime), music (Spotify), software (Office 365), online data storage (Apple iCloud), enhanced social media membership (LinkedIn), mobile phone packages and many apps.

There are challenges for consumers with subscriptions; for example, they may sign up for services which they rarely use and some subscriptions can be difficult to cancel.

Participative pricing

Pay what you want is a form of participative pricing (see Chapter 10, Discover More on Participative Pricing) and is an area that is still being researched. Researchers suggest that for this to be effective a reference price should be provided as an indication, and it's important to justify why this pricing method is being used (Narwal and Nayak, 2019) for customers to trust the method.

Buy now pay later

Buy now pay later is where credit is offered to the consumer at the point of purchase and they pay later. The downside is that this could result in debt being created. Credit cards offer limited BNPL functionality where customers can decide to clear their card each month or to pay interest on their borrowings. However, this can result in overconsumption (Fook and McNeill, 2020) as consumers make impulse purchases, regardless of whether or not they have the money available.

Group buying

Group or team buying has been witnessed with websites such as Groupon and Pinduoduo. com, where a minimum number of buyers commit to purchasing an item and gain a lower price through bulk purchase. Groupon focused on experiences, such as days out, but during the pandemic in 2020 moved towards local marketplace items. Pinduoduo has a different approach and started by connecting farmers with customers, from fruit and vegetables to coffee growers. It links manufacturers and brands with its customers, acting as a marketplace for shopping with friends. However, researchers have found that these group sites often succeed because they offer lower prices (Cao and Li, 2020).

Crowdfunding

Crowdfunding cannot be ignored as a finance mechanism and while this may seem like a new system, this is how many charities fund their work.

Third-party crowdfunding websites allow individuals and companies to promote activities or innovations to encourage donations. Researchers have identified that crowdfunding platforms have become a critical vehicle for entrepreneurs with a new idea or innovation, to raise funds and ensure they are noticed by possible investors (Fan et al., 2020). Most crowdfunding platforms charge based on the funds raised and some also levy a transaction fee. If donors are paying by credit card, this may incur additional charges, so it's wise to check the details as if you raise £100,000 you might only gain £92,000 after costs.

Popular websites for crowdfunding include those shown in Table 11.1, with examples of their target audience and the fees involved.

Table 11.1   Crowdfunding platforms, audiences and fees

Crowdfunding platform	Aimed at	Popular with	Platform fees	Transaction fees
Kickstarter	Start-ups	Creative businesses	5%	3% + $0.20 per transaction
Indiegogo	Start-ups	Tech companies	5%	2.9% – 4.4%
GoFundMe	Individuals	Individuals seeking to cover medical expenses, education and personal events	0%	2.9%* + £0.25 per transaction
Mightycause	Non-profits	Integrates with CRM systems and social media	$59 – $99 per month	1.2% + $0.29
Patreon	Creatives	Podcasters, writers, educators	5% – 12% of monthly income	2.9% – 5% + $0.10 – $0.30 per transaction

Some of these sites such as Patreon are positioned as business management tools, enabling platform users to upload their content to the site and promote it to a paying audience.

Smartphone Sixty Seconds® – Discover crowdfunding sites

- Go online and search for *top crowdfunding sites*.
- How many can you find?
- Have you ever used a crowdfunding site to raise money or to donate money?
- If yes, what was this for?

ETHICAL INSIGHTS Cross-country price discrimination

Charging different prices in different countries for the same products is not unusual and can be due to increased local taxes or in the case of physical goods, the transportation and distribution. However, there is a lack of transparency over online subscription pricing, where there are fewer logistical issues. This means that there can be wide variations depending on the location. Researcher Joel Waldfogel examined the different rates for Spotify based on 60 countries (Waldfogel, 2020). Unsurprisingly, the study found that reduced rates are typically charged in areas where the average household income is lower. He also found price discrimination benefitted the company as this provided a larger user base. This may seem logical, although there are issues of fairness if you're located in one country and across the border it's much cheaper.

- How do you feel about different prices being charged in different countries?
- Which subscription products do you pay for that you couldn't live without?
- What are your thoughts about subscription pricing as a business model?

Pricing transparency and challenges

Greater price transparency exists online where consumers compare one item with another. Researchers have found that price transparency can result in customers being 'willing to pay more when pricing is clear and transparent but also likely to accelerate their purchase' (Hanna et al., 2019, p. 235).

There are issues for organisations who are trying to move towards digital models, which doesn't always work. For example, newspapers and magazines can hide the paid-for content behind a paywall, yet as researchers in the USA found 'not a single U.S. newspaper has successfully transformed itself digitally' (Chyi and Ng, 2020, p. 543), which indicates that we're willing to pay for some subscriptions, but not others. It seems that access to news stories doesn't have a value, unless it's free.

Digital pricing models offer companies more alternatives and different approaches to income generation and some of these examples can be applied to traditional goods.

11.3.3 DIGITAL PROCESSES

Smaller traditional stores might provide no indication of the goods in stock, only what's available in store. Although some parts of digital processes such as the visibility of order history and stock checking might be considered part of physical evidence, they are core processes that help customers to make decisions and stay with the same provider. For example, busy shoppers might go online into a supermarket website and select a shopping basket from a week ago and re-order the same goods. Stock checking is available for digital devices in some retailers, although it can be easier to see stock availability on websites.

Virtual consultations became popular during the 2020 pandemic, especially for medical procedures and discussions (Sinha et al., 2020), as well as student projects. These could be applied to B2C online shopping for more expensive goods. For example, chatbots could detect customer interest based on a series of questions and hand the conversation to a virtual sales assistant.

This section has looked at digital products, digital pricing and digital processes. There's more on digital products and places, payments and processes in Chapter 1. Physical evidence or the online user experience was explained in Chapter 3. People in the form of influencers or ambassadors was considered in Chapter 4, and promotion was addressed in Chapters 3, 4, 5 and 6.

The critical factor is identifying the relevant digital elements for your organisation that make sense! In the digital marketing audit (see Chapter 8), weaknesses identified in that audit can be addressed at this stage.

Having considered how the digital marketing mix can be applied, the next step is creating tactics from the digital marketing mix objectives.

Let's look back at the examples of digital marketing mix objectives in Chapter 10 (10.5) and turn one of those into tactics. The chosen objective is 'To add five digital products to the product offer by September'.

To transform objectives in to tactics, I've made some notes that are shown in Figure 11.2. This note includes details of who is involved and the timescale. There is also a

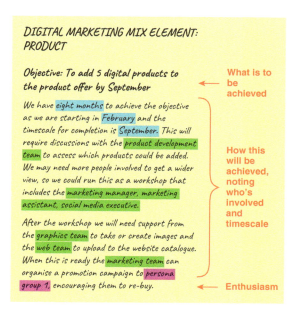

Figure 11.2 Digital marketing mix objectives transformed into tactics

Table 11.2 Gantt chart to add five digital products to the product offer by September

Action	Detail	Who	Feb	Mar	Apr	May	June	Budget
Product assessment	Workshop to identify most suitable products to add	Product development and marketing teams	■					In-house
Brief for graphics team	Prepare one-page brief for the graphics team about the number, type and size of images needed	Marketing assistant	■	■				In-house
Product imagery	Imagery will be needed for the website product listing as well as web banners, for emails and for social media	Graphics team		■				£2,000
Add content to website	Upload products to the website catalogue	Web team			■			In-house
Promotion campaign to persona group 1	Email countdown campaign announcing new product on the way	Marketing team			■			In-house
	Social media (Instagram and Facebook) to showcase 'coming soon'	Social media executive			■	■		In-house
	Email countdown campaign announcing new product on the way	Marketing assistant				■		£500
New products launched	Email campaign to persona group 1	Marketing team					■	£500
	Banners changed on website and across social media	Web team					■	In-house
	Paid search campaign across social media	Social media executive					■	£20,000

link to a persona group that was created earlier, so the objective is firmly connected back to Chapter 4, where digital personas were developed.

This is the basis for building the plan, with each objective becoming a series of actions (shown in Table 11.2 as a Gantt chart).

The budget for this campaign is a total of £23,000 which is used for additional imagery to supplement the work carried out by the graphics team as well as email platform costs (Mailchimp) and the paid search campaign costs.

The Gantt chart will need to be developed further as Table 11.2 shows just one objective. All objectives will need to be reviewed and created in the same way, so that all the actions and timescales can be seen and adjusted if needed.

Activity 11.2 Transform objectives into tactics

- Take one of your objectives and write a note to identify the tactics needed to make it happen.
- Indicate who is involved.
- Include the external costs and sum up the total budget.
- Consider whether the budget seems reasonable for the size of the organisation.
- Present as a Gantt chart.

Having identified the actions, you will need to create a campaign to promote the digital product. Case Example 11.1 shows MUD Jeans and expands on their current and future digital 7Ps, concluding with a digital campaign concept.

CASE EXAMPLE 11.1 MUD Jeans

Fast fashion has an impact on our environment and having spent 30-plus years in the sector Bert van Son from the Netherlands created a novel business – MUD Jeans. MUD Jeans are aimed at collaborative consumers who are conscious of ecological issues and seeking ways to reduce consumption.

MUD Jeans' mission is 'Creating a world without waste', as shown in Figure 11.3, and this informs every aspect of the business.

As a small business, it needs to grow and build its customer base. It is adopting a growth strategy and the primary objective is to convert a further 1,000 lease-a-jeans customers. Let's determine the digital marketing plan to successfully provide digital products and services. This involves assessing the changes required to the current and future digital marketing mix based on this objective.

(Continued)

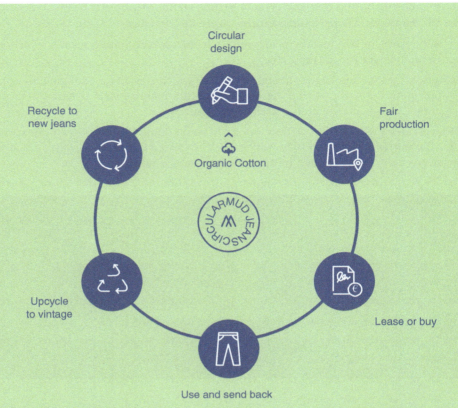

Figure 11.3   MUD Jeans circular mission

With permission from MUD Jeans

Product – current situation

The physical product range is kept simple – denim clothing, but this is fashion with a difference as the clothes are made from recycled denim and organic cotton. The products are pesticide free and because they're using recycled jeans there is no waste. The range includes jeans, jean jackets, skirts and bags.

The recycled denim is from customers' old jeans which they can send to their processing centre. If the jeans are not ready for recycling, they are reused and promoted as 'vintage'. Team MUD says its jeans are the most sustainable in the world, saving water, carbon dioxide emissions and recycling materials.

The company also offers a digital gift card.

Product – future recommendations

There are no recommendations for changes to the product at this time. MUD Jeans works on simplicity of product. Adding more lines would complicate this and could create more waste which is contrary to the business mission. Plus, the company already has digital gift cards.

Price – current situation

MUD Jeans has an innovative payment method, as customers can lease their jeans via the website. This is a form of subscription pricing and moves towards offering fashion as a service. Instead of paying €119.95 for the garment, customers pay €9.95 a month for their first pair of MUD Jeans for a one-year lease. After 12 months, you keep or swap the jeans. The idea is that 'high-quality becomes affordable' (Mud Jeans, 2021, p. 1), you buy better for longer and, at the same time, you no longer need to own your clothes, as you can swap for another pair.

To further encourage sustainability, another pricing incentive for customers is a discount on new jeans when they return their old denims (of any brand) to Team MUD.

The website takes payment in several currencies. There's the option to buy now and pay later using Klarna.

Price – future recommendations

Many pricing options have been considered except participative pricing. MUD Jeans could offer vintage lines based on 'pay what you want'. A pilot could assess what customers pay and whether it is a reasonable and fair amount. Content would be needed to explain where the profits go, so that customers didn't try to buy a pair of MUD Jeans for €1.

Place – current situation

MUD Jeans offers online and offline access to its products. The jeans can be leased or purchased via the website. They are also for sale in some physical fashion stores.

The website initially used WooCommerce and today runs as a Shopify site. Both are popular ecommerce platforms that allow companies to upload product catalogues, add discount codes and manage stock.

Place – future recommendations

MUD Jeans could expand its access to the products which are currently only sold via its website. It could adopt social selling and offer selected ranges via Instagram or Pinterest. This may not be suitable for jeans so might be used for specific products such as jean jackets and bags.

(Continued)

Promotion – current situation

In the Netherlands, MUD Jeans has gained publicity and won the ABN AMRO award for Sustainable Retailer of the Year 2020–21. The company has appeared in articles in many top fashion magazines and blogs across Europe, as well as featuring in podcasts and videos.

MUD Jeans is active on Facebook. The page is managed by four people in the Netherlands and one in Germany. As the owners are transparent about the companies manufacturing their products, they include these workers in their adverts. The Instagram page shares their core mission – a sustainable approach, as well as in-store images and fan photos. The Pinterest account is similar, with fewer followers.

They use Twitter which focuses on their business ethos of sustainability. Their YouTube channel is similar, although this contains behind-the-scenes tours and more background.

As well as recycling jeans, they recycle the imagery. The clothes are modelled by a small number of people and these photos are used again across social media and in their adverts.

They encourage customers to co-create content in their Ambassador Programme, by uploading photos, sharing on Instagram, recommending a friend and writing product reviews. In return, Ambassadors gain discounts, early access to new products, an extended return policy and brand merchandise.

Promotion – future recommendations

One area that could be explored is email. Regular email updates about the company should be shared with all persona groups.

The MUD Jeans Ambassadors could be given a mini-logo to use on specific posts. They will need to use the hashtag #ad to ensure they are not breaking local laws.

Processes – current situation

Awareness in the customer journey takes place across social media with a focus on sustainability. For consideration, to encourage people who have looked at the website to make a purchase or start a lease package, the company uses Facebook and LinkedIn, re-targeting adverts.

Conversion is present on the product pages, with large red buttons inviting customers to 'buy now' or 'lease now'. The product pages contain more details about how the jeans were made and illustrate the amount of water and carbon dioxide saved in production. Reviews are shown towards the end of the product page which include the reviewers' sizes, to give an accurate impression of the comments.

Enthusiasm is demonstrated with customer reviews and media stories about the brand. There's an option for happy customers to sign up to regular newsletters which are powered by MailChimp.

Processes – future recommendations

The processes have been well considered and all aspects of awareness, conversion and enthusiasm have been addressed. The only missing area is consideration which could be enabled by using chatbots on the website to answer any questions a web viewer may have.

Physical evidence – current situation

The online user experience is good which is not surprising, with a Shopify website which is designed to be easy to use for customers. There is a detailed size guide which explains how to take measurements. Reviewers have commented on the simplicity of the process.

Physical evidence – future recommendations

The online user experience is not an issue at this time as the website gains great feedback. So there are no recommendations to change physical evidence.

People – current situation

With over 30 years working in the fashion industry, it is not surprising that Bert van Son has created a short supply chain. Upcycling and dyeing the denim take place in Spain and the stitching takes place in Tunisia. The sales and marketing team is based in the Netherlands.

The staff share a commitment to reduce pollution from garment production, stop cheap, fast fashion and make clothing that lasts longer. However, there are many companies offering recycled, upcycled, sustainable clothing; the difference with MUD Jeans is its total circular approach to business. As a passion brand, it adds value to its customers by delivering on its commitment to the environment across its business operations. MUD Jeans sums up its value to customers as 'Doing jeans differently' which includes its approach to its products, pricing and people.

People – future recommendations

MUD Jeans has a fair and balanced approach to staff and workers, there are clear roles and a commitment to the mission. The only recommended change is to increase the brand ambassadors to create user-generated content across the social media platforms.

Having discussed the current and future recommendations for the 7Ps, the growth strategy is to convert 1,000 lease-a-jeans customers. Table 11.3 shows the recommended digital marketing mix objectives and digital marketing campaign concepts.

Physical evidence isn't included as the website has received positive feedback from over 500 customers, so doesn't need any changes at this time. It's estimated that appointing ten brand ambassadors to create user-generated content across the social media platforms will generate 200 sales, so, combined with the remaining digital marketing mix elements, the objectives meet the strategy.

The digital campaign concepts follow the same theme – 'without costing the earth' – which fits with the company's mission and demonstrates how the strategy has a direct impact on any creative work. More work would be needed to develop this campaign.

(Continued)

Table 11.3   MUD Jeans digital marketing mix objectives and digital marketing campaign concept

Digital Marketing Mix	Digital Marketing Mix objectives	Digital marketing campaign concept
Product	To sell 100 digital gift cards in locations near to physical stores over three months	Give what they want without costing the earth
Price	To test participative pricing for 100 pairs of jeans	Pay what you want without costing the earth
Place	To use two social media platforms as sales channels that generate 300 sales by December	Buy what you want without costing the earth
Promotion	To generate 100 sales from the persona group 1 by October	Buy what you want without costing the earth
People	To appoint ten brand ambassadors to create user-generated content across the social media platforms	Say what you want without costing the earth
Processes	To get 200 existing customers to lease more jeans	Re-buy what you want without costing the earth

Case questions

- Recommend three other digital marketing mix objectives that align with the strategy for MUD Jeans.
- Using the theme 'without costing the earth', develop a brief for an agency or in-house member of staff to explain what is required.
- Create a campaign for MUD Jeans based on the theme 'without costing the earth'. You can select the promotional tools that you feel will work best.

11.4 CREATING A DIGITAL MARKETING CAMPAIGN

When building your digital marketing plan, you will have considered promotion (see the digital marketing toolbox in Chapters 3, 4 and 5) and you may need to create individual campaign plans. This section looks at digital marketing campaigns; if you want to organise traditional marketing campaigns, see **Discover More** on Advertising and Promotion.

DISCOVER MORE ON ADVERTISING AND PROMOTION

For in-depth coverage of all types of campaigns, read the latest edition of *Advertising and Promotion* by Chris Hackley and Rungpaka Amy Hackley, published by Sage.

The digital marketing campaign planning process is shown in Figure 11.4 and starts with brand position which is outlined and then the following steps are discussed.

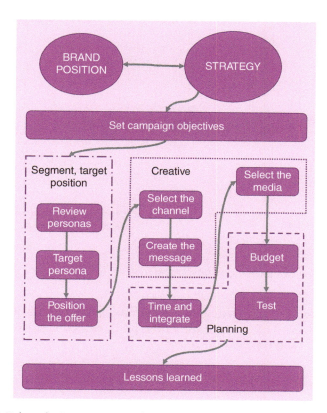

Figure 11.4 Digital marketing campaign planning process

11.4.1 BRAND POSITION

Before starting the digital marketing campaign, you agree the brand position and the strategy. Positioning is complex as this concerns the brand, its identity and imagery, its content, its pricing strategy, its processes and benefits.

The positioning should be considered within a wider brand exercise to decide if it's a luxury or affordable item, whether it's fun or serious and how the brand wishes to be perceived in the market. As an example, Figure 11.5 shows a brand positioning model for food delivery boxes in the UK.

The two dimensions used are the factors that the companies are focused on: price and the range of options. Some companies such as Balance Box focus on super-healthy foods. Mindful Chef provides healthy foods plus a range of other options for different diets. At the other end of the scale are the supermarket ready meals. So a supermarket could offer 'luxury' ready meals at higher prices which are differentiated by higher-quality ingredients or packaging, sometimes endorsed by a celebrity chef.

Figure 11.5   Two-dimensional brand positioning map

When positioning an organisation, it's about understanding the value offered to customers. In Figure 11.5, is the value in the pre-prepared meals delivered to your doorstep, a wide range of foods or price?

DISCOVER MORE ON BRAND POSITIONING

Read the latest edition of *Strategic Brand Management* by Elliott, Percy and Pervan, published by Oxford University Press.

Once the strategy is in place, whether that's awareness, consideration, conversion or enthusiasm, the campaign objectives can be created.

We'll work through each step in the digital marketing campaign planning process shown in Figure 11.4. Budgeting is covered later in this chapter.

11.4.2 SET DIGITAL MARKETING CAMPAIGN OBJECTIVES

Whilst you will have agreed objectives for the digital marketing plan, you will also have campaign objectives. Think of campaign objectives as a subset of your main objectives.

Let's apply the digital marketing strategy framework, focused on conversion. The persona is hungry students.

Objective 1: To gain a 10 per cent increase in online sales in November

- **Campaign objective A:** To target UK students aged 18–22, living away from home, via Instagram, in November, offering evening delivery
- **Campaign objective B:** To re-target web visitors using Instagram, during October and November, with a 10 per cent student discount offer

Objective 2: To increase adoption of the mobile app by 25 per cent from September to December

- **Campaign objective C:** To target UK students aged 18–22, living away from home, via Instagram, in November, offering a free app with nutritional data
- **Campaign objective D:** To re-target web visitors across the Google network, from September to December, with the app details

The granulation or development of the details in the specific campaign objectives makes it easier to construct the **creative offer and messaging**, which follow later in this chapter.

The difference between the digital marketing plan objectives and the campaign objectives is the detail. Campaign objectives focus on a platform and a specific activity – such as re-targeting.

11.4.3 SEGMENT, TARGET AND POSITION (STP)

Traditional marketing models include the concept of STP – segmentation, targeting and positioning (see Discover More on traditional strategy models in Chapter 10 for books that cover this in depth). In a digital context, this changes and segmentation is covered in Chapter 2, digital personas which are more detailed than a simple segment.

Targeting addresses which personas are relevant for an activity, whether that's a new product launch or a communications campaign. For example, if the brand has three personas such as busy families, city living and hungry students, they would not all respond to the same promotional campaign; that's why it's useful to target campaigns to specific personas or segments.

11.4.4 SELECT THE CHANNEL

With many options available, channel selection can be a challenge! Look back at Chapters 3, 4, 5 and 6 to decide which elements of the digital marketing toolbox will be selected. It may be that multiple channels are selected, such as social media and online communities. This is another reason why, when developing personas, you consider the webographics. If the webographics are not strong or detailed enough, you need to go back and add greater depth and information.

Thinking about potential channels for the persona hungry student:

- Hungry students might use Google to search for local information, so paid search may be a useful channel
- Hungry students may use Instagram for inspiration

The critical factor is ensuring you have research to back up and support your claims.

11.4.5 CREATE THE MESSAGE

The objectives and targeting have been agreed and the next stage is building the creative offer. However, the creative offer can be more challenging in a digital environment. For example, think about the size of an ad on LinkedIn – it's tiny! Instagram needs compelling visual images to attract attention.

Added to this you need to communicate a specific message that appeals to the persona in microseconds. Advertising appeals are either emotional, trying to elicit an emotion, whether positive or negative, or rational, trying to connect with a practical or utilitarian need, and are the foundation for the advertising message (Grigaliunaite and Pileliene, 2016).

Many consumer behaviour experts have explored examples of rational (effectiveness, convenience, price, safety) and emotional (exclusivity, adventure, beauty, relaxation) appeals. The key is that a single appeal is used in an advert, aimed at a specific target audience, so that there is instant understanding and no confusion.

Smartphone Sixty Seconds® – Find the appeals

- Use your mobile phone and log in to a social network. What adverts can you see?
- Take one advert and identify the advertising appeal.
- Is it emotional or rational?
- Compare with classmates: do they see the same or different messages?

DIGITAL TOOL   Canva.com

Canva is a free online design tool with many easy-to-use templates for social media. Many companies use Canva to create their Instagram and Twitter adverts and posts. It's free for individual use and also for non-profits. The paid-for version gives access to more templates and is designed for larger companies.

- Try it here: Canva.com

Activity 11.3 Propose the creative offer and messaging

Propose the creative offer and messaging for either:

- Campaign objective A: To target 'hungry students' – students based near your location, aged 18–22, living away from home, via Instagram, in November, offering evening delivery; or

- A campaign related to an organisation of your choice.

11.4.6 TIMING AND INTEGRATION

Advertising online allows you to plan the exact timing of when you want to launch your adverts. For example, Instagram and Facebook allow you to schedule adverts (if the 'lifetime budget' option is selected) for certain days at specific times. For example, if your campaign objective is to target hungry students, via Instagram, in November, offering evening delivery, you may run the adverts between 4 p.m. and 10 p.m., when the target audience is thinking about food!

Plus, campaigns should be integrated. This means that the whole campaign is connected with other marketing promotional activities. So, if you have a traditional campaign on billboards outside the halls of residence, you can synchronise both campaigns.

If a campaign lacks integration, the customer will become confused. Imagine looking at a photo on Instagram, clicking through to the website, but landing on a page that doesn't make sense – this is **cognitive dissonance** (see Key Term) and usually results in customers abandoning pages.

Another aspect of timing and integration is ensuring that you don't run different promotions at the same time. If you plan a 10 per cent off and a 15 per cent off campaign simultaneously, the 10 per cent is less likely to work and the advertising budget will be wasted.

KEY TERM   COGNITIVE DISSONANCE

Cognitive dissonance theory holds that individuals may have conflicting attitudes, beliefs or behaviour, leading to discomfort (Festinger and Carlsmith, 1959).

Inconsistency in beliefs leads to dissonance. For example, you may believe that smoking is dangerous but you are at a party and meet someone interesting, who is smoking, and instead of complaining about the smoke, you stand next to them, potentially inhaling. Your belief that smoking is bad is inconsistent with your action (putting up with the smoke) and results in a change of belief or behaviour.

11.4.7 SELECT THE MEDIA

Having agreed four campaign objectives (A to D), we can apply these to the overall media plan and select the media. This may include elements from the digital marketing toolbox (see Chapters 3 and 4).

For example, to enhance the adverts we need to ensure that the website is up to date and contains relevant information, and we may also write some new blog articles that focus on the challenges of being a student and cooking when away from home.

Table 11.4 shows a digital media plan example that explains the type of content that will be placed and where. This would typically be supported by a commentary to provide more details.

Table 11.4   Digital media plan example

Communication channel	General information	Helpful recipes	News about food	Ad campaign
Website	✓	✓	✓	
Blog	✓	✓	✓	
Twitter	✓	✓	✓	
Facebook		✓	✓	✓
Instagram		✓	✓	✓
Google				✓

11.4.8 TESTING

Pre-testing

Before running the ads, you might **use A/B or multivariate testing** (see Key Term) to assess which adverts will be most successful.

KEY TERMS   A/B AND MULTIVARIATE TESTING

A/B testing compares one thing against another, such as trying two different images for an advert. Testing can include headlines, body copy or website landing pages.

Multivariate testing considers a combination of items at the same time. For example, in a display advert the multiple variations could include two different images, as well as two different headlines. Two adverts, plus two headlines, are equal to four items being tested. If two versions of the body copy are also varied, this increases the variables to six.

By gathering data, you can evaluate which was most successful, whether that was based on the number of people visiting a website, downloading a brochure or completing a purchase.

Digital marketing advertising platforms allow you to run several different adverts at the same time and gain feedback as to what worked. Paid search and social media adverts can test the adverts automatically and only show the more successful adverts (e.g. those gaining most clicks) to the target persona group.

Testing in a digital marketing environment is fairly straightforward. Set a small budget, run the adverts for a week and gather the feedback. This is also known as a 'test and learn' strategy.

Post-testing

Post-testing is measuring results after the adverts have run. In digital advertising, this can take place quickly, literally in 24 hours. This will provide data on which were the most successful ads and why. You can repeat the ad format to re-test in case this was an exception.

Lessons learned

After the campaign has concluded, the team can evaluate what they discovered. The post-testing stage can inform which elements of the campaign were most successful and what needs to change before another campaign is launched.

Chapter 13 contains more on digital marketing metrics and analytics, explaining what can be measured and how.

There's one further element of the campaign to consider – budgeting, which we'll explore next.

11.5 BUDGETING CORE CONCEPTS

Having a budget enables companies to allocate resources and better manage the organisation. As a student, you'll have a budget which may be based on income from a part-time job, savings or other funds. If companies don't manage their budgets by spending too much or not gaining additional income, they can run out of money and can go out of business if there are no ways to borrow the funding. This means that budgets are critical business processes.

In building your digital marketing plan, once the tactics and resources are identified you need to prepare a budget. There may be additional resources required to support the plan such as materials or more staff. (See Chapter 12, 'Managing Resources and Reporting' for more on this.)

Traditionally, budgets were organised based on different approaches, such as:

- Objective and task
- Budget available
- Percentage of turnover
- Last year's budget

11.5.1 OBJECTIVE AND TASK

When the objectives have been formulated and the tactics listed, you allocate the required funds to complete all activities. This method is known as the 'objective and task' budget which allocates the money needed to meet the objectives.

The challenge may be that the budget required to meet the objectives is unaffordable for the organisation. In this case, you may need to review the objectives and refine them to manage with a smaller budget, or opt for the 'budget available' method.

11.5.2 BUDGET AVAILABLE

More often than not, this applies to smaller organisations and is about the possible or available budget. If you have a budget of £20,000, you need to maximise the impact of it and decide what will generate the best results and meet your objectives. This means that you need to become more creative and potentially use freely available tools where possible (see Digital Tools: Canva.com and pixabay.com).

DIGITAL TOOL Pixabay.com

One of the greatest costs in marketing is creating images. Pixabay offers free images and royalty-free photos. This is an online site where users can add their images – giving them away free – and other users can download them to use in different ways.

As its website notes, Pixabay content can be used for free for commercial and non-commercial use across print and digital, except in the cases mentioned in 'What is not allowed'. Typically you can't use the images to sell as Zoom backgrounds, t-shirts or posters. In some cases, permission may be needed, but the website explains the steps.

11.5.3 PERCENTAGE OF TURNOVER

The CMO Survey® group collects data from chief marketing officers (CMOs) to help predict future trends. The group has captured data on marketing budgets since 2008 and shares its results on its website (cmosurvey.org) (Moorman, 2020). The group's work indicates that average marketing budgets based on a percentage of turnover are:

- B2B Product – 11.3 per cent
- B2B Services – 11.3 per cent
- B2C Product – 17.3 per cent
- B2C Services – 14.9 per cent

Although these are averages, it will depend on the company's objectives and what the percentage represents. For example, ASOS as a B2C product is in the average of the 17.3 per cent bracket, but in 2020 the firm spent 3.7 per cent on marketing. Although it seems that it is under the average and spending much less, 3.7 per cent at ASOS in 2020 represented £119 million! This means that you need to consider the context – the type of company, its revenue and its objectives.

11.5.4 LAST YEAR'S BUDGET

This method is more usual in larger organisations where a budget has been allocated to different departments and you are given last year's budget plus 5 per cent.

The downside with this method is that departments are encouraged to spend the entire budget, even if not needed, just to gain the same amount the following year.

11.5.5 DIGITAL MARKETING BUDGETS

In digital marketing, there is greater flexibility as online advertising is auction-based and so depends on the search terms being used, the volume of searches and competition for the words. As an example, if you bid for a phrase like 'online postcard printing' this may cost £10 per click. But if you bid for 'e postcard maker' this may cost 10p. This means smaller businesses can more easily compete, as long as they are creative.

Other budgeting models include **cost per acquisition** (see **Key Term**) but the overall budget may still be based on percentage of turnover, or objective and task, or last year's budget.

KEY TERM COST PER ACQUISITION

In a digital environment, we consider cost per acquisition – what does it cost to gain or convert a new customer? Acquisition can be securing data (an email address), a donation or a sale.

As an example, if my average sale is £100 on a product that costs £25 to produce, my profit margin is 75 per cent. If my target profit margin is 50–70 per cent, I could afford to spend £5 to £50 in securing the customer.

However, if it is an expensive keyword that costs £100, I would never make a profit and this wouldn't work. I therefore need to understand the acquisition cost from the start.

Chapter 3 explained the different paid search payment options. You might experiment with a small budget initially and monitor the results. As you gain the data, results and confidence, you can increase the budget. This method of pilot testing is useful to gather evidence to assess whether some channels, messages or keywords are better than others.

CASE EXAMPLE 11.2   Petpuls – The crowdfunded AI dog collar

Petpuls is a dog collar with a difference. It is smart clothing that detects whether your pet is happy, anxious, angry, sad or relaxed, based on voice recognition powered by AI. Your dog wears a collar, you connect via WiFi and you can check your dog's emotion on the app.

It started as a student project in South Korea where students can gain an extra income by dog-sitting. Having developed the collar, the product was originally launched using Asia's largest crowdfunding platform company Wadiz, where the team exceeded its goal and gained 164 per cent of its target amount.

As the crowdfunding approach was so successful in South Korea, in June 2020 the company decided to seek funding in the US and Europe, using crowdfunding platform Indiegogo. This crowdfunding package included the 'Double Dog pack', with ten dog collars for $740 for up to ten dogs, which was claimed by ten people, and for a donation of $5 you could receive a thank you message!

The Indiegogo site didn't generate the same level of funding – we were deep in a pandemic at that time, and although the company aimed to raise around $80,000 it only secured 14 per cent of its target. However, the product gained worldwide publicity and won a silver Stevie® International Business Award for 'Best New Product or Service of the Year' in the category of consumer products, durables. The product raised other monies totalling $750,000 in seed funding.

The business has eight employees and the small collars retail at $99, the large version at $108, plus the shipping costs. Extra straps can be purchased and are available in five colours.

Case questions

- What type of advertising appeals might work best for Petpuls?
- What method of budget setting should Petpuls use?
- How might better results be achieved by crowdfunding?

11.6 PRESENTING THE PLAN

When the plan has been completed, you may need to share with colleagues or teachers or external funders if you're trying to raise money to start a new project. In this section, we look at different ways to present and share your plan.

11.6.1 PRESENTATION OPTIONS

The presentation options depend on the purpose of the plan and the target audience. For example, in some situations the work you're presenting will be uploaded to a submission point by a specific time and you'll have no opportunity to explain or clarify the information, which is why it is so important to check and follow the guidelines. These guidelines are not just for assignments as some companies, such as Amazon, are said to dislike PowerPoint presentations and prefer short briefing documents, which means that being able to write a plan in five pages or in fewer than 2,000 words is a real skill.

Depending on the audience and the purpose of the plan, you might be able to present remotely or in person, or possibly email and follow up with a discussion. With many options, it's essential to clarify this at the start.

Earlier in this chapter in Figure 11.1: Building the digital marketing plan, we considered some presentation options and most of these elements, whether tables, short summaries or personas, could be displayed in slides or in a document.

Regardless of the presentation format, all plans involve telling a story – what we know (the audit), where we're headed (the strategy) and how we get there (the action plan). All good stories include a beginning, a middle and an end. You can add your own creativity to the plan, as long as it's within the agreed guidelines. But don't forget, a plan with many great images that doesn't provide the story (or answer the assignment questions) will never work. One way to gain attention is to present the key elements of the plan on one page.

11.6.2 ONE-PAGE DIGITAL MARKETING PLAN

In Chapter 10, we looked at strategy and objectives, and considered how a strategy translates into objectives. If we start with two of these objectives and list some possible digital marketing tools to use, we can start to present that plan.

Table 11.5 shows the strategy, digital marketing objectives and tactics that have already been created. There are two objectives for each strategy and each objective has one or more suggested tactics.

Table 11.5 Strategy, digital marketing objectives and tactics

Strategy	Digital marketing objective	Digital Marketing Mix element	Digital Marketing Mix objectives	Digital campaign concept	Tactics
Conversion	To gain 20 million new members by December	Product	To gain 400,000 new Strava community members per week via Instagram	Wherever you run, walk or cycle, join our athlete community	• Social media advertising to drive traffic to the website • Promote the hashtags #strava #cycling #running #walking #cyclinglife #cyclingphotos #fitness #instacycling #instarunners

The strategy is based around the **digital marketing strategy framework** (see Chapter 9) and the objectives are aligned with this.

Under each objective, I have added one or more possible tactics, which we can expand on. Before we do, we need to consider that there are three fundamental stages in the user or customer journey: pre-purchase, purchase and post-purchase. These are described in the strategy as awareness, consideration and conversion, so they are arranged in a logical order.

Another key factor is that we are targeting specific individuals or audience personas (see Chapter 2) rather than everyone who may visit our website, social media space or affiliate site.

This is because it's fine to consider social media to increase engagement, but if our persona doesn't use social media, it won't work. So now you need to revisit the one, two or three personas you created earlier (see Activity 2.2: Create a digital persona) and ensure that these are still valid and resonate with the organisation's strategy and objectives. If not, you may need to adapt them.

Having confirmed the personas, look back at your strategy and the desired objectives. Ensure that you select elements from the digital toolbox which are relevant to the objectives. To help with this, note which objective is being achieved for each tactic. In some cases, it may be more than one objective.

Table 11.6 shows an example of a one-page digital marketing plan outline. This addresses the tactics only and does not address the resources required, nor the control mechanisms and the measures. This provides a balanced overview to decide which tactics should be selected, and, from this, the specific details concerning resources can be added in the next phase.

With Table 11.6, we need to apply the plan to an organisation, so let's imagine that this is a charity requiring volunteers, supporters and donors. I have added in three personas, which we could outline as:

- Vic the volunteer – older, male, uses Facebook to stay in touch with grandchildren only, checks email every day, visits the website, reads online articles
- Sam the supporter – student, rarely checks email, uses Instagram and only online on mobile
- Diana the donor – business owner, donates money, has no spare time, uses LinkedIn and Twitter, checks email, reads articles online

Your personas should contain significantly more detail and be evidence-based! An example of a one-page plan using this information is shown in Table 11.6.

The essential aspect to this one-page digital marketing plan outline is that where there are blank boxes, this is because the tactics (email, online advertising or pay per click) are not relevant for those persona groups.

From Table 11.6, you can create a Gantt chart (see the example in Table 11.2) which should include the overall area, the specific action, the date by when this should happen and the job role or skills needed. It may be that the digital marketing assistant can use video editing or a good photographer. This is why people's names are not added as it is about roles, not individuals. The Gantt chart might include the budget and other resources, which we consider further in Chapter 12.

Table 11.6 Example of a one-page digital marketing plan

Strategy: Pre-purchase, purchase and post-purchase

Digital toolbox element	Objective being achieved	Persona 1 Vic the volunteer	Persona 2 Sam the supporter	Persona 3 Diana the donor
Email	To encourage 20% of customers to leave a review before 30 September	Email and ask for a review on how volunteering makes a difference		
Website	To increase sales from the website from 5% of visitors to 10% before 31 May	Add case studies to the website to show the good work		
Online PR	To generate 10% more visitors to the website by 31 December	Create a case study on how volunteering makes a difference		Find companies for PR on benefits of getting involved with charities
Search engine marketing	To drive 15% more traffic to the website by the end of Q1	Do not use PPC for these personas		
Blogs	To drive 15% more traffic to the website by the end of Q1			Articles on benefits for companies to get involved in LinkedIn
Social networks	To increase engagement on social media by 10% in the next six months	Posts about volunteers making a difference and organising a volunteer event	Links to images from resources area with toolkits on organising events	Case studies on how volunteering makes a difference on LinkedIn
Social media advertising	To drive 15% more traffic to the website by the end of Q1		Ads on Instagram to download useful content from website	Urgent appeal ads on Twitter
UX	To increase sales from the website from 5% of visitors to 10% before 31 May		Improve the mobile UX	
Site design	To encourage 15% of web visitors to share their email address within 12 months	Add resources area with downloadable toolkits on organising events		

JOURNAL OF NOTE

Long Range Planning has been publishing research since 1968. Its articles include subjects such as business models and stakeholders, as well as the move to digital operations.

CASE STUDY

PLANNING FOR GROWTH

This continues our long case study and you may find it helpful to read earlier parts in previous chapters.

Gabriel has been promoted from content manager to assistant communications manager for Strava. His competitor evaluation was well received, plus his participation and contribution in the Zoom meetings were positively noticed. His camera was always on, he prepared for the meetings and had plenty of questions, further evidencing his commitment and enthusiasm.

In his new role, the first task is to build a digital marketing plan that focuses on communications. As content manager, his approach was to work on one aspect of content and then include his team, so that they discovered what was involved with the processes.

He's aware that the purpose of the plan is to create a document that can be used by team members to deliver the strategy and objectives. The plan contains the tactics to expand on the objectives.

In Chapter 10, objectives were suggested which are revisited here, so Gabriel can build the tactical plan. These objectives are:

- To gain 20 million new members by December
- To convert 20 per cent of free members to the premium account by December
- To retain 75 per cent of premium members in the next 12 months
- To gain new city planners from 1,000 cities in the next 12 months

He starts by taking the first objective and identifying what is required to make this happen. The objective is ambitious – to gain 20 million new members by December. At the moment, the company is gaining new members as word of mouth is spreading the use of the app, but the new members are mainly in the USA which is where the company started. Gabriel decides to break the objective into specific elements, by using the 7Ps.

Considering the product and the price, this objective is connected to the free version of the app. As the app works for cyclists and runners, he needs to create relevant personas.

In terms of their location, most of the current Strava members are based in the USA and the UK. Gabriel decides he wants to target Australia and New Zealand, whose populations are 25 million and 5 million – 30 million in total. The data indicates that around 15 per cent are cyclists, meaning that if they all subscribed there would be 4.5 million new members, so in order to reach his 20 million objective, he needs some additional markets and may also need to consider other sports in these locations too.

When Gabriel evaluated the competition, he looked at Runkeeper as it has 50 million users. Other competitors have closed in the last few years including Runtastic (which became adidas® Running) and Endomondo with 20 million users. It may be wise to target these users too and encourage them to switch – if he gained 20 per cent from here, he would have a further 14 million and a total of 18.5 million. For the remaining 2 million, he decides to target other geographic locations and adds the countries where the top races take place: Italy, France and Spain. With this combined approach, he should reach the target numbers.

Gabriel notes the other elements of the 7Ps:

- **Place:** Access to the product which is the app which is available in all app marketplaces.

- **Processes:** The ad messages should have a one-click to download.

- **Physical evidence:** The website is up to date with all Gabriel's recent content and no changes are needed here.

- **People:** He will need to ensure, when managing the resources, that he allocates a full budget and briefs the local country teams too.

The largest piece of work is promotion as many of the other elements are in place. Gabriel considers that the best approach will be online advertising direct to people using Runkeeper, Runtastic and Endomondo in the target locations (Australia, New Zealand, Italy, France and Spain). There will be two ad types, one aimed at the cyclist persona and another for runners.

At the same time, blogs and other local material would help support the campaign, combined with an email campaign to local members to recommend a friend and in return gain one month's free premium membership.

To summarise the work to be done, Gabriel creates a table which he will add to a PowerPoint presentation to share with his manager as a top-level digital marketing plan.

Action	Detail	Note
Create adverts	Aimed at people using Runkeeper, Runtastic, Endomondo and matching the personas created earlier	Two ad types, one aimed at cyclists and another for runners
		Ads should work on social media and ad networks too
		Ads focused on target audience in Australia and New Zealand, Italy, France and Spain
Plan advert schedule	Ensure the ads are timed to coincide with other local activities	Speak to local managers for more background
Local blog articles	Identify local KoMs and QoMs to see if they will participate in the campaign	Contact local managers for help
Manage the ad campaign	Once live, the ads need to be managed daily to review progress and make any amendments that may be needed	Consider when planning resources
Email marketing	Recommend a friend campaign	Understand who is managing the data and how this would work
		Would need additional email creative input

Gabriel is aware that this is an outline digital marketing plan and that he needs to add the budget and resources to it before presenting to his manager.

CASE QUESTIONS

- What other factors should Gabriel consider when creating this outline digital marketing plan?
- Based on this approach, create a plan for Gabriel to achieve another objective: 'To convert 20 per cent of free members to the premium account by December.'
- Create a social media ad campaign for Gabriel that is aimed at runners, especially those using Runkeeper, Runtastic, Endomondo, and matches the personas he created.

FURTHER EXERCISES

1. For an organisation of your choice, assess its digital marketing mix. Consider its current activities and make recommendations for the future.

2. Organise a digital marketing campaign for your university's marketing degree. First, evaluate the different channels, based on one persona, and recommend one channel to use in this campaign. Develop some outline visuals and copy that could be used.

3. Create a digital marketing plan for an organisation of your choice.

4. Budgeting is a waste of time. It's easier for organisations to just spend what they need to. Argue for or against this notion and justify your response.

SUMMARY

This chapter has explored:

- The digital application of the extended marketing mix
- How to assemble a digital marketing plan
- Digital marketing campaign planning
- Factors to consider when constructing a budget
- Ways to present a digital marketing plan

GO ONLINE

Visit **study.sagepub.com/hanlon2e** to access links to interesting articles, websites and videos related to this chapter.

PART 4

DIGITAL MARKETING MANAGEMENT

CONTENTS

12 Managing Resources and Reporting 333
13 Digital Marketing Metrics and Analytics 365
14 Integrating and Transforming Digital Marketing 395

Join the gig economy

Use a content scheduling tool

ACTIVITIES

Evaluate roles and responsibilities using the RACI matrix

Gig economy

OVERVIEW
Chapter 12 introduces resources exploring each of the 9Ms, with guidance on how to select resources and understand roles in projects.

KEY CONCEPTS

DIGITAL TOOLS

MarTech and Stackies

SAF framework

Digital dashboards

MarTech landscapes

12

MANAGING RESOURCES AND REPORTING

LEARNING OUTCOMES

When you have read this chapter, you will be able to:

Understand all types of resources within organisations

Apply the 9Ms resources model

Analyse the SAF framework

Evaluate roles and responsibilities using the RACI matrix

Create reports for an organisation using dashboards

PROFESSIONAL SKILLS

When you have worked through this chapter, you should be able to:

- Apply a resources framework to identify gaps in an organisation
- Use a content scheduling tool

12.1 INTRODUCTION TO MANAGING RESOURCES AND REPORTING

A marketing plan isn't a plan without resources. You need people, a budget, technology to make it happen and materials such as content.

Bizarrely, resources are often considered part of a management role, rather than the responsibility of marketing. We need to change this and own every part of the digital marketing plan.

Resources in organisations include the assets, from the people to the processes and the knowledge to the networks. Resources are the reasons why organisations succeed, and in digital marketing all actions, and therefore all resources, can be measured, so that it is easier to understand what contributes to an organisation's success. This is recognised in business management, practised by successful organisations and supported by academic theory.

The Danish economist and management theorist Birger Wernerfelt explored the resource-based view of the firm (RBV), which evolved into resource-based theory (RBT). Wernerfelt's work took place at a time when success within an organisation was said to be due to the product mix. Wernerfelt suggested that both products and resources should be considered. His examples of resources included: 'brand names, in-house knowledge of technology, employment of skilled personnel, trade contacts, machinery, efficient procedures, capital' (Wernerfelt, 1984, p. 172).

Whilst Wernerfelt provided some initial examples of resources, this has developed into a broader list to incorporate: tangible or intangible aspects of the business; physical or human processes; and intellectual property (Davcik and Sharma, 2016).

> ### DISCOVER MORE ON RESOURCE-BASED THEORY
>
> This older article provides useful background: 'Resource-based theory in marketing' by Irina Kozlenkova and colleagues in the *Journal of the Academy of Marketing Science* (Kozlenkova et al., 2013).

Thinking about turning resources into assets, for the tech giant Amazon its processes are its key resource: the systems in place to deliver goods ordered online the next day, or the same day in some locations.

This chapter considers the key issues and types of resources required for successful implementation of a digital marketing strategy, so that you'll be able to define the resources needed to deliver a digital marketing plan (see Chapter 11). Resources are defined with frameworks to select the most appropriate resources. We'll explore roles and responsibilities and governance. The chapter concludes with a section on how you report your findings.

12.2 THE 9MS RESOURCE TYPES

After you have listed the tactics and created your plan, you need to consider what resources will be required to make it happen.

The foundations of resource planning are in manufacturing, where it was critical to ensure the right people were in the right place with the right machines and materials, at the right time. This has led to a plethora of 'M models', from the 5Ms of Efficiency (Manpower, Materials, Machines, Methods, Money) to the Six Sigma techniques for improving processes (Method, Mother nature, Man, Measurement, Machines, Materials).

I have adopted a blended approach, with 9Ms: Manpower, Money, Method, Mother nature, Measurement, Machines, Materials, Management and Minutes, as shown in Figure 12.1.

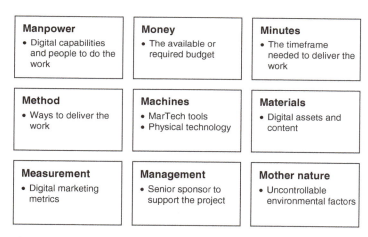

Figure 12.1 The 9Ms of resource planning

We'll now explore each of these elements, although measurement is considered in greater detail in Chapter 13, 'Digital Marketing Metrics and Analytics'.

12.2.1 MANPOWER – DIGITAL CAPABILITIES

When creating a plan, a key factor is deciding who will do the work – the people involved. One of the major challenges is the digital capabilities gap.

Digital skills are considered to be essential to countries to such an extent that the European Union, the World Bank and the World Economic Forum all evaluate how different nations compare on these skills. As a digital marketing student, you're already ahead, but in 2020 the digital skills gap in Europe still existed with over

40 per cent of citizens lacking basic digital abilities (European Commission, 2020). These skills include communicating online, finding information and content online, setting up an online account, using the internet to solve problems and ensuring you're staying safe online.

Digital natives were born using these skills, but not everyone is in the same place. This is why, when you create a persona (see Chapter 4), you assess their webographics – if they don't have any, you need to consider alternative approaches to communication!

One study defined the digital skills needed in the workplace (Gekara et al., 2019) and recommended a digital skills framework for organisations when considering capabilities. I've adapted this framework and identify the key parts in this section.

1 Digital knowledge

Digital knowledge concerns theoretical comprehension and understanding. This is the first level and these skills are gained when studying. You may be investigating different frameworks or theories to better understand how and why situations occur. For example, in Chapter 2, 'The Digital Consumer', we considered showrooming and webrooming. Once you understand a concept, you can logically suggest methods of addressing this – that's the next skill.

2 Cognitive know-how

Cognitive know-how is the second level, which considers logical, intuitive, innovative and creative thinking in the digital space. It's the ability to apply theory and think creatively. When running a digital marketing campaign, this might include people who can write content to maximise SEO (see Chapter 3) or others who may create imagery that is vivid and interactive (see Chapter 4).

3 Practical know-how

At the third level, practical know-how is the use of digital tools such as hardware, software, information and security systems. This level considers the ability to use the relevant skills and know-how by applying digital tools. For example, there may be tools that can facilitate easier management of showrooming and webrooming, such as 'before you go' pop-ups in websites, or QR codes in store, showing how the system price matches or carries out other activities. This third level could be used to assess which team members can create social media adverts, add products to an ecommerce website or build a new website.

4 Competence

At level four, you're demonstrating competence, so that you can independently learn new skills or transfer existing skills to new situations. When studying, you may be asked to create a digital marketing plan and when you're working in an organisation, you may need to do the same, on your own, without your teachers. This demonstrates digital competence.

5 Digital attitude

The final stage is a digital attitude – your values and beliefs that enable you to develop digital **competence** (see Key Term in Chapter 11). It's being open to adopting new technology and skills. This has been described as having a digital mindset (Solberg et al., 2020, p. 107). If we think back to the Technology Acceptance Model (TAM) in Chapter 2, this evaluated how team members felt about using new technology based on their perceptions of how straightforward a tool was to use and its value or usefulness.

This digital skills framework is a useful assessment tool to analyse the internal skills within an organisation, based on what's needed to successfully implement your digital marketing strategy and plan.

12.2.2 MONEY – THE BUDGET

Cost identification and analysis concern pinpointing all the elements needed in the budget (see Chapter 11 for more on budgeting). A budget is needed for:

- Lead generation, whether that's using paid search, social media of influencers
- Email marketing – even if the organisation isn't using a paid-for tool, a budget may be needed to create email templates
- Managing online communities and conversations, although this may be more around salaries and a technology tool to alert the team when there are new posts
- Machines – the tools and technology needed to deliver the work (see 'Machines' later in this chapter)
- Materials such as copy for websites, images for email (see 'Materials' later in this chapter)

There is an idea that some elements are free, especially people's time. Salaries are usually considered to sit outside a marketing budget and are considered sensitive data that's not shared (for a different approach, see Case Example 12.1: Bellingcat).

Another area that's considered to be free are the social media platforms. They may be free to access and there may be no charge for companies to add content, but ensuring the target audience see the content is more challenging. As an example, Facebook typically shares **organic posts** (see Key Term) with fewer than 10 per cent of those that 'like' the page. To gain attention from the audience, advertising can be required (see Chapter 3 for more on online advertising and Chapter 11 for more on budgets).

> **KEY TERM**   ORGANIC POSTS
>
> On social media platforms like Facebook, an organisation can reach its target audience in two ways: via (a) paid adverts; or (b) organic posts. Your organic reach is the number of people who saw the content, without you paying to promote it, as opposed to the paid reach – the number of people who saw the post after you invested in advertising to share it.
>
> Organic posts typically include unpaid updates that are not sales focused. If they are too promotional, social media platforms like Facebook are less likely to share the content widely as they deem this to be poor quality content, unless of course you pay to promote it! Don't forget, Facebook owns Instagram, Messenger and WhatsApp and could apply the same principles to these platforms.

Return on marketing investment

Regardless of the costs involved in terms of time when creating budgets, one concept that's frequently mentioned is return on marketing investment (ROMI) which considers the results from the marketing budget. For example, for every £100 spent on digital marketing, what does this generate? If we generate £200, that's £100 extra or a 50 per cent return on the marketing investment.

However, ROMI is a short-term measure and ignores the lifetime value of the customer; it looks at one sale at one time, often connected to a single product. Online advertising facilitates more detailed measurement and the returns can be easier to see. For example, being able to set budgets based on maximum cost per customer, such as CPA (see Key Term **Cost per acquisition** in Chapter 11), builds in the return on marketing investment from the start. So companies need to be aware of the cost of finding new customers and to understand how much they are likely to spend (see **Customer lifetime value** in Chapter 13). This varies depending on the products, the cost of the goods and profit margins. As companies can run multiple digital campaigns, they can more easily assess what worked and why.

CASE EXAMPLE 12.1   Bellingcat

The award-winning journalism website Bellingcat was started by Eliot Higgins, who previously blogged using the pseudonym Brown Moses (a name in a song by 1960s rock star Frank Zappa). Based in the Netherlands, the bellingcat.com website explains: 'Bellingcat is an independent international collective of researchers, investigators and citizen journalists using open source and social media investigation to probe a variety of subjects.'

These writers spend time gathering facts and removing fiction and their work has exposed lethal attacks on individuals, uncovered suspects behind fatal events and other international misdeeds. Subsequently, their stories and information are used by news media worldwide.

Bellingcat's staff and contributors in over 20 countries have adopted an open approach to their investigations and share their methods of newsgathering. Being accountable and pooling these sources is a core element of their values.

As transparency is so important, they share their resources model. Their income is funded by a range of grants, plus they hold chargeable workshops and request donations on their website. There's a **Call to action** (see Key Term in Chapter 3) on the website that states: 'Your donation to Bellingcat is a direct contribution to our research. With your support, we will continue to publish groundbreaking investigations and uncover wrongdoing all around the world.'

To collect these donations, they use the crowdfunding platform Patreon (see Chapter 11) which enables them to take recurring contributions. Additionally, they explain that some companies provide in-kind donations of **MarTech** and these are listed on their website.

Unlike many organisations, they also share details of staff salaries which are based on the NGO (non-governmental organisations) sector salary scale and they follow guidelines from the Charities Association in the Netherlands (Goede Doelen Nederland), as the Bellingcat website notes:

- The remuneration for staff and employees is within the middle of the NGO-sector salary scale.
- The yearly remuneration of the executive director is 90.000 EUR (including pension and holiday allowance).

This explicit approach not just to sharing the salaries, but also to justifying why they have been set at these levels, is unusual. However, it is part of the organisation's DNA – they need to make sure that their entire business model is open for anyone to examine.

Case questions

- Bellingcat's business is based on sharing its resources – how can the organisation ensure it continues to be successful if digital competitors appear?
- What other methods of income generation could Bellingcat adopt?
- The marketing model for many charities is based on donations. What challenges may arise when creating a budget based on donations?

12.2.3 MINUTES – THE TIMESCALE

Timeframes help to explain the total time required to deliver a piece of work, which can highlight whether it would take too long and may need extra help to complete. This also involves scheduling the resources so you know what and who are needed and when. This is often displayed as a Gantt chart (see Chapter 11 for an example).

The timescales may depend on the stakeholders and who's involved in the work. So, if a plan needs to be presented to a senior management team that only meets once a month, you may need to add in an extra four weeks. Or, if there's an agency involved, it may need time to set up the account before work commences. It's always worth adding in some extra time in case of delays.

12.2.4 METHOD – THE DELIVERY

The method of undertaking the work depends on the internal capabilities. Sometimes, there aren't enough staff or there are competence gaps, as we considered in the above section, 'Manpower'. Another issue is that sometimes internal resources can be disrupted; for example, staff may be off sick or on leave. In these situations, outsourcing can be a short-, medium- or long-term solution. There are different approaches to managing disruption with internal resources which include contract marketplaces, agency engagement, working with consultants or finding temporary staff.

Contract marketplaces

Online contract marketplaces act as intermediaries to enable buyers to find potential freelancers and the freelancers to gain work. For example, if a company needs to build a website, or create images, or design a logo, it may pay to promote the work on these marketplaces and people registered with the site can bid for the work or showcase their earlier achievements. These contract marketplaces are aimed at freelancers who may be working full- or part-time and some examples of these marketplaces are:

- peopleperhour.com
- upwork.com
- freelancer.com
- fiverr.com

This type of work is also referred to as being part of the gig or the platform economy. Researchers have explored the **gig economy** (see Key Term) and categorised the different elements based on two dimensions: the worker's location and the complexity or skills required to conduct the task (Vallas and Schor, 2020). This study considered the location as local or global; I've adapted this to online and offline. The second dimension concerns the amount of skill required for the task, which was classed as low to high, as shown in Figure 12.2.

Online work that requires fewer skills includes microtasking. For example, Amazon's Mechanical Turk (MTurk) is used by companies to catalogue products, re-name images and gather pieces of information. These jobs are called human intelligence tasks (HITs). However, the payment for the tasks can be a few cents, so workers may need to carry out hundreds of tasks to earn a few dollars. MTurk is widely used by companies such as Pinterest to tag images, by WikiHow to check queries and by researchers to gain survey responses.

Online work that needs greater skills includes design and coding. Influencers and content creators were seen by Vallas and Schor as being between low and high in terms of skills. If you imagine a typical influencer filming themselves opening a product and recording their reaction, this doesn't need too many skills, whereas a content creator who is writing blog articles may have undertaken a degree and gained skills in copy writing. These elements of remote or non-local work Vallas and Schor considered to be crowdworking.

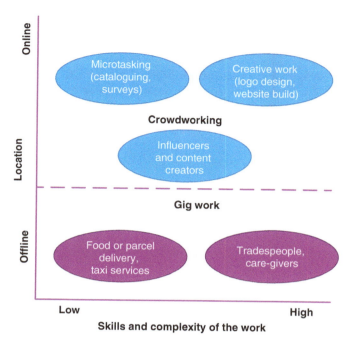

Figure 12.2 Types of work in the platform economy

Source: Republished with permission of *Annual Review of Sociology*, from 'What do platforms do? Understanding the gig economy', Vallas, S. and Schor, J. B., 46, 2020; permission conveyed through Copyright Clearance Center, Inc.

The offline setting the researchers considered as local work because it's often delivered at a local level, such as food delivery. For example, a local Just Eat Takeaway.com delivery person needs to be close to the food and the customers, whereas someone cataloguing images or building a website may be working anywhere in the world.

KEY TERM GIG ECONOMY

The gig or platform economy is where freelancers take flexible or short contracts to undertake pieces of work. The downsides of gig work include the lack of employment protection (no paid holidays, no sick pay), the lack of power in the relationship (some platforms use algorithms to promote the work) and dependence on the platform for work. The advantage is the flexibility to choose when to work and what work to take on.

In the UK, Uber drivers successfully took legal action against the firm, saying they were formal workers, not gig workers. Their case was based on the power of Uber in enforcing which cars the workers had to buy, as well as the firm allocating their work through its own platform. This is likely to evolve over the next few years as both sides seek clarification.

Gig economy platforms that specialise in offline services that require good skills include TaskRabbit. This site partners with IKEA, so if you buy kit furniture, you can find someone to assemble it for you!

Companies can outsource work to these contract marketplaces and only pay for what they need, when it's needed. Using online freelancers often means you can speed up processes to facilitate faster delivery of some parts of a project. In larger organisations, it can be easier to gain permission to spend £1,000 or $1,000 on a service than it can be to start a staff-hiring process.

Activity 12.1   Join the gig economy

Many students join the gig economy to supplement their income whilst studying:

- Review the gig economy platforms (e.g. peopleperhour.com, upwork.com, freelancer. com, fiverr.com) and select an area that you're qualified for, such as creating social media posts, writing content, designing an advert.
- Read the requirements and pitch for a piece of work.
- Note the time involved in your research and creating the pitch.
- Discuss what happens next.

12.2.5 MACHINES – TOOLS AND TECHNOLOGY

In a digital environment, machines are coming to the fore. When the M models were developed in manufacturing, machinery concerned the plant and equipment needed to deliver the work. Applied in a digital environment, this might include:

- Physical technology such as desktop or laptop computers or tablets
- Digital marketing technology tools such as programmes, apps or software

Planning for these resources in advance is a good idea as gaining budgetary approval in bigger organisations can take weeks (or months). It may be necessary to evaluate the different options available to ensure the organisation selects the relevant tools. This section explores marketing technology further.

MarTech

Marketing technology tools are referred to as MarTech (marketing + technology) and we can consider these as our digital machinery. Organisations often use many MarTech programmes or applications to facilitate the customer journey, conduct audits and create plans.

MarTech products are not used in isolation but often integrated or connected with others in **stackies** (see Key Term).

MarTech products are growing fast: with just 350 tools in 2012, there are now over 8,000 tools available for marketers (Brinker, 2020a, p. 1).

This is too many to consider, so Table 12.1 shows examples of some of these MarTech stacks and products, applied to areas of marketing management.

Table 12.1 Examples of MarTech stacks and products, applied to areas of digital marketing management

Marketing management area	Example of MarTech stack	Examples of products and why used
Planning	Projects and workflow	• Semrush – to see popular keyword planning • CompetitorMonitor – to instantly price-check competitors' online prices
Sharing information	Marketing briefing	• Teams – to discuss and share files • SurveyMonkey – to conduct research amongst stakeholders
Customer awareness	Campaign calendar	• Trello – to schedule content • Asana – to assign tasks amongst team members
Customer consideration	Lead generation	• Hubspot – to create landing pages and nurture leads • Lead Forensics – to see who's visiting your website
Customer conversion	Email marketing	• Zendesk chat – to offer live chat on websites • Sendgrid – to send triggered emails from an ecommerce website • Mailchimp – to send planned emails to a database
Customer enthusiasm	Community and reviews	• Feefo – to automate reviews from online sales • Disqus – to manage and respond to comments in the community

(Continued)

Table 12.1   (Continued)

Marketing management area	Example of MarTech stack	Examples of products and why used
Managing materials	Asset management	• Dropbox – to store images and materials in shared folders • Brandmaker – to store all digital assets in one place, assigning permissions to different users
Social listening	Conversational marketing and chat	• Fanpage Karma – to monitor social media conversations and engage fans better • Crowdfire – to discover and schedule content, and manage all your social accounts from one place
Data management	Management	• Salesforce – to register customer details and respond • Zoho – to manage customer data and streamline processes
Reporting	Marketing report	• Sprout social – to report on social media campaign results • Hootsuite – to manage and report on all social media channels

Table 12.1 shows that the MarTech stacks and products are applied to all areas of digital marketing management. In fact, many MarTech products can be used for multiple purposes. For example, Salesforce and Hubspot provide many similar services such as database management, the ability to send emails and reporting.

As there are so many options and the possibility of duplication – or paying twice for the same service – Netherlands-based Frans Riemersma of MarTechTribe provides vendor analysis – a service to help organisations decide which stackies work best for them. Both Riemersma and Brinker crowdsource to find the tools, before examining further and adding to their datasets.

MarTech fees vary from a few dollars a month to hundreds of thousands of dollars a year, depending on the number of users in the organisation who need access to the system. Typically these tools are charged on a licence basis, so if I have 150 staff I pay for 150 licences. There is often a minimum monthly fee which makes some of these tools too expensive for smaller organisations, and at the top end you might budget £500,000 a year for a comprehensive social media management and reporting tool system. However, some tools such as Hootsuite and MailChimp have a free option for small businesses and individuals.

Smartphone Sixty Seconds® – Search for stackies

- Use your mobile phone and search for *The Stackie Awards* to see some examples.
- Which is your favourite and why?

DIGITAL TOOLS   MarTech landscapes

Two organisations have created impressive visual diagrams of the MarTech tools available:

- Netherlands-based Frans Riemersma focuses on European stackies – go to martechtribe.com to explore the Martech Supergraphics.
- Scott Brinker's Marketing Technology Landscape shows a snapshot of all the MarTech products discovered – go to chiefmartec.com and download the latest version.

12.2.6 MATERIALS – DIGITAL ASSETS

In digital marketing, the key materials revolve around digital content which we discussed in Chapter 4. These are the materials or assets that are involved in every element of the customer journey. This can include the words, images and video on websites, social media posts, email newsletters, online adverts, blogs, vlogs and online communities.

For example, Aprimo, a United States-based marketing automation software company, uses Wordpress, Uberflip, Vidyard and InVision as part of its content stackie (Brinker, 2020b):

- WordPress can run its website
- Uberflip adds calls to action (see CTAs in Chapter 3) to all content
- Vidyard analyses video performance
- InVision helps plan campaigns by creating user journeys (see Chapter 2) and wireframes (see Chapter 7) so that everyone who needs to be involved, from marketing to software development and the web team, are included from the start

These tools have different functions, but work together. They also ensure that there is consistency with the CTAs and that the marketing plan is working. Digital material production requires careful planning which is why tools such as InVision used by Aprimo can be useful.

Furthermore, creating content is resource-intensive. Where content is evergreen (see Chapter 4, 'Content Marketing') and has no sell-by date, it can be used at any time. Another approach is to reuse content and this may be why MUD Jeans recycles its professionally photographed model images across social media, as well as its website (see Case Example 11.1).

The effort in creating content is another reason why many organisations use influencers and encourage user-generated content (see Chapter 4) as others become responsible for the production of the digital material.

In your plan, consider carefully what's required and how the content will be sourced. You can find free online images on websites such as Pixabay and use online image creation tools such as Canva (see Digital Tools in Chapter 11).

Activity 12.2   Use a content scheduling tool

Content scheduling tools allow you to plan in advance content that's timed to be shared at specific times. The larger paid-for tools enable scheduling in blogs, landing pages and emails. The free versions limit this to social media. In this activity, the aim is to schedule words, but you could try images too.

- Go to Hootsuite.com
- Select PLANS and FREE.
- Register for a free account and connect your social media account.
- Prepare and schedule some posts.
- Search for a subject of interest, add as a content stream and monitor for ten days.

If you're stuck, Hootsuite has a training area at education.hootsuite.com

12.2.7 MEASUREMENT – DIGITAL MARKETING METRICS

Measurement is covered in Chapter 13, and it's critical to ensure those involved in the project have agreed consistent key performance indicators (KPIs) or metrics.

A project will fail if you are measuring likes gained for an Instagram page and if I am measuring sales income via Instagram. We are measuring different numbers and they will never tally, so ensure that there is consistency from the start.

12.2.8 MANAGEMENT – SENIOR SPONSOR

Regardless of company size, it is essential to obtain a senior sponsor at a management level to support the project, or the lack of support could lead to a project not starting, being postponed or, worse still, failing.

Once the tactics and resources are all listed and the budget has been submitted, you might need to reduce the costs or re-allocate priorities. One framework to assess which parts of the plan to prioritise is the impact and effort matrix (Gray, 2010), which is shown in Figure 12.3. The matrix is ideally completed in a small team and creator Dave Gray suggests that this takes 30 minutes to one hour.

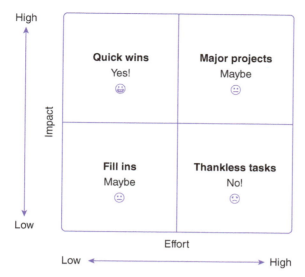

Figure 12.3   Impact and effort matrix

Source: Gray (2010)

12.2.9 MOTHER NATURE – THE UNCONTROLLABLE ENVIRONMENT

Mother Nature contributes to some organisations as a positive source of materials. However, in this context we consider the impact on our digital marketing plan.

In manufacturing, Mother Nature was considered on two levels. Internally, within a production environment it's whether the setting works, whether it is the right temperature and if the location has access to materials. Externally, this is considered as the uncontrollable environmental factors which may cause business interruption – extreme weather conditions, such as hurricanes, floods or earthquakes, mean staff cannot easily travel, supplies cannot get delivered or power cuts occur. This used to only be considered in manufacturing, but now applies to all organisations. For example, organisations can be disrupted due to pandemics where governments worldwide may restrict the movement of people, whether they are staff or customers, which can negatively impact business operations.

When building your plan, make sure you've addressed the potential impact of Mother Nature, with details of the potential mitigation; for example, being able to adopt digital methods of access, changing digital pricing or introducing digital products.

Depending on the company size, you may not need all of the 9Ms and you can adapt the framework as needed.

12.3 CHOOSING THE RIGHT RESOURCES

The resources required (see the 9Ms) for your digital marketing plan may include additional staff, new software systems or extra materials such as new imagery. The issue is whether this is possible, which is where the SAF framework can help.

12.3.1 THE SUITABILITY, ACCEPTABILITY, FEASIBILITY (SAF) FRAMEWORK

The Suitability, Acceptability, Feasibility (SAF) framework (Johnson et al., 2008) seeks justification of actions and strategies to see if they demonstrate suitability, acceptability and feasibility for the organisation, its purpose and environment. This framework considers whether the organisation has the resources available to fulfil the strategy and Table 12.2 shows an example of this.

You may already be using the SAF framework without realising! Imagine when you are thinking about buying or renting a new mobile phone:

- Is the phone battery life suitable for long commutes and the three-day festivals you are planning to go to?
- Will it be acceptable in size, style and brand and considered as OK by friends?
- Is the phone feasible in terms of the contract price affordability and will you be able to re-sell it at the end of the contract?

These are important factors as buying a mobile phone or taking on a new phone contract may involve a one-off payment or a monthly fee from £10 to £60 depending on the type, the length of contract and other variables. In this case, you are justifying your decision to yourself and your bank balance! You process the SAF framework in your head in about five minutes, but when applying this to an organisation, especially where you may have been given a budget, the best approach is to follow the four SAF steps that we will explore next.

Step 1 – Suitability, Acceptability, Feasibility criteria

Justification is essential. Imagine you have recommended developing a new app for a business. This involves a major investment. If you are working as a digital marketing manager, you are responsible for bigger and costlier decisions and need to address the factors discussed here.

Suitability

This assesses whether the strategy addresses the circumstances in which the organisation is operating. Key questions to ask include:

- Will the strategy meet the organisation's objectives?
- Does it fit with future trends, environmental opportunities and digital disruption?

- Does it exploit the strategic capabilities of the organisation?
- Is it sustainable over the long term?

Acceptability

Plans need to be acceptable to stakeholders. It is necessary to understand whether the expected performance outcomes are likely to meet stakeholders' expectations. Questions to consider are:

- Will the strategy be acceptable to key stakeholders?
- Will the strategy meet the expectations of key stakeholders?
- Are the expected performance outcomes (e.g. return on investment) acceptable?
- Are the associated or potential risks containable?

Feasibility

Having a plan is one issue; the next is whether the organisation has the resources and competencies to deliver. If there is no budget to work on the proposed plan, another may be needed. Questions to be asked include:

- Can we afford it?
- Can the strategy be made to work in practice?
- Do we have the resources and competencies to make it happen?
- Do we have experience or success in delivering similar strategies in the past?

It's possible that you may not know all the answers and so need to gather more information – that's step 2.

Step 2 – Information sources and analysis

It is worth going back to Chapter 9, 'Audit Frameworks' to ensure your information sources are valid and rigorous. If the original information is weak, such as it having an over-reliance on online sources, rather than verified research, it may have a negative impact on your plan.

You may need research to justify the investment. This could include a digital marketing audit and an analysis of customer behaviour. Another factor is the financial analysis that is, to explore income and the costs of development and delivery. The more detail and analysis included, the stronger the recommendation will be.

Step 3 – Ranking/Comparison

You use step 3 when you have several choices and you are not sure which to select, so ideally you compare the options. You might introduce a scoring system or a yes/no approach. The more yes answers, the more likely that option is to go ahead.

Let's work through an example of how to score different options using SAF. To do this, I have applied a score from 1 to 10, where:

- 10 = the option fully meets the criteria = YES
- 5 = there are some limitations in meeting the criteria = MAYBE
- 1 = a significant issue exists in meeting the criteria = NO

In this example, I've used Natura, a natural beauty products business founded in Brazil. Let's step into the future and imagine that the company decides to introduce natural cleaning products too.

Table 12.2 works through an adapted version of the SAF framework, where I have scored the option of introducing these new products.

Table 12.2   SAF framework scoring example applied to Natura

SAF framework element	Key considerations	Natura score	Comment/Implication
Suitability	Will the strategy meet the organisation's objectives?	10	Represents business growth
	Does it exploit the strategic capabilities of the organisation?	10	Yes, the systems are already in place
	Is it sustainable over the long term?	5	May require an emergent strategy as competition increases
Acceptability	Will the strategy be acceptable to key stakeholders?	10	They will love the idea!
	Are the expected performance outcomes (e.g. return on investment) acceptable?	5	It's been requested and there is growth in organic and sustainable products
	Are the associated/potential risks containable?	1	A few risks, may need contingency plans, such as to partner with a company that has experience in this sector
Feasibility	Can we afford it?	10	Investment available internally or short-term loan
	Can the strategy be made to work in practice?	5	Short-term partnership required for market knowledge about cleaning products
	Do we have the resources and competencies to make it happen?	10	Experienced project team can be established quickly
	Do we have appropriate experience/success in delivering similar strategies in the past?	10	Skills and systems in place
Total score		76	

I have kept this fairly simple so there are 10 questions to be answered, with a maximum of 10 for each response, so the maximum total is 100. With 76/100, this is an acceptable recommendation. If this had been 30/100 it might be rejected. This takes us to step 4.

Step 4 – Conclusion

If the Natura example was assessed against other options such as creating natural clothing or gifts, it is easier to decide which will work best. In the example in Table 12.2, this requires some judgement, so more research might be needed!

There is subjectivity in scoring the different elements, so a discussion can be useful if you are working in a team.

Don't lose heart if the options seem unattainable! If you have ever had a placement with or worked in a small organisation, you will know that it's not easy to recruit new staff as needed. One option may be crowdsourcing and considering the platform economy.

12.4 ROLES AND RESPONSIBILITIES IN GROUPS

Clarity is essential to understand who is doing what and when in any organisation or with any type of project. It also ensures that there are no gaps and no duplication. It removes confusion and assigns clear accountability for specific areas.

12.4.1 THE RACI MODEL

A popular model for identifying roles and responsibilities in a group or project is the RACI model, which represents Responsible, Accountable, Consulted and Informed (Project Management Institute, 2013).

RACI roles and responsibilities

RACI allocates roles and responsibilities as follows:

- Responsible: These people have responsibility for certain tasks
- Accountable: The person accountable for the job in hand who will give approval
- Consulted: These people would like to know about the task and their opinions are needed before a decision is made or action taken
- Informed: This group get one-way communication to keep them up to date with progress, and other messages after a decision is made or action taken

Imagine that you are launching a new advertising campaign using Instagram. Table 12.3 shows an example of how the RACI roles and responsibilities chart might look.

Why bother using the RACI matrix?

Reasons why roles should be clarified and agreed in advance include the following:

- If the roles and responsibilities are unclear, it takes ages to get a decision and no one knows whom to contact and how to get a 'yes' when needed.

- Plus, if the work doesn't go according to plan, it is not clear why or who is responsible.
- Too many people focus on doing the same thing. 'I didn't know you were doing that too!' becomes a common mantra.
- Stuff just doesn't happen: 'I didn't know we needed to do that, oops.'
- It's demoralising: some staff take on too many tasks to catch up, whilst others act as passengers, staying in the background and contributing little to the work.

Think back to the last time you were involved in a group work project. Did it work well? It can be the same in business too. In organisations where projects are assigned, some people do more than others and there are the same excuses you have heard in group work!

Table 12.3   RACI roles and responsibilities example

| Task list | Roles | | | |
	Digital Marketing Assistant	Designer	Digital Marketing Manager	Marketing Director
Justification for campaign	A	–	R	C
Target audience definitions	R	C	A	I
Copy for campaign	R	–	C	I
Image options for campaign	A	R	C	I
Campaign execution	R	–	A	–
Campaign monitoring	R	–	I	–
Campaign feedback	R	C	A	I

R = Responsible, A = Accountable, C = Consulted, I = Informed

Activity 12.3   Assess roles and responsibilities using the RACI matrix

Imagine that you are working on a group project for one of your assignments. There are specific tasks required at different times. You all have different roles and are sharing the tasks to save time.

Using Table 12.3 as your framework, note the top seven tasks and identify the roles you will all take. When you have done this, add in the RACI factors to show who will be responsible, accountable, consulted and informed during your project.

12.5 GOVERNANCE IN DIGITAL MARKETING

In a digital world, decisions and actions are more transparent, stakeholders seek greater accountability and organisations need to manage resources well. This all relates to governance, being transparent, accountable and well managed. Governance can include rules and regulations as well as good practice.

For example, the UK bank NatWest launched a marketing campaign called #HelpfulBanking but it didn't liaise with the IT team before this went online and it coincided with its online banking system failing. This led to a customer-created campaign entitled #UnhelpfulBanking. This is an example of a hashtag becoming a bashtag and a wider audience jumping into the conversation to make fun of the organisation.

Smartphone Sixty Seconds® – From hashtag to bashtag

- Go online and search for 'bashtag'.
- How many examples can you find?
- Why did the hashtag backfire and become a bashtag?

Another example is that of the celebrity influencer Khloe Kardashian, who promoted medication that was only available via prescription. As well as being inappropriate content to some influencers who may not be old enough to take the treatment, the pharmaceutical company is adopting weak practice by glamorising prescription medication. While this generated significant media attention, it could be described as a lack of governance.

Governance requires an understanding of the risks, not just for legal compliance but also to understand the potential reputational damage. In a digital context, bad news spreads fast. Earlier research suggested managing the risk in various ways (Loop and Malyshev, 2013).

12.5.1 POLICIES AND PROCEDURES

Organisations should be aware of the laws and regulations and industry codes of practice in their sector. Privacy and data management (see Chapter 1) are the main concern, but this should include brand and trademark protection, disability and discrimination, as well as copyright issues. For example, a website could take someone else's words (plagiarism) or images (digital theft – see Chapter 4, 'Content Marketing') and suggest they were created by the organisation. But sooner or later, this will be discovered.

Digital marketing is complex and one area lacking clarity is social media. The boundaries between professional and personal can blur for both staff and customers. For staff, it is possibly easier as when you start work and sign your employment terms and conditions, this includes a clause about 'not bringing the firm into disrepute' – saying or doing something you shouldn't.

But sometimes it's the consumers or fans who create inappropriate content online. In 2021 the British footballer Marcus Rashford experienced racism online after a match where his team lost. He was saddened by the comments and the police opened an investigation as one of the messages seemed to be sent from a teacher – with an open profile on Twitter.

ETHICAL INSIGHTS   Managing incivility in online communities

Company policies often restrict employees as to what they can and can't post on social media, but they don't apply to customers or other members of a brand community.

Dr Jan Breitsohl and Dr Denitsa Dineva have researched consumer aggression in some depth (see their chapter 'Managing incivility in online brand communities' in *The SAGE Handbook of Social Media*, 2022) and noted that organisations have many methods of managing weak customer behaviour, such as inappropriate or offensive language, but often remain in the background, choosing not to get involved.

- What actions should organisations take if someone posts rude (but legal) comments on an Instagram post?
- Organisations don't always respond to uncivil behaviour. Why do you feel this may be?
- Have you ever responded to incivility in online communities? If yes, what prompted you, and if no, why was this?

12.5.2 GOVERNANCE TRAINING

Training is useful to inform about policy, educate about the influence of a message and explain the impact on future careers. It's incredible to imagine that a teacher would have sent racist remarks without considering the consequences and impact on their career. This demonstrates that training is required at all levels to explain what is and isn't acceptable.

The training should include the senior management team too, in case they're responsible for the errors. Some people manage this by having two social media accounts, one personal and one public. Yet this may not work as software such as peekyou. com can identify connected accounts.

12.6 REPORTING THE RESULTS

When you have carried out your digital marketing plan, it is time to share the results. From an early age, everything we do is reported: school reports, subject performance reports and end-of-year reports. It's no different at work. When you carry out any marketing activity, it has to be measured, monitored and reported, regardless of the organisation type. For example:

- Companies with shareholders have to create and share annual reports, interim reports, statistics, presentations, press releases and other knowledge-based information

- Universities create and share their strategy for people, education, research and innovation, the corporate plan, financial review and results

- Charities create and share their annual report and accounts, strategic plans and policies

All this information requires knowledge and data. It can be too late if you reach the end of the year and start to gather the data because:

- The organisation may have performed worse than expected
- There may be issues that have been missed
- Urgent actions may be required due to the results of some data

Think about your university grades and what would happen if you waited until the end of the year before realising action was needed. This is why it is critical to collect the data on an ongoing basis, to anticipate requirements in the organisation and take the necessary action as soon as possible.

Options for reporting are varied and depend on the: (a) legal requirements; (b) audience type; (c) time available to organise; (d) amount of detail to share; and (e) required action. There are variations in reporting formats, from those that need to take place in person or virtually, or those where written or visual material will be needed to support the data delivery.

CASE EXAMPLE 12.2   ArcticZymes Technologies

ArcticZymes Technologies is a business-to-business research-based biopharmaceutical company that develops and manufactures enzymes. These are molecules that enable chemical reactions and perform tasks in our bodies, such as breaking down toxins and fighting disease. They're essential for our survival.

(Continued)

Based in Tromsø, Northern Norway, the scientists at ArcticZymes Technologies work with Mother Nature, a positive resource for the company. The unique location provides access to the marine Arctic and enables the company to identify new cold-adapted enzymes for use in molecular research and therapeutics. The work contributes to finding cures for different illnesses for animals and people.

The business does not sell direct to consumers, but via distributors, such as Scientifix in Australia. ArcticZymes Technologies could be considered as an 'ingredient company' as it develops core components that are used by other scientific companies and research bodies.

A smaller business, the annual sales income is under £10 million which was boosted during the health pandemic as its products were used in the development of COVID-19 vaccines. The company has just over 20 staff on its LinkedIn profile and doesn't use other forms of social media. This may be due to the company size, but also because it is a life sciences company and conducts sensitive work.

Owned by shareholders, the reporting is well structured. Every quarter, ArcticZymes Technologies is required to share its results. The data is presented in different ways to inform shareholders rather than to entertain them and consists of:

- An online presentation – a recording of 30 to 45 minutes that's uploaded to Vimeo and includes the downloadable presentation
- A downloadable report – usually around 15 pages of financial data
- A downloadable presentation – usually around 20 slides
- A press release – usually a one-page summary of the highlights

The report that is available in Quarter 4 includes a summary for the entire year so is usually longer, with more detail. All the material is available on the website for stakeholders – and competitors – to access.

The presentations contain many bar and pie charts, explaining the income sources, where the budget has been spent and the future forecasts. There's a summary from the chief executive to share their strategy and details about their highlights which are mainly positive or justify potentially negative issues. These presentations are more important than standard company data as they can be used by stakeholders to decide to buy or sell shares, so it is essential that the information is accurate.

Case questions

- Prepare a job description for a marketing manager for ArcticZymes Technologies that identifies their digital capabilities.
- What other methods of reporting could ArcticZymes Technologies adopt?
- Why do companies like ArcticZymes Technologies need to create so many downloadable presentations?

DISCOVER MORE ON WAYS TO REPORT AND PRESENT PLANS

For many more ways to present the plan, see *The Digital Marketing Planner: Your Step-by-Step Guide* (Hanlon, 2022).

12.6.1 DASHBOARDS

Although the report design depends on the audience to be addressed, the most frequently used internal data delivery system has become the dashboard. Dashboards have been described as tools that 'not only support the understanding of complex datasets but also are applicable to a variety of contexts and data domains' (Vázquez-Ingelmo et al., 2021, p. 1).

In all types of vehicles, from motorbikes and cars, from boats to aircraft, dashboards have been a common feature. They let you know the amount of fuel, your speed and indicate if there are any issues such as lack of oil or light bulbs have failed. In recent years, dashboards have become more sophisticated and often include average fuel consumption, outdoor temperature and elapsed journey time. The purpose of these functions is to inform and make you aware, so that you can re-fill with fuel before running out, slow down in traffic and ensure the vehicle is maintained.

In situations where there is an urgent or critical need to see key information quickly, dashboards can literally save lives. They are used in hospitals and medical facilities, in airports, stock markets, call centres and retailers.

DISCOVER MORE ON MARKETING DASHBOARDS

Writing in the *European Journal of Marketing,* the article 'Marketing dashboards, resource allocation and performance' is a helpful evaluation of dashboards (Clark, 2020).

An earlier article, 'Dashboards as a service', discusses the background to dashboards as well as explaining how to create them (Pauwels et al., 2009).

Advantages and disadvantages of dashboards

Advantages of dashboards include: a consistent set of metrics, which is useful for comparable analysis and enables teams to measure the agreed actions and activities.

You can see trends and make changes faster. Moreover, dashboards save time by gathering all information in one place and there is faster reporting as the focus is on the key metrics.

Disadvantages of dashboards include: they might display smaller amounts of data and mislead the overall picture. There can be a tendency to focus on the numbers (what) rather than the reasons (why) and they may provide a simplistic overview rather than the in-depth detail that may be needed. In addition, they can become a support system rather than an enabler.

The critical factor is ensuring the dashboards are not just watched, but action is taken and discussions about the content take place too. Looking at this, we can see that the Plan–Do–Check–Act (PDCA) cycle (see Chapter 13) starts to become more important.

DIGITAL TOOL　Digital dashboards

Digital dashboards are available online for you to experiment with and some free options are shown here. These require you to sign up with an email address and a password:

- Google data studio (datastudio.google.com) can connect analytics, search marketing and paid search
- Klipfolio (klipfolio.com) has a free option, PowerMetrics, and is used by HP and IBM
- Visualize Free (visualizefree.com) contains a wide range of templates

Other dashboards that offer free trials include Tableau (tableau.com) and Datapine (datapine.co.uk).

Creating a digital dashboard

When creating a dashboard, you need to consider the type of dashboard that is needed, the audience viewing the dashboard and where the data is located.

In terms of type of marketing dashboard, the main options are:

- Strategic: Focusing on larger organisational goals such as total monthly sales value, number of customers that month
- Tactical or project focus: Showing status of the campaign with details such as conversion rates, number of shares, email marketing results, performance of online adverts
- Operational: Aiming at specific business activities such as number of outstanding responses, number of orders to dispatch, number of customer queries

Dashboards are typically internally viewed and not shared with wider stakeholder groups, but inside the organisation there are different audiences with varying requirements. Senior executives may require top-level data such as the overall performance of an ad campaign on web sales, whereas marketing teams may be more interested in the granular detail, such as which images or headlines were most successful.

There are so many tools to choose from that both MarTechTribe and ChiefMarTech provide Dashboard and Data Visualisation stacks. Most of these systems are available online and can be used at any time from any device. The key is identifying the metrics that matter.

JOURNAL OF NOTE

Aimed at marketing students and people working in industrial and business-to-business markets, the journal *Industrial Marketing Management* contains many articles on resources.

CASE STUDY

This continues our long case study and you may find it helpful to read earlier parts in previous chapters.

IDENTIFYING THE RESOURCES TO DELIVER THE CAMPAIGN

Gabriel has considered the top-level digital marketing plan and has gained approval to proceed. He needs to consider the resources needed, how these will be managed and how the reporting will take place.

In interviews when asked about the numbers, co-founder Mark Gainey usually responds by saying that they don't publish their figures, although Strava's annual income is said to be $25 million and the funding is derived from third-party sources. Instead of getting a loan from the bank, Strava funders are major venture capital companies and private firms, including Sequoia Capital who has backed companies including Airbnb, Hubspot, Klarna and Zoom. These firms invest in the business and often gain a seat on the board and have some control over the company direction. The aim is for these firms to get a return on their investment at a future time.

In November 2020, Strava secured an additional $110 million to meet its overall strategy (see Chapter 10).

As part of building the digital marketing plan, Gabriel considers the resources required, using the 9Ms as a framework.

There are nearly 300 staff, with nearly 30 managing Facebook and Instagram. This is part of the social media team who are based mostly in the United States and the United Kingdom, but also in Indonesia, Austria, France and Japan. These teams need to be skilled in social listening and in using social care software, including Khoros and Sprout Social which they're using in their stackie. These tools provide digital customer care, community engagement and social media management, ensuring that Strava responds to any issues that may arise.

To deliver the objectives, Gabriel reflects on the work he has already carried out, breaking down the first objective 'To gain 20 million new members by December', and realises he needs to work with the country teams as well as the social media and online ads teams. The country teams will be able to advise on the online ads and it would be useful to have a coordinator to liaise between the teams, so the first new role is country team coordinator. He realises that the graphics teams are very busy creating ongoing content, so the second role will be an online content designer who can create ads and emails.

METHOD

In addition to the internal team, Gabriel is aware that Strava uses several external agencies including Seven Hills for PR support, creating awareness and raising the profile in new countries (previously it was Fusion Media who now manage RunFestRun). He will need to ensure they are in the loop when they are preparing the ads, so they can support local PR.

MOTHER NATURE

The global pandemic demonstrated the impact of Mother Nature. With local lockdowns and people unable to exercise, Gabriel believes the development team is working on more indoor activities for the future, although this is outside the scope of his plan.

MACHINES

No additional computer equipment or devices are needed and, to be honest, Strava is great at supporting any additional tech requirements.

MATERIALS

The main materials with be images, text and video. Some local photoshoots will be needed to ensure the imagery is relevant for the specific countries. Other graphics will be needed for the email campaign to show how to find and download the app and get started.

MONEY

As the company's turnover is $24 million, typically the total marketing budget might be around $2.4 million which is 10 per cent. From this, he is likely to have a budget of $240,000 or 1 per cent of the total income, as he's aware other campaigns are already in place. Although he knows that the budget could be increased due to the recent funding round, he thinks it's better to be cautious. Staffing will be outside the marketing budget, so he notes the spending in Table 12.4.

Table 12.4 Strava budget to achieve the objectives

Item	Note	Budget
Online ads	Target people in multiple countries including Australia and New Zealand, Italy, France and Spain	100,000
Graphics	Development of ideas and creation of materials for use across the whole campaign	20,000
Images	Local photo shoots	15,000
Email marketing	Recommend a friend campaign and email data	15,000
Agency contribution	Local PR campaigns	25,000
Landing page creation	Local landing pages to track new members	5,000
Country managers	Local support which may be needed	15,000
Contingency		5,000
Total		**200,000**

Gabriel has added $5,000 contingency for other items that might arise but have not yet been identified. This is a total budget request of $200,000 which is less than the possible $240,000 as Gabriel's taking a prudent approach.

MEASUREMENT

As the objective includes a measurement, 20 million new members by December, Gabriel can assess how well the campaigns are working based on the number of new members gained. He will need to ensure that he takes a snapshot of the exact number of members before the campaign starts. In addition, with the new landing pages, he will more accurately be able to report the results. However, he will need support from the analytics team who will be able to share the marketing metrics.

MANAGEMENT

Gabriel is fortunate that the communications manager is a supporter of his work and has given him the green light to go ahead with the project. He needs to make sure that he does not let her down.

MINUTES

The timescales are fixed as the objective must be completed by December which is in six months' time. It may be sensible to organise monthly updates for the communications manager to ensure the plan stays on schedule.

CASE QUESTIONS

- Look at the budget that Gabriel created and consider whether there are any items missing.
- Using the RACI model, it is clear that Gabriel has responsibility for most of these tasks. Identify who else should be included and their roles.
- Discuss the best way for Gabriel to report on the monthly updates to the senior management team.

FURTHER EXERCISES

1. For an organisation of your choice, assess its digital capabilities based on reviewing its online reports and checking its careers pages. What are their gaps and why does this matter?

2. Using the 9Ms of resource planning, start to assess the requirements for your plan. You may evaluate factors such as whether extra people are needed, the overall budget available, the materials and MarTech. Justify your decisions, especially where one element of the 9Ms is not included.

3. Apply the SAF framework to a digital marketing plan that you have created.

4. Using a dashboard only provides a snapshot of organisational performance for that one moment. It's out of date as soon as it's created. Discuss why dashboards matter and justify your response.

SUMMARY

This chapter has explored:

- The different types of resources within the 9Ms framework
- The concept of MarTech and how stackies are used by organisations
- How to choose the right resources by applying the SAF framework
- How to use RACI when allocating team roles and responsibilities
- Factors to consider when creating a digital dashboard

GO ONLINE

Visit **study.sagepub.com/hanlon2e** to access links to interesting articles, websites and videos related to this chapter.

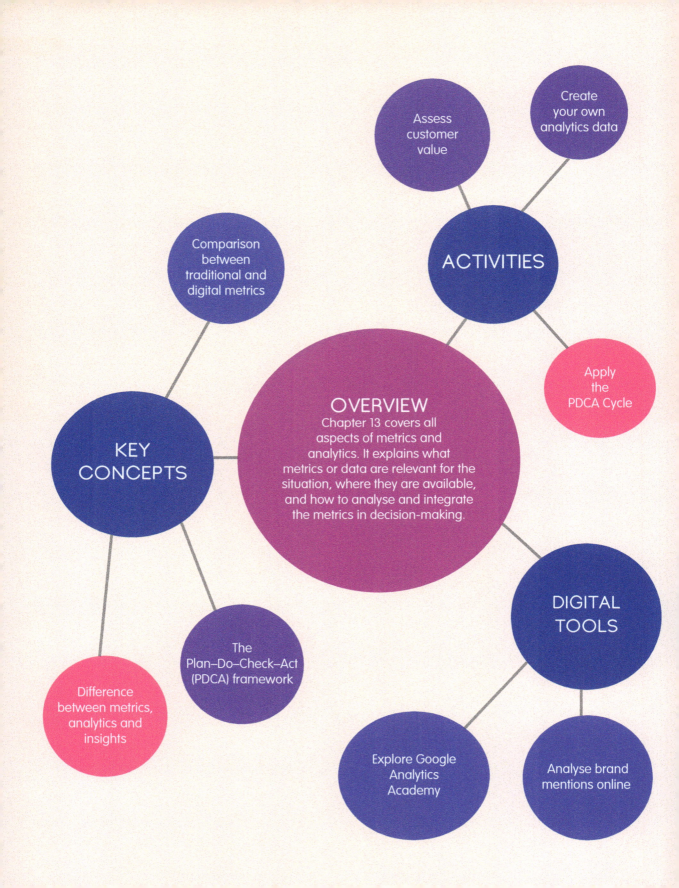

Assess customer value

Create your own analytics data

ACTIVITIES

Comparison between traditional and digital metrics

Apply the PDCA Cycle

OVERVIEW
Chapter 13 covers all aspects of metrics and analytics. It explains what metrics or data are relevant for the situation, where they are available, and how to analyse and integrate the metrics in decision-making.

KEY CONCEPTS

DIGITAL TOOLS

Difference between metrics, analytics and insights

The Plan–Do–Check–Act (PDCA) framework

Explore Google Analytics Academy

Analyse brand mentions online

13

DIGITAL MARKETING METRICS AND ANALYTICS

LEARNING OUTCOMES

When you have read this chapter, you will be able to:

Understand the benefits of metrics in marketing

Apply the customer value concept

Analyse the metrics to gain insights

Evaluate the types of metrics available

Create a Plan–Do–Check–Act (PDCA) framework

PROFESSIONAL SKILLS

When you have worked through this chapter, you should be able to:

- Recommend metrics for an organisation
- Gain insights to create actionable plans

13.1 INTRODUCTION

Measuring online marketing is the key difference in digital. Every web visitor, every device used and every page viewed can be analysed using onsite and offsite tools. This chapter looks at metrics, from web to social media analytics, from email to SEM and content. Then we explore the analytics and insights which are available to form a large picture to show if our digital marketing plan is working.

From an early age, everything we do is measured – our birth weight, height, the year we start to walk and talk – then at school there are so many tests to measure our performance: how well we perform in specific subjects, over the whole year and compared to our peers. In the same way, organisations measure performance. So

> a 'metric' is a performance measure that top management should review. The term comes from music and implies regularity: the reviews should typically take place yearly or half-yearly. A metric is not just another word for measure – while all metrics are measures, not all measures are metrics. Metrics should be necessary, precise, consistent and sufficient for review purposes. (Ambler, 2000, p. 61)

Metrics have been defined as 'a measuring system that quantified a trend, dynamic or characteristic' (Farris et al., 2009, p. 1). While we understand what metrics may be, we need to appreciate:

- WHAT metrics or data are relevant for the situation
- WHERE the metrics are available
- HOW to analyse the metrics
- HOW to integrate the metrics in decision-making
- HOW to present the analysis

Presenting data and providing reports were considered in Chapter 12, so this chapter explores different types of digital marketing metrics from web to social media, email to content marketing. We consider the data sources, how we can analyse the results to provide feedback that enables recommendations for improvement, and finally the PDCA framework as a method of integrating the metrics into our decision-making from the start.

13.2 TRADITIONAL TO DIGITAL METRICS

Metrics have evolved as online channels provide greater visibility and more data for marketers. Digital marketing metrics are a way for organisations to measure their online performance. Table 13.1 shows a range of measures from traditional to digital which explains some of the changes to the metrics that are relevant in different situations. This also shows how it relates back to the Digital Marketing Strategy Framework (see Chapter 10) so that you can build in the relevant metrics based on your selected strategy.

Table 13.1 Traditional to digital marketing metrics

Marketing metric type	Traditional metrics	Digital metrics	The digital marketing strategy framework
Customer volume	• Total number of customers	• **Customer value** • Number of views (posts, videos, ads) • Fans, likes, followers	Awareness, consideration
Distribution/availability	• Number of stockists	• Online availability	Awareness, consideration
Market share	• Volume or value	• Number of visitors to owned media • Share of wallet	Awareness, consideration, conversion
Key financials	• Sales • Return on investment	• Sales • Return on investment • **Customer value** • Conversion rate (number of visitors to the website and the percentage completing a conversion action) • Cost per action (the cost per click, video view, lead capture or per customer)	Conversion
Market growth rate	• The percentage at which your market is growing (or declining) offline	• The percentage at which your market is growing (or declining) offline and online	Conversion
Customer satisfaction	• Number of complaints (level of dissatisfaction)	• Customer satisfaction (e.g. Net Promoter Score, Customer Satisfaction Index) • Ratings/Reviews • **Customer value**	Conversion, enthusiasm
Customer behaviour	• Loyalty/retention	• **Customer value**	Enthusiasm
Product quality	• Relative perceived quality	• Review scores • Number of returns	Enthusiasm

Let's explore the changes in these metric types and why they matter. You may have noticed that traditional marketing metrics focus on the organisation, whereas digital metrics place the customer at the centre and consider the concept of customer value.

13.2.1 CUSTOMER VOLUME

Traditional marketing often considers the total number of customers at that moment in time. It doesn't consider how to expand the same customer base or how to encourage customers to share brand or product stories. Digital marketing takes a broader perspective and considers the customer value (see Figure 13.1), which can lead to finding new customers through existing customers.

Other measures of volume include the number of content views. This enables marketers to understand and compare which was the most and least successful content, based on the number of people who saw or heard it. Measures such as the number of fans may be a vanity metric, but in some situations this matters. For example, once an organisation has achieved 10,000 followers on Instagram, it can use the platform as a sales tool. For influencers, this is a key metric as the volume of fans or followers dictates how much they can charge to promote branded content and is an essential factor in their product offer.

Smartphone Sixty Seconds® – Check customer volume

- Go online and search for your favourite brand on a social media channel.
- How many followers does it have?
- How does this enable it to sell online?

13.2.2 DISTRIBUTION/AVAILABILITY

Traditional marketing considered the number of stockists – in a digital context, this is about where the items are available online and how soon they can be delivered. For example, you may find a branded item available on many websites, but Amazon may offer next-day delivery. This is one of the reasons that Amazon is so successful: the company understands the concept of immediacy which, over 40 years ago, Latané defined as 'closeness in space or time and absence of intervening barriers or filters' (Latané, 1981, p. 344).

13.2.3 MARKET SHARE

Market share is still a valid measure, but it's moved beyond the traditional volume or value and now considers the number of visitors to owned media such as websites. So when marketers want to launch new products, they can be promoted to specific audiences faster.

In addition to share of the market we consider share of wallet. This represents the percentage of disposable income that consumers have.

13.2.4 KEY FINANCIALS

Traditional key financials focused on the sales generated or the return on investment from marketing activities. In a digital context, while sales are still critical, it's not about a one-off sale, it's about longer-term value for the customer.

For example, imagine you're a customer of Amazon (or a similar company you've shopped with online for some time): how much do you spend with the company every year? Then imagine that's just one year; for how many years have you been a customer? Add that all up and discover what you've spent so far. This is the 'customer lifetime value (CLV)' which is considered as 'an older measure of the present value of future profits generated from customers over their relationship with the organisation' (Harrigan et al., 2015, p. 30).

Other ways of calculating customer value (Harrigan et al., 2015, p. 30) include those shown in Figure 13.1.

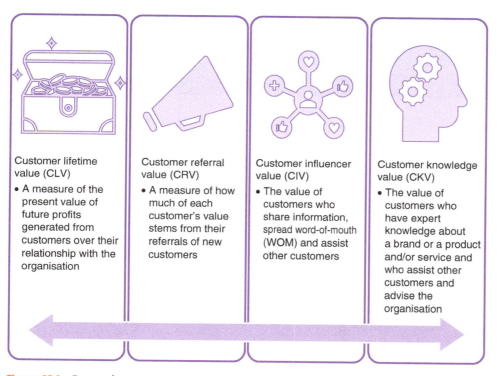

Customer lifetime value (CLV)

• A measure of the present value of future profits generated from customers over their relationship with the organisation

Customer referral value (CRV)

• A measure of how much of each customer's value stems from their referrals of new customers

Customer influencer value (CIV)

• The value of customers who share information, spread word-of-mouth (WOM) and assist other customers

Customer knowledge value (CKV)

• The value of customers who have expert knowledge about a brand or a product and/or service and who assist other customers and advise the organisation

Figure 13.1 Types of customer value

Customer value measures

These customer value measures are based on much longer-term relationships with customers, placing the customer within the sales process, rather than at the end. For example, TripAdvisor® invites travellers to leave reviews after their stay – effectively once the sale has been completed. So individual customers share opinions with others which could lead to further sales through customer referral value.

TripAdvisor® encourages customer knowledge value by asking users if they can answer questions about their reviews, such as 'Does this hotel have a lift?' or 'Does this hotel cater for vegans?' Responding and adding customer knowledge saves organisations time and the responses are viewed as authentic as they're from real customers.

Using TripAdvisor® as the example, customer influencer value occurs when you like, favourite, share and add your opinions. You could say the customers are the sales intermediaries, by promoting the destination for the company by creating user-generated content and actively sharing brand information.

Activity 13.1   Assess customer value

For an organisation of your choice, assess its customer value. Using Figure 13.1 as your framework, consider the value gained from (a) referrals, (b) influence and (c) knowledge. You'll need to search online to gain the data and provide evidence for your response. Refer to Table 13.1 for the digital metrics to be assessed.

Attribution

Chapter 12 considered Return on Marketing Investment (ROMI) which can be a singular measure, with results from one event or campaign. This can be used over a longer timeframe, such as 12 months, but it can be difficult to know why someone placed an order via your website. Was it the advert they saw on Facebook? An image they swiped up on Instagram? A company they searched after seeing a TikTok video? Listening in a room in Clubhouse? Or perhaps a friend mentioning the brand name in WhatsApp? The challenge is knowing what worked as it could be one of these touchpoints or it could be a combination. Knowing the source of the conversion action is called **attribution** (see Key Term).

KEY TERM   ATTRIBUTION

Researchers suggest that 'Marketing attribution is a strategy of determining the value of marketing communications and allocating it to identified touchpoints along customer journeys' (Buhalis and Volchek, 2021, p. 2). Effectively it's the strategy that calculates where the sale or conversion action came from, whether that was social media, an email campaign or something else. The benefit of this is knowing where to focus your digital marketing efforts.

However, attribution may be inaccurate and depend on what's being measured and the information or data that this shows. Table 13.2 shows different examples of attribution measures and explains how they work which is based on touchpoints – or the places where customers interact with the brand. Typically, to see the data you need access to a Google Ads account which provides attribution reports, showing the touchpoints in your attribution strategy.

Table 13.2 Examples of attribution measures and how they work

Attribution strategy	What this measures	How attribution is allocated	What this shows	Examples of how it can be used
Linear	From one touchpoint to the next	Attribution is shared equally among the touchpoints	The touchpoints involved, but not what adds value to the conversion	To see which touchpoints are most successful and landing pages (see Chapter 3) could help to show this
Position based (U shaped)	The first and last touchpoints	40% allocated to the first and last touchpoints, the remaining 20% is shared among the middle touchpoints	Which channels acquire relevant target audience and which channel is most suitable for converting sales	To focus on primary channels by adding more updates or content
Time decay	Touchpoint closest to the sale, the number of days between the initial and final interaction	100% of attribution allocated to the last action	Which touchpoint acts as the conversion	By introducing time-limited offers to reduce the time to conversion
First interaction	The first touchpoint	100% of attribution allocated to the first action	Which channel is most suitable for gaining awareness and consideration	In planning awareness campaigns
Last interaction	The last touchpoint	100% of attribution allocated to the last action	Which channel is most suitable for converting sales	To understand the main conversion touchpoint

DIGITAL TOOL   Google Analytics Academy

Google is keen for students to learn more about analytics and has created a series of free online workshops. Visit the link below to start exploring and learn more about analytics and attribution. It's a step-by-step process from beginners to advanced.

• https://analytics.google.com/analytics/academy

Conversion rates

Other key financials in a digital context include the conversion rate which is measured in the analytics dashboard. Typically conversion rates can be very low – between 4 per cent and 1 per cent, which is why companies often focus on driving visitor numbers because the more visitors, the more conversions. You might think 2 per cent sounds low, but ASOS, which spends over £100 million on marketing, had a conversion rate of 2.8 per cent in 2016; this increased to 3 per cent in 2017, it moved to 3.2 per cent in 2018 and 2019, then dropped to 3 per cent in 2020. You can see that the conversion rates are increasing by small amounts. Be aware that conversion rates vary based on the company type, products offered and the wider environment, plus ASOS has a high conversion rate compared with other online retailers.

The other key metric is the cost per action, such as the cost per customer – for example, if 10 per cent of people who clicked on the advert decided to add a product to the cart and check out, and if the advert cost is £2.50, and if the average sale per customer is £25. It's important to ensure that this makes sense within the organisation and its setting. If it's a non-profit and the average donation is £20 as a one-off, it has lost money if the adverts are £20 per action.

On the other hand, if it's a B2B situation where the average customer lifetime value is £25,000, it's a great return on the investment.

So it's critical to evaluate the cost per action. In digital marketing, this is easier to achieve and you can set maximum budgets.

DISCOVER MORE ABOUT CUSTOMER TOUCHPOINTS

This book is about digital marketing and considers the customer journey within an online setting. Writing in the *Journal of Retailing and Consumer Services*, researchers from Spain have considered the 'Short-term and long-term effects of touchpoints on customer perceptions' (Cambra-Fierro et al., 2021) which identifies a range of customer interactions or touchpoints to assess what's important to consumers in a retail context. Their study includes B2B touchpoints with helpful examples.

13.2.5 MARKET GROWTH RATE

The percentage at which your market is growing or declining is easier to measure online as it often starts with reductions in web visitors. This indicates that competitors may have moved into the area and are taking some share of wallet, or it suggests that the products may not be relevant.

For example, during the pandemic e-tailers selling casual clothing performed better than those selling formal outfits. With the world in lockdown, it was difficult to understand why a new suit or formal jacket might be needed. At this stage, many companies started to see their market decline rather than grow. However, ASOS introduced 'loungewear' and managed to grow its business during the pandemic.

13.2.6 CUSTOMER SATISFACTION

Organisations have transitioned from having complaints departments to customer service teams. The language was seen as negative (complaints department) and defending the organisation rather than supporting the customer. There was no consideration of satisfaction, just the aim of reducing customer complaints which were accepted as commonplace.

In an online setting, where good and bad news can be shared more easily, customer satisfaction can be gathered through feedback and comments across social media.

In addition, there are formal assessment methods using tools such as the Net Promoter Score® (see Key Term in Chapter 2) and review platforms.

Smartphone Sixty Seconds® – Customer Satisfaction Index (CSI)

- Wherever you are in the world, search for *Customer Satisfaction Index*.
- What did you find?
- What measures were used?
- If you did not find any results, why might this be the case?

13.2.7 CUSTOMER BEHAVIOUR

Traditional marketing was fixated on the concept of loyalty and retaining customers. This is an inward-looking focus that considers ways to hold onto the customer, rather than placing the customer first and creating benefits so that customers want to stay.

This is a step towards building advocates who positively promote the organisation and is recognised as the enthusiasm part of the Digital Marketing Strategy Framework (see Chapter 10).

13.2.8 PRODUCT QUALITY

Digital business methods have enabled much faster feedback on product quality. Traditional marketing measures consider the perceived quality of products, often based on smaller focus groups that tried to be representative of a wider audience. However, these are organised formal situations and may not always provide the degree of honesty needed.

Online people can anonymously leave feedback and make comments about the exact features of a product they don't like. For example, some online clothing retailers encourage customers to share their height and size and say how well a garment does – or does not – fit them. This provides feedback from more customers and allows companies to stop production of poor performing products much faster.

Digital marketing has delivered critical changes to metrics. Apart from the change in data accessibility, where we can see real-time data via websites, there has been a change of attitude. There is a move away from a negative, company-centred and insular approach to a positive, customer-centric and outward-looking focus.

The following sections explore different digital metrics based on specific channels.

CASE EXAMPLE 13.1   Microsoft's traditional metrics

It's difficult to imagine that one of the major tech companies we're involved with daily is nearly 50 years old. Founded in 1975, Microsoft helps us write documents (Word), deliver presentations (PowerPoint), save documents (OneDrive), send emails (Outlook), play games (Xbox), use VR (HoloLens), communicate from any location (Teams) and connect at work (LinkedIn).

With 1 billion devices using Windows programs and an annual revenue approaching $150 billion, Microsoft is a major tech company that's keen on measurement. It segments its product lines into three groups and considers their revenue separately:

- Productivity and Business Processes, which generates an annual revenue of over $45 billion and includes Office and LinkedIn. In fact, LinkedIn contributes around $8 billion a year.
- Intelligent Cloud, which generates an annual revenue of nearly $50 billion and includes Azure.
- Personal Computing, which generates an annual revenue of nearly $50 billion and includes Windows, devices and gaming. The Xbox Game Pass service has over 15 million subscribers.

The CEO is Satya Nadella who studied computer science and worked in the tech sector before joining Microsoft. Under Nadella's guidance, the firm has significantly increased its income. He is passionate about helping customers and in the 2020 annual report commented: 'Our success is dependent on our customers' success, and we need to obsess about them – listening and then innovating to meet their unmet and unarticulated needs.'

Microsoft employs over 160,000 people worldwide, including 40,000 who work in sales and marketing. The annual marketing budget is around $20 billion and represents 14 per cent of revenue. The Chief Marketing Officer is Christopher C. Capossela who joined Microsoft after leaving university and has worked there for over 25 years.

The annual report includes a statement on how the company uses metrics:

We use metrics in assessing the performance of our business and to make informed decisions regarding the allocation of resources. We disclose metrics to enable investors to evaluate progress against our ambitions, provide transparency into performance trends, and reflect the continued evolution of our products and services. Our commercial and other business metrics are fundamentally connected based on how customers use our products and services.

There are specific metrics for LinkedIn which comprise: Talent Solutions, Learning Solutions, Marketing Solutions, Sales Solutions and Premium Subscriptions.

With external shareholders, Microsoft's main focus is sales growth and the return on investment. However, there are many competitors across the different business segments. Competitors to Office have been identified by Microsoft as software and global application vendors, such as Apple, Cisco Systems, Facebook, Google, IBM, Okta, Proofpoint, Slack, Symantec, Zoom, and numerous web-based and mobile application competitors as well as local application developers.

Case questions

- Why is Microsoft mainly focused on traditional metrics?
- Which metrics would you recommend that Microsoft uses to measure their customers' success and why?
- What metrics could be used to assess LinkedIn and why?

13.3 DIGITAL METRICS, ANALYTICS AND INSIGHTS

Metrics are a unit of measurement such as a percentage, number or volume. Analytics are how we assess the data and insights provide explanations as to why specific metrics occur. For example, a metric may be the number of web visitors which could be 100,000 a day, but the analytics program, such as Google, shows that there was a sharp increase in web visitors to 150,000 on a specific day. To find out why, we may need to look at monitoring tools, such as Hootsuite (see Case Example 13.2), to gain insights and understand why this happened. It may be that a mention on a specific website with strong recommendations from an influencer created a spike in web traffic.

Although metrics, analytics and insights are all different, social media platforms often group these together and use the terms interchangeably. But analytics programs don't automatically provide insights that are based on an intelligent appreciation of what happened. They may provide clues and indicate that specific posts were more successful than others, or that there were mentions by an influencer with many followers. Social media platforms' 'insights' show the numbers of visitors, viewers, followers and more.

In addition to the traditional customer volume measures, digital marketing metrics cover specific processes such as web analytics, SEM and pay-per-click (PPC) analytics, social media analytics and email analytics. The following sections look at the metrics that are relevant for the situation, where these are available (analytics tools) and how these are analysed to gain insights.

13.3.1 WEB ANALYTICS

Web analytics can be described as the assessment of a variety of data, including web traffic, web-based transactions, web server performance, usability studies, user-submitted information and related sources to help create a generalised understanding of the online visitor experience. The official Web Analytics Association definition is 'the measurement, collection, analysis and reporting of Internet data for the purposes of understanding and optimizing Web usage' (Web Analytics Association, 2008, p. 3).

Web analytics tools come in two forms: *onsite* and *offsite analytics*.

Onsite analytics

Onsite analytics measure actual visitors to the page and this is based on access to the data; that is, you control or manage the website and can obtain the details relating to your customer touchpoints.

The best-known onsite web analytics program is probably Google Analytics. People always say this is free, which it is at one level, although in exchange for the free service, Google captures and uses your data. So, whilst it may be without charge, Google benefits from knowing about your data. There are companies that opt for the paid-for version, so they can control and manage their own data. For example, financial institutions often don't want to share their visitor numbers or web stats with Google, so whilst they use the program, they pay to store and retain their own data. For a fully customised Google Analytics package, the fees start at around $100,000 a year.

Other paid-for programs include Adobe Analytics and IBM Digital Analytics where annual subscriptions start at $100,000. These programs offer greater machine learning and are often managed by data analytics teams to ensure they are maximising conversion opportunities.

Offsite analytics

Offsite analytics do not require access to the data. Based on aggregated data from companies like Google, offsite analytics measure potential web audience numbers and show how your website compares to others. These tools have limited data and indicate monthly web traffic and keywords being used. For example, Similarweb (similarweb.com) and Semrush (semrush.com) are offsite analytics tools that require subscriptions to access detailed data.

Insights from the analytics tools

These tools allow organisations to compare one situation with another and evaluate performance, such as:

- Site usage/audience

  - How many visitors came to the site
  - How frequently they visited
  - Geographic data
  - Some demographic data
  - Technical data; browser, device type
  - Path through the website (visitor funnel)

- Visitor sources

  - Where the visitors came from
  - Percentage of visitors from social networks

- Site content

  - Top entry pages
  - Top exit pages (where shopping carts were abandoned)

- o   Top performing pages
- o   Least performing pages
- o   Length of visit (duration and bounce rate)
- Quality assurance

  - o   Broken pages
  - o   Site speed

There are two major methods for gathering information for web analytics: **web server log files** (see Key Term) and **page tagging** (see Key Term).

> ### KEY TERM   WEB SERVER LOG FILES
>
> Web server log files or web log files are records (logs) of every action (hit) on a website. This includes a visit to the site, clicking on specific items and the steps through the website. The web log file is created and is available to the website administrator. They can see the visitor behaviour but will not always know who the visitor is.

There are challenges with cookies because they can be rejected or blocked or removed. Sometimes the cookies time out before a page loads, especially when it is a slow loading page – busy visitors may click off the page before it loads fully. Other challenges include the page tagging not reporting on non-pages such as PDFs or downloaded files, so the data may not be accurate.

> ### KEY TERM   PAGE TAGGING
>
> Page tagging is adding tags to web pages; these tags are better known as adding cookies when visitors arrive at a web page.
> See Key Term **Cookie**, on p. 49.

To start, you add a tag to your website which allows Google to share data with the web team. Some of the analytics terminology includes:

- Users: Visitors to the website
- Sessions: The period of time a user is active on your site and if they are inactive for 30 minutes or more this is counted as a new session
- Page view: A web page being loaded (or reloaded) in a browser
- Bounce rate: A bounce is a single-page session on a website. Typically, a single-page session lasts less than one whole second!

- Session duration: The average time a user (visitor) spends on your site – it is a basic measure as it is total visitor numbers divided by the total time on the site
- Conversion: A completed activity, online or offline, such as buying a product online, downloading a white paper or clicking the 'live chat now' button
- Attribution: The process of assigning credit for conversions to touchpoints in the customer journey
- Tag: A snippet of code (JavaScript) that sends information to a third party, such as Google. Google Analytics' tracking code or Facebook pixels are examples of tags

13.3.2 MAIN DATA ANALYSIS METHODS FOR ONLINE TRAFFIC

Whether you're analysing web traffic, online adverts, social media or email marketing, you'll notice that there are three main ways of assessing online traffic to gain insights: longitudinal, comparative and content analysis.

Longitudinal analysis

Longitudinal analysis concerns comparing the same data (metrics) over a period of time. For example, you might review the web visitor numbers by week, month, quarter or year on year. This can show how well the website is performing which may result in conversion actions. Conducting analysis over a period of time allows you to make informed decisions if you notice negative changes. For example, if the web traffic starts declining but there doesn't seem to be a rational explanation (such as a pandemic which impacted on web traffic for many organisations), it may be appropriate to conduct a digital marketing audit (see Chapter 9) to understand the wider context. Having access to the data means you can take action before it's too late.

Comparative analysis

Comparative analysis enables you to measure one item against another, such as reviewing one successful web page with a less successful page. You can explore the differences to identify whether this is due to content being relevant or perhaps other factors, such as the customer journey. It's important not to compare web pages in isolation, but to consider them within the wider external environment. Perhaps you've had a web page on a specific topic for a long time, but there was no interest and when something happened externally, it became more relevant. For example, if you've suddenly discovered you need to work from home, website pages providing advice and guidance on managing work–life balance or how to minimise back pain may suddenly become more useful and so traffic to these pages increases due to external factors.

Content analysis

Content analysis considers qualitative and quantitative factors. Qualitative measures include analysing keywords in the text and the sentiment or the feeling of the person communicating the message. They are also known as glottometrics, which include word length, word order, richness of vocabulary and word frequency. Beyond glottometrics, other quantitative content measures include: volume of terms mentioned, reach of the message (how far it spread) and number of clicks on links, photos, videos or other material. This data can be used for future marketing campaigns, focusing on what's been successful in the past and avoiding content that failed to meet its objectives.

Activity 13.2   Create your own analytics data

- Start a blog!
- Use free blogging tools such as Wordpress.com or Medium and create some posts about your digital marketing experience. Ideally posts should contain at least 350 words – that's less than a page of A4 – so that Google can see and index the posts.
- Add some copyright-free images and credit the image source.
- Share the blog posts across social media to encourage people to read your content.
- To gain access to basic analytics, after a month review the data in the analytics section of the blog. You can see the number of visitors and which posts were more successful.

Web addresses for specific campaigns can be constructed in such a way, using UTM parameters (see Key Term **Urchin tracking module (UTM) parameters**), that marketers can analyse exactly which aspects of a campaign were most successful. The main benefit of using UTM parameters is that marketers can tell which ads worked and which ads didn't, as well as gaining information into the sale attribution or other conversion activity that took place (see Key Term **Attribution**).

KEY TERM   URCHIN TRACKING MODULE (UTM) PARAMETERS

One feature that Google retained when it purchased Urchin analytics was its Urchin tracking module parameters or UTMs. Google described UTMs as custom campaign parameters for advertising URLs (Google, 2017). These custom parameters (or elements) are added to a web address so that marketers can identify which website, advertising method, campaign, search terms and content type worked.

All five parameters must be used and Figure 13.2 shows an example of a web address that contains these five UTMs. Next time you click on a link, look closely at the whole web address!

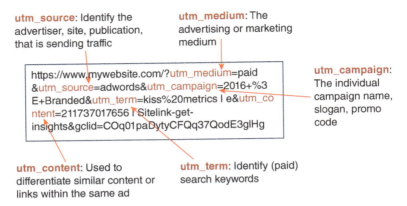

utm_source: Identify the advertiser, site, publication, that is sending traffic

utm_medium: The advertising or marketing medium

utm_campaign: The individual campaign name, slogan, promo code

https://www.mywebsite.com/?utm_medium=paid
&utm_source=adwords&utm_campaign=2016+%3
E+Branded&utm_term=kiss%20metrics | e&utm_co
ntent=211737017656 | Sitelink-get-
insights&gclid=COq01paDytyCFQq37QodE3glHg

utm_content: Used to differentiate similar content or links within the same ad

utm_term: Identify (paid) search keywords

Figure 13.2   Example of web address using UTMs

13.3.3 ADVANTAGES AND DISADVANTAGES OF WEB ANALYTICS

Web analytics has become a job role in its own right and can help information professionals use tested keywords to achieve their SEO (search engine optimisation) aims (for more on SEO, see Chapter 3). It can change the way organisations approach paid search, leading them to focus less on expensive keyword bidding (Google Ads). This information can be used to fine-tune the website, to provide visitors with more useful content and to improve navigation through the site. Web analytics is about understanding the data and using the information to improve different situations.

The downside is **big data** (see Chapter 1, 'The Digital Marketing Landscape'). There is such a volume of information that it's difficult to know where to start and what to consider when looking at an analytics page. Also, the data changes in real time, so as soon as you have a clear picture, the situation changes. This speed of data change or its velocity is a challenge and it means agreeing when the data is collected to ensure consistency. For example, you might decide to take a snapshot on the first Wednesday of each month. This provides a consistent approach in looking back on the previous month's or quarter's activity.

ETHICAL INSIGHTS   Ethical algorithms

We are concerned about big data due to its potential misuse which results from the algorithms which take the data to create rules or instructions. At a basic level, these rules are computer code that says 'if this happens do this'. However, there are several incidents of algorithms creating bias.

For example, higher paid jobs have been shown to men rather than women on online job sites (if male, show these jobs) and social media networks have promoted political content during major elections to specific people (if they like these programmes, show these adverts). There have been questions about the people creating the algorithms who may not demographically represent all members of society and who may be creating the instructions based on how they see and experience the world.

- How do we ensure the algorithms treat people fairly in our society?
- Does this matter? Isn't this just part of how computer systems work?
- How do you feel about your search results being biased towards your gender, name, location or other factors?

DISCOVER MORE ABOUT ETHICS AND DATA

The article 'Ethics of quantification or quantification of ethics?' by Andrea Saltelli in *Futures* (2020) presents good arguments around the main issues of ethics and data, with examples and sources of online guidance.

13.3.4 PAID SEARCH ANALYTICS

Paid search analytics allow you to see the results from adverts when visitors are searching online. In Chapter 3, we discussed the different advertising formats including impressions and conversion actions. Here we consider the main search metrics, which include:

- Impressions: The number of people who were shown your ad
- Clicks: The number of people who clicked on the ad and then to your website
- Clickthrough rate (CTR): The percentage of people who click on your ad from the number of people who saw your ad
- Conversions: The number of people who took an action(s)
- Conversion rate: The percentage of people visiting your site and completing a conversion action
- Average cost per click (CPC): The average cost per click
- Average cost per action (CPA): The average cost per conversion action

Like Google Analytics, Google Ads provides campaign overviews that show the clicks, impressions and average CPC on one page. There are specialist advertising analytics programs, such as Kenshoo, which group the data in one place. These programs are mainly used by international brands, such as LG electronics, Under Armour clothing and Santander bank, who manage several campaigns across different networks in various locations and may be working with multiple agencies.

13.3.5 SOCIAL MEDIA ANALYTICS

At one level we have web analytics, which provide data about web visitors, and the next level of data is within your social media pages which are similar to web data.

As social media pages have visitors, they gather data on their behaviour. This enables the social media companies to sell advertising space to organisations as they have rich details on which Instagram pages are popular, which YouTube channels are most watched and which interests are visible on Twitter.

The main social media platforms consider two key measures: (1) daily active users (DAUs) and (2) monthly active users (MAUs). Instagram, Twitter, Pinterest, WhatsApp and TikTok all measure DAUs and MAUs – the details are often included in the reports to shareholders as an indicator of growth. The difference between DAUs and MAUs is engagement. Daily active users visit the sites every day, whereas monthly users could be described as being less active. While these are the top-line measures indicating the popularity of the platforms globally, social media provide rich data sources for organisations and indicate these metrics:

- Reach/Impressions: How many people were shown the post, tweet, image, video
- Likes, fans, follows: Number of users that follow you
- Engagements/Actions on page: Total number of times a user interacted with a post or content, in terms of clicks, shares, replies, follows, likes, links
- Engagement rate: Number of engagements divided by impressions

Social media provide onsite data with access for page administrators only. As Facebook was the first social media platform to offer advertising, many of the other social media networks followed the way it organised the analytics. So if you know how Facebook works, you'll find that Instagram (owned by Facebook), Twitter, LinkedIn and TikTok use similar approaches.

Offsite data is not available at this time because most social media networks lock the detailed data. So you need to adopt a manual process, looking through the social media pages and assessing the data available on the screen, such as the number of likes, the number of posts or the number of engagements. There are some tools (see Digital Tool **Brand24**) that allow free trials to capture some data.

DIGITAL TOOL Brand24

Brand24 is designed to monitor mentions of a brand, product or service online. It bases the data on offsite sources such as blogs, web pages and social media comments. The results are presented as a dashboard or an infographic. The dashboard includes the top sites mentioning the brand, the source categories (blog, web page, social media) and the most influential people discussing the subject, which is useful if you want to identify influencers. The comments are segmented into a summary of positive and negative over a selected timescale. The company offers a free seven-day trial to show you a dashboard based on a search of keywords.

- https://app.brand24.com

13.3.6 ADVANTAGES AND DISADVANTAGES OF SOCIAL MEDIA ANALYTICS

The advantages of social media analytics are that they provide a useful overview of how content is performing and you can see the engagement (retweets, link clicks, likes, replies) on different content types.

The disadvantages of social media analytics are that they lack depth and detail; the data often doesn't tally with other analytics programs and the focus can be on encouraging organisations to spend money on promoting successful posts.

CASE EXAMPLE 13.2 Hootsuite social media reporting

Started in 2008 by Ryan Holmes, Hootsuite is a social media management program. It has become a favourite tool for posting and monitoring social media content, plus it provides social listening, enabling brands to track brand sentiment. Holmes was part of an ad agency that needed a tool to manage its clients' social media. As the agency couldn't find a program to suit it, it created its own which became known as Hootsuite. Hootsuite groups together your different social media networks, so you can monitor them all at the same time.

With its headquarters in Vancouver, Canada, Hootsuite has over 1,500 employees in Australia, the USA, Mexico and across Europe (Belgium, France, Germany, Italy, Romania, Spain, UK). The estimated annual revenue is over $400m. The program is used by nearly 20 million companies worldwide, including Dominos (pizzas), Melia (hotels) and Longchamp (luxury goods). One of the reasons for its success is the integration as the program connects to many third-party tools including:

(Continued)

- Social networks such as Facebook, Instagram, YouTube, Twitter, LinkedIn
- Online tools such as Canva (image creation), Adobe stock images
- Website programs such as Magento, Shopify, WooCommerce

Integration means that companies need fewer systems to manage and this is an area where the Hootsuite software developers have excelled. There are so many integrations with third-party tools that they have a dedicated website (apps.hootsuite.com) that lists what's available.

Hootsuite offers a free starter plan which provides basic monitoring and scheduling of social media content. Reporting is included in the Professional, Team, Business and Enterprise accounts, allowing results to be viewed on a dashboard:

- Customer volume: Number related to content, such as views
- Customer value: Engagement, such as the mentions, comments and tags for one brand account or many
- Customer value and enthusiasm: Sentiment analysis (see Key Term in Chapter 5)

The reports provide insights based on the data and indicate the best times to post, when greatest engagement will be achieved. Although there are dashboards online, there is the ability to export the data to Excel files which enables greater longitudinal and comparative analysis.

The program is available on the desktop and the app. In an average month, there are around 30,000 downloads of the app. To encourage many people to learn more about the program, Hootsuite has a freemium version. So you can try it to see if you like it and keep the free version if you're a small business (or a student trying it out!).

One industry analyst on the Techcrunch website commented: 'One challenge that Hootsuite has had over the years has been the company's focus on the freemium model, and how to convert its initially non-paying users into paying tiers with more premium offerings.'

This is a competitive marketplace with many new companies entering the space and offering different features (search online for social media dashboard to see the latest list) but Hootsuite is a trusted brand with perhaps more to offer.

Case questions

- What measures would you take to convert more of the freemium members to paying members?
- Hootsuite offers integration with many third-party apps. Which apps do you believe are critical to integrate for an organisation that wants to better connect its marketing tools?
- How would you assess which monitoring and reporting system to use for your university? What elements would be included in your assessment criteria?

13.3.7 EMAIL ANALYTICS

In the past, direct mail revolved around the use of sending a letter by post. The challenge was that you didn't know if it had reached the intended recipient, whether they opened or disposed of the letter, and the only way of knowing if they took direct action as a result of the letter was to include some form of code that could be redeemed against a purchase and checked later – sometimes months and months afterwards!

With email it is different and researchers noted some years ago: 'accurately measuring achieved results of any given email marketing campaign can help companies understand and improve the marketing activities they conduct in order to ultimately reach their business goals' (Bilos et al., 2016, p. 97).

Detailed email tracking and measurement are only available if you use an email marketing system, sometimes called an email delivery system. If you send a batch email to say 1000 people, direct from your Google or Outlook accounts, it might look like it's a spam attack. Your local internet service providers (ISPs) such as AT&T, Aussie Broadband, Canal Digital, Sky or ViaSat, may decide to block the emails so that they are not delivered at all. And again, if they are delivered, you don't know who has opened the email or clicked on links unless you have requested read receipts and created dedicated landing pages.

Using an email software system such as campaignmonitor.com, emailit.co or mailchimp. com includes built-in analytics tools that allow you to gain more accurate data as to who has looked at what and when. In addition, it facilitates better management of the data as people can automatically subscribe to or unsubscribe from your mailings.

Analytics provided through email software include a large amount of data in terms of who received the email and the action they took as a result. Table 13.3 shows the types of email analytics data available

Table 13.3 Email analytics data available

Data provided	Metrics available: what this means	How to analyse the data and gain insights
Total recipients	Total number of people that the email was sent to	Assess strength of the email list – if it's only sent to 15% of the list, it indicates the data is old and may be out of date
Successful deliveries	The total number of emails that actually got through or delivered	Content analysis: assess the strength of the email subject getting through spam filters
Bounces	The number of people (a) whose mailbox is full – this is a soft bounce – or (b) who have left the organisation or deleted the email account – this is a hard bounce	Assess strength of the email list – if there are too many hard bounces, it indicates the data is old and may be out of date
Times forwarded	How many times the email was forwarded to others	Content analysis: assess the perceived value of the content
Forwarded opens	How many of those who received the forwarded email opened it	Content analysis: assess the perceived value of the content
Recipients who opened	The details (email addresses) of the people who received the email and opened it	Content analysis: assess the value of the content for the target audience

(Continued)

Table 13.3   (Continued)

Data provided	Metrics available: what this means	How to analyse the data and gain insights
Total opens	The number of people who received the email and opened it	Comparative analysis: assess against previous emails to see which are more successful, although typical open rates vary according to sector, timing and more
Last open date	The last time the email was opened – this indicates the 'shelf life' of an email communication	Content analysis: assess the ongoing value of the email as this indicates the 'shelf life' of an email communication
Recipients who clicked	The details (email addresses) of the people who received the email, opened it and clicked on one of the links in the email	Content analysis: assess the additional value of the email for the target audience
Total clicks	The total number of clicks	Comparative analysis: review against previous emails to see which are more successful
Total unsubscribers	The number of people who unsubscribed following this email	Content analysis: assess the content quality and also the frequency rate. People unsubscribe for different reasons and a typical unsubscribe rate is 0.5%. If it's more than that, the target audience may think they're receiving too many emails from you
Total abuse complaints	The number of people who reported this as spam – too many of these and you won't be able to send any emails	Content analysis: assess the content quality as this metric indicates that the target audience were unhappy with the content – too many of these and you won't be able to send any emails

Email software systems provide summary reports that show all of this data. They allow you to compare one campaign to another to better understand successful subject lines, content and possibly delivery times. These systems can include integration with social media so that newsletters, offers or other information can be shared across social media platforms at the same time. There is research into why email works (see Figure 3.2: Theoretical model of email opening on p. 65).

There are options to test and review the data to see what worked within email software delivery systems. One popular option is A/B testing (see Key Term in Chapter 11).

13.4 USING THE METRICS THAT MATTER TO CREATE AN ACTIONABLE PLAN

There is a question with so many metrics: what really matters? Figure 13.3 shows examples of weak, acceptable and strong metrics. The weak metrics shown here are often called **vanity metrics** (see Discover More). They don't contribute meaningful data; for example, on Facebook you may have 100,000 fans, but fewer than 2,000 may see your content due to the algorithm (see Chapter 3) so the number of fans has no impact on content shared. An organisation may have 50,000 Twitter followers, but if the followers miss a few hours looking at Twitter, they may not see any tweets that have been shared.

These metrics follow the Digital Marketing Strategy Framework (see Chapter 10) of awareness, consideration, conversion, enthusiasm. The stronger metrics are those that generate conversion actions such as a sale or provision of an email address or other data, to start a one-to-one conversation.

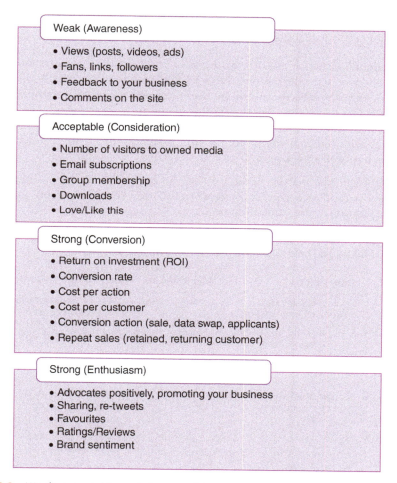

Weak (Awareness)

- Views (posts, videos, ads)
- Fans, links, followers
- Feedback to your business
- Comments on the site

Acceptable (Consideration)

- Number of visitors to owned media
- Email subscriptions
- Group membership
- Downloads
- Love/Like this

Strong (Conversion)

- Return on investment (ROI)
- Conversion rate
- Cost per action
- Cost per customer
- Conversion action (sale, data swap, applicants)
- Repeat sales (retained, returning customer)

Strong (Enthusiasm)

- Advocates positively, promoting your business
- Sharing, re-tweets
- Favourites
- Ratings/Reviews
- Brand sentiment

Figure 13.3   Weak, acceptable and strong metrics

DISCOVER MORE ABOUT VANITY METRICS

Vanity metrics are considered as those that make you look good but have little substance.

Read the article 'How healthy is your business ecosystem?' in the *MIT Sloan Management Review,* which explores metrics and provides evidence as to why vanity metrics are not relevant (Pidun et al., 2021).

Although the number of fans as a simple metric is weak when considered in isolation, it matters when you are reviewing conversion rates. For example, if ASOS sees a drop in its conversion rate which means its sales volume decreases, one method of addressing this is to increase the volume of visitors across social media to drive traffic to the website.

13.4.1 WHO USES THE METRICS?

Having understood which metrics matter most and how can we use them, we need to understand who uses the metrics. Table 13.4 shows the strong metrics identified in Figure 13.3, explains who these may be useful for and how they are applied. What's interesting is that this shows that the figures matter for people outside the marketing team and may include community managers and content creators, which may involve external agencies, customer service, finance, general managers, product selectors, sales teams and web developers.

It is wise to relate the metrics being used to the organisation's overall objectives or KPIs as they will be recorded on a formal basis, and everyone is using – and hopefully understanding – the same measures.

Table 13.4 Metrics and how to use them to create an actionable plan

Metric	Explanation	Who useful for	How to create an actionable plan
Number of visitors to owned media	Number of visitors to a website, by hour, day, week, month	Content Creators	Assess if website and other owned media are performing or growing; if not, ask why and make recommendations to change
Email subscriptions	Number of people signing up for your email newsletter	Content Creators, Sales, Web Manager	Examine whether 'email collectors' such as 'subscribe here' are working and if not change
Group membership	Number of people joining a group created by the organisation	Community Manager	Appraise whether it is worth continuing or adapting the group NOTE: specific group objectives are needed (see Chapter 6, 'Online Communities')
Downloads	100 people downloaded a 'how to guide'	Content Creators, Web Manager	Identify how many people downloaded information and if it is worth (a) creating the information and (b) asking for personal data before the download
Ratings/Reviews	Ratings that may be verified or unverified, e.g. rated five stars on TripAdvisor® or product given one star	General Managers, Product Selectors	Evaluate what is happening with frontline teams, to gauge feedback on products that do/don't work and make changes quicker
Love/Like this	People clicking the ♥ to show their friends they like the item	Marketing, Product Selectors	Explain trends and whether the 'love' is converted and becomes a purchase; if not, recommend changes to the website or other places
Brand sentiment	People talking about the brand online	Marketing	Reflect on brand strength and make changes if needed

Metric	Explanation	Who useful for	How to create an actionable plan
Return on investment (ROI)	The investment divided by the resources employed, e.g. if a new website costs £50,000 to develop and generated sales of £180,000 over 12 months, the ROI was £130,000 or 2.6 times	Marketing, Finance	To see if the money and resources invested generated the expected return which is a useful way of planning future budgets but a strategic measure which may need consideration after 12 months
Conversion rate	Often a percentage showing the number of people who visited your site and the number who purchased	Marketing, Sales, Web Developers	Identify the situation and make changes as needed because small tweaks can make a big difference. If you generate 10,000 visitors to a website with a 2% conversion rate, this is 200 sales, so conversion rate optimisation techniques (see Chapter 14, 'Integrating, Improving and Transforming Digital Marketing') to increase to 2.5% could generate an extra 50 sales
Cost per action	The cost per click, video view	Marketing	Assess how much it costs for each action and whether it is viable
Cost per customer/cost per acquisition	The cost of acquiring a new customer	Marketing	Assess how much it costs to acquire a customer and whether it is viable
Conversion action (sale, data swap, applicants)	When people complete a conversion, such as buying a product online, sharing their email address, registering to donate	Sales, Marketing	Assess which actions were more successful and adapt other campaigns
Repeat sales (retained, returning customer)	The number of customers that return and make a second and ongoing purchases, or continue to subscribe (rather than unsubscribe) and maintain their donations	Sales, Marketing, Customer Service	Analyse whether customer service and the customer journey are working and calculate the customer lifetime value

13.4.2 WHAT TOOLS CAN BE USED?

In addition to the platform insights (e.g. Wordpress or ecommerce dashboards, Facebook and Instagram analytics, email marketing programmes), there are many sophisticated monitoring and management tools such as:

- Adobe Analytics
- Agorapulse
- Bing Analytics
- Google Ads
- Google Analytics

- Hubspot
- Hootsuite
- Loomly
- Salesforce Marketing Cloud
- Sprinklr
- Sprout Social

These provide data and automatically generate reports in the forms of dashboard or downloadable workbooks. It is worth noting that the creation of analytics tools is one of the fastest growing businesses in digital marketing, and with fees from a few dollars a month to hundreds of thousands of dollars a year. Some programs offer free versions which include limited functionality and are a great way to assess whether they're right for your organisation.

13.5 PLAN–DO–CHECK–ACT (PDCA)

In addition to the analytics described in this chapter about how to access and use the metrics to create an actionable plan, there is a structured framework which enables marketers to consider the application and usage of the data, before the digital marketing campaign starts or before you launch a new website. Effectively this allows you to plan the metrics you'll be analysing from the start. This helps as it ensures you're assessing factors that can be measured!

In the field of quality management, the Plan–Do–Check–Act (PDCA) cycle was created by Walter Shewart and refined by his student Edward Deming (Johnson, 2002). It is a basic circular concept that is over one hundred years old and it is still valid as it encourages managers to plan what is needed (identify the situation), do something about it (develop solutions), check the results (evaluate the metrics) and act to fix it (make the necessary changes).

For example, if you're asked to organise an Instagram advertising campaign, the PDCA cycle can help. To start, you might look back at other campaigns and assess the metrics. This may provide evidence or insights that show that some images achieved the objective better than others. But you need to be aware of the metrics – are you measuring the reach (awareness) or engagement (consideration) or conversion? You need to identify whether there are any elements of customer value to be considered. Based on this, you might reflect on the previous campaigns and identify why they were successful. This takes you towards step 1 in planning your new campaign – using previous data for actionable insights, such as the most successful headlines, images or other factors. Move to step 2 and do something. This may involve running a pilot test to see if the results are still valid, which are confirmed (or not) in step 3 where you check whether the proposed campaign is achieving the objectives. When you have gained the knowledge and checked the situation in step 3, you can move to step 4, as shown in Figure 13.4.

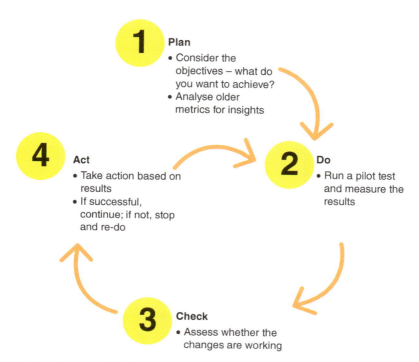

Figure 13.4   Application of the PDCA to an advertising campaign

The PDCA cycle allows you to use the data to create an actionable plan. It's part of the tech culture of 'fail fast', so instead of rolling out a whole campaign and hoping it works, a pilot takes place and if it works this continues; if not, it's stopped quickly.

Activity 13.3   Apply the PDCA cycle

Consider a tech program that did not work. Based on this, prepare a second campaign that either re-launches or changes the messaging. Use the PDCA cycle as your framework for constructing the campaign. Consider that you may need to carry out some research to discover why it failed or wasn't as successful as anticipated, in order to build up your argument for the proposed campaign. Prepare alternatives in case step 2 needs to be refined!

JOURNAL OF NOTE

Big Data & Society considers the implications of big data for societies and analyses big data practices. As an open-access journal, it's available to explore and discover articles around ethical issues as well as discussions on the use of data and metrics.

CASE STUDY
MEASURING STRAVA'S RESULTS

This continues our long case study and you may find it helpful to read earlier parts in previous chapters.

The digital marketing plan has been created and the resources have been identified. Gabriel needs to consider the metrics and analytics, to measure the performance of the plan. This means he can ensure that the plan is working and, if not, will have the time to make changes.

There are around 40 million web visitors a month to the website, with a conversion rate of around 2 million – that's 5 per cent, which is a good result as typically conversion rates are between 1 per cent and 5 per cent. Gabriel will need to increase the number of web visitors and encourage more people to download the app. He needs to ask the analytics team to share the marketing metrics. Strava uses Google Analytics and a range of other analytics packages as part of its MarTech stack, including:

- Branch – this is a mobile deep linking system to increase engagement and retention
- New Relic – a dashboard used to keep an eye on application health and availability while monitoring real user experience
- Facebook Domain Insights – this website contains tracking information that allows admins to see Facebook Insights
- Facebook Signal – this provides content ideas and can show relevant trends, photos, videos and posts from Facebook and Instagram for use in storytelling and reporting
- Facebook Pixel – this is Facebook's conversion tracking system for ads on Facebook to websites
- Snowplow – similar to Google Analytics, this is an open-source analytics that you store yourself

There are only two key metrics Gabriel wants to review: the number of visitors to the website (or landing page) and the conversion rate. At the start, it may be that some A/B testing will be useful to make early assessments to show what's most likely to work.

Gabriel realises that the challenge will be those visitors who saw the ad on Facebook, then went to the website on a different device where cookies were blocked. It's all about attribution and ensuring the analytics package captures this data.

CASE QUESTIONS

- Discuss the types of metrics that Strava is using and identify whether there are any elements that may be missing or duplicated.
- What actions could be taken to increase Strava's conversion rate?
- Strava seems to be using multiple dashboards and systems. Why is this and what would you recommend?

FURTHER EXERCISES

1. For an organisation of your choice, evaluate the types of metrics used relating to the Digital Marketing Strategy Framework and assess what changes could be made.

2. Recommend, with justification, the key metrics and the tools or methods to measure the effectiveness of a digital marketing activity for an organisation of your choice.

3. For an organisation of your choice, recommend metrics to measure customer awareness and enthusiasm. Consider what the chosen organisation needs to measure and any benefits or drawbacks.

4. Digital marketing metrics aren't the responsibility of the marketing team and should be managed by the tech team. Discuss and justify your response.

SUMMARY

This chapter has explored:

- The differences between traditional and digital metrics
- Types of digital metrics
- Differences between metrics, analytics and insights
- How to use the data to create actionable plans
- How to use the Plan–Do–Check–Act (PDCA) framework

GO ONLINE

Visit **study.sagepub.com/hanlon2e** to access links to interesting articles, websites and videos related to this chapter.

Evaluate the value from digital marketing

Apply the exit strategies framework

Social media exit strategies for organisations

ACTIVITIES

Create a plan for digitisation and digitalisation

OVERVIEW
Chapter 14 links the earlier chapters, discussing the value of digital marketing and the application of digital transformation into organisations. The chapter concludes with a look at the future of digital marketing.

KEY CONCEPTS

Digitisation and Digitalisation

Corporate digital responsibility

Access the World Bank Open Data to understand issues with big datasets

DIGITAL TOOLS

Use the Digital Competence Framework for Citizens to assess your digital skills

Explore the Hyper Island Toolbox to gain engagement with team members

14

INTEGRATING AND TRANSFORMING DIGITAL MARKETING

LEARNING OUTCOMES

When you have read this chapter, you will be able to:

Understand digital marketing transformation

Apply the exit strategy archetypes framework

Analyse the 6Cs of integration

Evaluate the value from digital marketing

Create a plan for digitisation and digitalisation

PROFESSIONAL SKILLS

When you have worked through this chapter, you should be able to:

- Assess your digital skills
- Create a plan for digital transformation

14.1 INTRODUCTION TO INTEGRATING AND TRANSFORMING DIGITAL MARKETING

Is all marketing digital now? It is less about whether all marketing is digital, and more about the distinct characteristics of digital marketing. Digital marketing is different from traditional marketing because it is:

- **Technology-enabled** as tools and processes are accessible via the internet
- **Data-driven** as you can see real-time consumer activity through metrics, analytics and insights
- **Globally connected** as organisations gain wider access to their online presence
- **Agile and flexible** as you can start or stop campaigns in minutes, create websites in days, launch companies in weeks
- **Dynamic and logical** as you can specify which customers you want to target, where and when

Does this mean that traditional marketing has disappeared? Marketing, regardless of whether it's traditional or digital, will always exist. People will buy products, whether online or offline, whether physical or virtual, or whether they're essential utilitarian goods or desired hedonic purchases. This behaviour means that organisations need to address customers' needs and make them aware of their products, nurture consideration, encourage conversion and foster enthusiasm – all elements of the Digital Marketing Strategy framework.

There have been many examples of well-known and long-established companies that stuck to traditional marketing and ignored digital. As a result, the businesses failed, with new digital disrupters emerging, as the example companies in Table 14.1 demonstrate.

Table 14.1 Companies failing to adopt digital marketing

Examples of failed businesses	Digital disrupter that precipitated the failure
Borders, the book and music retailer, which had over 500 stores and was probably the first store to close due to Amazon	Amazon selling books online, which when it started many people said would fail as people needed to pick up and look at books before purchasing!
Blockbuster, the video chain, where the idea was that you visited the store in person to collect your video, but you were fined if you returned the video late	Netflix, an idea that developed when one of the team was fined for returning a video too late, which has evolved over time, adapting to new technology
Comet, the electrical retailer, selling goods in store	The growth in online shopping and price comparison sites
TopShop, a clothing retailer in over 35 countries, which closed during the pandemic as it focused on face-to-face retail	ASOS which is a digital-first business and eventually purchased the TopShop name

Smartphone Sixty Seconds® – Failed to adapt

- Using your mobile phone, search online for other 'companies that failed due to digital disruption'.
- How many did you find?
- What types of companies were impacted?

To help you better understand the issues with traditional and digital marketing, this chapter will examine methods of integrating marketing, consider the path towards digital transformation and finally will look at the future of digital marketing.

14.2 THE VALUE OF MARKETING

The American Marketing Association (2017, p. 2) suggests that, 'Marketing is the activity, set of institutions, and processes for creating, communicating, delivering, and exchanging offerings that have value for customers, clients, partners, and society at large'. This positions marketing at the heart of organisations with its role being to create value. The Chartered Institute of Marketing (2015, p. 2) claims, 'Marketing is the management process responsible for identifying, anticipating and satisfying customer requirements profitably'. So marketing is a management process. Yet there are many organisations without marketing representation on their boards as marketing is seen as being tactical rather than strategic.

Perhaps it's the secret to success? Companies that are flourishing embrace marketing, whether it's traditional or digital. These companies listen to customer feedback and appreciate the strategic role of marketing; for example:

- JustEat Takeaway.com has a chief executive with marketing expertise
- Unilever has a chief executive with marketing expertise, plus a chief digital and marketing officer
- Ikea has both a communications manager and a digital manager
- Gymshark has both a chief technology officer and a chief brand officer

Yet not all organisations recognise marketing – digital or traditional – at the executive level. There is a danger that marketing becomes the responsibility of the technology team unless marketers learn how to manage digital marketing.

Marketers must address digital marketing at a strategic level. It can be seen as individual topics, rather than a holistic and integrated discipline. This is because we can separate the different elements into silos which may be disconnected, such as: email, websites, SEO, PPC, content, social media, communities, augmented and virtual realities. Many organisations employ different people responsible for these areas which makes sense if you're managing massive email lists and sending many emails a week to different persona groups, or if you are managing all the social media pages for a large number of products in the same brand. We could argue that these areas of digital marketing are valid at a tactical level, but as Professor Debra Zahay (2021, p. 134) notes, 'digital marketing should not be considered as a series of fragmented topics but rather as a system, sometimes coherent and sometimes chaotic, for bringing together and synthesizing information about the customer'.

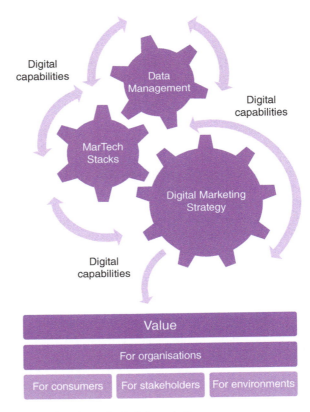

Figure 14.1   Enhancing value through digital marketing

So how do we tackle the challenges of digital marketing? It's about enhancing value. Digital marketing has the potential to not just create value for organisations, but also to augment value by having a clear strategy. This involves selecting the right MarTech stacks and managing the data – whether that's customer information, product insights or online advertising activities, this requires digital capabilities, including knowledge, know-how and competence (see Chapter 12, 'Managing Resources and Reporting'). Figure 14.1 shows how the value is enhanced.

When combined, there is additional value, not just for organisations and their consumers, but also for stakeholders and environments. Organisations can better understand their consumers' needs and the expectations of their stakeholders as well as the wider environment and the impact on our world. The American Marketing Association definition mentions value for 'society at large' which partly addresses the wider environment.

For example, Unilever established a new role for a chief digital and marketing officer, which replaced the traditional chief marketing and communications officer. This was needed as the company listens to customer feedback and manages its data in over 35 datacentres worldwide (see Case Example 1.1 in Chapter 1). This enables Unilever to make informed decisions about new products. The data also contributes to a better understanding of the energy used in manufacturing its products which means that staff strengthen their value to the environment, by identifying where they can reduce greenhouse gases and move closer to zero emissions. So, data and the MarTech stacks used to manage it enhance the value of digital marketing.

DIGITAL TOOL   World Bank open data

The World Bank shares global development data on its website. You can search by country or indicator (e.g. climate change, economy and growth, education) and download the data to explore the complexities of managing datasets.

https://data.worldbank.org

Not all companies have digital and marketing officers and you may find that, as a student and later as a graduate in digital marketing, you are given a role to introduce or blend digital marketing into the business. It is often the case that digital natives (see Chapter 1) are given responsibility for digital and social media in different formats, especially if you have a digital marketing qualification.

Activity 14.1   Evaluate the value of digital marketing

- Using Figure 14.1 'Enhancing value through digital marketing' as your guide, identify an organisation that has created value for itself through digital marketing.
- This value can be created for consumers, stakeholders or environments.
- Discuss the value that's been created.

DIGITAL TOOL   Assess your digital skills

The Digital Competence Framework for Citizens (DigComp) has a free online tool to assess your digital competences. Complete the exercise by clicking on the boxes that best describe your ability. At the end, you're presented with a radar chart showing how you compare to others.

www.digitalskillsaccelerator.eu/learning-portal/online-self-assessment-tool

14.3 INTEGRATING TRADITIONAL AND DIGITAL MARKETING

Most organisations have a digital presence, whether that's a formal website or social media pages. A critical factor is ensuring that every aspect of the digital presence is connected or integrated. This can be challenging as some organisations separate teams into digital and marketing rather than embracing a holistic approach across the firm.

Another major factor with integration is that often we only consider communications, but it's also about the wider digital marketing mix – the 7Ps. In Chapter 1, we considered our digital world and how digital marketing impacts on people, products, places, payments and processes. Earlier chapters also considered digital tools and channels. Successful integration requires an approach that is focused on the consumer, with a competitive offer, where the content is consistent and stakeholders can connect, co-create and collaborate, which is continually improved. Figure 14.2 shows a framework for the 6Cs to integrate the digital and traditional marketing mix.

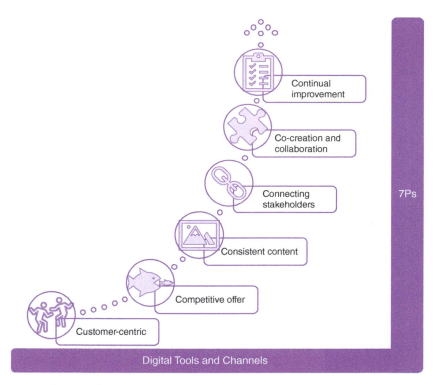

Figure 14.2   The 6Cs of integration

14.3.1 CUSTOMER-CENTRIC

In our digital world, digital marketing strategy places the customer at the centre of the process (see Chapter 10). A new conceptual module of digital marketing based on how consumer behaviour is changing, with the ideas of humanity and humanness at the core, has been proposed (Dwivedi et al., 2020). Humanity is described as being kind and understanding of others, regardless of their background. Humanness is the notion of being human in our world of artificial intelligence, bots and machine learning. This is a customer-centric model which integrates elements of marketing, from consuming to creating.

DISCOVER MORE ON THE DIGITAL MARKETING AND HUMANITY CONCEPTUAL MODEL

Set aside an hour or so and read the article 'Setting the future of digital and social media marketing research: Perspectives and research propositions', published in the *International Journal of Information Management* (Dwivedi et al., 2020), as this indicates many areas for future research into marketing.

14.3.2 DIGITAL COMPETITIVENESS

Being competitive means having an advantage that is difficult for competitors to copy. Without this, it is difficult to maintain a business.

Some years ago, researchers explored hyper-competitive conditions and suggested there were three aspects within competitive value (Grover and Kohli, 2013, p. 656): (1) software; (2) processes; and (3) information. We can look at examples, when we apply these conditions in a digital context, to elements of the 7Ps:

- Product and place: Competitiveness from software

    o The world's largest taxi firm, Uber, doesn't own a single vehicle – it has clever software that connects drivers to passengers.

    o The world's largest accommodation agency, Airbnb, doesn't own a single hotel room – it has clever software that matches hosts to guests.

- Processes and physical evidence: Competitiveness from processes

    o The world's largest retailer, Amazon, doesn't own a single product – it has clever processes that match buyers to sellers, facilitates easy purchasing with the one-click to buy now and encourages customers to pay in advance for delivery with Prime. This results in customers using the platform for all their shopping requirements.

- People and their behaviour: Competitiveness from information

    o One of the world's largest social networks, Facebook, helps sellers specify exact buyer types based on user profiles and behaviour – their source information.

This research was based on creating digital business strategies and mashing up aspects of the business to identify where the opportunities exist, which may include sharing aspects of the business processes, which in the past was unheard of.

14.3.3 CONSISTENT CONTENT

Consistency is a key theme within marketing integration, yet many researchers consider this as only being applied to integrating marketing communications. Yet consistency should apply across the organisation, from the digital marketing mix to the vision. From a strategic perspective, the mission needs to hold true for some years as changing company direction on a regular basis confuses staff, consumers and other stakeholders. For example, nearly 30 years ago, Amazon created its vision statement 'to be Earth's most customer-centric company, where customers can find and discover anything they might want to buy online, and endeavors to offer its customers the lowest possible prices' (Amazon Inc., 2017). Amazon started with a bold vision as it wasn't aiming for consumers located only in its home country of the United States, but across the globe. It wasn't just about books – the initial product offer – this was about anything a customer might want to purchase online. This vision still holds true today and has remained consistent for three decades.

14.3.4 CONNECTING STAKEHOLDERS

To connect people was considered as a communication goal by earlier research (Batra and Keller, 2016). Connections are facilitated by digital environments where consumers connect to each other, join communities and read feedback. For example, consumers can ask questions, answered by other consumers – this is typically how customer support on Apple products works. I've extended this to connecting stakeholders, so that customers, staff and investors all have the potential to be connected.

In a business-to-business environment, connecting stakeholders is normal, as this often requires one larger, more complex sale, rather than many small purchases.

For example, a packaging company may have a contract with a cheese producer who sells to supermarkets. The packaging company is required to produce environmentally friendly wrapping for the cheese which requires product information, such as the 'use by' date, the name of the producer and the exact contents. This also means the packaging company needs to liaise with other stakeholders such as the machinery manufacturers, to ensure they can take the material and turn this into some form of wrapping. There are multiple stakeholders involved – the machinery manufacturer, the packaging company, the cheese producer, the supermarket and finally the consumer. In this B2B context, the stakeholders are always connected.

14.3.5 CO-CREATION AND COLLABORATION

The customer has been considered a co-creator of value for many years (Bettencourt et al., 2014). Examples of co-creation or collaboration include positive reviews, sharing authentic feedback and praising organisations publicly for their service.

Digital marketing spaces provide opportunities for co-creation as consumers can share problems, ask questions and make suggestions, which have been called conversations (Patroni et al., 2020). If organisations listen to the conversations, they can assess and decide which products are worth creating. So, whether it's social media, email responses, comments in online communities or popular search terms in SEO, digital marketing enables greater understanding of stakeholders' needs.

For example, there are over 1 billion Instagram users and the average post includes ten hashtags; that's many conversations and many opportunities to listen and capture feedback. Several fast fashion companies have used social media to refine product offers, such as Mango. It used Instagram Stories to offer different clothing choices to its community. These were ideas or plans for clothing that had not yet entered full production. Mango 'mocked up' different outfit ideas then asked its followers to choose their preferred designs and, based on customer feedback, they decided which clothing to move into production.

The additional value from co-creation is innovation. With consumers involved in the process, the innovation is more likely to succeed as consumers will recommend what they need and, if involved in the process, eagerly await the final product. This process of capturing problems, questions or suggestions from consumers can be heard by organisations who can then decide whether to convert and launch them as new ideas (Patroni et al., 2020).

For instance, during the various pandemic lockdowns, Unilever partnered with Walmart in the US to 'co-create and launch a new bath product range. This was based on customer insights from their datacenters which identified people needed more "me time" at home during lockdown' (Unilever, 2020, p. 25).

DISCOVER MORE ON CO-CREATION

The textbook *Social Media Marketing Theories and Applications* by Stephan Dahl (Sage, 2018) includes a useful chapter dedicated to co-creation and collaboration.

ETHICAL INSIGHTS   Co-destruction

Co-creation is the positive aspect of collaborating with stakeholders, but there is a dark side known as co-destruction. Co-destruction occurs when customers or other stakeholders become unhappy and vent their dissatisfaction online which can destroy an organisation.

For example, this is often seen in online travel communities, such as Trip Advisor®, where individuals complain about the customer service, entitling their review as 'stay somewhere else!' These negative reviews can result in fewer bookings, cancellations and a decline in business revenue.

- How do organisations manage co-destruction?
- Does it matter or is part of consumers being honest about organisations?
- How would you feel if an organisation you worked for gained terrible feedback?

14.3.6 CONTINUAL IMPROVEMENT

The final stage in this framework is continual improvement. In a digital environment, companies can add and remove online material in a matter of minutes. Where there are mistakes, products that don't work or content leading to co-destruction, companies can adapt and improve. However, it's not sufficient to improve only when there are errors; organisations need to continuously improve to stay ahead.

This is where tactical actions can be helpful. For example:

- Review of **web analytics data** to see where customers entered and abandoned the website, which pages were viewed and which were ignored (see Chapter 13, 'Marketing Metrics and Analytics')
- **Online surveys** to ask why customers didn't buy from you today
- **Live chat analysis** to read the conversations and see where customers dropped out of the user journey
- Assessment of the **user experience** (see Chapter 3) to see how well the website does or doesn't work

However, improving is not always adding; sometimes it means taking away or withdrawing from a platform, instead of rarely updating. Researchers in Germany, Carsten Schultz and Björn Kruse, have been researching organizational exit strategies on social media platforms (Schultz and Kruse, 2022). Their work identified different behaviours within organisations in how they either abandoned, or planned a gradual withdrawal from, social media. Figure 14.3 shows the options for organisations.

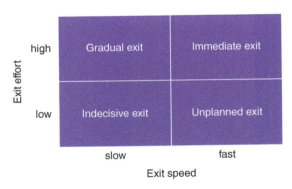

Figure 14.3 Exit strategy archetypes

Source: Schultz and Kruse (2022)

The exit strategy archetypes in Figure 14.3 are measured on two dimensions: first, the amount of effort a brand applies to leave the social media pages; and, second, the speed of exit. For example, the fresh, handmade cosmetics company LUSH closed its social media accounts as it couldn't see the benefit for the company or the customers. This was an immediate exit – fast with great effort. Yet other companies such as Nike have demonstrated an indecisive effort and lack of speed to address their Facebook page (see facebook.com/nike). This page is rarely updated and there seem to be no plans to manage the exit strategy.

Activity 14.2   Application of the exit strategies framework

Identify an organisation of your choice that has reduced its activity on a specific social media platform. Apply the exit strategy archetypes framework and assess which type of exit strategy they are using. Should they stay or should they go? Take this one stage further and make recommendations on how they could improve the process.

DISCOVER MORE ON SOCIAL MEDIA EXIT STRATEGIES

Read the chapter 'Organizational exit strategies on social media platforms' by C.D. Schultz and B. Kruse (2022) in A. Hanlon and T. Tuten (eds), *The SAGE Handbook of Social Media Marketing*.

CASE EXAMPLE 14.1   Ikea's approach to co-creation

IKEA is best known for its Scandinavian-style furniture. The Swedish company has 422 stores in over 50 countries and is often popular with students as it offers a range of useful items at reasonable prices. IKEA operates multiple websites, with many of the same products, in different languages. A typical year can involve 4 billion visits to IKEA.com. Ikea furniture holds its value and older items can be resold on eBay.

The IKEA vision is 'to create a better everyday life for the many people by offering a wide range of well-designed, functional home furnishing products at prices so low that as many people as possible can afford it'.

During the pandemic, many retail stores were closed, but the IKEA website stayed open. In addition, the retailer augmented its offer and introduced click and collect across stores

(Continued)

in some locations, commenting that 'In-store fulfilment helped to create more capacity and shorten delivery lead times' as customers wanted the goods in the shortest possible time. To complement online access to goods, it introduced online access to planning services to design kitchens, wardrobes and living room storage, enabling consumers to book appointments to speak with an advisor online.

Co-creation is also a key part of the IKEA offer, with customers and with other brands. Recognising its role in the circular economy and the need to address sustainability, IKEA collaborated with MUD Jeans, a company which recycles old jeans to make new ones. By collaborating, IKEA and MUD created a new sofa cover for the KLIPPAN range. IKEA commented: 'KLIPPAN sofa is an iconic IKEA product. By offering new sofa covers made from recycled materials, we can help customers to renew their sofa and reuse materials,' said Piotr Jakubiak, Deployment Leader at New Business and Innovation Deployment, IKEA of Sweden. 'We are happy to work together with MUD Jeans to make the KLIPPAN sofa cover with recycled denim. This simple action will give new life to the sofas and worn jeans' (Inter IKEA Systems B.V., 2021, p. 1).

To facilitate co-creation with customers, IKEA has established the website ikeacocreation. com which shares its approach to co-creation. For example, the new co-creation approach with the KLIPPAN sofa cover has been launched as a limited collection available in certain European markets. While IKEA calls this 'an iconic product', adding a recycled MUD cover makes this older sofa design that was launched in 1979 more relevant for environmentally conscious consumers.

Case questions

- What are the key factors for IKEA to consider with connecting stakeholders when integrating the digital and traditional marketing mix?
- Which elements of digital competitiveness does IKEA use and why?
- What are the risks with co-creation projects?

14.4 THE PROCESS OF DIGITAL TRANSFORMATION

Within a marketing context, digital transformation is the process of moving an organisation from a traditional marketing focus to one that embraces digital. This does not mean the organisation stops selling traditional products, but instead adapts to more closely meet the customers' requirements, such as being able to make contact, place orders or buy products online.

The process of digital transformation involves three progressive phases: (a) digitisation, (b) **digitalisation** (see Key Terms) and (c) transformation, as shown in Figure 14.4.

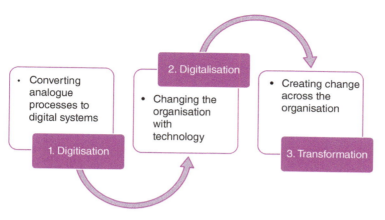

Figure 14.4   The process of digital transformation

KEY TERM   DIGITISATION

Digitisation involves taking analogue items and converting them to digital; as Brennen and Kreiss (2016, p. 560) suggested, 'the conversion of analogue data into digital form'. One challenge with digitisation is that, in an online setting, many customers expect the product to be free, such as Google Maps or news material (Kumar and Reinartz, 2016).

KEY TERM   DIGITALISATION

Digitalisation is about changing the organisation with technology. Having digitised a process, the next step is 'the application of digital technologies—in our work related to the application in businesses' (Ritter and Pedersen, 2020, p. 181). This is not simply using the tools, but also how we use or apply them to make life easier.

14.4.1 DIGITISATION

Digitisation involves converting analogue processes to digital systems. Many organisations still rely on what we could describe as old-fashioned systems which are often physical items. These may include paper records, printed brochures or loyalty cards.

For example, a dental practice might store its patients' records on paper in card files. These could be stored in metal physical filing systems with a key to keep them secure. These require a lot of physical storage space and might not be up to date. Plus, they are easy to mis-file and if the key is lost that could be a problem! Digitisation means adding the details to an online patient management system. While this could include auto-saving features and other benefits that staff may find useful, the initial process requires time and effort, along with investment, which is why it might not happen.

Another example of digitisation is the move from thousands of printed brochures to perhaps a few or none as they become digital downloads. With 24/7 availability, digital downloads enable customers to gain access to the material when needed.

14.4.2 DIGITALISATION

Digitalisation involves taking action and making changes in organisations with technology. This is about changing business processes in different areas. This also involves a move from physical to digital. Business processes include communicating with customers, holding meetings and producing reports.

For example, if a dental practice converted its analogue process of collecting paper records to an electronic patient management system, staff could change the way they communicate with their patients. Instead of sending letters, they could email patients. The patient management system could do this automatically after the latest appointment, including a calendar invitation as well as an SMS message 48 hours before as a reminder. However, this may create fear amongst the staff who may think that this could take their job, so they might resist the new system.

Traditionally, many sales meetings were held face to face, but the pandemic demonstrated that it was possible to hold meetings online. Although it may not be the same as an in-person meeting, the additional benefits include saving time, as well as saving fuel and reducing carbon emissions.

Many organisations produce reports manually and digital tools such as Google Analytics enable the creation of dashboards, or automated reporting. This also saves time and allows marketers to focus on strategic factors, such as analysing the data, rather than creating the data.

The nine steps towards digitisation and digitalisation

The issue is: how do you start the process towards digital transformation? The critical factor is to start with evidence and to involve others in the process. It's best to start with a small project and the nine steps to digitisation and digitalisation are:

1. Find the advocate

2. Create an online customer journey

3. Construct the customer experience

4. Map the digital toolbox

5. Review content assets

6. Identify community support

7. Identify the strategic options

8. Create a strategy

9. Pause and present the strategy

These nine steps towards digitisation and digitalisation launch the process of digital transformation. For example, you might be trying to persuade an organisation to use digital loyalty cards, instead of physical ones. This is a small step towards removing an analogue process in favour of a digital one, which is digitisation. But it may require additional technology and become a digitalisation project. Let's explore these steps further and apply them to the example of a physical loyalty card. These take up a lot of space in a wallet and consumers might forget them.

Step 1 – Find the advocate

When embarking on any new project, to get commitment for future actions and to ensure it is successful you need an advocate, supporter or project champion. This is often a senior person who might be in the marketing department, but they might not be. It is important that the advocate has some authority or power and is able to persuade or influence others.

For example, if one of the aims relates to cost saving, but an initial investment is needed, find the finance director, as they may have a vested interest and be willing to support the project. For example, having physical loyalty cards may be less expensive than the initial coding required to establish online or virtual cards. But, in the longer term, it saves money and adds greater value by providing more customer insights.

Step 2 – Create an online customer journey

When the advocate has been identified, you need to ensure that you have evidence to support future recommendations. A useful mechanism for this is to start with the online **customer journey** (see Chapter 2, 'The Digital Consumer').

But don't do this alone! Involve others and compare their ideas for the customer journey. At this stage, you have included other team members, and as they have contributed to the project they will have a greater interest in how it will work.

Step 3 – Construct the customer experience

Using the customer journey as your foundation, the next step is to construct the customer experience from start to finish. This helps to identify other stakeholders (see Chapter 11) that may need to be involved in the process of digitisation and digitalisation. It also allows you to make contact with them and gain their opinions too.

For example, there may be a stakeholder group with good understanding of accessibility issues and group members could provide useful information to ensure you are not excluding groups by accident.

Step 4 – Map the digital toolbox

If at this stage you have found your advocate, created the online customer journey and constructed the customer experience, it is worthwhile looking at the current activities and how they apply to the customer journey (see Chapter 2). Some may be relevant, some less so. Mapping all items in the toolbox provides an indication of where the organisation is right now. It is a useful snapshot to see the digital tools that are or are not used.

For example, with the loyalty card you need to consider how the changes will be communicated to consumers. Reviewing the digital toolbox elements will highlight any actions that may be required.

Step 5 – Review content assets

One of the fears when working on digital transformation is that all current working practices will be ignored or removed. One of the factors you will have noticed throughout this textbook is that content will be required at every step of the journey. Organisations often have vast content assets, yet they don't realise what's there. It's important to review the current content as a useful way to understand what the organisation has available when making future plans.

With the loyalty card example, these elements may become obvious when mapping the digital toolbox and highlighting areas where existing content could be re-used or where new content is required.

Step 6 – Identify community support

Online communities provide conversations when they discuss organisations, their products and services, as well as generating new ideas.

Review whether the company has any online communities, whether formal or informal, and if yes, identify where they are located as this is a great story to share with the organisation: 'We may not be online, but our customers are, perhaps we should join the party?'

For example, the online community could also be involved in creating or testing the digital loyalty card. Discovering where they are and gaining their involvement earlier may lead to a more successful launch.

Step 7 – Identify the strategic options

The organisation needs to understand where digital fits into the business. In an ideal world, it is simply part of the business, but at this stage it may be a new idea. Let's imagine it is a new idea and there is already a strategy in place. Using the evidence gathered in steps 1 to 5, look back at Chapter 10 to identify the strategic options for the business.

Check how the loyalty card fits into the overall strategy. If it doesn't, perhaps it's time to abandon the idea before developing further!

Step 8 – Create a campaign strategy

Having reached this step where the digital loyalty card fits with the corporate or business strategy and adds value by providing more data, you need to prepare to launch the campaign. Preparing a campaign strategy with clear objectives will ensure this is more successful.

Refer back to Chapters 10 and 11 to build your recommended campaign strategy.

Step 9 – Pause and present the strategy

At this stage, you need to pause and to share the evidence gathered and present the strategy. There is no point spending time creating objectives and a plan if the senior management team has not seen the evidence and don't agree with the strategy.

You could speak with your advocate and ask to meet some of the senior management team for their opinion. This allows you to test the likelihood of the recommendations being adopted. This can result in several outcomes:

- The advocate organises the meetings, which work well and result in the adoption of all recommendations
- Meetings are organised with some members of the senior management team and some recommendations are adopted
- The senior management team is unwilling to adopt any of the ideas, in which case a meeting is required with the advocate and the CEO to agree the best way to move forward
- Alternatively, an unexpected response or a mix of these possibilities may occur!

DIGITAL TOOL   Hyper Island Toolbox

If you're working with other team members, you may need alternative techniques to bring them on board. Or sometimes you might need to break the ice if they don't warm to your ideas! Hyper Island has created a 'toolbox for anyone who wants to do things more creatively and collaboratively in their team or organization'. It links to a range of free tools you can use when collaborating and trying to innovate or consider what the future may look like.

https://toolbox.hyperisland.com

Activity 14.3   Create a plan for digitisation and digitalisation

For an organisation of your choice, identify an area where it would benefit from moving from analogue to digital, or further embracing technology. Using the nine steps to digitisation and digitalisation, create a plan showing your approach to make this happen.

14.4.3 DIGITAL TRANSFORMATION

Digital transformation is the last step and takes the change from one or two processes, in one or two departments, to modifications across the entire organisation.

For example, within the dental practice, this involves the reception team, along with the technicians and dentists. Along with an electronic patient management system that is managed internally, they could enable access for patients to book their own appointments. Any product recommendations or advice from dentists could be automatically emailed to patients as future reminders, with discount codes for recommended products. Patients could add their reviews to the product recommendations which would give the dentists greater feedback and is better than being asked questions when you're sitting in the dentist's chair – it's more customer-centric.

As digital transformation applies to technology and people, it also encompasses more than marketing and is often considered in IT and information systems, due to its connection to technology. While technology helps the process, successful digital transformation only happens with people, not processes (see Technology Acceptance Model in Chapter 2). This has been described as having 'digital mindsets' (Solberg et al., 2020, p. 105). Just because there is amazing new technology in place, this doesn't mean the staff will happily use it! The international consultants McKinsey reported that 70 per cent of complex projects, such as digital transformation, fail and this can be expensive. The main reasons for failure in digital transformation are:

- People – lack of communication or agreement between teams
- Skills – not having the abilities to run and manage the systems and believing the technology will work on its own

For example, the American multinational conglomerate GE launched a new independent digital business focused on developing software for the industrial internet of things. It was considered a great idea, but as a separate business unit it didn't share the same objectives as the rest of the company, which it was meant to be working with. With such different aims, the project backfired with drastic consequences – the company's share price dropped, the reputation was damaged and the goals weren't achieved. Although over time this was turned around, this is an example of poor communication resulting in a failed initial project.

CASE EXAMPLE 14.2   Japan's digital transformation journey

Japan is an island nation with a rich history. With a population of nearly 130 million, one-third of which live around Tokyo, it is one of the most technologically advanced countries in the world.

However, it is widely acknowledged that the country is less digitised than many others. One of the main analogue systems used country-wide is the Hanko stamp, a small circular or square seal that bears the individual's or company's name (search online for examples). It's the equivalent of your official signature as the Hanko creates an Inkan – a stamp on a piece of paper.

These are used by all types of organisations, from banks to local government departments, major corporations to small businesses. Hanko stamps are used to approve purchases, for contract documents and internal documents. It's a tradition dating back for many centuries and is one example of how the country uses pieces of paper rather than electronic methods.

To address these issues, the government is leading digital transformation and the prime minster took two key steps:

- The creation of a Digital Agency, a new team to support digital transformation
- The appointment of a Digital Transformation Minister

The Digital Agency aims to change the mindsets of all government departments and in an interview (Rakuten, 2021) with Mickey Mikitani, the CEO of Rakuten, a major internet company, the Digital Transformation Minister Mr Takuya Hirai commented:

People thought that Japan was doing its best with digitalization and new technology, but when the virus forced us to look at our own society, it was obvious that neither the public nor the private sectors had the capability to deal with it effectively. It was only this year that it became obvious to people in Japan that our country was so far behind on digitalization.

The first step in the process is digitisation, replacing Hanko stamps with electronic methods. There are signs this is happening as several organisations have stopped using Hanken in favour of electronic signatures, including social media platform Line, the beverages company Suntory Holdings and Mercari, an online marketplace.

Many of these changes were driven by the pandemic. For example, Mercari's employees who were classed as vulnerable during the pandemic still had to visit the office to use Hanko to finalise paper documents. The company realised that the traditional process was risking the lives of their staff. As the government issued guidelines essentially saying Hanko seals were not necessary when concluding contracts, Mercari decided to adopt this change.

There have been major benefits too; as Suntory Holdings observed (Shibata, 2020, p. 1), annual savings of '30 million yen ($279,000) in contract paper, stamp and mail expenses; 60,000 hours of paperwork; 3 million sheets of paper and 18 tons of CO_2 emissions'.

With the government leading the move, this will make it easier for commercial organisations to follow and newer electronic contract systems, such as DocuSign, are enabling this process.

Case questions

- What steps would you recommend to maintain the momentum of digital transformation across Japan that was accelerated by the pandemic?
- How have other organisations you know changed their business practices as a result of the pandemic?
- What actions could persuade an old-fashioned business to adopt new technologies, such as electronic signatures?

14.5 SUCCESSFUL DIGITAL TRANSFORMATION

Successful digital transformation is challenging as the nature of the process involves disruption. But 'digital change does not occur by accident. Instead, it requires strong investment across the organisation because the disruptive potential of change, especially for more mature stages of digital transformation, extends beyond technologies' (Halpern et al., 2021, p. 1).

So, having understood the process of digital transformation and realised that many of these projects fail, this section considers how digital transformation can be successful. The key components of successful digital transformation are:

- Key event
- Digital strategy
- Leadership
- Stakeholders
- Competencies
- Methods and means

14.5.1 KEY EVENT

Digital transformation is often driven by a key event. Typically this was because a competitor had made a major change or a new disrupter had entered the market. IBM led the PC market for many years and failed to see the changes as it was no longer just companies buying large mainframe computer systems, but also individual customers wanting smaller desktop PCs to use at home.

For example, COVID-19 has been a key event that impacted on many organisations and forced them to consider transforming their business and adopting digital. Read Case Example 14.2 to see how Japan has had to embark on a digital transformation journey.

14.5.2 DIGITAL STRATEGY

More companies are realising that they need a digital strategy which is a key part of digital transformation. This is an area where different researchers agree. These disruptions trigger strategic responses which can involve a blend of digital business strategy or a dedicated digital transformation strategy (Vial, 2019), such as the one shown in Case Example 14.2 with Japan.

Other researchers have recommended different strategic options, such as creating a digital co-creation platform (Verhoef et al., 2021). Looking at how small and medium enterprises (SMEs) responded during the pandemic, it's been suggested that employing digital strategy depended on the competencies of the firms. However, many SMEs lacked the digital literacy needed to create the strategy (Priyono et al., 2020).

14.5.3 LEADERSHIP

A study examined how businesses approach digital transformation and discovered that, along with a digital strategy, top management validation was vital (Fischer et al., 2020). Along with the senior supporter, governance in the shape of clear rules and responsibilities is essential for digital transformation. The CEO or MD has to want to make the change. If they don't want to make the change or if they won't support the actions, it's very unlikely that it will succeed.

Investigating change across 94 airports worldwide to better understand the approach to transforming an organisation, Halpern et al. (2021) upheld this argument. Their work highlighted the need for clear leadership for digital programmes. These researchers further identified that it wasn't just about having a leader who was committed to the change, but also a senior management team that 'support and engage in digital initiatives' (p. 6).

14.5.4 STAKEHOLDERS

As well as the leaders, stakeholders (see Chapter 11) are involved in the process of digital transformation. Professor Anjar Priyono et al. (2020, p. 19) commented that the people are 'more important than its digital technologies because the latter are only tools'.

This is not simply about the staff or leaders; it involves the wider communities as 'Digital transformation changes societies' (Fischer et al., 2020, p. 1). In this study, Fischer and colleagues examined how large companies manage digital transformation projects and people was a core element. Sharing knowledge with stakeholders and gaining their involvement mean that projects are more likely to work when launched, as the relevant people have been involved in the process and can more quickly adapt.

The opposite approach is to work in secret and tell suppliers or other stakeholders about the changes, when they are finalised. The lack of communication at an early stage adds time to the final process and may result in some stakeholders withdrawing from the partnership.

For example, Nike, the worldwide sportswear company, adopted digital transformation by creating one technology strategy across the entire business. This started with the digitalisation of their supply chain process with the development of the 'Express Lane' concept. Ensuring suppliers were involved has reduced the time spent on product design to product availability from months to weeks.

14.5.5 COMPETENCIES

Digital expertise is growing in demand and having the processes in place to do something (capability) is one side; the other is possessing the skill or knowledge to make it happen (competence).

As a student, you're building your competencies and when applying for jobs recruiters can test these in various ways, such as: asking you to deliver a presentation, explain a situation or work in a team to complete an activity. If you demonstrate the required competencies, you make the shortlist. In the same way, digital transformation only happens where the competencies are available. In some companies, this can be too difficult to achieve, so they start afresh with a new business.

For example, the National Australian Bank (NAB) is a traditional business that realised it was missing opportunities to gain a digital customer base. Instead of bolting on digital to its existing offer (which was done in part for the existing customers), NAB created an entirely new bank, UBank. This new business offers online-only banking to different personas. This enabled UBank to recruit people with digital competencies and was driven by its strategy as NAB decided to uplift its digital capability (see Chapter 9 for more on competencies).

This balance between asking existing employees to take on work outside their normal functions, or retraining, or planning to recruit staff with digital skills, has been identified by several researchers (Verhoef et al., 2021; Vial, 2019). Sometimes it can be easier to start a new business unit and recruit for the skills needed, such as the UBank example.

14.5.6 METHODS AND MEANS

The final element involved in digital transformation is having the technology and processes in place, as well as the budget to make it happen.

Technology is often seen as the driver of digital transformation, which to a certain extent it is. Yet, without the stakeholders, no amount of amazing technology will make it happen. Successful digital transformation requires experience with digital technology, which is why we see the roles of chief technology officer (CTO) which is more common in tech companies, or chief digital officer (CDO) which is more common in traditional organisations.

Budgets involved in digital transformation typically require millions or billions of dollars for large international organisations. Equally, for smaller businesses, small steps can be taken by subscribing to new software tools.

Smartphone Sixty Seconds® – CTOs and CDOs

- Using your mobile phone, search online for 'chief technology officers + list' and 'chief digital officers + list'.
- How many did you find?
- What types of companies employ these roles?

14.6 THE FUTURE OF DIGITAL MARKETING

Digital marketing could be considered to be at a crossroads, with digital strategy starting to replace the focus on digital tactics. At the start, it was all about the tactics, such as building websites, running online adverts or creating social media pages. Now that digital marketing has been in existence for longer, organisations are stepping back to consider the broader digital picture. Digital strategy is now recognised as being different from a traditional marketing strategy, as section 14.1 'Introduction' explained.

Behaviour is changing too, within consumers, companies and governments, with greater co-creation and collaboration, as this section will discuss.

14.6.1 CHANGING ONLINE CONSUMER BEHAVIOUR

Consumer well-being

Our digital world has progressed from being able to see company brochures online to your smartwatch praising the number of steps you've taken. Digital is baked into our very being. From the moment we wake until we turn in, we're all connected. The evolution from Web 1.0 to the concept of Web 4.0 was highlighted in Chapter 1, although some authors believe we've now reached marketing 5.0, described as 'technology for humanity' (Kotler et al., 2021).

The notion of caring and doing the right thing was part of Google's original mission statement of 'Don't be evil' as the platform encouraged developers to ensure their work was ethically responsible. This is a recurring theme which Professor Yogesh Dwivedi and colleagues identified in their digital marketing and humanity conceptual model (Dwivedi et al., 2020).

Being kind and understanding is part of being human and within this we can consider consumer well-being. According to Vrontis et al. (2021), the emotional responses and impact of digital marketing, and how this positively or negatively alters consumer well-being, is an area for future research.

For example, we've seen sports clubs and sports stars taking social media breaks, to demonstrate their unhappiness with social media platforms failing to address online abuse which, apart from being unacceptable, can traumatise those being discriminated against.

The value of our data

Digital marketing operates in a data-driven world. As marketers, we can capture evidence and gain insights within days, not years. This has been called 'the datafication of business' which has launched the fourth industrial revolution (Fernández-Rovira et al., 2021, p. 1).

Worldwide legislation around data protection has continued to grow. In the future, we may see a situation where individual consumers can generate income from their data.

Imagine being rewarded for accepting marketing cookies, with additional bonuses if the data can be shared with relevant third parties!

The ethics of data use and protecting our privacy are two of the major issues which will remain critical in our future. This leads to a requirement for greater trust and transparency within organisations in how they collect and use our data.

14.6.2 CHANGING DIGITAL COMPANY BEHAVIOUR

Caring and connecting

In emerging economies where budgets may be smaller, the concept of frugal innovation was seen as an affordable solution to build products that are good enough (Zeschky et al., 2011). It is a creative approach to invention and design which involves improvising or finding alternative solutions (Soni and Krishnan, 2014).

One study has suggested that in a post-pandemic world, we are becoming more careful with how we use resources (Radjou, 2020) and may be entering a phase of a frugal economy. We're consuming less and re-using more. In this frugal economy, it's not just innovation which is created based on a limited budget, it's also about finding clever and simple solutions in many areas. Radjou (2020) provides several examples which support elements of the 6Cs of integration, including:

- Customer-centric – companies adopting stronger sustainable goals to have a positive impact on society and the environment
- Connecting stakeholders – organisations working together with the community to find solutions
- Co-creation and collaboration – companies sharing office space, business equipment or staff
- Continual improvement – manufacturers scaling out and sharing resources, rather than buying more and scaling up

These examples demonstrate that the solution isn't always spending more money, but spending more time considering the solution, as well as involving stakeholders. This is part of the move away from companies operating in silos and keeping new projects top secret, to being customer-centric and connecting stakeholders in co-creation projects, to gain continual improvement.

Corporate digital responsibility

As part of caring for our resources and connecting stakeholders, a new concept has been proposed called 'corporate digital responsibility' (Lobschat et al., 2021, p. 875). Corporate social responsibility is a well-known concept where companies seek to engage with stakeholders and foster ways to be more sustainable. Corporate digital responsibility (CDR) is an extension of this idea and proposes that with the growth of digital technology, as well as many cases of mismanagement of our data, companies should take a more ethical view and become responsible at a corporate level in their use of digital technology.

> **KEY TERM** CORPORATE DIGITAL RESPONSIBILITY
>
> Corporate digital responsibility is defined as 'the set of shared values and norms guiding an organization's operations with respect to four main processes related to digital technology and data. These processes are the creation of technology and data capture, operation and decision making, inspection and impact assessment, and refinement of technology and data' (Lobschat et al., 2021, p. 875).

CDR involves many stakeholders:

- Organisations such as third parties who provide technology services or other suppliers involved in digital aspects of the business
- Individual actors such as managers of data inside the organisation, as well as employees and customers
- Artificial and technological actors such as the use of algorithms and machine learning
- Institutional, governmental and legal actors such as legal data privacy frameworks (e.g. GDPR, California Consumer Protection Act – see Chapter 1) and trade associations which may offer codes of conduct

The concept of CDR once again involves collaboration and co-creation. Collaboration involves wider stakeholder groups and recommends that the firm's use of data gathering and targeting should be transparent in order to build trust.

14.6.3 CHANGING GOVERNMENT BEHAVIOUR

Events can be a driver for change, especially for digital transformation and not just for companies and consumers. During the pandemic, many governments had to make rapid changes just to communicate with citizens, although the responses varied worldwide. The United Nations classified these government policy actions in three phases: react, resolve and reinvent (United Nations Division for Public Institutions and Digital Government, 2020).

In the react phase, there was an urgent need to provide accurate information due to the spread of fake news. For example, according to the United Nations, in March 2020 just 110 of its 193 member states had created information portals and yet within 14 days, this had grown to 167. There were further advances in online communication and one example from Norway is the prime minster holding an online press conference aimed at children, to help reduce their worries.

Another aspect of react was connecting with stakeholders and seeking volunteers to collaborate in a range of settings, from acting as support staff in hospitals to transporting older people to appointments.

The second phase, resolve, involved developing multi-stakeholder partnerships as governments aimed to find remedies for difficult issues. This included seeking solutions for COVID-19 patients as well as using data to identify hotspots and ensure citizens were not placing themselves in danger. For example, in Singapore the government worked with the app stores and local community groups to successfully deploy a contact tracing app (along with a physical token for older people who didn't have a smartphone), within eight weeks. The TraceTogether app has been credited as one of the reasons for Singapore's low COVID-19 mortality levels per million population.

The third stage, reinvent, emphasised the need for governments to be able to adopt new technology swiftly. As Case Example 14.2 demonstrated, the pandemic was the catalyst for the Japanese government to encourage businesses to move away from the centuries-old tradition of hanko stamps, to adopting electronic signatures.

Digital marketing is our future and we need to ensure that we carefully consider the tools and technology that we use, to enhance value for organisations, consumers, stakeholders and our environments. In the words of Sir Tim Berners-Lee, 'The future is still so much bigger than the past.'

JOURNAL OF NOTE

A helpful journal covering all aspects of integrating and transforming digital marketing is the *Journal of Research in Interactive Marketing*. Previously known as *Direct Marketing: An International Journal,* the name changed to reflect the move to digital with a focus on integrated marketing.

CASE STUDY

CONNECTING TEAMS, CONNECTING CAMPAIGNS, CONNECTING THE BUSINESS

This continues our long case study and you may find it helpful to read earlier parts in previous chapters.

Claire is a digital consumer. Originally, she was using Garmin, which she recently dropped in favour of Strava. Since joining Strava, she has noticed adverts appearing promoting Strava on her Instagram account which she thinks is odd as she's already a premium subscriber and has linked her app to her Samsung watch. She thinks that Strava should be better organised than this and there should be a way of ensuring its systems are more joined up.

She also received a 'recommend a friend' email, which she's forwarded on to five friends who love running too. Two of them are still using Garmin, one uses Runtastic and the others use Runkeeper. Claire thinks it must be difficult to stop using an app that contains all your records and switch to a new one as it would feel like starting over. But Runtastic seems to have disappeared after it merged with Adidas; she isn't sure. She's heard that Runkeeper changed when it merged with another company.

Claire is currently on a work placement in an old-fashioned food company and, as she seems to be the youngest person in the building, she's been given the task of integrating digital marketing within the business, specifically to ensure the different campaigns are connected and to provide advice on how to use more digital tools.

Gabriel is enjoying his new role as assistant communications manager for Strava. But he's had feedback from some premium users that they're seeing adverts for premium subscriptions which he needs to investigate. Although this is one small element of communications, it's essential that the digital marketing plan is integrated. He wonders if the premium team have been running separate campaigns. He's been so busy trying to create a digital marketing plan, it may be that he left some people out of the process. He needs to ensure that the feedback doesn't turn into negative online conversations.

His boss is very supportive and Gabriel will ask her if he can involve some of the senior team to share the plan. More integration is needed, not just with the different campaigns, but across the departments. Gabriel believes that a meeting where he explains the issue will bring everyone together as well as saving time and money, though he needs a structure for the meeting and is not sure where to start.

CASE QUESTIONS

- What frameworks could Gabriel use to explain the issues around the lack of integration?
- Imagine you're in Claire's shoes, working on placement with the task of integrating digital marketing within a traditional business – how would you start?
- What methods can companies adopt to join up their departments?

FURTHER EXERCISES

1. Evaluate the value of digital marketing for an organisation of your choice.

2. Analyse elements of digital competitiveness for a sports or retail brand.

3. Design a digital transformation plan for an organisation of your choice. What do you consider to be the main challenges?

4. The future of marketing is digital. Discuss with justification for your arguments.

SUMMARY

This chapter has explored:

- The elements involved in integrating the digital and traditional marketing mix
- Organisational exit strategies on social media platforms
- The differences between digitisation and digitalisation in the process of digital transformation
- Factors in successful digital transformation
- The future of digital marketing

GO ONLINE

Visit **study.sagepub.com/hanlon2e** to access links to interesting articles, websites and videos related to this chapter.

REFERENCES

Abbasi, A., Chen, H. and Salem, A. (2008) 'Sentiment analysis in multiple languages: Feature selection for opinion classification in Web forums', *ACM Transactions on Information Systems*, *26* (3), pp. 1–34.

Ackland, R. (2013) *Web Social Science*. London: Sage.

Adgate, B. (2021) 'As podcasts continue to grow in popularity, ad dollars follow', *Forbes*. www.forbes.com/sites/bradadgate/2021/02/11/podcasting-has-become-a-big-business/?sh=6ca926702cfb

Adner, R. and Kapoor, R. (2016) 'Right tech, wrong time: How to make sure your ecosystem is ready for the newest technologies', *Harvard Business Review*, *94* (11), pp. 60–7.

Akar, E., Mardikyan, S. and Dalgic, T. (2019) 'User roles in online communities and their moderating effect on online community usage intention: An integrated approach', *International Journal of Human–Computer Interaction*, *35* (6), pp. 495–509.

Amangala, E.A. and Wali, A.F. (2020) 'Market orientation, service quality perception, and customer satisfaction: The role of market-sensing capabilities', *Business Perspectives and Research*, *8* (2), pp. 216–31.

Amazon Inc. (2017) 'Amazon jobs'. Available at: www.amazon.jobs/working/working-amazon.

Ambler, T. (2000) 'Marketing metrics', *Business Strategy Review*, *11* (2), pp. 59–66.

American Marketing Association (2017) 'Definitions of marketing', AMA.Org. www.ama.org/the-definition-of-marketing-what-is-marketing

Ancillai, C. et al. (2019) 'Advancing social media driven sales research: Establishing conceptual foundations for B-to-B social selling', *Industrial Marketing Management*, *82* (December 2018), pp. 293–308.

Ansoff, H.I. (1957) 'Strategies for diversification', *Harvard Business Review*, September, pp. 113–24.

Argyris, Y.A. and Monu, K. (2015) 'Corporate use of social media: Technology affordance and external stakeholder relations', *Journal of Organizational Computing and Electronic Commerce*, *25* (2), pp. 140–68.

Armstrong, A. and Hagel, J.I. (1996) 'The real value of on-line communities', *Harvard Business Review*, *74* (May–June), pp. 134–41.

Arora, S. and Sahney, S. (2017) 'Webrooming behaviour: A conceptual framework', *International Journal of Retail and Distribution Management*, *45* (7–8), pp. 762–81.

ASOS PLC (2019) ASOS Annual Report and Accounts 2019. London. Available at: www.asosplc.com/~/media/Files/A/Asos-V2/reports-and-presentations/annual-strategic-report-2019-24102019.pdf.

Aw, E.C.X. and Labrecque, L.I. (2020). Celebrity endorsement in social media contexts: Understanding the role of parasocial interactions and the need to belong.

Journal of Consumer Marketing, *37* (7), 895–908. https://doi.org/10.1108/JCM-10-2019-3474

Aydin Gökgöz, Z., Ataman, M.B. and van Bruggen, G.H. (2021) 'There's an app for that! Understanding the drivers of mobile application downloads', *Journal of Business Research*, *123* (December 2019), pp. 423–37. doi: 10.1016/j.jbusres.2020.10.006.

Azuma, R.T. (1997) 'A survey of augmented reality', *Presence: Teleoperators and Virtual Environments*, *6* (4), pp. 355–85.

Bacev-Giles, C. and Haji, R. (2017) 'Online first impressions: Person perception in social media profiles', *Computers in Human Behavior*, *75*, pp. 50–7.

Balakrishnan, J. and Griffiths, M.D. (2018) 'An exploratory study of "selfitis" and the development of the selfitis behavior scale', *International Journal of Mental Health and Addiction*, *16* (3), pp. 722–36.

Bardhi, F. and Eckhardt, G.M. (2017) 'Liquid consumption', *Journal of Consumer Research*, *44* (September), pp. 582–97.

Bardhi, F., Eckhardt, G.M. and Arnould, E.J. (2012) 'Liquid relationship to possessions', *Journal of Consumer Research*, *39* (3), pp. 510–29.

Bareket-Bojmel, L., Moran, S. and Shahar, G. (2016) 'Strategic self-presentation on Facebook: Personal motives and audience response to online behavior', *Journal of Computers in Human Behavior*, *55*, pp. 788–95.

Barkemeyer, R. et al. (2020) 'Media attention to large-scale corporate scandals: Hype and boredom in the age of social media', *Journal of Business Research*, *109*, pp. 385–98.

Barth, S. and de Jong, M.D.T. (2017) 'The privacy paradox – investigating discrepancies between expressed privacy concerns and actual online behavior: A systematic literature review', *Telematics and Informatics*, *34* (7), pp. 1038–58.

Batra, R. and Keller, K.L. (2016) 'Integrating marketing communications: New findings, new lessons and new ideas', *Journal of Marketing*, *80* (November), pp. 122–45.

Bayighomog Likoum, S.W. et al. (2020) 'Market-sensing capability, innovativeness, brand management systems, market dynamism, competitive intensity, and performance: An integrative review', *Journal of the Knowledge Economy*, *11* (2), pp. 593–613.

BBC (2020) Virtual reality production: Where do I start? Academy Guides, BBC.com. Available at: www.bbc.com/academy-guides/virtual-reality-production-where-do-i-start (accessed 22 May 2021).

Bec, A. et al. (2021) 'Virtual reality and mixed reality for second chance tourism', *Tourism Management*, *83* (May 2019), article no. 104256.

Belk, R.W. (2014) 'You are what you can access: Sharing and collaborative consumption online', *Journal of Business Research*, *67* (8), pp. 1595–600.

Benlian, A. (2015) 'Web personalization cues and their differential effects on user assessments of website value', *Journal of Management Information Systems*, *32* (1), pp. 225–60.

Bennett, D.H.S., Anaza, N.A. and Andonova, Y. (2021) 'Big names and small price tags: An analysis of celebrity endorsement on consumers' perceptions of price, quality, and intent to purchase', *Journal of Marketing Theory and Practice*, pp. 1–17. https://doi.org/10.1080/10696679.2021.1896952

Bettencourt, L.A., Lusch, R.F. and Vargo, S.L. (2014) 'A service lens on value creation', *California Management Review*, *57* (1), 44–67.

Bickle, J.T., Hirudayaraj, M. and Doyle, A. (2019) 'Social presence theory: Relevance for HRD/VHRD research and practice', *Advances in Developing Human Resources*, *21* (3), pp. 383–99.

Bilos, A., Turkalj, D. and Kelic, D. (2016) 'Open-rate controlled experiment in e-mail marketing campaigns', *Market-Trziste*, *28* (1), pp. 93–109.

Booms, B.H. and Bitner, M.J. (1980) 'New management tools for the successful tourism manager', *Annals of Tourism Research*, *7* (3), pp. 337–52.

Borowski-Beszta, M. and Polasik, M. (2020) 'Wearable devices: New quality in sports and finance', *Journal of Physical Education and Sport*, *20* (2), pp. 1077–84.

Botsman, R. (2015) 'Defining the sharing economy: What is collaborative consumption – and what isn't?', Fast Company. Available at: www.fastcompany.com/3046119/defining-the-sharing-economy-what-is-collaborative-consumption-and-what-isnt (accessed 24 June 2017).

Botsman, R. and Rogers, R. (2010) *What's Mine Is Yours*. London: Collins.

Bourdieu, P. (1986) 'The forms of capital', in J. Richardson (ed.), *Handbook of Theory and Research for the Sociology of Education*. Westport, CT: Greenwood. pp. 241–58.

boyd, d.m. and Ellison, N.B. (2007) 'Social network sites: Definition, history, and scholarship', *Journal of Computer-Mediated Communication*, *13* (1), pp. 210–30.

Breitsohl, J. and Dineva, D. (2022) 'Managing incivility in online brand communities', in J. Burgess, A. Marwick and T. Poell (eds), *The SAGE Handbook of Social Media*, 2nd edn. London: Sage.

Brennen, J.S. and Kreiss, D. (2016) 'Digitalization', *The International Encyclopedia of Communication Theory and Philosophy*. Edited by K.B. Jensen and R.T. Craig. Hoboken, NJ: Wiley.

Brinker, S. (2020a) 'Marketing Technology Landscape Supergraphic (2020): Martech 5000—really 8,000, but who's counting?', Chiefmartech.com. Available at: https://chiefmartec.com/2020/04/marketing-technology-landscape-2020-martech-5000 (accessed 30 May 2021).

Brinker, S. (2020b) 'The STACKIE Awards 2020, The MARTECH conference'. Available at: https://cdn.chiefmartec.com/wp-content/uploads/2020/10/martech-stackies-2020.pdf.

Brinker, S. (2021) 'Summer of stacks: Opening the 2021 MarTech Stackie Awards', Chiefmartech.com. Available at: https://chiefmartec.com/2021/05/summer-stacks-opening-2021-martech-stackie-awards (accessed 30 May 2021).

Brodie, R.J., Hollebeek, L.D., Biljana, J. … Ilic, A. (2011) 'Customer engagement: Conceptual domain, fundamental propositions, and implications for research', *Journal of Service Research*, *14* (3), pp. 252–71.

Brownlie, J. (2018) 'Looking out for each other online: Digital outreach, emotional surveillance and safe(r) spaces', *Emotion, Space and Society*, *27* (March), pp. 60–7.

Brownlie, J. and Shaw, F. (2019) 'Empathy rituals: Small conversations about emotional distress on Twitter', *Sociology*, *53* (1), pp. 104–22.

Bruns, A. (2006) 'Towards produsage: Futures for user-led content production', in *Proceedings: Cultural Attitudes towards Communication and Technology 2006*. Tartu, Estonia. pp. 275–84. Available at: http://eprints.qut.edu.au (accessed 4 July 2018).

Bruns, A. and Stieglitz, S. (2013) 'Towards more systematic Twitter analysis: Metrics for tweeting activities', *International Journal of Social Research Methodology*, *16* (2), pp. 91–108.

Buhalis, D. and Volchek, K. (2021) 'Bridging marketing theory and big data analytics: The taxonomy of marketing attribution', *International Journal of Information Management*, *56* (September 2020), article no. 102253.

Buhalis, D., Andreu, L. and Gnoth, J. (2020) 'The dark side of the sharing economy: Balancing value co-creation and value co-destruction', *Psychology and Marketing*, 37 (5), pp. 689–704.

Burberry (2020) *Annual Report 2019/2020*. Available at: www.burberryplc.com/en/investors/results-reports.html.

Burt, G., Wright, G., Bradfield, R., Cairns, G. and van der Heijden, K. (2006) 'The role of scenario planning in exploring the environment in view of the limitations of PEST and its derivatives', *International Studies of Management and Organization*, *36* (3), pp. 50–76.

Button, K. (2020) 'The "Ubernomics" of ridesourcing: The myths and the reality', *Transport Reviews*, *40* (1), pp. 76–94. https://doi.org/10.1080/01441647.2019.1687605

Cai, C.W. (2020) 'Nudging the financial market? A review of the nudge theory', *Accounting and Finance*, *60* (4), pp. 3341–65.

Cambra-Fierro, J., Polo-Redondo, Y. and Trifu, A. (2021) 'Short-term and long-term effects of touchpoints on customer perceptions', *Journal of Retailing and Consumer Services*, *61* (December 2020), article no. 102520. https://doi.org/10.1016/j.jretconser.2021.102520

Cao, E. and Li, H. (2020) 'Group buying and consumer referral on a social network', *Electronic Commerce Research*, *20* (1), pp. 21–52. doi: 10.1007/s10660-019-09357-4.

Cato, S., Iida, T., Ishida, K., Ito, A., Katsumata, H., McElwain, K.M. and Shoji, M. (2021) 'The bright and dark sides of social media usage during the COVID-19 pandemic: Survey evidence from Japan', *International Journal of Disaster Risk Reduction*, *54* (October 2020), p. 102034. https://doi.org/10.1016/j.ijdrr.2020.102034

Chaffey, D. and Smith, P.R. (2008) *Emarketing Excellence*, 3rd edn. Oxford: Butterworth Heinemann.

Chartered Institute of Marketing (2015) 'Definition of marketing', CIM.co.uk. www.cim.co.uk/files/7ps.pdf

Chen, T.Y., Yeh, T.L. and Chang, C.I. (2020) 'How different advertising formats and calls to action on videos affect advertising recognition and consequent behaviours', *Service Industries Journal*, *40* (5), pp. 358–79. https://doi.org/10.1080/02642069.2018.1480724

Chitturi, R., Raghunathan, R. and Mahajan, V. (2008) 'Delight by design: The role of hedonic versus utilitarian benefits', *Journal of Marketing*, *72* (May), pp. 48–63.

Chopdar, P.K. and Balakrishnan, J. (2020) 'Consumers' response towards mobile commerce applications: S-O-R approach', *International Journal of Information Management*, *53* (March), article no. 102106.

Chou, Y.C. and Shao, B.B.M. (2020) 'Adoption and performance of mobile sales channel for e-retailers: Fit with m-retail characteristics and dependency on e-retailing', *Information Systems Frontiers*, pp. 1–14.

Christensen, C.M., Raynor, M. and McDonald, R. (2015) 'What is disruption?', *Harvard Business Review*, *93* (12), pp. 44–56.

Chyi, H.I. and Ng, Y.M.M. (2020) 'Still unwilling to pay: An empirical analysis of 50 U.S. newspapers' Digital Subscription Results', *Digital Journalism*, *8* (4), pp. 526–47.

Clark, B. (2020) 'Marketing dashboards, resource allocation and performance', *European Journal of Marketing*, *55* (1), pp. 247–70.

Coles, B.A. and West, M. (2016) 'Weaving the internet together: Imagined communities in newspaper comment threads', *Computers in Human Behavior*, *60*, pp. 44–53.

Colicev, A., O'Connor, P. and Vinzi, V.E. (2016) 'Is investing in social media really worth it? How brand actions and user actions influence brand value', *Service Science*, *8* (2), pp. 152–68.

Committee of Advertising Practice (2020) 'Influencers' guide to making clear that ads are ads'. Available at: www.asa.org.uk/resource/influencers-guide.html.

Content Marketing Institute (2017) The 2017 Content Marketing Framework. Available at: http://contentmarketinginstitute.com/2016/10/content-marketing-framework-profitable.

Corcoran, S. (2009) 'Defining earned, owned and paid media', Forrester Blogs. Available at: http://blogs.forrester.com/interactive_marketing/2009/12/defining-earned-owned-and-paid-media.html (accessed 8 October 2015).

Court, D., Elzinga, D., Mulder, S. and Vetvik, O.J.J. (2009) 'The consumer decision journey'. www.mckinsey.com. Available at: www.mckinsey.com/business-functions/marketing-and-sales/our-insights/the-consumer-decision-journey.

Cox, M. and Ellsworth, D. (1997) 'Application-controlled demand paging for out-of-core visualization'. Proceedings. Visualization '97 (Cat. No. 97CB36155) (July), pp. 235–44. Available at: http://ieeexplore.ieee.org/lpdocs/epic03/wrapper.htm?arnumber=663888.

Cranmer, E.E., tom Dieck, M.C. and Fountoulaki, P. (2020) 'Exploring the value of augmented reality for tourism', *Tourism Management Perspectives*, *35* (January 2019), article no. 100672.

Crowston, K. and Fagnot, I. (2018) 'Stages of motivation for contributing user-generated content: A theory and empirical test', *International Journal of Human Computer Studies*, *109*, pp. 89–101.

Cunningham, S. and Craig, D. (2016) 'Online entertainment: A new wave of media globalization?', *International Journal of Communication*, *10*, pp. 5409–25.

Curcio, I.D.D., Dipace, A. and Norlund, A. (2016) 'Virtual realities and education', *Research on Education and Media*, *8* (2), pp. 60–68.

Dacko, S.G. (2016) 'Enabling smart retail settings via mobile augmented reality shopping apps', *Technological Forecasting and Social Change*, *124*, pp. 243–56.

Daft, R.L. and Lengel, R.H. (1986) 'Organizational information requirements, media richness, and structural design', *Management Science*, *32* (5), pp. 554–71.

Davcik, N.S. and Sharma, P. (2016) 'Marketing resources, performance, and competitive advantage: A review and future research directions', *Journal of Business Research*, *69* (12), pp. 5547–52.

Davis, F.D. (1989) 'Perceived usefulness, perceived ease of use, and user acceptance of information technology', *MIS Quarterly*, *13* (3), pp. 319–40.

REFERENCES

Davis, F.D., Bagozzi, R.P. and Warshaw, P.R. (1989) 'User acceptance of computer technology: A comparison of two theoretical models', *Management Science, 35* (8), pp. 982–1003.

Dawkins, R. (2006) *The Selfish Gene*, 30th anniversary edn. Oxford: Oxford University Press.

Day, G.S. (1994) 'The capabilities of market-driven organizations', *Journal of Marketing, 58* (4), pp. 37–52. doi: 10.2307/1251915

De Cremer, D., Nguyen, B. and Simkin, L. (2017) 'The integrity challenge of the Internet-of-Things (IoT): On understanding its dark side', *Journal of Marketing Management, 33* (1–2), pp. 145–58.

Dineva, D.P., Breitsohl, J.C. and Garrod, B. (2017) 'Corporate conflict management on social media brand fan pages', *Journal of Marketing Management, 33* (9–10), pp. 679–98.

DiNucci, D. (1999) 'Design and new media: Fragmented future – web development faces a process of mitosis, mutation, and natural selection', *Print, 53* (4), pp. 32–5.

Ditchfield, H. (2020) 'Behind the screen of Facebook: Identity construction in the rehearsal stage of online interaction', *New Media and Society, 22* (6), pp. 927–43.

Duane, A. and O'Reilly, P. (2016) 'A stage model of social media adoption', *Journal of Advances in Management Sciences & Information Systems, 2*, pp. 77–93.

Dwivedi, Y.K., Ismagilova, E., Hughes, D.L., … Wang, Y. (2020) 'Setting the future of digital and social media marketing research: Perspectives and research propositions', *International Journal of Information Management*, May, article no. 102168.

EAB (2021) *About Us, EAB.com*. Available at: https://eab.com/about (accessed 23 May 2021).

Eagle, L. et al. (eds) (2020) *The SAGE Handbook of Marketing Ethics*. London: Sage.

Eckhardt, G.M., Houston, M.B., Jiang, B., et al. (2019) 'Marketing in the sharing economy', *Journal of Marketing, 83* (5), pp. 5–27.

Econsultancy (2009) 'Acquire, convert, retain', Econsultancy.com. Available at: https://econsultancy.com/events/masterclasses.

Enke, N. and Borchers, N.S. (2019) 'Social media influencers in strategic communication: A conceptual framework for strategic social media influencer communication', *International Journal of Strategic Communication, 13* (4), pp. 261–77.

Ethical Influencers (2020) 'How to calculate your engagement rate', Ethicalinfluencers. co.uk. Available at: https://ethicalinfluencers.co.uk/how-to-calculate-social-media-engagement-rate (accessed 14 September 2020).

European Advertising Standards Alliance (2018) 'Best practice recommendation on influencer marketing'. Brussels. Available at: www.easa-alliance.org/sites/default/files/EASA BEST PRACTICE RECOMMENDATION ON INFLUENCER MARKETING_2020_0. pdf.

European Commission (2020) 'The digital skills and jobs coalition', ec.europa.eu. Available at: https://ec.europa.eu/digital-single-market/en/digital-skills-and-jobs-coalition (accessed 25 February 2021).

Fan, T., Gao, L. and Steinhart, Y. (2020) 'The small predicts large effect in crowdfunding', *Journal of Consumer Research, 47* (4), pp. 544–65. doi: 10.1093/jcr/ucaa013.

Farah, M.F. and Ramadan, Z.B. (2020) 'Viability of Amazon's driven innovations targeting shoppers' impulsiveness', *Journal of Retailing and Consumer Services, 53* (September 2019), article no. 101973. doi: 10.1016/j.jretconser.2019.101973.

Farris, P., Bendle, N., Pfeifer, P. and Reibstein, D. (2009) *Key Marketing Metrics.* Harlow: Pearson Education.

Fast Company. Available at: www.fastcompany.com/3046119/defining-the-sharing-economy-what-is-collaborative-consumption-and-what-isnt.

Feher, K. (2021) 'Digital identity and the online self: Footprint strategies – An exploratory and comparative research study', *Journal of Information Science, 47* (2), pp. 192–205. https://doi.org/10.1177/0165551519879702

Fernández-Rovira, C., Álvarez Valdés, J., Molleví, G. and Nicolas-Sans, R. (2021) 'The digital transformation of business: Towards the datafication of the relationship with customers', *Technological Forecasting and Social Change, 162* (September 2020), article no. 120339.

Festinger, L. and Carlsmith, J.M. (1959) 'Cognitive consequences of forced compliance', *Journal of Abnormal Psychology, 58* (2), pp. 203–10.

Fischer, M., Imgrund, F., Janiesch, C. and Winkelmann, A. (2020) 'Strategy archetypes for digital transformation: Defining meta objectives using business process management', *Information & Management, 57* (5), article no. 103262.

Fook, L.A. and McNeill, L. (2020) 'Click to buy: The impact of retail credit on over-consumption in the online environment', *Sustainability, 12* (18), pp. 1–15. doi: 10.3390/SU12187322.

Fotopoulou, A. and Couldry, N. (2015) 'Telling the story of the stories: Online content curation and digital engagement', *Information Communication and Society, 18* (2), pp. 235–49.

Fournier, S. and Avery, J. (2011) 'The uninvited brand', *Business Horizons, 54* (3), pp. 193–207.

Freeman, R.E. (1984) *Strategic Management: A Stakeholder Approach.* Boston: Pitman.

Ganley, D. and Lampe, C. (2009) 'The ties that bind: Social network principles in online communities', *Decision Support Systems, 47* (3), pp. 266–74.

Garg, S., Goldwasser, S. and Vasudevan, P.N. (2020) 'Formalizing data deletion in the context of the right to be forgotten', ArXiv.Org, 2002.10635, 1–36.

Garratt, R.J. and Lee, M.J. (2021) Monetizing Privacy. Federal Reserve Bank of New York Staff Reports. New York. doi: 10.2139/ssrn.3767028.

Gatti, L., Pizzetti, M. and Seele, P. (2021) 'Green lies and their effect on intention to invest', *Journal of Business Research, 127* (February), pp. 228–40. doi: 10.1016/j.jbusres.2021.01.028.

Gavilan, D. (2022) 'The role of push notifications', in A. Hanlon and T. Tuten (eds), *The SAGE Handbook of Digital Marketing.* London: Sage.

Gay, R., Charlesworth, A. and Esen, R. (2007) *Online Marketing: A Customer-Led Approach.* Oxford: Oxford University Press.

Geçer, A.K. and Topal, A.D. (2021) 'Academic and postgraduate student awareness of digital product copyright issues', *Information Development, 37* (1), pp. 90–104.

Gekara, V. et al. (2019) 'Skilling the Australian workforce for the digital economy'. Available at: www.ncver.edu.au/news-and-events/media-releases/employers-need-to-do-more-to-prepare-for-the-digital-future.

Gensler, S., Neslin, S.A. and Verhoef, P.C. (2017) 'The showrooming phenomenon: It's more than just about price', *Journal of Interactive Marketing*, 38, pp. 29–43. doi: 10.1016/j.intmar.2017.01.003.

Gensler, S., Völckner, F., Liu-Thompkins, Y. and Wiertz, C. (2013) 'Managing brands in the social media environment', *Journal of Interactive Marketing*, 27 (4), pp. 242–56.

Gentile, C., Spiller, N. and Noci, G. (2007) 'How to sustain the customer experience: An overview of experience components that co-create value with the customer', *European Management Journal*, 25 (5), pp. 395–410.

George, J.J. and Leidner, D.E. (2019) 'From clicktivism to hacktivism: Understanding digital activism', *Information and Organization*, 29 (3), article no. 100249. https://doi.org/10.1016/j.infoandorg.2019.04.001

Gilmore, J.N. (2020) 'Securing the kids: Geofencing and child wearables', *Convergence*, 26 (5–6), pp. 1333–46. https://doi.org/10.1177/1354856519882317

Goffman, E. (1956) *The Presentation of Self in Everyday Life*. Monograph. Edinburgh: University of Edinburgh Social Sciences Research Centre.

Google (2017) 'Custom campaigns', support.google.com. Available at: https://support.google.com/analytics/answer/1033863#parameters.

Google (2020) 'How Google Search works', Google.com. Available at: www.google.com/intl/en_uk/search/howsearchworks/algorithms (accessed 17 September 2020).

Google Developers (2021) 'Mobile-first indexing best practices', Google Search Central. Available at: https://developers.google.com/search/mobile-sites/mobile-first-indexing (accessed 20 May 2021).

Granger, C.H. (1964) 'The hierarchy of objectives', *Harvard Business Review*, 42 (May–June), pp. 63–74.

Granovetter, M.S. (1973) 'The strength of weak ties', *American Journal of Sociology*, 78 (6), pp. 1360–80.

Gray, D. (2010) 'Impact Effort Matrix'. Available at: http://gamestorming.com/impact-effort-matrix-2.

Greenhouse (2020) 'Job Application for Trust & Safety Support Manager at Strava'. https://boards.greenhouse.io/strava/jobs/1523079

Gregoire, Y., Salle, A. and Tripp, T.M. (2015) 'Managing social media crises with your customers: The good, the bad, and the ugly', *Business Horizons*, 58 (2), pp. 173–82.

Grewal, D., Bart, Y., Spann, M. and Zubcsek, P.P. (2016) 'Mobile advertising: A framework and research agenda', *Journal of Interactive Marketing*, 34, pp. 3–14. Available at: http://dx.doi.org/10.1016/j.intmar.

Grigaliunaite, V. and Pileliene, L. (2016) 'Emotional or rational? The determination of the influence of advertising appeal on advertising effectiveness', *Scientific Annals of Economics and Business*, 63 (3), pp. 391–414.

Grover, V. and Kohli, R. (2013) 'Revealing your hand: Caveats in implementing digital business strategy', *MIS Quarterly*, 37 (2), pp. 655–63.

Guadagno, R.E., Okdie, B.M. and Kruse, S.A. (2012) 'Dating deception: Gender, online dating, and exaggerated self-presentation', *Computers in Human Behavior*, 28 (2), pp. 642–7.

Gunawardena, C.N. (1995) 'Social presence theory and implications of interaction and collaborative learning in computer conferences', *International Journal of Educational Telecommunications*, 1 (2–3), pp. 147–66.

Gupta, V. (2017) 'A brief history of Blockchain', *Harvard Business Review*, February, pp. 2–5.

Hackley, C. and Hackley, R.A. (2017) *Advertising and Promotion*, 4th edn. London: Sage.

Hale, J.P. (1995) *Applied Virtual Reality Research and Applications*. Washington, DC: National Aeronautics and Space Administration.

Hallem, Y., Ben Arfi, W. and Teulon, F. (2020) 'Exploring consumer attitudes to online collaborative consumption: A typology of collaborative consumer profiles', *Canadian Journal of Administrative Sciences*, 37 (1), pp. 82–94. doi: 10.1002/cjas.1554.

Halpern, N., Mwesiumo, D., Suau-Sanchez, P., Budd, T. and Bråthen, S. (2021) 'Ready for digital transformation? The effect of organisational readiness, innovation, airport size and ownership on digital change at airports', *Journal of Air Transport Management*, 90 (September 2020), article no. 101949. https://doi.org/10.1016/j.jairtraman.2020.101949

Han, S. and Anderson, C.K. (2020) 'Customer motivation and response bias in online reviews', *Cornell Hospitality Quarterly*, 61 (2), pp. 142–53. doi: 10.1177/1938965520902012.

Hanlon, A. (2020) 'Ethics in digital marketing and social media', in L. Eagle et al. (eds) *The SAGE Handbook of Marketing Ethics*. London: Sage.

Hanlon, A. (2022) *The Digital Marketing Planner: A Step-by-Step Guide*. London: Sage.

Hanna, R.C., Lemon, K.N. and Smith, G.E. (2019) 'Is transparency a good thing? How online price transparency and variability can benefit firms and influence consumer decision making', *Business Horizons*, 62 (2), pp. 227–36.

Haobin Ye, B., Fong, L.H.N. and Luo, J.M. (2021) 'Parasocial interaction on tourism companies' social media sites: Antecedents and consequences', *Current Issues in Tourism*, 24 (8), pp. 1093–108. https://doi.org/10.1080/13683500.2020.1764915

Harrigan, P., Soutar, G., Choudhury, M.M. and Lowe, M. (2015) 'Modelling CRM in a social media age', *Australasian Marketing Journal*, 23 (1), pp. 27–37.

Harun, A. et al. (2020) 'Understanding experienced consumers towards repeat purchase of counterfeit products: The mediating effect of attitude', *Management Science Letters*, 10 (1), pp. 13–28.

Hassenzahl, M. and Tractinsky, N. (2006) 'User experience: A research agenda', *Behaviour and Information Technology*, 25 (2), pp. 91–7. doi: 10.1080/01449290500330331.

He, Q. et al. (2020) 'Strategic alliance research in the era of digital transformation: Perspectives on future research', *British Journal of Management*, 31 (3), pp. 589–617.

Heeter, C. (1989) 'Implications of new interactive technologies for conceptualizing communication', *Media Use in the Information Age*, August, pp. 217–35.

Heidemann, J., Klier, M. and Probst, F. (2012) 'Online social networks: A survey of a global phenomenon', *Computer Networks, 56* (18), pp. 3866–78.

Hendriks, M. and Peelen, E. (2013) 'Personas in action: Linking event participation motivation to charitable giving and sports', *International Journal of Nonprofit and Voluntary Sector Marketing, 18* (1), pp. 60–72.

Hennig-Thurau, T., Gwinner, K.P., Walsh, G. and Gremier, D.D. (2004) 'Electronic word-of-mouth via consumer-opinion platforms: What motivates consumers to articulate themselves on the Internet?', *Journal of Interactive Marketing, 18* (1), pp. 38–52.

Herhausen, D. et al. (2019) 'Detecting, preventing, and mitigating online firestorms in brand communities', *Journal of Marketing, 83* (3), pp. 1–21. doi: 10.1177/0022242918822300.

Herring, S., Job-Sluder, K., Scheckler, R. and Barab, S. (2002) 'Searching for safety online: Managing "trolling" in a feminist forum', *The Information Society, 18*, pp. 371–84.

Hirschman, E.C. and Holbrook, M.B. (1982) 'Hedonic consumption: Emerging concepts, methods and propositions', *Journal of Marketing, 46* (3), pp. 92–101.

Hofacker, C.F. (2001) *Internet Marketing*, 3rd edn. New York: John Wiley & Sons.

Hoffman, D.L. and Novak, T.P. (1996) 'Marketing in hypermedia computer-mediated environments: Conceptual foundations', *Journal of Marketing, 60* (July), pp. 50–68.

Horky, T., Grimmer, C.G. and Theobalt, C. (2020) 'Social personalities in sports: An analysis of the differences in individuals' self-presentation on social networks', *Media, Culture and Society, 43* (1), pp. 3–22. doi: 10.1177/0163443720960922.

Hossain, S.F.A. et al. (2020) 'Ubiquitous role of social networking in driving m-commerce: Evaluating the use of mobile phones for online shopping and payment in the context of trust', *SAGE Open, 10* (3).

Hovland, C.I. and Weiss, W. (1951) 'The influence of source credibility on communication effectiveness', *Public Opinion Quarterly, 15* (4), pp. 635–50.

Huaman-Ramirez, R., Albert, N. and Merunka, D. (2019) 'Are global brands trustworthy? The role of brand affect, brand innovativeness, and consumer ethnocentrism', *European Business Review, 31* (6), pp. 926–46. doi: 10.1108/EBR-11-2017-0202

Huang, K. and Wang, K.Y. (2020) 'Brand evaluation, animosity, ethnocentrism and purchase intention: A country of origin perspective', *International Journal of Organizational Innovation, 12* (4), pp. 80–9.

IBM (2020) 'What is machine learning?', IBM.com. www.ibm.com/cloud/learn/machine-learning

Inegbedion, H.E. (2021) 'Digital divide in the major regions of the world and the possibility of convergence', *Bottom Line, 34* (1), pp. 68–85.

Inter IKEA Systems B.V. (2021) 'IKEA makes a new dress for KLIPPAN sofa with MUD Jeans by using recycled jeans', about.ikea.com. Available at: https://about.ikea.com/en/newsroom/2021/04/21/ikea-makes-a-new-dress-for-klippan-sofa-with-mud-jeans-by-using-recycled-jeans (accessed 26 April 2021).

InternetLiveStats.com (2020) 'Total number of websites: Internet live stats', Internetlivestats.com/total-number-of-websites. Available at: www.internetlivestats.com/total-number-of-websites (accessed 10 August 2020).

Ismagilova, E., Slade, E., Rana, N.P. and Dwivedi, Y.K. (2020) 'The effect of characteristics of source credibility on consumer behaviour: A meta-analysis', *Journal of Retailing and Consumer Services*, *53* (January 2019), article no. 101736.

Ivanova, A. et al. (2020) 'Mobile phone addiction, phubbing, and depression among men and women: A moderated mediation analysis', *Psychiatric Quarterly*, *91* (3), pp. 655–68.

Jackson, S. (2009) *Cult of Analytics*. New York: Routledge.

Jacobs, J.V. et al. (2019) 'Employee acceptance of wearable technology in the workplace', *Applied Ergonomics*, *78* (March), pp. 148–56.

Jacobson, D. (2009) 'COPE: Create Once, Publish Everywhere', ProgrammableWeb. Available at: www.programmableweb.com/news/cope-create-once-publish-everywhere/2009/10/13.

Jenkins, H. (2008) *Convergence Culture: Where Old and New Media Collide*. New York: New York University Press.

Jhandir, M.Z., Tenvir, A., On, B.W., Lee, I. and Choi, G.S. (2017) 'Controversy detection in Wikipedia using semantic dissimilarity', *Information Sciences*, *418–419*, pp. 581–600. https://doi.org/10.1016/j.ins.2017.08.037

Jiang, Y. and Balaji, M.S. (2021) 'Getting unwired: What drives travellers to take a digital detox holiday?', *Tourism Recreation Research*, pp. 1–17. DOI: 10.1080/02508281.2021.1889801

Johnson, C.N. (2002) 'The benefits of PDCA', *Quality Progress*, *35* (5), p. 120.

Johnson, D., Rodwell, J. and Hendry, T. (2021) 'Analyzing the impacts of financial services regulation to make the case that buy-now-pay-later regulation is failing', *Sustainability*, *13* (1992), pp. 1–20.

Johnson, G., Scholes, K. and Whittington, R. (2008) *Exploring Corporate Strategy*, 8th edn. Harlow: Pearson Education.

Just Eat (2021) 'Join the UK's leading food delivery provider'. Available at: https://restaurants.just-eat.co.uk (accessed 15 February 2021).

Kalaignanam, K. et al. (2021) 'Marketing agility: The concept, antecedents, and a research Agenda', *Journal of Marketing*, *85* (1), pp. 35–58.

Kaplan, A.M. and Haenlein, M. (2010) 'Users of the world, unite! The challenges and opportunities of social media', *Business Horizons*, *53* (1), pp. 59–68.

Kaplan, D. (2021) 'Public intimacy in social media: The mass audience as a third party', *Media, Culture and Society*, *43* (4), pp. 595–612. doi: 10.1177/0163443721991087

Katz, E., Blumler, J.G. and Gurevitch, M. (1973) 'Uses and gratification research', *Public Opinion Quarterly*, *37* (4), pp. 509–23.

Keeker, K. (1997) 'Improving web site usability and appeal, MSN usability & marketing'. Available at: https://docs.microsoft.com/en-us/previous-versions/office/office-12/cc889361(v=office.12)?redirectedfrom=MSDN.

Kering (2020) Kering Universal Registration Document. https://keringcorporate.dam.kering.com/m/726533d8fa257732/original/Kering_2020_Universal_Registration_Document.pdf

Keya, F.D. et al. (2020) 'Parenting and child's (five years to eighteen years) digital game addiction: A qualitative study in North-Western part of Bangladesh', *Computers in Human Behavior Reports*, *2* (May), article no. 100031.

Kietzmann, J.H., Hermkens, K., McCarthy, I.P. and Silvestre, B.S. (2011) 'Social media? Get serious! Understanding the functional building blocks of social media', *Business Horizons*, *54* (3), pp. 241–51.

Kim, H. and Hanssens, D.M. (2017) 'Advertising and word-of-mouth effects on pre-launch consumer interest and initial sales of experience products', *Journal of Interactive Marketing*, *37*, pp. 57–74.

Kim, J.J., Wang, Y., Wang, H., Lee, S., Yokota, T. and Someya, T. (2021) 'Skin electronics: Next-generation device platform for virtual and augmented reality', *Advanced Functional Materials*, article no. 2009602, pp. 1–34. https://doi.org/10.1002/adfm.202009602

Kim, M.J., Lee, C.K. and Jung, T. (2020) 'Exploring consumer behavior in virtual reality tourism using an extended stimulus-organism-response model', *Journal of Travel Research*, *59* (1), pp. 69–89.

Kotler, P. (1965) 'Competitive strategies for new product marketing over the life cycle', *Management Science*, *12* (4), pp. B-104–B-119.

Kotler, P., Kartajaya, H. and Setiawan, I. (2021) *Marketing 5.0: Technology for Humanity*. Hoboken, NJ: Wiley.

Koukaras, P., Tjortjis, C. and Rousidis, D. (2020) 'Social media types: Introducing a data driven taxonomy', *Computing*, *102* (1), pp. 295–340.

Kozinets, R.V. (2002) 'The field behind the screen: Using netnography for marketing research in online communities', *Journal of Marketing Research*, *39* (1), pp. 61–72.

Kozlenkova, I.V., Samaha, S.A. and Palmatier, R.W. (2013) 'Resource-based theory in marketing', *Journal of the Academy of Marketing Science*, *42* (1), pp. 1–21.

Kreiner, H. and Levi-Belz, Y. (2019) 'Self-disclosure here and now: Combining retrospective perceived assessment with dynamic behavioral measures', *Frontiers in Psychology*, *10* (Mar), pp. 1–12.

Kumar, V. and Reinartz, W. (2016) 'Creating enduring customer value', *Journal of Marketing*, *80* (6), pp. 36–68.

Kumar, V., Choi, J.W.B. and Greene, M. (2016) 'Synergistic effects of social media and traditional marketing on brand sales: Capturing the time-varying effects', *Journal of the Academy of Marketing Science*, *45* (2), pp. 1–21.

Ky, S.S., Rugemintwari, C. and Sauviat, A. (2021) 'Friends or foes? Mobile money interaction with formal and informal finance', *Telecommunications Policy*, *45* (1), pp. 1–31. doi: 10.1016/j.telpol.2020.102057.

Lai, J. and Widmar, N.O. (2021) 'Revisiting the digital divide in the COVID-19 era', *Applied Economic Perspectives and Policy*, *43* (1), pp. 458–64.

Laney, D. (2001) 'META Delta', *Application Delivery Strategies*, *949* (February), p. 4.

Langenscheidt (2015) *Das Jugendwort steht fest: "Smombie" macht das Rennen*. www.langenscheidt.de/Pressemeldungen/Das-Jugendwort-steht-fest-Smombie-macht-das-Rennen

Latané, B. (1981) 'The psychology of social impact', *American Psychologist, 36* (4), pp. 343–56. https://doi.org/10.1037/0003-066X.36.4.343

LaTour, K.A. and Brant, A. (2021) 'Social listening to create bespoke customer experiences: Best practices for hospitality operators', *Cornell Hospitality Quarterly*. doi: 10.1177/1938965521993087.

Lave, J. (1991) 'Situating learning in communities of practice', in L.B. Resnick, J.M. Levine and S.D. Teasley (eds), *Perspectives on Socially Shared Cognition*. Washington, DC: American Psychological Association. pp. 63–82. Available at: http://psycnet.apa.org/record/1991-98452-003.

Law, E.L.C. and Van Schaik, P. (2010) 'Modelling user experience – An agenda for research and practice', *Interacting with Computers, 22* (5), pp. 313–22.

Lazarsfeld, P.F., Berelson, B. and Gaudet, H. (1944) *The People's Choice*. New York: Duell Sloan and Pearce.

Le, T.D. (2018) 'Influence of WOM and content type on online engagement in consumption communities: The information flow from discussion forums to Facebook', *Online Information Review, 42* (2), pp. 161–75.

Lee, Y.C. et al. (2020) '"I hear you, I feel you": Encouraging deep self-disclosure through a chatbot', in Conference on Human Factors in Computing Systems – Proceedings, pp. 1–12. doi: 10.1145/3313831.3376175.

Lemon, K.N. and Verhoef, P.C. (2016) 'Understanding customer experience throughout the customer journey', *Journal of Marketing, 80* (6), pp. 69–96.

Leung, C.H. (2017) 'Assessing mobile phone dependency and teens' everyday life in Hong Kong', *Australian Journal of Psychology, 69* (1), pp. 29–38.

Li, H.A. and Kannan, P.K. (2013) 'Attributing conversions in a multichannel online marketing environment: An empirical model and a field experiment', *Journal of Marketing Research, 51* (1), pp. 40–56.

Lim, B.A. (2021) 'Beauty tech in demand: COVID-19 pushing Benefit Cosmetics to adopt more AR beauty tools', Cosmeticsdesign-asia.com. Available at: www.cosmeticsdesign-asia.com/Article/2020/06/15/Benefit-Cosmetics-to-adopt-more-AR-beauty-tools-in-light-of-COVID-19 (accessed 23 May 2021).

Lin, Y.H. and Chu, M.G. (2021) 'Online communication self-disclosure and intimacy development on Facebook: The perspective of uses and gratifications theory', *Online Information Review*. doi: 10.1108/oir-08-2020-0329.

Liu, Y., Zhou, S. and Zhang, H. (2020) 'Second screening use and its effect on political involvement in China: An integrated Communication Mediation Model', *Computers in Human Behavior, 105*, pp. 1–8.

Lo, W.H. and Cheng, K.L.B. (2020) 'Does virtual reality attract visitors? The mediating effect of presence on consumer response in virtual reality tourism advertising', *Information Technology and Tourism, 22* (4), pp. 537–62. doi: 10.1007/s40558-020-00190-2.

Lobschat, L., Mueller, B., Eggers, F., Brandimarte, L., Diefenbach, S., Kroschke, M. and Wirtz, J. (2021) 'Corporate digital responsibility', *Journal of Business Research*, *122* (July 2018), pp. 875–88.

Lombard, M. and Ditton, T. (1997) 'At the heart of it all: The concept of presence', *Journal of Computer-Mediated Communication*, *3* (2), pp. 1–68.

Loop, B.J.L. and Malyshev, A.G. (2013) 'How to manage a company's social media presence', *Intellectual Property & Technology Law Journal*, *25* (4), pp. 3–8.

Lou, C. and Yuan, S. (2019) 'Influencer marketing: How message value and credibility affect consumer trust of branded content on social media', *Journal of Interactive Advertising*, *19* (1), pp. 58–73.

Madrigal, A.C. (2012) 'Dark social: We have the whole history of the web wrong', *The Atlantic*. Available at: www.theatlantic.com/technology/archive/2012/10/dark-social-we-have-the-whole-history-of-the-web-wrong/263523.

Manshad, M.S. and Brannon, D. (2021) 'Haptic-payment: Exploring vibration feedback as a means of reducing overspending in mobile payment', *Journal of Business Research*, *122* (August 2020), pp. 88–96.

Marketing Week (2016) 'YouTube and Snapchat push "snackable" video ads on mobile', April, p. 7. doi: ISSN: 0141-9285.

Mathwick, C. (2002) 'Understanding the online consumer: A typology of online relational norms and behavior', *Journal of Interactive Marketing*, *16* (1), pp. 40–55.

Mathwick, C., Malhotra, N. and Rigdon, E. (2001) 'Experiential value: Conceptualization, measurement and application in the catalog and Internet shopping environment', *Journal of Retailing*, *77* (1), pp. 39–56.

McCarthy, E.J. (1964) *Basic Marketing: A Managerial Approach*. Homewood, IL: Irwin.

McCorkindale, T. and DiStaso, M. (2014) 'The state of social media research: Where are we now, where we were and what it means for public relations', *Research Journal of the Institute for Public Relations*, *1* (1). Available at: www.instituteforpr.org/wp-content/uploads/TinaMarciaWES.pdf.

McQuail, D. (1983) *Mass Communication Theory: An Introduction*. London: Sage.

Mendelow, A.L. (1981) 'Environmental scanning: The impact of the stakeholder concept', Proceedings of the International Conference on Information Systems, pp. 407–17.

Mental Health America Inc. (2021) 'About Mental Health America'. www.Mhanational.Org/About. www.mhanational.org/about

Meyer, C. and Schwager, A. (2007) 'Understanding customer experience', *Harvard Business Review*, *85* (2), pp. 116–26.

Milgram, P. and Kishino, F. (1994) 'A taxonomy of mixed reality visual displays', *IEICE Transactions on Information and Systems*, *77* (12), pp. 1321–9.

Mills, A.J. and Plangger, K. (2015) 'Social media strategy for online service brands', *The Service Industries Journal*, *35* (10), pp. 521–36.

Minguillón, J., Lerga, M., Aibar, E., Lladós-Masllorens, J. and Meseguer-Artola, A. (2017) 'Semi-automatic generation of a corpus of Wikipedia articles on science and technology', *El Profesional de La Información*, *26* (5), pp. 995–1004. https://doi.org/10.3145/epi.2017.sep.20

Mintzberg, H. (1987) 'The strategy concept I: Five Ps for strategy', *California Management Review, 30* (1), pp. 11–24.

Miquel-Romero, M.-J. and Adame-Sánchez, C. (2013) 'Viral marketing through e-mail: The link company–consumer', *Management Decision, 51* (10), pp. 1970–82.

Mitchell, R.K., Agle, B.R. and Wood, D.J. (1997) 'Toward a theory of stakeholder identification and salience: Defining the principle of who and what really counts', *Academy of Management Review, 22* (4), pp. 853–86. doi: 10.5465/AMR.1997.9711022105.

Mitchell, T. (1997) 'Machine learning'. www.cs.cmu.edu/afs/cs.cmu.edu/user/mitchell/ftp/mlbook.html

Moorman, C. (2020) 'Covid-19 and the state of marketing'. Available at: www2.deloitte.com/content/dam/Deloitte/us/Documents/CMO/us-cmo-survey-highlights-and-insights-report-feb-2020.pdf.

Muñiz, A.M.J. and O'Guinn, T.C. (2001) 'Brand community', *Journal of Advertising Research, 27* (4), pp. 412–32.

Nabity-Grover, T., Cheung, C.M.K. and Thatcher, J.B. (2020) 'Inside out and outside in: How the COVID-19 pandemic affects self-disclosure on social media', *International Journal of Information Management, 55* (June), article no. 102188.

Narwal, P. and Nayak, J.K. (2019) 'How consumers respond to social norms: An evidence from pay-what-you-want (PWYW) pricing', *Journal of Consumer Marketing, 36* (4), pp. 494–505. doi: 10.1108/JCM-05-2018-2677.

Narwal, P., Nayak, J.K. and Rai, S. (2021) 'Assessing customers' moral disengagement from reciprocity concerns in participative pricing', *Journal of Business Ethics*. doi: 10.1007/s10551-021-04782-8.

National Aeronautics and Space Administration (NASA) (2012a) 'Technology Readiness Level'. NASA.gov. Available at: www.nasa.gov/directorates/heo/scan/engineering/technology/txt_accordion1.html.

National Aeronautics and Space Administration (NASA) (2012b) 'Technology Readiness Level definitions', p. 1. Available at: www.nasa.gov/pdf/458490main_TRL_Definitions.pdf.

Naylor, G.S. (2017) 'Complaining, complimenting and word-of-mouth in the digital age: Typology and terms', *Journal of Consumer Satisfaction, Dissatisfaction and Complaining Behavior, 29* (January), pp. 131–43.

Nicholas, G. and Shapiro, A. (2020) 'Failed hybrids: The death and life of Bluetooth proximity marketing', *Mobile Media and Communication*, pp. 1–23.

Nielsen, J. (2012) 'Usability 101: Introduction to usability'. *Nielsen Norman Group website*. doi: 10.1557/mrs.2011.276.

Norton, D.W. and Pine, B.J. (2013) 'Using the customer journey to road test and refine the business model', *Strategy & Leadership, 41* (2), pp. 12–17.

O'Dea, S. (2020) 'Number of mobile devices worldwide 2020–2024', Statista.com. Available at: www.statista.com/statistics/245501/multiple-mobile-device-ownership-worldwide/ (accessed 11 December 2020).

OECD (2001) 'Understanding the digital divide', *OECD Digital Economy Papers, 49* (4). https://doi.org/10.1080/08109020127271

Office of the Attorney General (2021) California Consumer Privacy Act (CCPA). State of California Department of Justice. https://oag.ca.gov/privacy/ccpa

Okello Candiya Bongomin, G. and Ntayi, J.M. (2020) 'Mobile money adoption and usage and financial inclusion: Mediating effect of digital consumer protection', *Digital Policy, Regulation and Governance*, *22* (3), pp. 157–76. doi: 10.1108/DPRG-01-2019-0005.

Olsen, R.K., Kammer, A. and Solvoll, M.K. (2020) 'Paywalls' impact on local news websites' traffic and their civic and business implications', *Journalism Studies*, *21* (2), pp. 197–216. https://doi.org/10.1080/1461670X.2019.1633946

O'Reilly, T. (2005) 'What Is Web 2.0? Design patterns and business models for the next generation of software'. O'Reilly Blog. http://oreilly.com/web2/archive/what-is-web-20.html

Orange (2019) *2019 Integrated Annual Report*. Paris. Available at: www.orange.com/en/integrated-annual-reports.

Orús, C., Gurrea, R. and Ibáñez-Sánchez, S. (2019) 'The impact of consumers' positive online recommendations on the omnichannel webrooming experience', *Spanish Journal of Marketing – ESIC*, *23* (3), pp. 397–414. doi: 10.1108/SJME-08-2019-0067.

Pantano, E. and Stylos, N. (2020) 'The Cinderella moment: Exploring consumers' motivations to engage with renting as collaborative luxury consumption mode', *Psychology and Marketing*, *37* (5), pp. 740–53. doi: 10.1002/mar.21345.

Papismedov, D. and Fink, L. (2019) 'Do consumers make less accurate decisions when they use mobiles?', in 40th International Conference on Information Systems, ICIS. Munich, pp. 1–9.

Parise, S., Guinan, P.J. and Kafka, R. (2016) 'Solving the crisis of immediacy: How digital technology can transform the customer experience', *Business Horizons*, *59* (4), pp. 411–20.

Pariser, E. (2012) *The Filter Bubble: What the Internet is Hiding from You*. London: Penguin.

Patroni, J., von Briel, F. and Recker, J. (2020) 'Unpacking the social media–driven innovation capability: How consumer conversations turn into organizational innovations', *Information & Management*, January, article no. 103267.

Pauwels, K., Ambler, T., Clark, B.H., LaPointe, P., Reibstein, D., Skiera, B., Wierenga, B. and Wiesel, T. (2009) 'Dashboards as a service: Why, what, how and what research is needed?', *Journal of Service Research*, *12* (2), pp. 175–89.

Perfect Corp (2021) 'About Us', PerfectCorp.com. Available at: www.perfectcorp.com/consumer/about-us (accessed 23 May 2021).

Petty, R.D. (2012) 'Using the law to protect the brand on social media sites', *Management Research Review*, *35* (9), pp. 758–69.

Pidun, U., Reeves, M. and Wesselink, E. (2021) 'How healthy is your business ecosystem?', *MIT Sloan Management Review*, Spring, pp. 31–8.

Pletikosa-Cvijikj, I. and Michahelles, F. (2013) 'Online engagement factors on Facebook brand pages', *Social Network Analysis and Mining*, *3* (4), pp. 843–61.

Porter, M.M.E. (1997) 'Competitive strategy', *Measuring Business Excellence*, *1* (2), pp. 12–17. doi: https://doi.org/10.1108/eb025476.

Prabowo, H. and Alversia, Y. (2020) 'The influence of value and browsing activity on impulse buying behavior moderated by source of online review case study: Food and beverage products on Instagram', in *ICEEG 2020*. Arenthon, France: Association for Computing Machinery (ACM), pp. 103–8. doi: 10.1145/3409929.3414745.

Prensky, M. (2001) 'Digital natives, digital immigrants', *On the Horizon*, *9* (5), pp. 1–6.

Priyono, A., Moin, A. and Putri, V.N.A.O. (2020) 'Identifying digital transformation paths in the business model of SME during the COVID-19 pandemic', *Journal of Open Innovation: Technology, Market, and Complexity*, *6* (4), pp. 1–22.

Project Management Institute (2013) 'A guide to the project management body of knowledge (PMBOK® guide)', Project Management Institute. doi: 10.1002/pmj.20125.

Pulizzi, J. and Barrett, N. (2009) 'Get content get customers: Turn prospects into buyers with content marketing'. Available at: http://getcontentgetcustomers.com/wp-content/uploads/2008/06/gcgg-ebook-rev2-may08.pdf.

PwC (2018) Consumer Intelligence Series: Prepare for the voice revolution. Available at: www.pwc.com/us/en/advisory-services/publications/consumer-intelligence-series/pwc-voice-assistants.pdf.

Quinton, S. and Reynolds, N. (2018) *Understanding Research in the Digital Age*. London: SAGE Publications.

Radjou, N. (2020) 'The rising frugal economy', *MIT Sloan Management Review*. https://sloanreview.mit.edu/article/the-rising-frugal-economy

Rakuten (2021) 'Is Japan ready to go digital? Digital Transformation Minister Takuya Hirai and Mickey Mikitani weigh in', The Official Blog of Rakuten Group, Inc. Available at: https://rakuten.today/blog/digital-transformation-minister-takuya-hirai-japans-new-digital-agency.html (accessed 28 April 2021).

Rauschnabel, P.A., Rossmann, A. and tom Dieck, M.C. (2017) 'An adoption framework for mobile augmented reality games: The case of Pokémon Go', *Computers in Human Behavior*, *76*, pp. 276–86.

Rawlins, B. (2008) 'Give the Emperor a mirror: Toward developing a stakeholder measurement of organizational transparency', *Journal of Public Relations Research*, *21* (1), pp. 71–99.

Reichheld, F.F. (2003) 'The one number you need to grow', *Harvard Business Review*, *81* (12), pp. 46–54.

Relling, M., Schnittka, O., Ringle, C.M., Sattler, H. and Johnen, M. (2016) 'Community members' perception of brand community character: Construction and validation of a new scale', *Journal of Interactive Marketing*, *36*, pp. 107–20.

Rheingold, H. (1987) 'Virtual communities', *Whole Earth Review*, *57* (Winter), pp. 78–81.

Rheingold, H. (1992) *Virtual Reality: The Revolutionary Technology of Computer-Generated Artificial Worlds – and How It Promises to Transform Society*. New York: Touchstone.

Ritter, T. and Pedersen, C.L. (2020) 'Digitization capability and the digitalization of business models in business-to-business firms: Past, present and future', *Industrial Marketing Management*, https://doi.org/10.1016/j.indmarman.2019.11.019

Rogers, E.M. (1962) *Diffusion of Innovations*. New York: Free Press of Glencoe.

Rudin, M. (2011) 'From Hemingway to twitterature: The short and shorter of it', *Journal of Electronic Publishing*, *14* (2). doi: http://dx.doi.org/10.3998/3336451.0014.213.

Santoveña-Casal, S. (2019) The impact of social media participation on academic performance in undergraduate and postgraduate students. *International Review of Research in Open and Distance Learning*, *20* (1), 126–43. https://doi.org/10.19173/irrodl.v20i1.3751

Sari, S.V. and Camadan, F. (2016) 'The new face of violence tendency: Cyber bullying perpetrators and their victims', *Computers in Human Behavior*, *59*, pp. 317–26.

Sarkar, S., Chauhan, S. and Khare, A. (2020) 'A meta-analysis of antecedents and consequences of trust in mobile commerce', *International Journal of Information Management*, *50* (March 2019), pp. 286–301.

Schaarschmidt, M. and Walsh, G. (2020) 'Social media-driven antecedents and consequences of employees' awareness of their impact on corporate reputation', *Journal of Business Research*, *117*, pp. 718–26.

Schneider, P.J. and Zielke, S. (2020) 'Searching offline and buying online – An analysis of showrooming forms and segments', *Journal of Retailing and Consumer Services*, *52* (June 2019), p. 101919. doi: 10.1016/j.jretconser.2019.101919.

Schultz, C.D. and Kruse, B. (2022) 'Organizational exit strategies on social media platforms', in A. Hanlon and T. Tuten (eds), *The SAGE Handbook of Social Media Marketing*. London: Sage.

Serazio, M. (2020) 'How news went guerrilla marketing: A history, logic, and critique of brand journalism', *Media, Culture and Society*, *43* (1), pp. 117–32. doi: 10.1177/0163443720939489.

Sethna, Z. and Blythe, J. (2019) *Consumer Behaviour*, 4th edn. London: Sage.

Shaalan, A., Tourky, M. and Ibrahim, K. (2022) 'The chatbot revolution: Companies and consumers in a new digital age', in A. Hanlon and T.L. Tuten (eds), *The SAGE Handbook of Digital Marketing*. London: Sage.

Shao, G. (2009) 'Understanding the appeal of user-generated media: A uses and gratification perspective', *Internet Research*, *19* (1), pp. 7–25.

Shibata, N. (2020) 'Japanese companies graduate from "hanko" stamps era', Nikkei Asia. Available at: https://asia.nikkei.com/Business/Business-trends/Japanese-companies-graduate-from-hanko-stamps-era (accessed 28 April 2021).

Short, J., Williams, E. and Christie, B. (1976) *The Social Psychology of Telecommunications*. Hoboken, NJ: John Wiley & Sons.

Similar Web (2020) 'Total visits to wikipedia.org'. www.similarweb.com/website/wikipedia.org

Sinha, V. et al. (2020) 'The role of virtual consultations in plastic surgery during COVID-19 lockdown', *Aesthetic Plastic Surgery*. Springer US. doi: 10.1007/s00266-020-01932-7.

Skarlatidou, A. et al. (2019) 'The value of stakeholder mapping to enhance co-creation in citizen science initiatives', *Citizen Science: Theory and Practice*, *4* (1), pp. 1–10. doi: 10.5334/cstp.226.

Smedley, D. (2020) 'Biking with Mark'. In *Talks at Google*. YouTube. www.youtube.com/watch?v=13vnrh2f4N8

Snickars, P. and Vonderau, P. (2009) *The YouTube Reader*. Stockholm: National Library of Sweden. Available at: http://pellesnickars.se/wordpress/wp-content/uploads/2010/07/youtube_reader.pdf#page=13.

Solberg, E., Traavik, L.E.M. and Wong, S.I. (2020) 'Digital mindsets: Recognizing and leveraging individual beliefs for digital transformation', *California Management Review, 62* (4), pp. 105–24. doi: 10.1177/0008125620931839.

Solove, D.J. (2011) 'Why privacy matters even if you have nothing to hide', *The Chronicle Review of Higher Education*, 15 May, pp. 1–8.

Soni, P. and Krishnan, R.T. (2014) 'Frugal innovation: Aligning theory, practice, and public policy', *Journal of Indian Business Research, 6* (1), pp. 29–47. https://doi.org/10.1108/JIBR-03-2013-0025

Statista (2020) 'Most popular social networks worldwide as of July 2020, ranked by number of active users', Statista.com. Available at: www.statista.com/statistics/272014/global-social-networks-ranked-by-number-of-users (accessed 2 October 2020).

Steuer, J. (1992) 'Defining virtual reality: Dimensions determining telepresence', *Journal of Communication, 42* (4), pp. 73–93.

Stewart, M.C. and Arnold, C.L. (2018) 'Defining social listening: Recognizing an emerging dimension of listening', *International Journal of Listening, 32* (2), pp. 85–100.

Stollfuß, S. (2020) 'Communitainment on Instagram: Fitness content and community-driven communication as social media entertainment', *SAGE Open, 10* (2).

Stroud, N.J., Peacock, C. and Curry, A.L. (2020) 'The effects of mobile push notifications on news consumption and learning', *Digital Journalism, 8* (1), pp. 32–48.

Stubb, C. and Colliander, J. (2019) '"This is not sponsored content" – The effects of impartiality disclosure and e-commerce landing pages on consumer responses to social media influencer posts', *Computers in Human Behavior, 98* (May 2018), pp. 210–22.

Sullivan, D. (2019) 'What webmasters should know about Google's core updates', Official Google Webmaster Central Blog. Available at: https://webmasters.googleblog.com/2019/08/core-updates.html (accessed 17 September 2020).

Sun, Y., Gonzalez-Jimenez, H. and Wang, S. (2021) 'Examining the relationships between e-WOM, consumer ethnocentrism and brand equity', *Journal of Business Research, 130* (September 2019), pp. 564–73. doi: 10.1016/j.jbusres.2019.09.040.

Tenopir, C., Volentine, R. and King, D.W. (2013) 'Social media and scholarly reading', *Online Information Review, 37* (2), pp. 193–216. https://doi.org/10.1108/OIR-04-2012-0062

Thaler, R.H. and Sunstein, C.R. (2008) *Nudge: Improving Decisions About Health, Wealth and Happiness*. New Haven, CT: Yale University Press.

Toffler, A. (1980) *The Third Wave: The Classic Study of Tomorrow*. New York: Bantam.

Tong, S., Luo, X. and Xu, B. (2020) 'Personalized mobile marketing strategies', *Journal of the Academy of Marketing Science, 48* (1), pp. 64–78.

Travers, J. and Milgram, S. (1969) 'An experimental study of the small world problem', *Sociometry, 32* (4), pp. 425–43.

Tremblay, S.C., Essafi Tremblay, S. and Poirier, P. (2021) 'From filters to fillers: An active inference approach to body image distortion in the selfie era', *AI and Society, 36* (1), pp. 33–48. doi: 10.1007/s00146-020-01015-w.

REFERENCES

Tsimonis, G., Dimitriadis, S. and Omar, S. (2020) 'An integrative typology of relational benefits and costs in social media brand pages', *International Journal of Market Research*, *62* (2), pp. 216–33.

Tung, L., Xu, Y. and Tan, F. (2009) 'Attributes of web site usability: A study of web users with the repertory grid technique', *International Journal of Electronic Commerce*, *13* (4), pp. 97–126.

Tzeng, S.Y. et al. (2021) 'Factors affecting customer satisfaction on online shopping holiday', *Marketing Intelligence and Planning*, *4* (2019), pp. 516–32. doi: 10.1108/MIP-08-2020-0346.

Tzima, S., Styliaras, G. and Bassounas, A. (2019) 'Augmented reality applications in education: Teachers' point of view', *Education Sciences*, *9*(2). doi: 10.3390/educsci9020099.

Unilever (2020) Unilever Annual Report and Accounts 2020. www.unilever.com/investor-relations/annual-report-and-accounts

United Nations Division for Public Institutions and Digital Government (2020) *UN / DESA Policy Brief # 61: COVID-19: Embracing digital government during the pandemic and beyond*. Department of Economic and Social Affairs.

UNWTO Secretary-General Zurab Pololikashvili (2021) *Secretary-General's Policy Brief on Tourism and COVID-19, United Nations World Tourism Organization*. Available at: www.unwto.org/tourism-and-covid-19-unprecedented-economic-impacts (accessed 2 January 2021).

Vallas, S. and Schor, J.B. (2020) 'What do platforms do? Understanding the gig economy', *Annual Review of Sociology*, *46* (July), pp. 273–94.

Vanden Bergh, B.G., Lee, M., Quilliam, E.T. and Hove, T. (2011) 'The multidimensional nature and brand impact of user-generated ad parodies in social media', *International Journal of Advertising*, *30* (1), pp. 103–31.

Vázquez-Ingelmo, A., García-Peñalvo, F.J. and Therón, R. (2021) 'Towards a technological ecosystem to provide information dashboards as a service: A dynamic proposal for supplying dashboards adapted to specific scenarios', *Applied Sciences*, *11* (7), pp. 1–14. doi: 10.3390/app11073249.

Venkatesh, V. and Ramesh, V. (2006) 'Web and wireless site usability: Understanding differences and modeling use', *MIS Quarterly*, *30* (1), pp. 181–206. doi: 10.2307/25148723.

Verhoef, P.C., Broekhuizen, T., Bart, Y., Bhattacharya, A., Qi Dong, J., Fabian, N. and Haenlein, M. (2021) 'Digital transformation: A multidisciplinary reflection and research agenda', *Journal of Business Research*, *122* (September 2019), pp. 889–901. https://doi.org/10.1016/j.jbusres.2019.09.022

Verhoef, P.C., Kannan, P.K. and Inman, J.J. (2015) 'From multi-channel retailing to omni-channel retailing', *Journal of Retailing*, *91* (2), pp. 174–81.

Vial, G. (2019) 'Understanding digital transformation: A review and a research agenda', *Journal of Strategic Information Systems*, *28* (2), 118–44. https://doi.org/10.1016/j.jsis.2019.01.003

Voorhees, C.M., Fombelle, P.W., Gregoire, Y., Bone, S., Gustafsson, A., Sousa, R. and Walkowiak, T. (2016) 'Service encounters, experiences and the customer journey: Defining the field and a call to expand our lens', *Journal of Business Research*, *79* (November), pp. 269–80.

Voytenko Palgan, Y., Mont, O. and Sulkakoski, S. (2021) 'Governing the sharing economy: Towards a comprehensive analytical framework of municipal governance', *Cities*, *108* (September 2020), article no. 102994. doi: 10.1016/j.cities.2020.102994.

Vrontis, D., Makrides, A., Christofi, M. and Thrassou, A. (2021) 'Social media influencer marketing: A systematic review, integrative framework and future research agenda#', *International Journal of Consumer Studies*, December 2020, pp. 1–28.

Wadbring, I. and Bergström, L. (2021) 'Audiences behind the Paywall: News navigation among established versus newly added subscribers', *Digital Journalism*, *9* (3), pp. 319–35. https://doi.org/10.1080/21670811.2021.1878919

Waldfogel, J. (2020) 'The welfare effects of Spotify's cross-country price discrimination', *Review of Industrial Organization*, *56* (4), pp. 593–613. doi: 10.1007/s11151-020-09748-0.

Walters, T. and Rose, R. (2016) 'Deliver peak experiences with interactive content', Content Marketing Institute, p. 19. Available at: https://contentmarketinginstitute.com/wp-content/uploads/2016/06/Ion_CMI_InteractiveContent_Final.pdf.

Web Analytics Association (2008) 'Web Analytics – definition'. Available at: www.digitalanalyticsassociation.org/Files/PDF_standards/WebAnalyticsDefinitions.pdf.

Weihrich, H. (1982) 'The TOWS Matrix: A tool for situational analysis', *Long Range Planning*, *15* (2), pp. 54–66.

Weiser, M. (1991) 'The computer for the 21st century', *Scientific American*, *265* (3), pp. 94–104.

Wells, K.J., Attoh, K. and Cullen, D. (2021) '"Just-in-Place" labor: Driver organizing in the Uber workplace', *Environment and Planning A*, *53* (2), pp. 315–31.

Wernerfelt, B. (1984) 'A resource-based view of the firm', *Strategic Management Journal*, *5*, pp. 171–80.

Wheeler, E. (1937) *Tested Sentences that Sell*. Englewood Cliffs, NJ: Prentice-Hall.

Whiting, A. and Williams, D. (2013) 'Why people use social media: A uses and gratifications approach', *Qualitative Market Research: An International Journal*, *16* (4), 362–9. https://doi.org/10.1108/QMR-06-2013-0041

Wikimedia Foundation Inc. (2020) Financial Statements. San Francisco, CA. https://wikimediafoundation.org/about/financial-reports

Winning Group (2021) 'Cutting-edge science & technology', Winning.com. Available at: www.winning.com.au/innovation (accessed 24 May 2021).

Wohllebe, A. and Dirrler, P. (2020) 'Mobile apps in retail: Determinants of consumer acceptance – a systematic review', *International Journal of Interactive Mobile Technologies*, *14* (20), pp. 153–64.

Wojdynski, B.W. and Evans, N.J. (2020) 'The Covert Advertising Recognition and Effects (CARE) model: Processes of persuasion in native advertising and other masked formats', *International Journal of Advertising*, *39* (1), pp. 4–31.

Workie, H. and Jain, K. (2017) 'Distributed ledger technology: Implications of blockchain for the securities industry 1', *Journal of Securities Operations & Custody*, *9* (4), pp. 1–22.

World Health Organization (2020) 'Call for action: Managing the infodemic', *World Health Organization News*. www.who.int/news/item/11-12-2020-call-for-action-managing-the-infodemic

REFERENCES

Wu, Y., Ngai, E.W.T., Wu, P. and Wu, C. (2020) 'Fake online reviews: Literature review, synthesis, and directions for future research', *Decision Support Systems*, *132* (February), p. 113280. https://doi.org/10.1016/j.dss.2020.113280

Yang, F., Heemsbergen, L. and Fordyce, R. (2021) 'Comparative analysis of China's Health Code, Australia's COVIDSafe and New Zealand's COVID Tracer Surveillance Apps: A new corona of public health governmentality?', *Media International Australia*, *178* (1), pp. 182–97.

Yao, Z. et al. (2021) 'Join, stay or go? A closer look at members' life cycles in online health communities', *Proceedings of the ACM on Human–Computer Interaction*, *5* (CSCW1), pp. 1–22.

Yildirim, C. and Correia, A.P. (2015) 'Exploring the dimensions of nomophobia: Development and validation of a self-reported questionnaire', *Computers in Human Behavior*, *49*, pp. 130–7.

Yin, L., Lin, N., Song, X., Mei, S., Shaw, S. L., Fang, Z., Li, Q., Li, Y. and Mao, L. (2020) 'Space-time personalized short message service (SMS) for infectious disease control – Policies for precise public health', *Applied Geography*, *114* (January 2019). https://doi.org/10.1016/j.apgeog.2019.102103

Yuan, D. et al. (2020) 'Managing the product-harm crisis in the digital era: The role of consumer online brand community engagement', *Journal of Business Research*, *115* (April), pp. 38–47.

Zahay, D. (2021) 'Advancing research in digital and social media marketing', *Journal of Marketing Theory and Practice*, *29* (1), pp. 125–39.

Zeschky, M., Widenmayer, B. and Gassmann, O. (2011) 'Frugal innovation in emerging markets', *Research-Technology Management*, *54* (4), pp. 38–45.

Zheng, A. et al. (2020) 'Self-presentation on social media: When self-enhancement confronts self-verification', *Journal of Interactive Advertising*, *20* (3), pp. 289–302.

Zhong, W., Wang, Y. and Zhang, G. (2020) 'The impact of physical activity on college students' mobile phone dependence: The mediating role of Self-Control', *International Journal of Mental Health and Addiction*. https://doi.org/10.1007/s11469-020-00308-x

Zoghaib, A. (2017) 'The contribution of a brand spokesperson's voice to consumer-based brand equity', *Journal of Product and Brand Management*, *26* (5), pp. 492–502.

Zoghaib, A. (2019) 'Persuasion of voices: The effects of a speaker's voice characteristics and gender on consumers' responses', *Recherche et Applications en Marketing*, *34* (3), pp. 83–110.

INDEX

Page numbers in *italics* refer to figures; page numbers in **bold** refer to tables.

5Ss (sell, serve, speak, save, sizzle) model, 294–295
9Ms resource types
  overview of, 335, *335*
  machines, 342–345, **343–344**
  management, 346, *347*
  manpower, 335–337
  materials, 345–346
  measurement, 346
  method, 340–342, *341*
  minutes, 339
  money, 337–339
  mother nature, 347
  Strava (case study), 360–361

A/B testing, 320
Abbasi, A., 135
Ackland, R., 259
acquisition, conversion, retention (ACR) framework, 287
aesthetics, 226–227, *226*
affiliate programs, 82–83
African Union (AU), 22
algorithms, 69–70, 76
Ambler, T., 366
American Marketing Association (AMA), 397
Ancillai, C., 168
Andreu, L., 40
anonymity, 156, 157, 259
Ansoff, H.I., 279, 280
API (application programming interface), 195, 196
App Annie, 188
ArcticZymes Technologies, 355–356
Arnold, C.L., 251
Arora, S., 34
ASOS, 116–117
attribution, 370, **371**, 379
audience display networks, 81–82, 84
augmented reality (AR)
  overview of, 212, 214–215
  application of, 216–225, *217*, *225*
  benefits of, 230–231
  challenges with, 231–232
  creation of, 232–234
  future of, 234–236, *235*
  key concepts in, 225–229, *226*, **228**
  Strava (case study), 236–237
  See also mixed reality (MR); virtual reality (VR)

Australasian Marketing Journal (journal), 86
Australia, 22
automotive retail, 220
Avery, J., 167
Aw, E.C.X., 102
Aydin Gökgöz, Z., 191
Azuma, R.T., 214

badmouthing, 174
Baidu, 80
Balaji, M.S., 207
Bardhi, F., 35
Bayighomog Likoum, S.W., 242
BBC, 231
beauty retailers, 220
Bec, A., 213, 214, 230–231
Bellingcat, 338–339
Benlian, A., 262
Bennett, D.H.S., 101
Berners-Lee, T., 5, 420
BEST principles, 112–113
big data, 12–15, **13**, 380–381
Big Data & Society (journal), 391
Bilos, A., 385
Black Hat SEO, 75
Black Lives Matter (#BLM) movement, 101
blockchain technology, 11, 19–20
blogs, 108–109
Blumler, J.G., 126
boasting, 174
bonding social capital, 153–154
Borowski-Beszta, M., 186
brand activism, 100–101
brand communities, 151, 162
brand journalism, 100
brand positioning, 315–316, *316*, 317
Brand24, 383
branded content, 100–101
Brannon, D., 188
Brant, A., 252
Breitsohl, J.C., 354
Brennen, J.S., 407
bridging social capital, 153–154
Brownlie, J., 151, 152
Bruns, A., 134, 135
budgeting, 321–324, 337–339
Buhalis, D., 40, 370
Burt, G., 248
Business Horizons (journal), 118
business strategy, 273

Button, K., 39
buy now pay later (BNPL), 16–18, 304–305
buyer journeys, 44–45

CACI, 13
California, 22–23, 24
call to action (CTA), 61–63, 339, 345
Camadan, F., 143
Canva.com, 318
capability, 252, 253, 255, 416
celebrity endorsers, 101–102
Chaffey, D., 294
channel selection, 317–318
Charlesworth, A., 256
Chartered Institute of Marketing (CIM), 397
chatbots, 203–204, 246, 251, 261
Chauhan, S., 202
Cheung, C.M.K., 158
China, 22
Chou, Y.C., 202
Christensen, C.M., 256
Christie, B., 132
Chu, M.G., 152
Chyi, H.I., 306
citizen journalists, 104
clicks, 381
clickthrough rate (CTR), 381
clothing retailers, 218–219
cloud computing, 8–9
CMO Survey, 322
co-creation, 402–403, 404–405, 418
co-destruction, 403
cognitive dissonance, 319
cognitive know-how, 336
Coles, B.A., 143
collaboration, 402–403, 418
collaborative consumption, 37
Committee of Advertising Practice (CAP),
    106–107
communitainment, 126–127
communities, 150. See also online communities
communities of fantasy, 161
communities of interest, 160
communities of practice, 159–160, 162–163
communities of relationship, 161
communities of transaction, 160–161
community feedback, 173–175, 174
comparative analysis, 378
competence, 252, 253, 255, 336–337, 415–416
competition, 244, 255–262, 256
complaints, 173, 251
Computers in Human Behavior (journal), 236
connecting media, 33
consistency, 261, 402
consumer behaviour, 33–36
consumer ethnocentrism, 249, 250
consumer power, 33
consumer return on investment, 226–227, 226

consumer well-being, 417
consumers, 40. See also digital consumers
consumption communities, 162
content analysis, 378–379
content audit, 95–96
content calendar, 113–114
content distribution, 114–115
content format, 108–109
content gating, 115
content length, 109–110
content life, 110
content management, 113–114, 173
content management systems (CMSs), 115
content marketing
    overview of, 92, 92
    evaluation of, 92–96, 94
    resource management and, 345–346
    story in, 96–99, 97
    storytellers in, 99–108, 99, 104
    Strava (case study), 118–119
    style in, 108–112, 111
Content Marketing Institute (CMI), 110,
    112–113
content marketing strategy, 112–118
contract marketplaces, 340–342, 341
convenience, 260–261
The Conversation (online news network), 280
conversion rate optimisation (CRO), 93
conversion rates, 371–372, 381
conversions, 381
cookies, 48, 49, 83, 262
COPE (Create Once, Publish Everywhere),
    116, 118
Corcoran, S., 98
corporate culture, 259–260
corporate digital responsibility (CDR), 418–419
corporate strategy, 272–273
cost per acquisition (CPA), 323, 338
cost per action (CPA), 78–79, 381
cost per click (CPC), 78, 381
cost per follow (CPF), 79–80
cost per thousand (CPM), 78
cost per view (CPV), 79
Couldry, N., 97
country of origin (COO) effect, 248, 250
Court, D., 287
covert advertising, 98
COVID-19 pandemic
    augmented, virtual and mixed reality and,
        212, 217, 235
    digital divide and, 8
    digital processes and, 246, 307
    doomscrolling and, 206
    governments and, 419–420
    mobile marketing and, 186, 205
    nudge theory and, 20
    online communities and, 150, 160, 175
    self-disclosure and, 157

sharing economy and, 38
social media and, 143
social presence and, 132–133
track and trace app and, 71–72
Cranmer, E.E., 214, 223
cross reality (XR). *See* mixed reality
crowdfunding, 305–306, **305**
Crowston, K., 108
cryptoassets, 11–12
cryptocurrencies, 18–19
cumulative satisfaction, 254
curated content, 96–97
Curry, A.L., 202
customer behaviour, **367**, 373
customer-centric model, 400–401, 418
customer experience, 40–41
customer journey
overview of, 40, 44–49, **45**, *46*
augmented, virtual and mixed reality and, 215, 218–221, 227, 229, 233
digital transformation process and, 409–410
email marketing and, 62, **62**, 64
mobile marketing and, 191, 192, 197
resource management and, 345
voice search and, 77
customer lifetime value (CLV), 369
customer satisfaction, 254–255, **367**, 372–373
customer service, 203–204
customer service encounters, 43
customer value, 369–370, *369*
customer volume, 367–368, **367**
customers, 40. *See also* digital customers
customisation, 261–262
cyberbullying, 156

Daft, R.L., 133
daily active users (DAUs), 125, 382
dark social, 48, 49
dashboards, 357–359
data protection
overview of, 21, 22–23
augmented, virtual and mixed reality and, 228
big data and, 15
digital marketing audits and, 246, 249
email marketing and, 65
future of, 417–418
governance and, 353
online communities and, 156
See also privacy
dating sites, 161
Davis, F.D., 52–54, **53**, *53*
Dawkins, R., 131
Day, G.S., 242, 243, 262
deepfakes, 229
demand-side platforms, 82, 83–84
Deming, E., 390
demographics, 50–51, **50**

Diffusion of Innovations, 103
digital attitude, 337
digital clutter, 35
Digital Competence Framework for Citizens (DigComp), 399
digital competition, 244, 255–262, *256*
digital competitiveness, 401
digital consumers
overview of, 32
consumer behaviour and, 33–36
customer experience and, 40–41
customer journeys and, 40, 44–49, **45**, *46*
digital personas and, 50–51, **50**
evolution of, 51–54, **53**, *53*
sharing economy and, 36–40, *36*
six degrees of separation and, 32
Strava (case study), 55–56
touchpoints and, 41–43
digital customers, 251–255, *252*
digital detox, 207
digital disruption, 10–11, **10**, 37
digital divide, 7–8, 199
Digital Economy and Society Index (DESI), 54
digital generations, 6–7
digital knowledge, 336
digital marketing
digital transformation process and, 406–416, *407*
future of, 417–420
integration and, 400–405, *400*, *404*, 420–421
vs. traditional marketing, 396–397, **396**
value of, 397–399, *398*
digital marketing audits
overview of, 242
digital competition and, 244, 255–262, *256*
digital customers and, 251–255, *252*
digital marketing plans and, 307
framework for, 243–245, *244*
importance of, 242–243, 275
information analysis and, 262–263
macro-environment analysis and, 243–245, 247–251
micro-environment analysis and, 243–247
resource management and, 349
Strava (case study), 264–266
digital marketing campaigns, 314–321, *315–316*, **320**, 411
digital marketing environment
overview of, 4
big data and, 12–15, **13**
origins and evolution of, 4–6, **5–6**
payments and processes and, 16–20
people and, 6–8
privacy and, 20–25, *24*
products and places and, 8–12, **10**
Strava (case study), 26–27
digital marketing metrics
overview of, 366

analytics and, 375–386, *380*, **385–386**
digital marketing campaigns and, 321
mobile marketing and, 194
resource management and, 346
social media and, 139
Strava (case study), 392
traditional metrics and, 366–375, **367**, *369*, **372**
uses of, 386–391, *387*, **388**, *391*
digital marketing plans
overview of, 300, *301*
budgeting and, 321–324
digital marketing campaigns and, 314–321, *315–316*, **320**
digital transformation process and, 411
marketing mix and, 303–314, *305*, **307**, **308**, *310*, **314**
presentation of, 324–327, *325*, *327*, 411
role of stakeholders in, 301–303
Strava (case study), 327–330, **329**
digital marketing strategy and objectives
overview of, 270–271
core concepts in, 271–273, *272*
digital marketing plans and, 325–326, **325**
digital strategy models and, 279–289, *281–282*, *288*
digital transformation process and, 410
frameworks for, 292–295
hierarchy of objectives and, 272, *272*, 289–292, **290–291**, 307
Strava (case study), 291–292, 296–297
traditional strategy models and, 273–279, **277**
See also content marketing strategy
Digital Marketing Strategy Framework
overview of, 282–287, *282*
digital marketing metrics and, 366, 373, 387, *387*
digital marketing plans and, 325–326
digital marketing toolbox
overview of, 60, *61*
email marketing and, 60–67, **62**, *65*
paid search and, 78–85
search engine optimisation and, 72–77
Strava (case study), 86–87
websites and, 67–72, **69**
See also content marketing; online communities; social media
digital natives, 336
digital payments, 16–19
digital skills, 335–337
digital theft, 9–10, 353
digital transformation, 406–416, *407*
digital wallets, 16–18
digitalisation, 407, *407*, 408–409
digitisation, 407–409, *407*
Dineva, D.P., 354
DiNucci, D., 122

direct marketing, 4
directness, 173–174
Dirrler, P., 203
disinformation, 143
disintermediation, 4
disruptive marketing, 256–257
distributed ledger technology (DLT), 19–20
distribution/availability, **367**, 368
Ditchfield, H., 130
doomscrolling, 202, 206
dual screening, 33
Duane, A., 141, **141–142**
Dwivedi, Y.K., 417

e-marketing, 60
e-money, 16
earned media, 97–99, **99**
Eckhardt, G.M., 35, 36–37
Econsultancy, 287
Edelman Trust Barometer, 260
education, 223–224
email analytics, 384–386, **385–386**
email marketing, 60–67, **62**, *65*
emotional intensity, 152, 154
engagement, 70, 71
engagement rate, 105, 145, 382
Esen, R., 256
Essafi Tremblay, S., 128
Ethical Influencers, 105
European Union (EU), 22, 23, 25
Evans, N.J., 98
evergreen content (flow content), 96, 345
exit strategies, 404, *404*
experiential values, 225–227, *226*, 232
expertise, 100, 108
extrinsic values, 226

Fagnot, I., 108
fake followers, 107
fake news, 94–95, **94**, 143, 419–420
fans, 382
Farah, M.F., 254
Farris, P., 366
FatSecret (app), 195–196
Feher, K., 130
filter bubble, 127
firestorms, 168
Fischer, M., 415
flow content (evergreen content), 96, 345
followers, 79–80, 382
Fotopoulou, A., 97
Fountoulaki, P., 214
Fournier, S., 167
fraud, 156
Freeman, R.E., 301
frugal economy, 418
fulfilment, 203
functional strategies, 273

games, 224–225, *225*
Ganley, D., 156
Gantt charts, **308**, 309, 326
García-Peñalvo, F.J., 357
Garg, S., 25
Gavilan, D., 201
Gay, R., 256
Gentile, C., 41
geofencing, 188, 190
gig economy, 138, 340, 341–342
Gilmore, J., 190
Global Positioning System (GPS), 26–27
Gnoth, J., 40
Goffman, E., 157
Google, 69–70, 75, 76, 80
governance, 353–354
governments, 419–420
Granger, C.H., 272
Granovetter, M.S., 175
Gray, D., 346
greenwashing, 274–275
Gregoire, Y., 173
Grewal, D., 197–198, *198*
group buying, 305
Gunawardena, C.N., 132
Gurevitch, M., 126
Gymshark, 142

Haenlein, M., 123, 132–133, **132**
Halpern, N., 414, 415
Hanna, R.C., 306
Haobin Ye, B., 102
haptic feedback, 188
Harrigan, P., 369
hate crimes, 156
He, Q., 302
hedonic communities, 159, 176–177
hedonic consumption, 51, 214–215, 226
Helly Hansen, 248–250
Hendriks, M., 50
Herhausen, D., 168
hierarchy of objectives, 272, *272*, 289–292, **290–291**, 307
Hofacker, C., 69, **69**
Hoffman, D.L., 123
home products brands, 221
homophily, 100, 108
honeycomb model, 127–131, *128*, 136
Hootsuite, 94, 115, 383–384
Hossain, S.F.A., 188
HTML code, 74
human intelligence tasks (HITs), 340
humanity, 400–401
hybrid apps, 189–190
Hyper Island, 411

IBM, 15
Ikea, 404–405

immediacy, 132
impartiality disclosure, 106–107
implantable technology, 182
impressions, 381, 382
in-market audiences, 84
Industrial Marketing Management (journal), 359
Inegbedion, H.E., 8
influencers, 82–83, 102–107, *104*, 111–112, 134
infodemic, 143
information analysis, 262–263
informed consent, 259
interactivity, 110–111, *111*, 227–229, **228**
International Organization for Standardization (ISO), 71
Internet Archive, 6
internet marketing, 60
Internet of Things (IoT), 5
intimacy, 132, 152, 154
intrinsic values, 226

Jacobs, J.V., 182
Japan, 412–413
Jiang, Y., 207
Journal of Business Research (journal), 263
Journal of Interactive Marketing (journal), 26
Journal of Research in Interactive Marketing (journal), 420
Jung, T., 213–214
Just Eat Takeaway, 4, 285–287

Kalaignanam, K., 185
Kannan, P.K., 48
Kantar, 13
Kaplan, A.M., 123, 132–133, **132**
Kaplan, D., 152
Katz, E., 126
Keeker, K., 69
key financials, **367**, 368–369, *369*, **371**
key opinion customers (KOCs), 107
Key Opinion Leaders (KOLs). *See* influencers
Khare, A., 202
Kibel, B., 46
Kietzmann, J.H., 127–131, *128*
Kim, J.J., 234
Kim, M.J., 213–214
Klarna, 17–18
Kotler, P., 271, 417
Koukaras, P., 124
Kozinets, R., 158–159
Kreiss, D., 407
Kruse, B., 404

Labrecque, L.I., 102
Lampe, C., 156
landing pages, 64, 72–73, 78–79, 106
LaTour, K.A., 252
Le, T.D., 162

leadership, 415
Lee, C.K., 213–214
LEGO, 168–169
Lemon, K.N., 41, 44–45, 306
Lengel, R.H., 133
Leung, C.H., 206–207
Li, H.A., 48
likes, 382
Lim, B.A., 220
Lin, Y.H., 152
liquid consumption, 33, 35–36
Liu, Y., 33
Lobschat, L., 419
location-based marketing (proximity
    marketing), 205
long-form content, 110
Long Range Planning (journal), 327
long-tail keywords, 73, 93
longitudinal analysis, 378
Lou, C., 103
Luo, X., 184–186
luxury fashion brands, 218

M&S (Marks & Spencer), 139–140
machine learning, 14–15
macro-environment analysis, 243–245, 247–251
manpower, 335–337
Manshad, M.S., 188
market growth rate, **367**, 372
market sensing, 242, 243. *See also* digital
    marketing audits
market share, **367**, 368
marketing, definitions of, 397
marketing audits. *See* digital marketing audits
marketing campaigns. *See* digital marketing
    campaigns
marketing mix
    digital marketing plans and, 303–314, **305**,
        307, **308**, *310*, **314**
    integration and, 400, *400*, 418
    See also people; physical evidence; place;
        price; processes; promotion
marketing plans. *See* digital marketing plans
marketing toolbox. *See* digital marketing
    toolbox
MarTech (marketing + technology), 339,
    342–345, **343–344**
Mathwick, C.,, 232
McCarthy, E.J., 184
McDonald, R., 256
McKinsey & Company, 287–289, *287*
McQuail, D., 130
media meshing, 33
media richness, 132–133, **132**
memes, 131
Mental Health America, 200
metrics. *See* digital marketing metrics

Meyer, C., 41
micro-environment analysis, 243–247
Microsoft, 374–375
Microsoft Usability Guidelines (MUG), 69
microtasking, 340
Mills, A.J., 124
Minguillón, J., 163
Mintzberg, H., 271
misinformation, 94–95, **94**
MIT Sloan Management Review (journal), 296
Mitchell, T., 15
mixed reality (MR)
    overview of, 212, 215–216
    application of, 216–218, *217*, 224–225, *225*
    benefits of, 230–231
    challenges with, 231–232
    key concepts in, 225–229, *226*, **228**
    See also augmented reality (AR); virtual
        reality (VR)
mobile advertising, 196–197, **197**
mobile apps, 188–196
mobile commerce, 202–205, **204**
mobile marketing
    overview and framework for, 182–184, *185*
    challenges for consumers with, 206–207
    mobile commerce and, 202–205, **204**
    place and, *185*, 186
    prediction and, *185*, 186
    pricing and, 185–186, *185*
    products and, 186–196, **187**
    promotion and, 193, 196–202, **197**, *198*, *201*
    Strava (case study), 207–208
Mobile Media & Communication (journal), 207
mobile peer-to-peer payment systems, 188
Mobile Phone Dependence Questionnaire,
    206–207
mobile place, *185*, 186
mobile prediction, *185*, 186
mobile pricing, 185–186, *185*
mobile products, 186–196, **187**
mobile promotion, 193, 196–202, **197**, *198*, *201*
mobile social commerce, 204, **204**
mobile wallets, 187–188
MoneySavingExpert, 85
MoneySuperMarket.com, 4
Mont, O., 36
monthly active users (MAUs), 125, 382
MUD Jeans, 309–314, *310*, **314**
multimedia message service (MMS), 199
multivariate testing, 320
Muñiz, A.M.J., 151, 162, 175

Nabity-Grover, T., 157, 158
NASA, 216
native apps, 188–189
Net Promoter Score (NPS), 43, 139, 254, 373
netnography, 158–159

New Zealand, 22
Ng, Y.M.M., 306
Nielsen, 13
Nielsen, J., 69, **69**
nomophobia, 206–207
non-fungible tokens (NFTs), 11–12
#notsponsored, 106–107
Novak, T.P., 123
nudge theory, 20–21

objectives, 271. *See also* digital marketing
    strategy and objectives
off-page SEO, 73, 74–75
offsite analytics, 376
O'Guinn, T.C., 151, 162, 175
Olsen, R.K., 115
on-page SEO, 73–74
one-off emails, 63
online brand community engagement
    (OBCE), 168
online communities
    overview of, 150–151
    creation and management of, 170–176,
        172, *174*
    development of, 155–159
    digital transformation process and, 410
    life cycles of, 164–166, *164*, **166**
    organisations and, 167–169
    Strava (case study), 176–177
    tie strength and, 151–155, *154*
    typology of, 159–164
online surveys, 404
onsite analytics, 376
opinion formers, 103
opinion leaders, 102–103
Orange Money Africa, 276–278, **277**
O'Reilly, P., 141, **141–142**
O'Reilly, T., 122
organic posts, 337–338
Organisation for Economic Co-operation and
    Development (OECD), 7
owned media, 97–98, **99**, 245

pacemakers, 182
page tagging, 377
paid media, 97–98, **99**
paid search, 78–85, 98, 197, 323
paid search analytics, 381–382
parasocial interaction, 102
Parise, S., 50
Pariser, E., 127
participative pricing, 304
participatory culture, 134
path to purchase, 48–49
pay per click (PPC), 78
payments, 16–19. *See also* mobile wallets
paywalls, 115

Peacock, C., 202
Pedersen, C.L., 407
Peelen, E., 50
people
    digital competitiveness and, 401
    digital marketing audits and, 245–246
    digital marketing plans and, 313, **314**
    digital marketing strategy and, 291–292, **291**
    See also influencers
Perfect Corp, 228
performance marketing, 82–83
personality traits, 52
personas
    overview of, 50–51, **50**
    augmented, virtual and mixed reality and,
        232–233
    digital marketing plans and, 326
    email marketing and, 66
    social media and, 138–139
PESTLE framework, 13, **13**, 243, 248
Petpuls, 324
physical evidence
    digital competitiveness and, 401
    digital marketing audits and, 246–247
    digital marketing plans and, 313, **314**
    digital marketing strategy and, 291–292, **291**
    See also user experience (UX)
Pixabay.com, 322
pixels, 79
place
    digital competitiveness and, 401
    digital marketing audits and, 245
    digital marketing environment and, 8–12, **10**
    digital marketing plans and, 311, **314**
    digital marketing strategy and, 291–292, **291**
    mobile marketing and, *185*, 186
plagiarism, 10
Plan–Do–Check–Act (PDCA) cycle, 358,
    390–391, *391*
Plangger, K., 124
planned content, 96
planned emails, 61
playfulness, 226–227, *226*
podcasts, 109
POEM model, 97–99
Poirier, P., 128
Polasik, M., 186
Pololikashvili, Z., 222
POSE model, 97–99, **99**
positioning, 315–316, *316*, 317
post-testing, 321
power, 302
practical know-how, 336
pre-loaded credit cards, 188
pre-testing, 320–321
Prensky, M., 7
price

digital marketing audits and, 247
digital marketing plans and, 304–306, **305**, 311, **314**
digital marketing strategy and, **290**, 291–292
mobile marketing and, 185–186, *185*
privacy, 20–25, *24*, 204, 228, 353, 417–418. *See also* data protection
privacy paradox, 20, 158, 176
Priyono, A., 415
processes
digital competitiveness and, 401
digital marketing audits and, 246
digital marketing plans and, 306–307, 312–313, **314**
digital marketing strategy and, 291–292, **291**
product quality, **367**, 373–374
products
digital competitiveness and, 401
digital marketing audits and, 247
digital marketing environment and, 8–12, **10**
digital marketing plans and, 303–304, 310–311
digital marketing strategy and, **290**, 291–292
mobile marketing and, 186–196, **187**
programmatic paid search, 83–84
programmatic real-time bidding (RTB), 83
progressive web apps (PWAS), 189
promotion
digital marketing audits and, 247
digital marketing plans and, 312, 314–321, **314**, *315–316*, **320**
digital marketing strategy and, 291–292, **291**
mobile marketing and, 193, 196–202, **197**, *198, 201*
See also digital marketing toolbox
propaganda, 94–95, **94**
prosumers, 38
proximity marketing (location-based marketing), 205
pseudonyms, 156, 157
psychographics, 50, **50**
Psychology and Marketing (journal), 54
push notifications, 200–202, *201*

Quick Response (QR) codes, 204–205

RACI (Responsible, Accountable, Consulted and Informed) model, 351–352, **352**
Radjou, N., 418
Ramadan, Z.B., 254
Ramesh, V., 69, **69**, 70
Rauschnabel, P.A., 224–225, *225*
Raynor, M., 256
re-intermediation, 4
Reach, Engage, Activate, Nurture (REAN) framework, 292–293
reciprocity, 152–153
Relling, M., 162

reporting, 139, 355–359
resource-based theory (RBT), 334
resource-based view (RBV) of the firm, 334
resource management
9Ms resource types and, 335–347, *335*, *341*, **343–344**
overview of, 334–335
governance and, 353–354
reporting and, 355–359
roles and responsibilities in groups and, 351–352, **352**
SAF framework and, 348–351, **350**
Strava (case study), 359–362
return on marketing investment (ROMI), 338, 370
review skeptics, 42–43
reviews, 42–43, 108
Reviews.io, 42
RFID (radio-frequency identification) tags, 5
Rheingold, H., 150
rich communications services (RCS) messaging, 199
right to be forgotten, 21, 25
Ritter, T., 407
ROBO (Research Online Buy Offline), 34
rules of engagement, 172, **172**

Sahney, S., 34
Santoveña-Casal, S., 134
Sari, S.V., 143
Sarkar, S., 202
Schaarschmidt, M., 260
Schneider, P.J., 34
Schor, J.B., 340
Schultz, C.D., 404
Schwager, A., 41
search engine optimisation (SEO), 72–77, 93, 380
search engine results pages (SERPs), 72–73
search engines, 80
second screening, 33
security, 204
segmentation, 50
segmentation, targeting and positioning (STP), 317. *See also* personas
self-disclosure, 132–133, **132**, 154, 157–158, 176
self-enhancement, 157
self-presentation, 132–133, **132**, 154, 157, 161
selfie dysmorphia (selfitis), 128, 157
sentiment analysis, 135–136, 263
SEO data tags, 74
Serazio, M., 100
service excellence, 226–227, *226*
Shao, B.B.M., 202
Shao, G., 130
shared media, 97–98, **99**
sharing economy, 36–40, *36*

Shaw, F., 151
Shewart, W., 390
short-form content, 109
Short, J., 132
short message services (SMS), 198–200
showrooming, 33–35
situational analysis. *See* digital marketing audits
skin electronics, 234–235, *235*
smart tattoo technology, 182
Smith, G.E., 306
Smith, P.R., 294
social capital, 153–154, *154*
social listening, 251–253, *252*
social media
    overview of, 122
    adoption and implementation of, 141–142,
        141–142
    advantages and disadvantages of, 143–144
    definitions of, 122–123
    individuals and, 125–134, **126**, *128*, **132**
    organisations and, 134–140, **135**, *137*
    paid search and, 81
    Strava (case study), 144–146
    types and role of, 123–125, **124**
social media analytics, 382–384
Social Media Engagement Behaviours
        (SMEB), 168
social media entertainment (SME), 126–127
social media influencers (SMIs). *See* influencers
social media search, 76
Social Media + Society (journal), 144
Social Media Strategy Framework. *See* Digital
    Marketing Strategy Framework
social presence, 132–133, **132**
social selling, 168
social shares, 93
societies, 150
Sociology (journal), 176
sofalising, 33
solid consumption, 33, 35–36
Solove, D., 21
source credibility, 99–100, 102
spite, 175
Sraha, L., 105
stackies, 342–344
stakeholder mapping, 303
stakeholders, 301–302, 353, 402, 409, 415, 418
Statista, 122
Steuer, J., 70, 213
Stewart, M.C., 251
Stieglitz, S., 135
story (content), 96–99
storytellers (content creators), 99–108, **99**, *104*
strategy, 271. *See also* digital marketing strategy
    and objectives
Strava (case study)
    augmented reality and, 236–237
    content marketing and, 118–119

digital consumers and, 55–56
digital marketing audits and, 264–266
digital marketing environment and, 26–27
digital marketing metrics and, 392
digital marketing plans and, 327–330, **329**
digital marketing strategy and objectives and,
    291–292, 296–297
digital marketing toolbox and, 86–87
integration and, 420–421
mobile marketing and, 207–208
online communities and, 176–177
resource management and, 359–362
social media and, 144–146
Stroud, N.J., 202
style, 108–112, *111*
subscription pricing, 304
Suitability, Acceptability, Feasibility (SAF)
    framework, 348–351, **350**
Sulkakoski, S., 36
Sunstein, C.R., 20
sustainability, 38

tactics, 271. *See also* digital marketing strategy
    and objectives
Tan, F., 69, **69**
targeted advertising, 21, 23–24, *24*
targeting, 317
tattling, 175
technology, 342–345, **343–344**
Technology Acceptance Model (TAM)
    overview of, 52–54, **53**, *53*
    augmented, virtual and mixed reality and,
        224–225
    content marketing and, 111
    digital marketing audits and, 246
    digital transformation process and, 412
    mobile marketing and, 203
    online communities and, 150
    resource management and, 337
    websites and, 68–69
Technology Readiness Levels (TRLs), 216–217,
    217, 246
text messages, 198–200
text to pay, 188
#TextForHumanity, 200
Thaler, R.H., 20
Thatcher, J.B., 158
Therón, R., 357
tie strength, 129, 151–155, *154*, 165
TikTok, 111–112
tom Dieck, M.C., 214
Tong, S., 184–186
Tönnies, F., 150
topical content, 96
touchpoints, 41–43
tourism, 221–223
TOWS matrix, 275–279, **277**
transaction-specific satisfaction, 254

travel organisations, 221–223
Trello, 293
Tremblay, S.C., 128
triggered emails, 61–63
trolling, 143–144, 156, 163
trustworthiness, 108
Tung, L., 69, **69**
twdocs.com, 258

Uber, 39–40
Unilever, 14–15
uninvited brands, 167
United Kingdom, 22, 25
United Nations (UN), 143, 419
United States, 22–23, 24
Urchin tracking module (UTM) parameters, 379, *380*
usability, 69–72
user-created content (UCC), 107–108
user experience (UX), 68–70, **69**, 404
user-generated content (UGC), 107–108, 345
uses and gratifications theory (UGT), 125–127, **126**, 131, 135, **135**, 224
utilitarian communities, 159
utilitarian consumption, 51, 214–215, 226

Vallas, S., 340
vandalism, 163
vanity metrics, 79–80, 386–387
Vázquez-Ingelmo, A., 357
Venkatesh, V., 69, **69**, 70
Verhoef, P.C., 34, 41, 44–45
virtual reality (VR)
    overview of, 212–214
    application of, 216–218, *217*, 220–225, *225*
    benefits of, 230–231
    challenges with, 231–232
    creation of, 232–234
    future of, 234–236, *235*
    key concepts in, 225–229, *226*, **228**
    See also augmented reality (AR); mixed reality (MR)
vividness, 110–111, *111*
vlogs (video blogs), 108–109
voice search, 77
Volchek, K., 370
Voytenko Palgan, Y., 36
Vrontis, D., 417

Walsh, G., 260
Wang, Y., 206

Wayback Machine, 6
wearable technology, 182, 186, **187**, 228. *See also* mobile marketing
Weaver, K., 83
Web 1.0 ('read only' web), 4
Web 2.0, 5, 122. *See also* social media
Web 3.0 (semantic web), 5
Web 4.0, 5
web analytics, 375–381, *380*, 404
Web Analytics Association, 375
web scraping, 13
web server log files, 377
webographics, 50, **50**
webrooming, 33–35
website performance checkers, 76
websites, 67–72, **69**, 203
Weihrich, H., 276
Wernerfelt, B., 334
West, M., 143
Wheeler, E., 295
Wikipedia, 162–163
Williams, E., 132
Winning Group, 254–255
wireframes, 192–193, 345
Wohllebe, A., 203
Wojdynski, B.W., 98
woke- washing, 101
World Bank, 399
World Health Organization (WHO), 143, 150

Xing, Z., 77
Xu, B., 184–186
Xu, Y., 69, **69**

Yao, Z., 150, 166
YouVisit, 223–224
Yu, F., 77
Yuan, D., 168
Yuan, S., 103
Yuan, X., 77

Zahay, D., 4, 398
Zeekit, 219
Zhang, G., 206
Zhang, H., 33
Zheng, A., 157
Zhong, W., 206
Zhou, S., 33
Zielke, S., 34
Zoghaib, A., 77